The Life of John Dryden

John Dryden, by Sir Godfrey Kneller. Reproduced by courtesy of
The National Portrait Gallery, London.

THE LIFE OF
JOHN DRYDEN

By

CHARLES E. WARD

Chapel Hill

THE UNIVERSITY OF NORTH CAROLINA PRESS

PR
3423
W3

To

PAULL FRANKLIN BAUM

teacher, scholar, mentor, friend

I gratefully dedicate this book

Preface

IT IS NOT difficult to agree with Dryden that "the learned seldom abound with action; and it is action only that furnishes the historian with things agreeable and instructive." Yet despite the paucity of "action" in Dryden's own career, there remain enough "things agreeable and instructive" to encourage the attempt to write a life of a great man of letters.

My present effort has been to assemble all the pertinent materials hitherto available and to add when possible new information and new interpretations. Where materials are not extensive, the temptation is to include every scrap, though insignificant and trivial, and to expand upon every trifle of gossip, though often interesting or scandalous. I have tried to resist this temptation and to include generally what can be corroborated or fairly inferred. If I seem in places to have relied heavily upon conjecture, I can only hope that the reader can agree upon its reasonableness.

For reasons which long ago appeared to me to be necessary, I have excluded, in general, critical pronouncement upon Dryden's work. His output was so vast and has been so relatively unexplored that to have attempted this second bow of Odysseus would have resulted in a work of unmanageable proportions. More than one critical study will be imperative to assess Dryden's immense contribution to English letters. Happily, signs are not wanting that substantial works will be forthcoming.

The early contributions to an understanding of Dryden's life, made notably by Dr. Johnson, Edmond Malone, Sir Walter Scott, and others, have been expertly detailed by James M. Osborn in *John Dryden: Some Biographical Facts and Problems*. Since their germinal work, the passage of time has seen the addition of much material by innumerable persons, to all of whom I gratefully acknowledge my indebtedness. More precise acknowledgments abound in the notes. To the Duke University Research Council I add special appreciation for grants, made over the years, to aid my investigations, and to many libraries, both in America and England, for their constant help.

To James M. Osborn, particularly, I wish to express my gratitude for unfailing aid, encouragement, and friendship over a quarter of a century of mutual interest in "glorious John."

My most profound debt I record in the dedication.

C. E. W.

Contents

The Life of John Dryden

As the sunbeams, united in a burning-glass to a point, have greater force than when they are darted from a plain superficies, so the virtues and actions of one man, drawn together into a single story, strike upon our minds a stronger and more lively impression, than the scattered relations of many men, and many actions; and by the same means that they give us pleasure, they afford us profit too.

Dryden, *Life of Plutarch*

The writing a Life is at all times, and in all circumstances, the most difficult task of an historian; and notwithstanding the numerous tribe of biographers, we can scarce find one, except Plutarch, who deserves our perusal, or can invite a second view. But if the difficulty be so great where the materials are plentiful, and the incidents extraordinary, what must it be, when the person that affords the subject denies matter enough for a page? The learned seldom abound with action; and it is action only that furnishes the historian with things agreeable and instructive.

Dryden, *Life of Lucian*

Backgrounds and Beginnings

1631-1659

JOHN DRYDEN was born on August 9 (N.S. August 19), 1631, in Aldwinckle, Northamptonshire, a village on the river Nene.[1] Tradition has maintained that he was born in the Parsonage of his maternal grandfather, Henry Pickering, who was then—and had been for many years—Rector of Aldwinckle All Saints. Tradition, which often proves to be a safe guide in the absence of documentary evidence, seems in this instance to be fairly accurate. Although local legend, with all the authority of age, can point unerringly to the very room in the surviving house across the road from All Saints where Dryden was delivered, no document has been found to corroborate the legend. Yet recent evidence has come to light which does establish beyond much doubt that he was baptized at All Saints, presumably by his grandfather, on August 14 (O.S.).[2] His parents, Erasmus Dryden and Mary Pickering, both members of prominent Northamptonshire families, had been married at Pilton on October 21, 1630, and had perhaps established residence in nearby Titchmarsh, where the Pickering family owned large estates, and where was situated the manor of Sir John Pickering, the uncle of Mary Dryden.[3] That the village of Titchmarsh was to be their home for many years is attested by the fact that the baptisms of their many children for the next twenty years are recorded in the Register of St. Peters, Titchmarsh.

The history of the Dryden and the Pickering families parallels that of many other county families of the sixteenth and seventeenth centuries. Of little importance before the reign of Henry VIII, they had somehow (perhaps as tradesmen) accumulated enough to buy or lease substantial holdings of land when Henry VIII distributed the huge church and monastery estates. By careful marriages they were able to add to their property; and in the expanding agricultural economy of the Tudor age they prospered and became important in the management of county affairs. They served as sheriffs, as Justices of the Peace—offices of great influence then—as M.P.'s, and as members of juries and of the increasing numbers of royal and governmental commissions. Though never by marriage or royal creation did they enter into the loftier ranks, they nevertheless, as time went on, accumulated knighthoods and baronetcies. By the beginning of the seventeenth century, both Drydens and Pickerings were well established in the squirearchy of Northamptonshire.

The Drydens of Cumberland established their family in Northamptonshire in the person of John Dryden, who before 1550 settled around Adneston (or Adson), a parish very close to the ancient priory of Canons Ashby. The priory had been, for three hundred years, a monastery with huge estates. Along with all other church properties it had been liquidated by Henry VIII, and after passing through several hands was acquired probably by one Erasmus Cope and passed on to his son John Cope, afterwards Sir John, before 1547. It was known locally and in many legal notices as "Copes Asshby." John Cope became Sheriff and a man of substance.[4] Among his many children was Elizabeth, whom John Dryden married about 1550. Dryden had acquired by this time extensive lands and would add to them by his marriage into the Cope family.

The Northamptonshire Drydens were now well launched: the children's names of this generation became fixed in succeeding generations: Erasmus (from Erasmus Cope, though the poet was to tell Aubrey more than a century later of friendship between Erasmus Roterdamus and his great-grandfather), John, Elizabeth, George, Edward. The appearance of these names in every branch and generation of the family provides not only an interesting puzzle to the biographer and editor of the poet but also a caveat; for in any one generation three or four Johns, Elizabeths, and Erasmuses will find their way into an official document of some kind.

To the marriage of this first John and Elizabeth Cope were born at least eight sons and three daughters. Not a university man himself, John seems to have been convinced about the values of an education. In 1571 he sent three sons to Magdalen College, Oxford—Anthony, Erasmus, and Edward. They were followed by George in 1575 and John in 1578. Anthony, the eldest, went on to the Middle Temple in 1575. George began his legal training at Furnival's Inn but moved to the Middle Temple in 1579. Erasmus, the second son, spent nearly seven years at Oxford; then he followed Anthony to the Middle Temple, where he was enrolled on February 8, 1578.[5] His career here was short-lived, for he had returned to Canons Ashby and contracted marriage with Frances Wilkes of Hoddenhull, probably in 1579. She was a daughter of a well-to-do merchant, Thomas Wilkes; and the families had been neighbors for a generation. To this marriage were born at least three sons—John, William, Erasmus —and many daughters. John, the eldest, born in 1580, followed the educational pattern set by his father and uncles and went to Broadgates Hall (later Pembroke), Oxford. Described as sixteen years old and son and heir of Erasmus, John matriculated on April 29, 1596. After six years at Oxford, he went to the Middle Temple on April 20, 1602. William followed his older brother to Broadgates in 1607, but after one year removed to the Middle Temple, where he was admitted on October 21, 1608. More than ten years separated William from the third and youngest son, Erasmus, who was to become the father of the poet. Though no record of his birth date has been discovered, he probably was born about 1602 or 1603; this conjecture is based upon his going to the university in 1618 at the same age as did his brothers, at fifteen or sixteen. Instead of going to Oxford, he broke the tradition of the family and went to Cambridge and to Emmanuel College. After three years he left, without a degree, to enter Gray's Inn, on February 11, 1621/22.

The reasons behind the choice of Cambridge and of Emmanuel for the education of the youngest son, could they be discovered, might provide more information about the Puritan leanings of the family than is now available. Emmanuel was the youngest of the Cambridge colleges, having been founded in 1584 by Sir Walter Mildmay as a seminary for the training of clergymen. Of definite Puritan feelings himself, Sir Walter was interested in providing for the youth of the Midland counties, particularly for those of Essex and Northamptonshire, a training in a theology that was at once strongly anti-Catholic and circumspectly anti-prelatical. The Calvinistic sympathies of the college were proclaimed, and to it came many youths from the merchant and proprietor classes of these counties.[6] Some of them were dedicated persons destined to make important contribution to the cause of religion and education, both in England and in New England. In the years when Erasmus Dryden was in residence, the college was becoming a center of marked intellectual activity, which continued for at least another generation and which was to make significant contributions to intellectual and religious history. For from Emmanuel came the heads for eleven other Cambridge colleges during the Commonwealth; and from its ferment arose later the distinguished leadership of the group of religious thinkers, honored then as now as the Cambridge Platonists—Cudworth, Smith, Whichcote.

There is no certainty, of course, that Erasmus Dryden entered Emmanuel to prepare for the ministry; there is evidence enough that the Drydens, and also the Pickerings, were Puritans. Erasmus, we can be sure, was brought up in a household which by the turn of the seventeenth century was committed to a way of religious life that soon brought its members into conflict with their established Church. They seemed to have had little patience with the outward forms of religious worship and little concern for the edicts of the bishops. As Puritans they were communicants of the Church by law established; they could take the sacraments of the Church of England. But they could also base their faith essentially upon the truths of Scripture, and they could give aid and comfort to clergymen within the church who dispensed with the external trappings of worship because they believed them closer to the practices of Rome than to the ideals of the Protestant Reformation. As early as 1604 old Erasmus Dryden had been arrested and imprisoned for circulating in Northamptonshire a petition in behalf of "puritan" clergymen, who were being harried by the Church for their contumacy. In February, 1605, Erasmus prayed King James for release on the ground that the circulated petition had merely been "a testimonial of the godliness of the preachers in the county."[7] Their "godliness" had consisted—from the Church's point of view—of their refusal to abide by the proclamation for uniformity in the Book of Common Prayer and the Book of Canons. Among the clergymen befriended by this Erasmus was John Dod, a highly educated and gifted man, who served the church at Canons Ashby from 1605 until 1611, when he was "silenced" by Archbishop Abbot.[8] It may be doubted that he remained silenced; for as late as 1625 he was still at Canons Ashby: in a lawsuit in that year in which Erasmus (now Sir Erasmus) was plaintiff, Dod made a deposition and was described as of that place. He was then seventy years old.[9]

Erasmus, from such a committed family, might well have found the atmosphere of Emmanuel College much to his liking in 1618. Yet if his father had any hope that his son would prepare for the ministry, he was to be disappointed. His residence at Gray's Inn has left no record. He may have remained only a short time, for in 1623 his father settled upon him property near his home. Sir Erasmus turned over to him a capital messuage and eight yardlands (240 acres), and another messuage and three yardlands. These tracts, in the village of Blakesley, had been part of the priory lands of Canons Ashby. With the acquisition of land of his own, young Erasmus seems to have taken his place, as had his older brothers John and William, among the landed gentry of the county.[10] The 330 acres of good Northamptonshire land yielded him a competence which became of direct benefit to English letters in the next generation; for upon his death in 1654 Erasmus left to his wife and to his son John the income from this Blakesley land.[11]

Now that he had achieved an assured income, Erasmus was ready to establish his own family. Across the county from Blakesley and Canons Ashby the Pickerings held much land in and about the villages of Aldwinckle and Titchmarsh. Friends of long standing, the families had years before cemented their relationship by the marriage of Sir John Pickering to Erasmus' older sister Susanna. Erasmus now found a wife in Aldwinckle. Mary Pickering was the daughter of the Reverend Henry Pickering, younger brother of Sir John and Rector of Aldwinckle All Saints, a post he had already held for more than thirty years. On October 18, 1630, Erasmus and Mary took out a marriage license at Peterborough, and three days later, on the twenty-first, they were married in Pilton Church. He was described as a "gentleman" of Canons Ashby and she "a maiden of Aldwinckle."[12]

Within a year their first son was born and baptized in Aldwinckle. This fact suggests that Erasmus had not returned with his bride to Blakesley but that he had found a place among the Pickerings. The records are complete for the regular succession of children of the marriage: the year after John, it was Agnes (November, 1632); the next year, Rose; the following year, Mary; in all, fourteen children— ten daughters and four sons.[13] Until he was in his seventh year John remained the only boy among five sisters; then in 1637 Erasmus was born. The disparity in ages of the boys would have made impossible any great comradeship between them: his early playmates within the home were girls. Since no information exists about his youth, it would be idle, if not pernicious, to speculate. Yet it may be permissible to try to relate to these years some random comments that he himself and others were to make more than a half century later. The tablet erected to his memory in Titchmarsh Church by his kinswoman Mrs. Elizabeth Creed, daughter of Sir Gilbert Pickering, mentions that he had his first education "here."[14]   This suggests the existence of a grammar school in the Aldwinckle-Titchmarsh area. That there was such a school during the years of Dryden's youth seems almost certain.   One Nathaniel Whiting, who had succeeded Dryden's grandfather at Aldwinckle All Saints, served as master of a free grammar school in the village; and it may be that the Reverend Henry Pickering had earlier served the same school.[15]   Even had no such school provided the rudiments to the youth, his father and (until 1636) his grandfather might have instructed him in language and encouraged him to read.   When in 1693 Dryden wrote the "Character of Polybius" to accompany Sir Henry Shere's translation of the *History,* he recalled that he had read Polybius "in English with the pleasure of a Boy, before I was ten years of age; and yet even then, had some dark notions of the prudences with which he conducted his design."   Other reminiscent comments in later life suggest that the reading of history during his formative years provided him his greatest pleasure.   Yet other studies apparently were not neglected, and taste was being cultivated for the English poets, among them Spenser.   "When I was a boy," he says in the Dedication to the *Spanish Friar* (1681), "I thought . . . Spencer a mean poet in comparison of Sylvester's Dubartas," which, to his youthful mind, outdid the "inimitable Spencer."[16]   It is likely too that his study of Latin began at home or in the village school.   In the "Life of Plutarch" (1683) he compared the educational regimen of his own boyhood unfavorably with that of Plutarch, for "the custom of those times was very much different from these of ours, where the greatest part of our youth is spent in learning the words of dead languages." And he found Plutarch's schoolmaster different from his: "rods and ferulas were not used by Ammonius, as being properly the punishment of slaves, and not the correction of ingenuous free-born men; at least to be only exercised by parents, who had the power of life and death over their own children."[17]

The basis for Dryden's future education was thus established in the decade of the 1630's.   Perhaps his interest in earlier history was whetted by family reminiscences of events still green in memory. Fotheringhay Castle, where Mary Queen of Scots had been mewed up and at last executed in 1578, stood in ruins only a few miles away. And history in the making became part of both the Dryden and the Pickering families.   The imprisonment of his grandfather and of his uncle Sir John Pickering for refusal to pay the forced "subsidy" of

Charles I in 1627/28 had been at once a result of personal conviction and a token of the hardening resistance that arose to Charles's desperate measures, not only in Northamptonshire but throughout the country. The swirling currents of political and religious controversy flowed strong about his village and the families of which he was a part. By the time he was nine, the long-gathering storm broke, and the Long Parliament of 1640 began to take over the reins of national government. There seems to have been no doubt on what side the Drydens and Pickerings would align themselves. Though probably too young to understand the import of events that followed fast upon actions of the Long Parliament, Dryden must have heard much family talk about illegal royal acts, Star Chamber proceedings, and the "unreasonable" edicts of the bishops, concerning freedom, usurpation, reform, rights of the people, and above all the rights of property. The unorthodox must have come to be the normal opinion. The rapid and involved events of a developing revolution were bewildering in the extreme; they were probably nearly incomprehensible to the boy of ten. Yet as his father and his uncles began to be drawn officially into the struggles on the local and the national scenes, and as he himself entered his adolescent years, it is hardly to be supposed that he could remain aloof. Opinions he doubtless had; but whether he merely assimilated those of his family or formed his own we cannot know.

As these crucial events unrolled, Dryden continued to prepare himself for a career as yet undefined. According to family tradition he could look forward to the university and to a life among the squires of the county. But again the family educational pattern was to be changed; instead of going directly to the university, Dryden received a King's Scholarship and went to London to take up residence at Westminster School. The fact of his attendance can be cited, but no record of the date of his admission is available; and the ages at which boys at this time entered the public schools were so varied that it is almost impossible to make a good guess. Cowley, in an earlier generation, was eleven or twelve when he entered. Locke, a schoolmate of Dryden's, was a King's Scholar at fifteen in 1647. Others ranged in age between twelve and sixteen. Perhaps it would be reasonable to assume that Dryden was about fifteen, an age that would place him in Westminster by 1646. Judging by his later eminence, we would suppose that his King's Scholarship was awarded to him on the basis of merit. Family influence, however, might not have been a handicap. In November, 1645, by Ordinance of Lords and Commons, the government of Westminster School was vested in a committee of thirty-three members, whose powers included the selection of King's Scholars and the supervision of electing from the school to Trinity College, Cambridge, and Christ Church, Oxford. Serving on the committee was Dryden's uncle Sir John Dryden, and another kinsman, Humphrey Salwey. Although these two probably had no need to force upon the committee the claims of the youngster from Titchmarsh, their presence hardly was calculated to do harm to his candidacy.[18]

But whatever influences won him his scholarship and his admission to Westminster, Dryden had now become a part of an energetic and effective school. Under Lambert Osbaldeston, headmaster from 1622-38 (to whom Cowley dedicated *Poetical Blossoms* in 1633), it had fostered an interest in poetry, and the best of Osbaldeston's pupils, like Cowley, had been fired by his enthusiasm for letters. And in an earlier generation of pupils Ben Jonson had begun to develop his talents under William Camden. Although such students would make their reputation in literature, the largest part of the students were directed toward the Church; and the school in the seventeenth century sent very many boys to the universities and into important ecclesiastical positions. During Dryden's time the headmaster was the famous Dr. Richard Busby, whose name was to become synonymous with the vigorous, dynamic, flogging schoolmaster. He was a rigorous classicist dedicated to instilling in his scholars a thorough knowledge of Latin and Greek, to which end he never scrupled to use the rod. In the troubled times of the Interregnum Busby succeeded in steering a careful course between his apparent sympathy for the royal cause and his need to follow the regulations of parliamentary committees. Yet so great was the zeal of both Presbyterian and Independent for education, and so aware were they of the value of Westminster School, that Busby seems to have found in the committees set up to regulate it a willing group of collaborators intent upon the same task of providing a thorough education to youth. As a consequence, Westminster flourished, political and religious differences submerged in the face of common educational ideals.

Although there exist no records of Dryden at Westminster, enough information about the curriculum and the routine of the scholars is available to reconstruct in general outline his residence under Busby. The day began at a quarter past five and ended twelve or fifteen hours later. After Latin prayers, morning ablutions from the common washbasin, and breakfast, the boys were marched, two by two, to their lessons. At six they began a two-hour session of repeating their grammar—Latin out of Lilly and Greek out of Camden, or after 1647 from Busby's own Greek grammar. In a semicircle before the master, they recited the rules and then made extempore verses in Latin and Greek upon themes suggested by the master. On alternate mornings, instead of making verses, they were called upon to expound some part of a Latin or Greek author, such as Cicero, Livy, Isocrates, Homer, or Xenophon. From eight to nine they were allowed time for "beaver," a refreshment period. At nine they met for another two-hour period devoted to the reading of those exercises, in prose and in verse, which they had prepared in their rooms the night before. After lunch they came back at one o'clock for another two-hour lesson. On this occasion the master expounded a selection from Virgil, Cicero, Euripides, or Sallust, commenting on rhetorical figures, grammatical constructions, and explaining prosody. Then followed an afternoon respite. The final meeting of the day was devoted to the repetition of a "leaf or two" out of a book of rhetorical figures or proverbs, or sentences chosen by the master. Then a theme was assigned, upon which the student was to compose prose or verse essays in Latin or Greek before the next morning.[19] These exercises, which demanded the utmost care, were not lightly undertaken or soon forgotten, at least not by Dryden. Nearly a half century later when he came to publish his translation of Juvenal and Persius, his memory went back to Busby and Westminster. The Third Satire of Persius, he remembers, he translated "at Westminster School, for a Thursday-night's exercise; and believe that it, and many other of my exercises of this nature in English verse, are still in the hands of my learned master, the Reverend Doctor Busby."[20] Busby fired the young Dryden with the love of classical satire and influenced thus early that lively mind which was to produce some of the finest verse satires in English.

Sunday provided no rest from the serious business of learning. The boys were expected to be in school before morning prayers in order to construe some part of the Gospel in Greek, or to repeat a Greek catechism. They often made verses for the afternoon, either upon the preacher's sermon of the morning, or upon the epistles or some other part of the Gospel. The foremost scholars of the last form, where Dryden found himself in 1649, were sometimes appointed tutors pro tem and expounded to the other scholars passages from Homer or Virgil or Horace. Here Dryden may have found ample scope in which to indulge his great love for Virgil—a love which remained with him to the last day of his life.[21]

But the year 1649 became of importance for another reason: it saw the first publication of his verse. His poem, "Upon the Death of the Lord Hastings," appeared in a small commemorative volume entitled *Lachrymae Musarum: The Tears of the Muses,* a collection of elegies lamenting the untimely death of Henry, Lord Hastings, the only son of the Earl of Huntingdon. The young lord, just past nineteen, died of the smallpox in June. One R. B. [Richard Brome?] undertook to solicit and edit suitable verses for the volume, which was published by Thomas Newcomb. Not unlike other commemorative volumes of the century, it included at first poems by twenty-seven persons, written in Greek, Latin, and English. Before printing was completed, eight more had responded tardily to the solicitation of R. B. Dryden was among them. Most of the contributors, as their verses attest, were newcomers to poetry and were not to be heard from again. But there were also among them established bards, such as Denham and Herrick, whose *Hesperides* and *Noble Numbers* had appeared two years before; and another neophyte who, like Dryden, would be heard from again—Andrew Marvell.[22]

Although "Upon the Death of the Lord Hastings" was the first of his work to be printed, we may be sure that it was not his first excursion into poetry; and we can never be certain that it was the best of his schoolboy verse. The exercises handed in to his Master Busby, translations though they were, may have shown his early talents to better advantage than this "original" poem, which had the fortune to be put into print. As could be expected, this poem of fifty-four couplets is highly derivative and imitative. Even the sympathetic reader may find it difficult to discover the promise of the later master of English heroic verse. But it is not the most contemptible poem in the volume, and it may be favorably compared with the verses of the established poets who are there represented. It is of course packed with schoolboy learning, the prosody is uncertain, and the "conceits" may be deplored; but they are not worse than some committed—in the name of wit—by the best poets of the age. Yet it succeeds in demonstrating some poetic feeling and an energy which was to become a characteristic of his later verse.[23] And one can also detect an awareness of form and proportion, and an ability, if only tentative, to combine disparate materials into a unity: the conventional elements of the elegiac form are here and await only practice and maturity to give them finished treatment.[24]

Within six months of the publication of his poem, Dryden, as a King's Scholar eligible for election to the university, was preparing to stand his examinations. He was successful and was elected to Trinity College, Cambridge, where he was admitted pensioner on May 18, 1650.[25] In the meantime his interest in writing and in publishing must have been whetted by the appearance of "Upon the Death of the Lord Hastings." His young friend John Hoddesdon had written poems and epigrams on texts of the Old and New Testaments, and had found a publisher for them. On June 7, 1650, his little book had received the "Imprimatur," and Hoddesdon proceeded with arrangements for the printing, among them a provision for a generous prefatory section of congratulatory poems to the young author (he was eighteen). Among these were three contributed by King's scholars, all recently elected: R. Marsh, W. James, and "J. Dryden of Trin. C."[26] Dryden's verses, a series of thirteen couplets, are in different tone from that of the poem to Hastings and show much less care in preparation. Jocular and witty, and at times scoffing, they yet serve the purpose of conventional congratulations to a youth not well endowed with poetic fire. As *juvenilia* they may have incidental interest, but they probably are not much better than others Dryden must have committed to the flames.

When Dryden entered Cambridge in 1650, he took with him one of the best educational experiences available to the youth of his time. In addition to the thorough training in ancient languages and literature provided by the renowned Busby, he would have studied mathematics, history, geography, and the Scriptures. He was resident during a time of revolutionary change, and Westminster was but a microcosm reflecting many shades and divergencies of political and religious opinion and conviction, from Busby, who is said to have remained a staunch loyalist, to pupils in the lowest form who came from Puritan and anti-loyalist families in England and Wales. Bound together by common educational interests, they may have achieved a measure of toleration that cannot easily be discovered in the larger world of the England of which they were a small part. Dryden was in the last form when Charles I stood trial and went to his death at the hands of the militant Independents at the Banquet Hall, only a short walk from Westminster School. What effect the event had upon the young student can hardly be known. Yet he may have found that the reality of regicide was far different from the resistance to illegal taxation of a live king, for which his grandfather and his maternal relatives were celebrated, in family circles, twenty years earlier.

In the summer of 1650 Dryden was matriculated as pensioner, at Trinity, and he took up residence in the autumn. On October 2, he was elected Scholar and placed under his tutor, Mr. Templer. His removal to Cambridge brought him much closer to his home in Titchmarsh than he had been at Westminster. His family had changed, for it was still growing by the addition of a new child nearly every year. His youngest siblings he could hardly have known, except during his limited vacations. The nearest brother was now twelve years of age, scarcely a stimulating companion for the young man in Trinity. Closer to him in age and probably in interests was his cousin John, the younger son of his uncle Sir John Dryden of Canons Ashby, who within a year was to enter Wadham College, Oxford. That a sympathetic tie existed between him and the cousins at Canons Ashby may be seen in the one extant letter (with verses) that Dryden wrote to Honor, his cousin John's sister, from Cambridge in 1653, and later in the magnificent tribute he paid his cousin in 1694, when he wrote verses to him entitled "To my Honour'd Cousin, John Driden of Chesterton."

Of Dryden's years at Trinity next to nothing is known. Despite his earlier publication of poetry, there is no evidence to show that he continued to write verse, and certainly none exists of publication. Nor is there any comment later from his coevals about his life at Cambridge, though Pepys, early in the Restoration years, makes an offhand remark that he had known Dryden at Cambridge. Only two contemporary notices remain, both to be found in the Trinity College "Conclusion Book." On July 19, 1652, is recorded this "conclusion":

Agreed then that Dreyden be put out of Comons for a forthnight [*sic*] at least, & that he goe not out of the Colledg during the time aforesaid excepting to sermons without express leave fro the Master or Vicemaster. & that at the end of the forthnight [*sic*] he read a confession [*recantation* lined through] of his crime in the hall at Dinner time; at the three fellowes table. His [*alledged* lined through] crime was his disobedience to the Vicemaster & his contumacy in taking of his punishment inflicted by him.[27]

We are left completely in the dark as to the nature of his disobedience, but there is a suggestion of a certain belligerence when punishment was to be meted out. *Contumacy* hints at an independent if not a recalcitrant spirit. And one wonders whether his powers of persuasion were exercised in order to reduce the gravity of his offense in official eyes, as might be indicated by the substitution of *confession* for the deleted *recantation*.

That he was a competent student we assume, but he seems not to have been among the best or the most prominent. He was not on the Honours List of 1653/54, yet none of his classmates in later life were to compete with him in public recognition or in contemporary esteem. Most of them are almost unknown to history. Only two who took their degrees with him in 1653/54 stand out. Walter Needham, on the Honours List for that year, became a respected physician; and Benjamin Pulleyn was Regius Professor of Greek from 1674-86.[28] That the resources of Cambridge allowed him to pursue his wide-ranging interests may be fairly inferred, both from the quality and the variety of his verse and prose published within the next half dozen years.

During his residence, Cambridge was an exciting place in a period of great intellectual movements in philosophy and religion. The Cambridge Platonists, with their new teaching, were exploring all kinds of questions touching man and his beliefs, and were asserting the divinity of human reason and insisting upon a large harmony underlying a universe that must have seemed in those years—to some minds—to be breaking into a thousand fragments. In the months when Independency and Cromwell, with his New Model Army, were defeating the Presbyterians and asserting their preeminence in church and state, Henry More, Cudworth, Culverwel, and Whichcote provided at Cambridge a center of vital religious thought and philosophical speculation. Their attempts to chart a middle way between the extremes of enthusiasm on the one hand and ritualism and dogma on the other produced a wide range of differing opinions.[29] It was an inquiring and a speculative academic society, and the liberal climate of thought which resulted must have exercised its influence upon Dryden as an undergraduate. Perhaps it produced, or reinforced in a mind already predisposed, a skepticism regarding the possibility of answers to be found at any extreme position, or of their validity. Perhaps even now he inclined toward Pyrrhonism, and in these crosscurrents of contemporary controversy he may have seen a need in the individual to eschew the excesses both of reason and of emotion. Such skepticism and diffidence, differing sharply from the dogmatism of many of his contemporaries, became a marked characteristic of his mind during the rest of his life. His refusal to accept an ipse dixit runs like a bright thread through most of his work, and the inability to see this thread has resulted in distorted interpretations of Dryden and of his work.

After Dryden left Cambridge with his B.A. degree in March, 1653/54, he may have returned to Titchmarsh. His whereabouts and his activities from this time until he began to publish in 1659 are so uncertain that we must exercise much caution in interpreting the few authenticated documents regarding him and his family. A return to his home may have been mandatory, for it is possible that his father was even in March suffering his last illness. He had already drawn up his will, which is dated December 30, 1652; by the middle of June, 1654, he died, and was buried in the local church on June 18.[30] Apparently never so active in affairs as were some of his relations, Erasmus had nevertheless been appointed in 1650 to the important post of Justice of the Peace,[31] and he may have been (though it is by no means certain) the Erasmus Dryden appointed to the post of the receipt of the customs of the port of London on January 25, 1653/54.[32] Erasmus' will left his family well provided, and the bequests indicate a prosperous county gentleman whose holdings had yielded, if not great wealth, a comfortable living. His widow was named executrix, a fact suggestive not only of his extreme confidence in her judgment but of her demonstrated competence in the management of affairs. Each of the many children was remembered, and all goods and chattels not expressly devised were to go to the widow. The older daughters were left varying amounts from £80 to £100 on condition that they should marry with their mother's consent. If they presumed to marry without it, their legacies were reduced, but not cancelled. To his son Erasmus he left £100, to be his when he "Accomplished" twenty-one years of age (he was now seventeen). The younger sons, Henry and James, were bequeathed £80 each. To John he left "two partes of my land in Blakesley."[33]

So before he had reached his twenty-third birthday Dryden, as the eldest son, found himself the head of his family and possessed of a small estate which had been part of the family holdings for a hundred years. With the exception of the two oldest sisters, Agnes and Rose, all of his brothers and sisters were minors. It may well be that this new responsibility changed his immediate plans for further academic work at Trinity, which was holding a place open for him. In the college "Conclusion Book"—under date of April 23, 1655 (more than a year after his graduation)—is the notation: "That schollars be elected into the places of Sr Hookes, Sr Sawier, Sr

Dreiden . . . with this proviso, that if ye said Bachelours shall return to the Coll, at or before Midsumer next to continue constantly according to statute, that then the schollers chosen into their places respectively shall recede and give place to them. . . ." None of the scholars named chose to continue, and one Wilford was elected in Dryden's place.[34] The interval between his father's death and the date of the college's action in withdrawing the opportunity to take up his scholarship very likely was spent in Northamptonshire, where he could have helped his mother in the immediate problems of administering his father's estate. In this, his own share was not inconsiderable.[35] His failure to return to Cambridge for his M.A. may very simply have been the result of added responsibilities within his family.[36]

The next four years in Dryden's career constitute for us the longest hiatus in the story of his life. There is no certainty of his whereabouts or of his activities, until the appearance in 1659 of his next published poem, "Heroique Stanzas to the Glorious Memory of Cromwell," which came out in company of two other poems on the same subject by Edmund Waller and Thomas Sprat. It may well be that he remained at home in Titchmarsh; but that he did so is unsupported by any evidence. It has been thought that he held minor employment in Cromwell's government during these years, a belief based upon statements of his enemies a decade or more later, and also upon the more recent discovery of official documents which appear to bear his name. The seventeenth-century report that he had been in the employ of his relative Sir Gilbert Pickering, Cromwell's Lord Chamberlain, may have been substantially true; yet no documentation will conclusively support it. The known documents (three in number) which bear the name "Dryden" may possibly point to the poet; but they may as easily designate another man.[37] Whether he worked for a short period for the government is of little or no importance to his development as a poet. But, for some, the belief that he did actually hold an inconspicuous job among Cromwell's civil servants during the last months of the Protector's rule has been a convenient club with which to beat him for assumed loyalties they could not share.

Whatever else may have occupied Dryden during this four-year interval, we are certain that his schoolboy interest in poetry had not been lost. To suppose that, since 1650, he had written no verse because none from his pen had been published is amply refuted by the quality of "Heroique Stanzas." The great and obvious differences between the poetic competence exhibited in this poem and in the earlier efforts testify to continuing experimentation and practice. The circumstances surrounding the inclusion of Dryden's poem in the volume *Three Poems Upon the Death of his late Highnesse Oliver Lord Protector of England, Scotland, and Ireland* are far from clear. Apparently planned in the beginning by the publisher Henry Herringman as a commemorative volume with poems by Marvell, Sprat, and Dryden (and so entered on January 20, 1658/59, in the *Stationers' Register*), it was actually published under the imprint of William Wilson. Instead of a poem from Marvell, however, a short panegyric by Waller (which had already appeared as a broadside) was substituted. Why Herringman transferred the property to Wilson and why Waller's poem was printed instead of Marvell's has never been satisfactorily explained. It has been assumed that a "delay" occurred in the publication of the volume and likewise that the change of stationers and the substitution of poems were a last-minute affair dictated by caution in the face of political changes. No evidence can be brought in support of these assumptions; and one wonders why a stationer, in the early months of 1659, needed to exercise "caution" in publishing a volume noteworthy for its tribute to Cromwell. Had it celebrated Charles Stuart, caution might have been called for.[38]

It is more important, however, to ask why Dryden wrote the poem and why it was subsequently included in what appears to have been a bookseller's venture. The Lord Protector died on September 3, 1658. That catastrophe even Providence seemed to recognize— or so some thought because of the appearance of prodigies of nature about this time. It was invested with symbolic significance; and the elaborate official preparations for a long-drawn-out period of national mourning until the final obsequies set for November 23 reinforced the impression that "both himself and the day will be most renowned to posterity."[39] His "effigy, draped in black velvet, lay in a darkened room in Somerset House. . . . The Wax image . . . adorned with sceptre and crown and clothed in crimson velvet, was placed erect on the bed . . . while the lights of 500 candles . . . revealed Oliver in a deep glow of glory after his allotted period of purgatorial seclusion."[40] No one in England—regardless of his political prejudices or his lack of them—was unaware of the event. It was certainly such an occasion as is embraced by poets, poetasters, and booksellers in any age. If Dryden, nine years before, had found it pleasant to record in elegiac form his thoughts on Lord Hastings, it is hardly sur-

prising that he should now, in more mature fashion, seize upon this
event of larger moment to memorialize Cromwell.

Just when he composed "Heroique Stanzas" is difficult to determine. In the opening stanza he criticizes those who in their
"officious haste" rushed into print early in the autumn. This may
have been a matter of pique or he may actually have believed that
decency required a becoming delay. But he must have been writing
it in November and December at the latest, for Herringman would
have had copy in hand when he registered the *Three Poems* volume
on January 20. Dryden's choice of title is significant and indicates
with great precision his intention. Using Davenant's *Gondibert*
quatrain, Dryden composed thirty-seven stanzas, strung like beads
on a string and unified by the controlling theme of Cromwell the
heroic Englishman who had brought order and stability out of a
domestic chaos, who by his military victories abroad had forced
respect and had left England internationally stronger than she had
been for half a century. It is a patriotic tribute to the heroic spirit.
As a selective recital, the poem, as Scott so well said, "considers the
Protector when in his meridian height, but passes over the steps by
which he attained that elevation." Nowhere does Dryden mention
Cromwell's Independency, though he refers to his piety; nowhere
does he express an opinion about the excesses of parliamentary rule;
nowhere is there an attitude toward royalty or to the royalists. Yet
the poem was used in his own time and later as a document "proving"
Dryden's espousal of the principles of the Commonwealth and his
mendacity in welcoming Charles II in the following year. If he
changed, he changed, as Dr. Johnson said, with the nation.

In "Heroique Stanzas" we meet some of the characteristics that
will mark in individualized and finished form a good deal of his
future poetry: enthusiasm; generosity and assurance of statement;
extreme vigor and strength; suppleness; variety of texture and tone;
well-freighted lines that move nimbly despite their weight; prosodic
and verbal experiments; and above all a feeling for the value, the
importance, and the dignity of verse.

Toward a Poetic Career
1660-1665

With the publication of "Heroique Stanzas" Dryden began his career. He was twenty-eight years old, no longer the fledgling versifier of Westminster School, but a mature man who was finding himself poetically later than did most of his contemporaries and his predecessors. Lacking direct evidence of a systematic and careful preparation for his future in writing, such as we know Milton enjoyed, we can only assume that the years since he left Cambridge had provided him opportunity for wide reading and practice in his craft. Assumptions, however, do not add to our knowledge of Dryden; and speculation, though pleasant, may tend to falsify what little we can discover. Whether he was in London in 1659 is unknown; one's presence was hardly demanded in order to have a poem printed. Yet London was familiar to him; and he possessed a modest income at this time of more than £70 a year, which in equivalent figures for the twentieth century (and particularly before the inflationary era of the mid-century) would have insured a comfortable living then or now. He should not be seen as a penniless poet starving in a garret as he wrote the epic or the play which he hoped would catapult him into fame.

If he was in London, he had, no doubt, the leisure to pursue his interests and to make friends who had similar interests. But wherever he was, he could not have been unaware of the deepening crisis that had enveloped the state after Cromwell's death. His own hopeful prediction in the poem, that

> No civil broils have since his death arose,
> But faction now by habit does obey

proved to be quite wrong. The succession of Richard Cromwell to his father's position produced, within the year, a series of events that led directly to the return of Charles Stuart. Richard's dissolution of the Parliament caused a split in the army and a struggle for power among factions of the civilians and the army. The refusal of the unrepresentative Parliament to provide for election of a free Parliament resulted in the assembling of the remaining members— the Rump. In the meantime General Monck with his forces in Scotland was urged to march to London, in the hope that he might be able to bring some kind of order to a situation that moved into more serious chaos as the weeks passed. Monck seemed to favor rule by Parliament, but came to the view that it must be representative. By the end of the year it became apparent that the Rump could not rule; and early in the new year, Monck, who had secured the City of London, was actually in communication with Charles. The country, in the intervening months, was well prepared for the fall of the Rump and the return of the King: the Great Experiment had come to an end. As a prelude to his restoration—and upon prompting by Monck and others—Charles made his Declaration of Breda on April 14. The guarantees and promises, prompted by a desire for tolerance, were met by enthusiastic and happy response from his willing subjects. By the end of April a new, free Parliament had been elected; and by June, eighty peers had taken their seats. Both houses agreed that Charles should be proclaimed on May 8, as was done. At once Edward Montague (later to be created Earl of Sandwich), who had joint control of the fleet with Monck, sailed for Holland with a large retinue (which included Samuel Pepys) to bring the King to England. By May 25, they had returned in triumph to Dover; and the Restoration was complete, except for the official ceremonies.[1]

During these months it is probable that Dryden was meeting and making friends with persons interested in literature. At least one such friendship he records in the early months of 1660, that with Sir Robert Howard, the sixth son of Thomas, Earl of Berkshire. Howard, five years Dryden's senior, had engaged in the Civil War on the King's side, and as recently as 1657 had been, he says, a political prisoner in Windsor Castle.[2] A man of varied accomplishments, he had already begun to write poetry, and upon the eve of the Restoration was ready with a volume, which was entered in the *Stationers' Register* on April 16 by Henry Herringman as a "book called several Pieces written by ye honoble Sʳ Robert Howard, vizt *Songs, Poems, & Panegyricks; a play called the Blind Lady, &c.*"[3]

Dryden took a friendly interest in the volume, and he may indeed have been the "worthy friend" who, according to Howard in "To the Reader," took "so much view of my blotted Copies, as to free me from grosse Errors." When the volume appeared in June, it contained prefatory verses from Dryden, "To my Honored Friend Sr Robert Howard."[4] Sir Robert's volume opened with a panegyric to the King and ended with another to General Monck—an example of poetical and political foresight consonant with Sir Robert's worldly shrewdness.[5]

Dryden's tribute to Howard extends to 106 lines and was probably written between April 16 and June 21, when Howard's volume was advertised in *Mercurius Publicus* (the same issue that advertised Dryden's *Astraea Redux*).[6] Built upon a careful plan, the poem not only pays tribute to his friend but reinforces Dryden's own attitude to a new régime in politics and in poetry. The first section is taken up with extravagant praise of Sir Robert's strength and sweetness, his grace and smoothness, the delight and instruction provided by his poems. From this encomium—in the almost exact center of his poem—he moves to a statement of principle that was in his thoughts during this period, for he expresses much the same idea in his poem of *Astraea Redux,* even then being printed. This is the belief in the moral nature of poetry and the moral obligation of the poet, a belief that came no doubt from his long study of the poetry of antiquity. So too did his ideas of poetry as Art, which infuse these verses. Poetry, he asserts, is not a matter of chance, "No atoms casually together hurl'd," but the work of a craftsman. And though the art conceals art, behind the verses stands the judicious maker, rejecting the extremes of swelling metaphor and of careless "numbers." The golden mean underlies and reinforces the art, whose purpose is to delight and to instruct. But the golden mean cannot exist in a vacuum, any more than can the poet; and the extravagant extremes in society tend to produce a climate in which the desirable and necessary ideals of evenness, calmness, moderation, and artistic responsibility find it difficult to develop. He says:

> Of Moral knowledge Poesy was queen,
> And still She might, had wanton wits not been;
> Who, like ill guardians, liv'd themselves at large,
> And, not content with that, debauch'd their charge.
> Like some brave captain, your successful pen
> Restores the exil'd to her crown again;
> And gives us hope, that having seen the days
> When nothing flourish'd but fanatic bays,

All will at length in this opinion rest:
'A sober Prince's government is best.'

Whether Howard's poetry fulfilled such a high function or whether the newly-restored King subsequently provided a settled government in which art could flourish, is at the moment not important. What is important is to recognize that Dryden, brought up in fanatic and distracted times, thus early expressed a point of view toward art and the conditions under which it might flourish. The impact of subsequent events modified somewhat part of his conviction; but to the end of his life he maintained the claims of art and the moral quality and purposes of poetry.

The poem to Howard, then, attains an importance, not because of what it says about Howard, but what it says about Dryden in the spring of 1660. He was thinking seriously about poetry, turning over the principles and practices of classical antiquity and testing them no doubt against the poetry of his own country and the age as he had known it. That his life thus far had been lived in a period of conflicts and confusion, he was keenly aware. When he surveyed the poetry of this time, he could reflect that since his boyhood in Northamptonshire the Muses had fled or had all but been murdered either by fanatic officialdom or by a hopelessness born of controversy, division, and violence. By June of 1660 political and social life had been nudged off dead center by the stirring events of the past year. The wild and unrestrained rejoicing of a people long subjected to, but by no means inured to, the extravagances of dictatorial and unrepresentative rule and widespread restrictions upon personal liberties marked a conviction that the restored monarchy could only be better than what it replaced, that indeed a new age was dawning, a life under what would be a settled government cognizant of the interests of the subject. To men of Dryden's generation this was an exciting prospect, for they knew of such a thing only through story and reminiscences of their elders. Under the circumstances, and under the spell of high hope, was it not reasonable to imagine that a new Golden Age would emerge?

Dryden's poem, issued by June 19 (when Thomason recorded his copy), fully illustrates these stirrings of revived hopes. The very title—*Astraea Redux*—contains a criticism and a hope; and to make certain that no misunderstanding occurred, Dryden included as a motto from Virgil: "Jam Redit Virgo, Redeunt Saturnia Regna." The Return of Justice, Astraea, who in the Iron Age had fled, would return when the Golden Age came back. But there are two further meanings to be discerned, beyond the obvious. Astraea had become associated—as Dryden and his readers knew—with the Monarch, with kingly authority. So not only had "justice" returned, but justice identified with Charles Stuart, the symbol and the hope of a new government dedicated to rule by law. The reign of arbitrary government, which had banished justice, was over (or so it was thought) and a great new age had begun. But, for Dryden, Astraea was also equated with poetry, which in the poem to Howard had been "queen" and had been banished in the late times. She too, like Charles, had suffered in exile; and like "justice" and Charles, she was now being restored to her rightful sovereignty.

Poetically *Astraea Redux* marks a growing competence in Dryden's handling not only of diverse themes but of the couplet form which he later will develop to its highest potential. The poem of 323 lines is a rich and varied tapestry combining elements from mythology, classical literature, Christianity, history, and the contemporary scene. The lines are heavily freighted, yet they move with an appearance of ease and with more vigor than he had shown before. His talent in combining and synthesizing large issues in sharp and precise phrasing, a talent which we associate with his later years, is adumbrated in *Astraea Redux*. For example:

> For his long absence Church and State did groan;
> Madness the pulpit, faction seiz'd the throne:
> Experienced age in deep despair was lost,
> To see the rebel thrive, the loyal cross'd:
> Youth, that with joys had unacquainted been,
> Envied gray hairs that once good days had seen;
> We thought our sires, not with their own content,
> Had, ere we came of age, our portion spent.
>
> (ll. 21-28)

His generalized attack upon the rebels of the Interregnum spares no one from the peers to the rabble, from the enthusiastic Saints to the self-serving worldlings:

> Nor could our nobles hope their bold attempt,
> Who ruin'd crowns, would coronets exempt;
>
> (ll. 29-30)

for since the rabble were taught by their "designing leaders" to strike at power they themselves wished

The vulgar, gull'd into rebellion, armed;
Their blood to action by the prize was warm'd.
The sacred purple then and scarlet gown
Like sanguine dye to elephants was shown. . . .

(ll. 33-36)

Their freedom they used to create a holocaust which destroyed the state, the church, and a settled and prosperous mode of life. His greatest contumely is reserved for the Rumpers, dispersed by Cromwell in 1653 and dismissed by Lambert in 1659, who had invaded Parliament, that

Once sacred house; which when they enter'd in,
They thought the place could sanctify a sin

(ll. 183-84)

and for the Saints who

First timely charm'd their useless conscience out.
Religion's name against itself was made;
The shadow serv'd the substance to invade:
Like zealous missions, they did care pretend
Of souls in shew, but made the gold their end.

(ll. 190-94)

Such attack upon the agents responsible for the destruction wrought in the past provided a necessary poetical background for the praise of Charles, which from the vantage point of the summer of 1660 was not extravagant. Hardly any man in England would have controverted the rightness of Dryden's sentiments. The King's reluctance to take revenge against his father's enemies and judges, his Declaration of Indulgence, his determination to reinstate the Church, to govern according to law, his announced clemency—all were hopeful auguries for the future harmony and prosperity of his reign. No one could have foreseen the cruel changes that the succeeding months and years would bring. Banished David's only crime in 1660 was to be God's anointed. Indeed, the tolerant attitude toward dissenters, the promise of rule by law, the proposals to advance trade and commerce, the expectation of a strong continental policy (whereby Holland would be humbled) would usher in "Time's whiter series," a new golden time under the new Augustus. And under Augustus the arts would flourish.

Dryden was not alone in thinking so. Sir William Davenant, having already prepared himself in some measure for the new day by his semipublic presentation of musical plays between 1656 and 1659, was already busy arranging for royal favor in seeking a patent to form a theater under the benign auspices of Charles. In this he was joined by Thomas Killigrew, whose interest in drama and the theater, like Davenant's, went back to the 1630's. An experienced and devoted playgoer, the King was eager to promote drama; and he very early gave assent to the plans of the two entrepreneurs. On July 9 and again on July 16, warrants were issued to prepare grants of monopoly to them and within a month the formal patents were issued.[7] The handicaps under which the patentees labored in these early months were enormous. After nearly twenty years of harassment by parliamentary government, not even an adequate building was available for the proper mounting of plays. The commercial tennis courts were there; and it was Lisle's and Gibbons' that the new proprietors appropriated for the legitimate theaters.[8] More serious than the lack of playhouses was the lack of actors. Some of the performers in the theaters before the "late troubled times" were available and provided the nucleus of the new companies. Younger people—both men and women—were recruited and trained with astonishing speed. But the most serious deficiency and one that could not easily or rapidly be remedied was the absolute dearth of experienced playwrights. With no continuous outlets available, no playwrights had been developed, and no plays to supply two theaters were in being or even contemplated during these months. The patentees took the only course open to them: they turned to the Elizabethan and Jacobean stage. Here they found the plays they wanted and by mutual agreement allotted certain plays to each company. In general Davenant took most of Shakespeare; Killigrew, most of Beaumont and Fletcher and Jonson. The theaters began to live perforce on revivals; but they could not long continue to do so. The demand for new plays for the new age at once opened up exciting opportunities for younger men with energy, ideas, and talent.

Those who had come to maturity during the years when plays were proscribed knew no living tradition of playwriting; but they did know the old plays. Not many, however, had seen them acted, and consequently relied, for even the rudimentary problems they were to face, either upon the chatty reminiscences of the old actors or upon the experience of the entrepreneurs themselves. Their own self-consciousness about the worth and promise of their Golden Age, of which they felt themselves an important part, only exacerbated the difficulty of finding a way to write drama. The old plays, proper for another age, were not for them. Something different was demanded for this expansive time. With this recognition and with no sure guide to a pattern of dramatic writing, they quite understandably began to ask questions, to renew their acquaintance with classical and modern critical theorists; and within the next two or three years some of the embryonic dramatists appear to have met with like-minded poets and to have argued critical theory and examined dramatic practice in the hope of finding a way to provide satisfactory plays which would not be too imitative of a past age, but which would stay within the accepted canons of dramatic writing. Although no definite coterie was formed, an identifiable group of persons—many of them with an amateur's interest rather than the professional's need to know—seem to have talked often and at length about drama; and some began to translate theory into practice, though without the need to make their way by their pens. Among these were the Earl of Orrery, Lord Buckhurst, Katherine Philips (the "Matchless Orinda"), Sir Samuel Tuke, perhaps, whose *Adventures of Five Hours* was one of the first original plays of the new age, possibly Lord Vaughan and Edward Howard, and certainly Sir Robert Howard and Dryden. Buckhurst had a hand in translating Corneille's *Pompey*[9] and the Earl of Orrery soon would be ready with his first play. Sir Robert had already published a play; and Dryden was not to be far behind with his first piece for the stage. In the meantime he was making friends, and, as the months passed, new circles of acquaintances were opening for him.

After his poem upon the return of the King, no other work came from his pen for nearly a year. We can assume that he was in London and had settled in lodgings with Sir Robert Howard perhaps in or near Lincoln's Inn Fields, where were centered the activities of the theater people.[10] Yet there is no indication that he was now engaged upon a play: his initial attempt was to be made only after he had exploited more likely avenues of popular recognition. By 1661 the excitement generated by the restoration of Monarchy had inevitably given place to the more humdrum business of day-to-day living. The promises of the King at Breda regarding religious toleration had produced a widespread euphoria; but very soon it became apparent that not all members of the new royal Parliament were as dedicated to toleration as the King seemed to be. In October, 1660, after conferring with church dignitaries, Charles issued a Declaration of Ecclesiastical Affairs, which recognized differences of opinion concerning forms and ceremonies in worship, proclaimed a continuation of latitude in such matters for the present, and postponed decisions until a national synod should meet, on April 5, 1661. Faced by the firm antagonism of a newly-established church supported by many members of the Parliament, the conference failed to support the liberal position that had been in effect. For it was considered unnecessary, if not unseemly, to compromise with dissenters who had been mainly responsible for the confusions and for the disestablishment of the past. Indeed, the shoe was on the other foot: Parliament was once more representative, but it represented a different and understandably resentful segment of society; and the King was firmly installed, though not yet crowned. It might have been recalled, as in fact it was by some, that he was on the throne, not through the virtue and energy of the royalists, but by courtesy of those dissenters who were now seeking relief from what they had fought against for years: imposition of forms of divine worship by the Established Church.

In the meantime, elaborate preparations were being made for the ceremony of Charles's coronation. St. James's Day, April 23, had been chosen, and as the day approached it became apparent that no pains would be spared to provide a colorful spectacle for a people long habituated to the drabness of the rule of the Saints. As the time drew nearer, Dryden and his fellow poets (though not so many as had welcomed the King at his return)[11] began to write their poems for the occasion. His own, *To His Sacred Majesty,* was published by Herringman very close to April 23.[12] Though the coronation was in effect an anticlimax, none of the intervening events of the past year seem to have changed Dryden's opinion of the King's virtues or his hope for the new reign. The poem has a journalistic tone; Dryden is the poetic reporter of a public show: the pleasant spring weather, the ornate cavalcade and procession, the investiture by the Church "presev'd from ruine and restor'd by you," the happy throngs of spectators, the triumphal arches and the pageants—all are duly recorded. But he does not fail to celebrate the King's toleration, and his sovereignty over a happy people, or his choice of bride (negotiations were now under way) to provide for a new dynasty. Although *To His Sacred Majesty* shows no great advance in Dryden's technique, it stood out as the only skillful poem on the event and must have directed attention to Dryden again as one of the most active poets in the new reign.

Having twice within the year paid court to Charles, Dryden turned next to a tribute to another man only slightly less exalted than the King in the political life of the time—Edward Hyde, the King's

Lord Chancellor, who had been created Lord Clarendon at the
coronation.   Clarendon had accompanied the Prince Charles into
exile where he became his trusted mentor.   If Dryden wished for
further public recognition as a poet, he could have singled out no
better subject than Clarendon.   The poem, *To My Lord Chancellor,*
designed as a gift for New Year's Day, 1662, shows a change of
direction.   Though of necessity political considerations appear in a
poem to the most distinguished political figure of the time, Dryden's
concern is now more with poetry and the place of the poet than with
the more immediate events of the day.   The opening lines comment
sardonically upon the costly gifts given the Chancellor by the
"flattering crowds," whose hope—not their love—is thereby shown.
But not so the neglected Muses, whom, he reminds Clarendon, he
himself had courted long ago in the days of Charles I.   The world of
letters does not forget this service, though the Chancellor might.
From this point to the end of the first movement of the poem, Dryden
makes an unabashed bid for the interest and the patronage of Clarendon, not merely for himself but for the fraternity of poets.   For the
Chancellor is one of them—or has been—and it is only meet that
since "Wit and religion" had been banished with Charles I, and since
Clarendon had already restored the second Charles and was at the
moment restoring the primacy of the Established Church, he should
also begin actively to restore the Muses.   It will be through him
that the monarch can dispense his "influence" to the poets.

> You are the channel where those spirits flow
> And work them higher as to us they go.

This appeal may not have been fruitless in the service of letters,
but it seems not to have led to any patronage for himself; yet more
than twenty years later he could write to Laurence Hyde, the Chancellor's son, that "on some occasions, perhaps not known to you,
[I] have not been unserviceable to the memory & reputation of My
Lord your father."[13]   The remainder of the poem lauds Clarendon
for his services to both Charles I and II, for his incorruptibility
as a Justice, and for his wisdom and skill in the conduct of affairs.

Dryden was now more than thirty years of age.   In the past
three years, that is, since he began his devoted service to letters, he
had seized upon every opportunity to celebrate events of large moment in his time: tribute to the figure of Cromwell, the restoration of
the Stuarts, the coronation of Charles.   If we add to these efforts
the verses to Sir Robert Howard and the recent poem to Clarendon,

a pattern emerges. Most, if not indeed all, of the verses deal with personalities, and the range is narrow. Within the limits consciously set by Dryden, they necessarily are repetitive, since the exploration of personality stays on the surface. We find no penetrating probing into the recesses of thought or feeling. Instead, we find historical summary, description of actions, journalistic exploitation of events, laudation of virtues generally recognized, and praise and occasionally fulsome flattery. This is not to say that, within these limits, Dryden's poetry was of slight quality. On the contrary, his use of imagery, his control of form, his growing prosodic competence and, in places, sophistication, and his tremendous drive are apparent. No contemporary was producing anything comparable to it, and among the younger poets of the new age he began to emerge as a man with poetic authority. But the early period of the neophyte was drawing to a close; the range needed to be extended; and after one more poem written on the almost overworked formula, he was to turn to the more intricate and vastly more difficult form of the drama.

Although Dryden seems to have written verses when a proper and appealing subject presented itself, it is clear that his whole energies were not absorbed in this way. For in bulk his output is small, and we can hardly imagine that within a year only two or three hundred verses represented his total activity. To account for his movements and interests during these months we need to look at the social and intellectual life that he found, or made, available. Rather short in stature and inclined to plumpness (he was not without reason to be called "Poet Squab"), he had the fresh, rosy complexion of country life which was not now, and would never be, lost in the dirty, confining atmosphere of seventeenth-century London. If not overmuch distinguished in appearance, he assuredly was in intellect and breadth of knowledge. He had read widely and well and observed closely, both men and books. Added to a keenness of mind was a shrewdness in practical matters that went back to his family and to his upbringing. Though he was by nature diffident, he seems to have compensated somewhat by a self-confidence in his powers that was to strike some contemporaries as arrogance. Yet to those who knew him best his kindness even in minor matters and his constant willingness to do literary favors at cost to his own time and energies were most worthy of comment. His sense of humor, his great ability to find the risible in men and events, must have enlivened many a group in which he found congenial spirits. Wry and sardonic at times, his humor could as easily be playful, though not often cruel. But it could turn biting and astringent—as his antagonists were to learn to their everlasting hurt. Of substantial family and endowed with one of the best of educations possible in his time, Dryden doubtless found entree to numerous and varied circles.

One was the band of men interested in science and experimentation, who made up the "invisible college," as Robert Boyle called it in 1646 in a letter to Monsieur Marcombes, his old French tutor. The phrase described a loosely-knit organization of like-minded men whose center in these early years was Oxford. Among them, in addition to Boyle, were John Wilkins, William Petty, Robert Hooke, Christopher Wren, John Wallis, and Dr. George Ent. Part of the group were resident in London and met fairly regularly, until Cromwell's death, at Gresham College. During the summer months of 1660, activities of the now somewhat augmented group continued in London. At a meeting on November 28, they proposed to establish a more formal organization for the advancement of experimental philosophy, and each member present suggested names of persons who might be invited to become members. On July 15, 1662, the first charter of incorporation was granted, and the Royal Society came formally into existence.[14]

The original intention to limit membership to fifty-five was abandoned, and under the terms of their charter, they elected further members to the society. A second charter was drawn up and officially sealed on April 22, 1663. At a meeting on May 20, acting under the provision that persons accepted within two months of the date of this charter should be declared fellows of the Royal Society, the council recorded the names of those who came to be known as the Original Fellows. Dryden, having been elected, upon the recommendation of Dr. Walter Charleton, on November 19, became one of the original group.

Among these various men who made up the Society, Dryden would have found much intellectual stimulation and many subjects of common concern. He had already made a friend of Dr. Charleton, one of the first of the new fellows of the Society elected after the regular Gresham College meetings began. Though Charleton had received his medical degree at twenty-four and practiced during a long life, his interests seem to have been more antiquarian and literary than medical. In the decade 1650-60 he had written ten books on various subjects;[15] and now, when Dryden made his acquaintance, he was ready with another. By the summer of 1662 he had completed his researches on the origin of Stonehenge—an inquiry apparently provoked by Inigo Jones's contention that it was the remains of a Roman temple. Charleton believed, on the contrary, that the Danes had erected the stones as a meeting place where they would elect their kings. His book, entitled *Chorea Gigantum; or the most famous Antiquity of Great Britain, vulgarly called Stonehenge, standing on Salisbury-Plain, restored to the Danes,* was ready for publication by September 18, when it was recorded in the *Stationers' Register.* It was apparently published soon after, with a title page dated 1663, accompanied by commendatory poems by Sir Robert Howard and Dryden. Although Charleton's fellow antiquary, John Aubrey, scoffed that " 'Tis a monstrous height for the grandees to stand: they had need to be very sober,"[16] Dryden found the book of value and suitable for comment. His verses may not be "the noblest poem in which English science has been celebrated by an English poet,"[17] but it is a well-wrought and graceful poem. His mind was much on the newly-formed Society, and he took the opportunity presented by Charleton's book to assert the solid achievements of English science, and of some of the men whom he was soon to join. The names he mentions are impressive and important: Bacon, Gilbert, Boyle, Harvey, Ent, and Charleton. Dryden is not particularly interested in Charleton's antiquarianism, but in his researches on light (in his *Physiologia*) and perhaps also in his current examination of sound, on which Charleton read a paper before the Society on September 10.[18] Dryden seems less concerned with the study of Stonehenge, though it gives him a chance to draw the rather obvious comparison between Charleton's restoring the Danish kings to Stonehenge and the restoring of Charles to his throne. Of significance is the couplet devoted to Boyle, the second line of which refers to Boyle's "great brother" Roger, the Earl of Orrery. The Earl was already writing plays, and Dryden was either now or very soon to make his acquaintance, another in the growing number of those with whom he will be on terms of intellectual, if not social, equality, and who were being drawn together by the common bond of the theater.

The reference to Orrery at this point is important because it emphasizes not only Dryden's interest in the Earl himself but also in the activities of the group of new men with respect to plays and the theater. It is clear that Dryden and Howard were on the most intimate terms in these months. The correspondence of Orrery and the independent testimony of the other men make clear that Charles

II also was active in the discussions now going on about the nature of drama and the kind of drama proper for this new age. The King recommended the writing of serious plays after the French manner, in rhyme. There was much speculation about the nature of plays, the relative merits of English drama and French, the proper themes, and the techniques to be employed in presenting plays to the new and restricted audiences that the currently-used tennis courts could accommodate. Following the King's advice, Orrery, upon his return to Ireland (and during attacks of the gout) wrote two plays within the next two years, and submitted one to the King, who liked it so well that he promised to have the Theatre Royal produce it as soon as the new theater in Bridges Street was occupied.[19]

Even more active than the noble Earl was Sir Robert Howard, who in 1661 had associated himself with Thomas Killigrew and his company in the projected building of a new house for the Theatre Royal. On December 20, 1661, Sir Robert, Killigrew, and others entered into agreement to lease ground for the new building and to build it by Christmas of 1662 for an estimated £1,500. Of the thirty-six building shares, Howard was allotted nine, and he thus became, with Killigrew, the largest owner of the enterprise. Of course his intention was to make money, for he saw the potential earning power of a new house that would be in operation before the rival Duke's Theatre could get under way. By the spring of 1662 work was progressing on the theater, and Dryden, associated as he was with Howard, could not have escaped the contagious excitement if he would.[20] While the new house went up, Howard was not idle: he completed a play which the company produced in Gibbons' Tennis Court on April 23—*The Surprisal*. Perhaps the apparent success of his friend's play spurred Dryden to proceed with one of his own. At any rate there is no doubt that he was then—or soon would be— engaged in blocking out his first comedy, *The Wild Gallant*. By the end of the year or in January, 1663, it was ready, but the completion of the new theater (in which he may have hoped to see it acted), had been delayed. It was not to open until May 7, 1663.

In the meantime, however, *The Wild Gallant* was acted: Evelyn saw it on February 5, 1662/63, in what may have been a performance at court. Later in the month (February 23) Pepys saw it at White-hall and found it wanting, as apparently did most of the audience.[21] Nor was Dryden ever under any illusions about this first effort. He admits that it is a laboriously imitative piece, which faced the com-petition of Howard's *The Committee* (acted before the previous November) and Sir Samuel Tuke's *The Adventures of Five Hours,* which had very recently (in January) made a success at the rival theater. When he came to publish the play six years later, Dryden admits not only that the play had been a failure in performance but that the plot "was not originally my own; but so altered by me . . . that *whoever the author was* [my italics], he could not have challenged a scene of it."[22] It was an inauspicious and perhaps a discouraging beginning, but it no doubt enforced a double realization upon Dryden that plotting a play and clothing it adequately for performance before a vocal and highly censorious group of persons in a theater was far different from writing a series of graceful and flattering couplets to the King or to Dr. Charleton; and that taking materials for a play from his predecessors was merely the first step in a process that demanded a knowledge of techniques and theories of the drama before they could be successfully translated into dramatic success.

As if to salvage something from the failure of *The Wild Gallant,* Dryden addressed, probably in the spring, some verses to Barbara Villiers, Lady Castlemaine, upon the encouragement given the play in performance. If he believed that flattering verses to this beautiful and notorious Cyprian would promote his interests in court circles, he must have had second thoughts, for they were not published then but remained in manuscript until 1674, when they appeared in *A New Collection of Poems and Songs.*[23]

His thoughts, we may suppose, were not primarily upon court beauties but upon drama and upon his personal concerns. Sir Robert Howard's shrewdness in plunging into the Theatre Royal affairs began to be justified. Though the completed building cost much more than the £1,500 the company had committed itself to, it soon became apparent that the investment would prove profitable. The value of the building shares increased enormously as the company began to draw larger audiences in their more commodious surroundings. In the summer of 1663 the expectation of continued prosperity was evident, and Dryden seems to have made plans to hitch his fortunes to the company which had shown such rich enterprise, and to Howard, who both as a business man and a playwright was enjoying a remarkable success. It is little wonder that Dryden for his next excursion into drama should have collaborated with Sir Robert. And no doubt through him Dryden now furthered his acquaintance with the Howard family. Two of Robert's brothers, James and Edward, were engaged in writing for the stage; and, in July, James's first play, *The English Monsieur,* was performed at the new playhouse.[24] Within six months Edward's first attempt, a tragedy entitled *The Usurper,* would be acted in the same house.

But it was not James and Edward that Dryden was most interested in, it was their sister Elizabeth, who was now twenty-five years of age. The fortunes of the family were at a low ebb because of the extensive expropriations of the Earl's property and fortune during the Commonwealth. Berkshire House, the Earl's town residence, was on the block, the Earl having already made overtures to the King to buy it from him and to help him thereby to retrieve some part of his fortune. (In due time the King bought it as a residence for Lady Castlemaine.) Of Elizabeth, the "baby" of the family, we know next to nothing; but her reputation has suffered severely under attacks by her husband's enemies and by unsubstantiated allegations.[25] Whether she was no better than she should have been cannot be proved, though it is abundantly clear that she was now and had been of marriageable age for some time. With the uncertain financial situation of the family, it had become evident that some kind of dowry was needed to attract a man who socially might become an acceptable husband to Elizabeth, who was connected by blood and marriage with the best families in England. Accordingly, Sir Robert had, with Sir Robert Long in the Exchequer, convinced the Earl that he should assign a grant of £3,000, which had come from the King, to his daughter.[26] Although no mention of dowry is made in relation to the grant, it seems clear that it was so regarded, especially in view of the Earl's urgent need of money for his own uses. The assignment was made over to Lady Elizabeth on February 27, 1662, but nothing had been paid on it and nothing was to be paid on it for a number of years. Dryden's family or character having proved sufficiently satisfactory to the Earl, he gave his consent to their marriage, and on November 30, 1663, they received a license at St. Swithins. He was described as a bachelor, about thirty and she about twenty-five.[27] On December 1 they were married.[28]

Until his marriage Dryden apparently had been living with Sir Robert in Lincoln's Inn Fields.[29] From this time until he and Elizabeth left London during the plague their residence is unknown; they may have been in rented lodgings.[30] But wherever Dryden was living, he was not far from the theater, which claimed his energies and thought until the plague stopped all dramatic production. At the moment he was particularly absorbed in Howard's new play, *The Indian Queen.* Following the lead of Orrery (who was Sir

Robert's cousin by his marriage to Margaret Howard, daughter of the Earl of Suffolk), Howard (with help from Dryden) was writing a "heroic" play after the new mode in rhyme. By the first of the year it must have been all but complete. It was produced at the Theatre Royal on January 27, 1663/64, when Pepys saw the street full of coaches and reported the gossip that the play was a magnificent spectacle.[31] *The Indian Queen* scored an immediate success, partly because of the elaborate mounting and costumes, and partly no doubt because (though composed after Orrery's *The General*) it was the first of the new plays in rhyme to be acted. The play was Howard's, but Dryden had a share in it (as he pointed out in the "Connexion of *The Indian Queen*," in 1667). The extent of his unspecified collaboration may have been more considerable than he was willing or able at the time to assert. A recent careful study of it suggests that as much as half of it might have been his.[32]

Dryden was now at work on his next play, *The Rival Ladies.* In view of the success of *The Indian Queen,* which was a heroic play in rhyme, it is curious that Dryden did not follow the same pattern. Instead of heroics, he put together a romantic tragicomedy with a single plot, but with many comic sub-actions, using blank verse for the most part with only occasionally a series of couplets in those scenes of verbal battledore and shuttlecock, of arguments in verse upon the outcome of which depends a turn in the action. It was acted probably in June, and the copy was almost at once (June 27) registered by Herringman in the *Stationers' Register*. Among those who saw it was Orrery, who had returned from Ireland in June for a visit which lasted for several months. His rhymed heroic plays had, as we have noted, been written, but as yet none had been acted. During this sojourn Orrery made arrangements for their production, and by early fall both *The General* and *The History of Henry V* had been produced.[33] During these months a group seems to have talked more than once about rhyme and its appropriateness as the form for serious drama. This was particularly pertinent and timely, for Howard's *Indian Queen* had been well received and now Orrery's own plays in the same mode were being acted. Another impetus to widespread discussion of plays and of rhyme and blank verse was provided by the appearance earlier in 1664 of Sorbière's *Relation d'un Voyage en Angleterre*. As Louis XIV's historiographer, Sorbière had been welcomed in London in 1663 and had been elected a fellow of the Royal Society. He observed not only the scientists and their work but many other things, including the theaters.

In his book he recalls his playgoing and makes highly critical remarks about English drama, particularly about the English violation
of the unities, the lack of decorum observed, and the failure to use
rhyme.   Thomas Sprat, however, took exception to many of his
observations on English life, thought, and customs, and set about
writing an answer, maintaining during the very months when the
plays of Howard, Dryden, and Orrery were introducing rhyme in the
new way that the English playwrights had rejected rhyme for blank
verse.

When Dryden's play, *The Rival Ladies,* was published (probably
in late October),[34] it carried a dedication to the Earl of Orrery, who
had now returned to Ireland.   This "Epistle Dedicatory" to *The
Rival Ladies* is significant not only for biographical information it
contains but also because it is Dryden's first prose criticism to see
print.   He initiates here the practice which was to continue to the
end of his career of embodying in prefatory form the results of his
thinking on poetic and dramatic theory and practice.   "This worth-
less present," he tells Orrery, was "designed" for the Earl when it
was "only a confused mass of thoughts, tumbling over one another
in the dark."   He reminds Orrery of the kindness he has always
shown his writings and recalls that some of them "have crossed the
Irish seas, to kiss your hands."   Extravagant praise of Orrery as
poet, playwright, and statesman finally gives place to a consideration
of the "new way" of writing plays, which he finds not so much a new
way as it is an old one newly revived and cites the example of
Sackville's *Gorboduc.*   Suppose it is a new way; should one not
follow the example of the "most polished and civilized nations of
Europe"?   Should the English oppose the world on this point as
"most of us do in pronouncing Latin."   It was Shakespeare—"who
had, undoubtedly, a larger soul of poesy than ever any of our nation"
—who invented blank verse to avoid the continual necessity of
rhyming.   So natural is rhyme for the English that he is amazed so
many stumble in it by inverting the order of words and by ending
the verses with verbs, a practice which he has tried to eschew.   The
only inconvenience of rhyme, he continues, is the occasional inversion
of words for the sake of rhyme, yet even here a poet may so order
his words as to forge a chain with all words in their proper places,
as in the "negligence of prose."   If this is done, then verse possesses
the advantage of prose in addition to its own.   The dignity and the
excellence of rhyme were taught by Waller, who "first made writing
easily an art" and showed how to "conclude the sense, most com-

monly in distichs." Both Davenant and Denham are included in his praise, for their "sweetness" in rhyme.

That the epistle to Orrery was being used as a public sounding board for some critical explorations which had been carried on in private may be seen in the repetition of such phrases as "some have said" and "objections some have made." In asserting the advantages of rhyme over blank verse he cites Sidney's well-established point of its aid to memory. But this is not to him the greatest advantage. That he reserves for the regulative power of rhyme in its control of the poet's imagination, which "like an high-ranging spaniel . . . must have clogs tied to it, lest it outrun the judgment." The belief that rhyme serves to tighten and order verse he is to advance more than once later. He is careful, however, to define such rhyme: it is that which does not force the sense, but follows it. Like the best medicines, it must be appropriately prescribed to achieve the intended result: a fit subject must first be chosen. This consideration leads him into the area immediately concerned, the drama. Here, he says, the best and most appropriate places for rhyme are scenes of argumentation and discourse "on the result of which the doing or not doing of some considerable action should depend." This use he demonstrated in practice in *The Rival Ladies*. At the close of the epistle he says that the "greatest part of my design has already succeeded to my wish, which was to interest so noble a person in the quarrel."

The dimensions of the "quarrel"—and the participants—are unfortunately unknown. But it seems clear that Dryden's epistle brought into public notice what had to this time been a private matter. In bespeaking Orrery's interest and support, he allies himself with one side of a critical controversy, which was to be aired publicly for a number of years. It is perhaps not too much to say that with this piece Dryden begins his first period of critical writing, and opens, for the new age, topics of speculation and of controversy which would produce some of the best criticism in English.

Reaction to Dryden's pronouncements was probably immediate in the coffeehouses and other assemblies of the wits.[35] Within a few months appeared the first public reply and disagreement—by Sir Robert Howard. Four of his plays were collected (at the instance of Herringman, according to Howard) in a volume registered on March 7, 1664/65, and probably published soon after. As a prefatory note, Howard wrote an essay "To the Reader." He makes a deceptively modest disclaimer of any ambition to be considered a playwright—he who had written more plays than any other man since the reopening of the theaters. Most of the short essay is taken up with advancing the claims of blank verse as the only proper vehicle for drama. Without mentioning by name his brother-in-law, he launches into a refutation of Dryden's ideas in the epistle to Orrery. His own excursion into rhyme in *The Indian Queen* Howard excuses as a kind of amiable acceptance of a fad, used against his better judgment. For him blank verse is more "natural" than rhyme, especially in dramatic dialogue where the repartee of the characters suggests lack of "art." On the contrary, rhyme shows too clearly the hand of the maker: the impression of unpremeditated and unrehearsed speech of the characters is destroyed by rhyme. The differences of opinion between the two men, here publicly displayed, continued for a number of years and provoked from Dryden two of his best critical essays, the first of which, the *Essay of Dramatic Poesy,* has taken its place among the foremost pieces of criticism in the language. If Sir Robert, by design or by accident, helped to evoke Dryden's early critical treatises, English literature remains his debtor. But however deep their differences in critical thought—and later in political beliefs—their friendship seems not to have suffered unduly; for Howard in his official and private capacity was to do many good services for Dryden.

The publication of Howard's remarks on rhyme and blank verse apparently occurred at almost the same time as the acting of Dryden's next play, *The Indian Emperour,* his first heroic drama written wholly in rhymed couplets, and produced by the Theatre Royal in April or May, 1665.[36] The play, as he pointed out, was a sequel to Howard's *Indian Queen,* using the same scenes and the same costumes. Love and honor, the twin ideals of the heroic play, were its themes. If Howard's essay denying the claims of rhyme was designed to embarrass Dryden and to provide a general criticism of his play, it probably did not succeed; for the couplets of *The Indian Emperour* surpassed any that had yet appeared in the theater. In one step Dryden established rhyme as the verse form for the evolving heroic drama, which was to become an important form of Restoration drama. In the epilogue to the play, Dryden notes the various groups of self-appointed critics. In the character of a Mercury (representing Phoebus), the epilogue gives them leave to exercise their prerogatives according to their rank. In the most privileged position are those like Howard:

> For the great dons of wit—
> Phoebus gives them full privilege alone,
> To damn all others, and cry up their own.

To the lesser breeds he allows much smaller privileges: some may judge doggerel rhyme, "all proves, and moves and loves"; and the habitués of the coffeehouses are accorded even less: "Their proper business is to damn the Dutch."

For more than a month the second Dutch War, a carefully stage-managed affair, had been in progress. Undertaken for the purpose of destroying the Dutch Navy in order to further the trade of English merchants, it had hardly begun when the plague struck. Bubonic in origin and brought from the Levant in merchandise through Holland (the propaganda insisted), it was making fairly rapid headway when *The Indian Emperour* was acted. In May forty-three deaths were reported, and Pepys on May 24 records much talk of it then going about town. The beginning of June saw the weekly "Bill" go up alarmingly, and as one precautionary measure the King ordered the theaters closed on June 5. Before the month was over six hundred had died; in July the deaths were counted in thousands. The hot, sultry weather provided favorable conditions for its spread. The court fled to Oxford (where Parliament met in November), and thousands of Londoners abandoned the capital for safer places. Dryden and his wife moved to the Earl of Berkshire's country place at Charlton, Wiltshire, where they were to remain longer than they may have anticipated. In September thirty thousand persons died, and from this high point the plague began to recede. But the theaters were not to reopen for more than a year.

Early Distinction

1666-1668

T HE LENGTH of Dryden's residence at Charlton during the plague months cannot be determined. It may be assumed that the growing virulence of the epidemic combined with the hot and humid weather of June and July may have driven Dryden and his wife to Wiltshire before the summer was out. Although details of his life there are lacking, his literary interests and activities can be inferred from the amount and the quality of the work he brought back to London after the end of the epidemic. It seems probable that he spent between a year and eighteen months at his father-in-law's estate.

Only two items related to his personal affairs can be assigned to these months. The first concerns his financial situation. The early grant to Lady Elizabeth of £3,000 remained only a paper promise; none of it had been paid to her by the summer of 1666. Since the closing of the theaters had stopped one source of income, Dryden must have become hard pressed for money; for it cannot be supposed that his income from the Blakesley land could maintain his wife and him in more than a very modest fashion. Furthermore, Lady Elizabeth was now pregnant, and their first child was expected within three months. With this prospect imminent, they apparently determined to press their claims on the Treasury for payment on the grant. Consequently they approached Sir Robert Howard, who served as their intermediary in negotiations with the Treasury commissioners, particularly with Sir Robert Long, Auditor of the Receipt of the Exchequer. How long it required to cut the red tape in the Treasury is unknown; but by June 25 a notation was made in the Treasury accounts that the grant of 1662 had not been paid and a directive was included that it should be paid, the funds to come from the revenues of Somerset and Dorset.¹ Sir Robert Long could hardly hope to find the entire amount in a Treasury depleted by the growing demand of the Dutch War still being fought. Perhaps it was little less than miraculous that he could find any money. Somehow he was able to allocate £768 15s. on the account, and sent down to Charlton a receipt for this amount to be signed by Lady Elizabeth and Dryden. On August 14, Dryden wrote him, enclosing the acquittance and a letter from Sir Robert Howard and directing that the payment be held until they should come for it.² Their efforts to obtain the remainder of the full amount dragged on for three more years, always complicated by the tangled financial affairs of the Earl of Berkshire.³ Scarcely a fortnight later, on September 6, their first son, Charles, was born.⁴

In the meantime, Dryden had been busy with a variety of literary projects: a poem (*Annus Mirabilis*), a prose essay in criticism (*An Essay of Dramatic Poesy*), and a play (*Secret Love*). These can be identified with certainty as being of this period; others, as yet unidentified, may also have been on the stocks. The Dutch War, having begun slowly in the early spring of 1665, made little headway during the height of the plague months. After the winter of 1666 it came to life again in the spring. At the end of May a force of about eighty English ships, under command of James, the Royal Admiral, Prince Rupert, and Albemarle, sailed into the channel to engage the Dutch. On June 1, a furious battle took place, with the English suffering heavy losses. After lines had been reformed, an English force reduced to forty ships began an engagement with nearly eighty Dutch ships and for four days fought to an inconclusive draw. Both fleets withdrew to rearm and to rest; but after a month they met again (July 24-25), when the English fleet emerged with a clear-cut victory. Heroic deeds had been done by the English commanders and seamen. In August, part of the Dutch fleet was burned by the fireships of the English, and the major engagements of the war had ended. Not since he had begun to write poetry seriously had Dryden found such an event to exploit. As we have seen, most of his verse was concerned with persons and was panegyric in interest and feeling. Now a subject presented itself which would provide him the opportunity to move into a genre at once more exalted and more significant to an aspiring poet than any he had yet approached—the heroic poem. In the "Account of the Ensuing Poem," prefixed to *Annus Mirabilis* as an address to Sir Robert Howard, Dryden writes: ". . . I have chosen the most heroic subject, which any poet could desire: I have taken upon me to describe the motives, the beginning, progress, and successes, of a most just and necessary war; in it, the care, management, and prudence of our King; the conduct and valour of a Royal Admiral, and of two uncomparable generals; the invincible courage of our captains and seamen, and three glorious victories, the result of all."

Although we cannot with certainty set dates for the writing of the poem, it would appear that it was taking shape between July and October. It is unlikely that he would have undertaken to write upon the subject until a solid basis for the superiority of English naval operations was established, that is, toward the end of July, 1666. English chauvinism had translated the indeterminate action of early June, 1665, into an English victory (one of the three Dryden mentions); but it was not until a year later that the flow of victory to the English was to be seen. The poem then was probably under way in the last part of the summer. But before he had completed the account of the war another holocaust of a different kind occurred. On September 2, the Great Fire broke out, and for nearly a week it raged, unchecked by all the devices and instruments available to pertinacious and self-sacrificing citizens, who, joined by a solicitous King, fought until they and the fire were finally exhausted. It laid waste more than 370 acres within the crowded city and destroyed more than 90 churches and 13,000 dwellings and commercial establishments. This turn of events presented Dryden with a problem which he solved brilliantly.

The Fire, he saw, was a "most deplorable, but withal the greatest argument that can be imagined; the destruction being so swift, so vast and miserable, as nothing can parallel in story." In their way the circumstances and the events of the Fire could be regarded as of sufficient magnitude and of such heroic proportions as to be comprehended within the definition of heroic action. It was a bold stroke to combine apparently antipathetic themes; for it broke a "oneness" of impression that he must have had in mind when the war alone remained his argument. Indeed, he recognized this in his "Account," when he points out to Howard that he has called the poem "*historical* rather than *epic* [which no doubt was his first designation of it], though both the actions and actors are as much heroic as any poem can contain." Yet he is reluctant to put it in the epic category because "since the action is not properly one, nor that *accomplished in the last successes* [italics mine], I have judged it too bold a title for a few stanzas which are little more in number than a single *Iliad,* or the longest of the *Aeneids.*"

The section on the war takes up more than two-thirds of the poem, which, had it stopped there, would doubtless not have been called *Annus Mirabilis.* The inclusion of the Fire enabled Dryden to celebrate not only "the piety and fatherly affection of our Monarch to his suffering subjects" but also the "courage, loyalty, and magnanimity of the City." His tribute to the city was to be emphasized by printing with the poem a dedication "To the Metropolis of Great Britain," in which he refers to the cruel trials through which the people have lived in the course of one year: "an expensive, though necessary, war, a consuming pestilence, and a more consuming fire." To account for Dryden's concern with the Fire, his dedication to the city, and his tribute to the role of Charles, a new interpretation has recently been advanced in great detail and with persuasiveness. Professor Hooker believes that "the title, dedication, and contents hint at . . . an object that would make the speedy publication of the poem desirable." The poem, he thinks, is "in one sense a piece of inspired journalism, written to sway public opinion in favor of a royal government, which dreaded a revolution . . . which, according to republican propaganda, was to be ushered in by omens and portents, by 'wonders' signifying the wrath of God against the King and his party." Pamphlets and tracts had been appearing for several years telling of prodigies and portents, "of crosses and humiliations befalling the King's friends, of signs betokening God's displeasure with the King and threatening to visit His heavy judgments upon the nation if it continued to support the royal government." Some of the tracts were entitled *Mirabilis Annus.* Dryden, then, "was engaged in countering the effects of seditious propaganda represented by a group of pamphlets whose very title he employed against them." Be this as it may, the tenor of Dryden's "Account" to Howard shows clearly that his thoughts are employed upon the epic poem and upon the details of a poetic art which can encompass a modern treatment of heroic actions. Indeed one may seriously doubt the narrow, political purpose as is suggested by this interpretation.[5]

The extent to which he was devoted to the heroic idea is to be seen in the thoughtful exposition he writes in the "Account," and in the poetry itself. He ranges, like his own nimble spaniel, over the fields of ancient and modern theory and practice in respect to verse forms proper to exalted subjects, his adaptation of language, the choice of images, the adornment of the thought. In what W. P. Ker called "one of the most systematic passages in Dryden," he divagates upon the composition of poetry in the well-known passage:

The composition of all poems is, or ought to be, of wit, and wit in the poet, or *Wit Writing* . . . is no other than the faculty of imagination . . . which, like a nimble spaniel, beats over and ranges through the field of memory, till it springs the quarry it hunted after . . . *Wit written* is that which is well defined, the happy result of thought, or product of imagination. . . . The proper wit of an Heroic or Historical Poem . . . [consists] in the delightful imagining of persons, actions, passions, or things. 'Tis not the jerk or sting of an epigram, nor the seeming contradiction of a poor antithesis (the delight of an ill-judging audience in a play of rhyme), nor the jingle of a more poor paronomasia. . . . The first happiness of the poet's imagination is properly invention, or finding of the thought; the second is fancy, or the variation, deriving or moulding, of that thought, as the judgment represents it proper to the subject; the third is elocution, or the art of clothing and adorning that thought . . . the quickness of the imagination is seen in the invention, the fertility in the fancy, and the accuracy in the expression.[6]

His great interest in the language of poetry is evident, and the problems to be faced by the English poet seeking significant and elevated words he discusses at length; and here begins a concern which is to last his lifetime and to which he addressed himself time and again.

To Howard, Dryden gives much credit for the entire poem; "if there be anything tolerable in this poem they owe the argument to your choice, the writing to your encouragement, the correction to your judgment, and the care of it to your friendship."[7] The address is dated from Charlton on November 10 and was presumably sent to Howard soon after, along with the poem, to be given to Herringman. It was licensed for the press by L'Estrange on November 22, and entered in the *Stationers' Register* on January 21, 1666/67. It must have appeared at once, for Pepys bought a copy on February 1. Embedded in the "Account" were some verses which he had written in the preceding year, after the naval engagement of June, 1665, to the Duchess of York in tribute to the Duke (the Royal Admiral), and which had been circulating in manuscript. Ostensibly included here to answer criticism that his language in these verses lacked height of fancy and dignity, they served another purpose: with them Dryden paid graceful homage to the Duchess, who could have had no place in the heroic account of the war. So his round of tributes came full circle; and his small poem, not immediately publishable elsewhere, made an appropriate appearance here.

Even before he wrote *Annus Mirabilis,* however, his retirement had enabled him to write a play, which he had also sent to Howard for criticism. His obligations to Sir Robert, both in his personal life and in his acknowledged deference to him in literary matters, are noteworthy during this time and are of some considerable importance to the interpretation of his *Essay of Dramatic Poesy,* written also during his stay at Charlton, and its aftermath. It seems probable that his critical essay preceded in composition the writing of the play, which appeared under the title of *Secret Love; or the Maiden Queen.* Both of these are clearly extensions of his interest in dramatic affairs so abruptly interrupted by the closing of the theaters in the early summer of 1665. Retirement to Charlton gave him the necessary leisure to pursue his speculations about the drama and to review the course of the informal talks with the wits of the town, which he had first hinted at in his dedication of *The Rival Ladies.* Almost as a corollary, the writing of a play would perhaps demonstrate in practice some of the theoretical considerations of the essay. As we shall see, *Secret Love* differs sharply from his most recent play, *The Indian Emperour,* whose stage life was cut short by the closing of the theaters. A tentative sequence of the most important work done at Charlton might be suggested. *An Essay of Dramatic Poesy*—at least in its initial form—would probably date in the late summer and autumn of 1665; *Secret Love* in the winter and spring of 1665/66; and *Annus Mirabilis,* of course, in the summer and early autumn of 1666.

The theater was never far from his thoughts, especially the Theatre Royal, to which he had allied himself. His personal connections with Howard, the largest shareholder in the building, would have kept him aware of the fortunes of the theater during the long-enforced holiday and of the improvements going forward. For Killigrew and his company, realizing that the stage had been built too narrow for the kind of scenes now being used in plays of the new era, and having nothing else to do, proceeded to make alterations to it in March, 1665/66, against the day when the Lord Chamberlain would allow reopening.[8] That day was still further away than they could have expected. Not until October, when both managers were seeking to gain permission to act, was there any hope. Then, by promising to give the proceeds of one day per week to the poor, they were accorded the privilege of reopening; but it was still to be a month before all barriers were removed. Toward the last of November, both theaters were apparently acting, but, understandably, to smaller audiences, since many of those who had fled the city had not yet returned.[9]

Among these was Dryden, who as far as can be determined, was still at Charlton. From November 10—when he dated, at Charlton, the "Account" prefixed to *Annus Mirabilis*—until many months later his residence cannot be determined with any confidence. It has generally been assumed that in the late autumn or winter he returned to London, presumably because the theaters had reopened and because he had written a number of things that may have been ready for publication. Yet he had entrusted to Howard the negotiations that resulted in the publication of *Annus Mirabilis* in January; and despite the fact that the Theatre Royal was again operating, *Secret Love* was not to be acted for several more months. Indeed, his presence in London might not have been so urgent as it was at Charlton; for his infant son was at the beginning of the new year hardly four months old. The difficulties of moving his family to the city were serious: the wholesale destruction wrought by the Fire had produced a housing shortage of enormous proportions, and in these months the problem of finding an adequate house would have been almost insoluble. If he remained at Charlton, Dryden could have made necessary trips to the city; and he could have taken temporary lodgings for himself during the ensuing months. Lack of evidence must leave the question open. Not until more than two years had passed, and after the birth of another son, did Dryden establish a permanent residence.

Whether in London or not, Dryden was able to keep in touch with the theater. Although *Secret Love* was not yet ready for acting, *The Indian Emperour* was; and on June 14 Pepys saw a performance of it. Within a week it was acted again at the Theatre Royal before the King.[10] Because of the plague, it had not had a chance to demonstrate its drawing power. Now it began to take its place as the most popular of the plays written since the Restoration, and in the next year was acted many times both in the commercial theater and at court.[11] Its success must have been gratifying to Dryden, and it doubtless encouraged him to the preparation of his new play for the stage. *Secret Love* appeared less than two months later: the King—and Pepys—saw it at the Theatre Royal on March 2, 1666/67, and the King enjoyed it so much that he returned on March 5 to see it again. Within the next month he commanded it to be acted at court.[12] His evident delight in it was emphasized in the autumn when Dryden, in the prefatory matter to the published play, recalls that the King "has graced it with the title of His Play."

The publication of *Annus Mirabilis,* and the popular success of both *The Indian Emperour* and *Secret Love* within the space of three months, affords unquestionable evidence that Dryden at the beginning of 1666/67 was the most able author of the time. Nor did his eminence go unmarked by King, and court, and city. His circle of prominent acquaintances began to widen. Already on terms of easy familiarity with many of the wits, he now claimed the attention of others who could find a place in such company. He still no doubt retained friendly relations with some of the members of the Royal Society, though his interest in the group had flagged during his sojourn in Wiltshire, and he had allowed his membership to lapse for nonpayment of dues.[13] With other prominent persons, such as the Duchess of Monmouth (and her Duke), Sir Charles Sedley, and Lord Buckhurst he established relations which were to last for many years. Others who were to be immediately important to him in the very full year now beginning were Sir William Davenant and the Duke of Newcastle, both attracted to him because of their need for his talents in the drama, now so well demonstrated. Both of these men had been long associated with each other, Davenant having been on Newcastle's staff during the early years of the Civil War, in 1642, and their friendship had continued during Charles's exile abroad. Newcastle, a man of great parts, a governor of Prince Charles in the early days, possessed a romantic spirit and had somewhat of the poet in him (as indeed did his second wife, the famous Duchess of Newcastle).[14] Though now an old man, Newcastle had by no means lost his zest for literature, and his old friend Davenant was manager of the Duke's Theatre. No longer young himself, Davenant was not only serving as brilliant guide to the fortunes of his theater, but was also now, and had been for several years, experimenting with the adaptation of Shakespearean and other plays to the stage with the addition of those operatic devices that he had launched even before the patent theaters were in existence. For some reason, never satisfactorily explained, Davenant approached Dryden, whom he knew but slightly, to help him in a projected revision of *The Tempest*. At about the same time (in late spring or early summer) he apparently put his old friend Newcastle in touch with the rising playwright for help on a project that he too had begun.

The circumstances surrounding the double collaboration which Dryden now undertook are vague. What, if any, financial arrangements were agreed upon are quite unknown, though it has been supposed that Newcastle was prepared to pay for Dryden's help in putting into shape a play to appear under the noble Duke's name.[15]

His aid in assisting Davenant with *The Tempest* perhaps carried with it no pecuniary implications, unless it would have been a share in the author's benefit rights and in publisher's payments. Yet this is merely conjecture. Perhaps the opportunity to collaborate with Davenant and of course the possibility of a subsequent entree into the Duke's Theatre were enough recompense, for Dryden was not yet irrevocably committed to giving the Theatre Royal all of his plays.

Judging by the order of their production, we can suppose that Dryden's collaboration with Newcastle claimed his time in the earlier months of the year. The Duke's proposal must have found a ready response from Dryden: to turn a translation he had made from Molière into an English comedy for the Duke's company. According to John Downes, the prompter of the Duke's playhouse, writing his reminiscences many years later, "The Duke of New-Castle, giving Mr. Dryden a bare Translation of it [*L'Etourdi*], out of a Comedy of the Famous *French* Poet Monseur Moleiro: He Adapted the part purposely for the Mouth of Mr. *Nokes,* and curiously polishing the Whole."[16] What Newcastle's "bare translation" consisted of, we have no way of knowing; but probably it would have been no better than Dryden could have made. He was already knowledgeable in the French playwrights, for he had studied them to good purpose in his preparation for the *Essay of Dramatic Poesy*. Not only was he aware of Molière's quality but also of Quinault's, upon whom he was to draw for a considerable amount of material. By a stroke of inspiration, he translated the original title, not to "The Blunderer," but to "Sir Martin Mar-all"; and as *Sir Martin Mar-All, or the Feign'd Innocence* the play was produced on August 15. It scored an immediate success, and the town was under no illusions about the authorship. Pepys saw it the first day and calls it "a play made by my Lord Duke of Newcastle, but, as everybody says, corrected by Dryden." He laughed until his head ached all evening and night.[17] The fiction of the great Duke's authorship was continued when it was registered under his name by Herringman, though it appeared without the Duke's—or Dryden's—name on the title page. Not until 1691 was it included among Dryden's works. Pepys's pleasure in *Sir Martin Mar-All* was shared by the theatergoers in general; Downes records that, along with Etherege's *Love in a Tub,* it got the company more money than any preceding comedy. Both at the Duke's and at court it continued its initial success for many years.

In the meantime, the Dutch War dragged on, ignominiously for the English, whose navy after the earlier victories had seriously deteriorated in fighting power and in morale. Negotiations for peace were instituted as early as March, but even in June, as Coventry returned from Holland with a draft of the proposed treaty, a large fleet of Dutch ships sailed into the Thames, destroyed several ships and captured the *Royal Charles* and the *Unity*. The ill-managed war had cost hundreds of thousands of pounds more than anticipated, and by the time a treaty was signed in Breda (July 21) and ratified in London (August 23-24) the King's Treasury was not only bare, but deep in the red, with no immediate prospects of replenishment. During these months, Samuel Pepys worried constantly about the large debt incurred by the navy; and as he watched the actions of a dissolute King and his wanton court, he could see no good to come of it all. Antagonism to Clarendon increased as the summer wore on, the King and his favorites and a faction in Parliament (of whom one was Sir Robert Howard) determined to drive him from his chancellorship. On August 30 he was relieved of his office, and the King gathered about him the new advisers—enemies of Clarendon— Catholics, crypto-Catholics, and dissenters, but none a Church of England man. So the Cabal—as it came to be called from the first letters of their names: Clifford, Ashley, Buckingham, Arlington, and Lauderdale—came into being.

All of these events were to have immediate and lasting influence upon Dryden's fortunes. Clarendon, to whom he had addressed the graceful poem of 1662, was out; he would soon be up for impeachment and subsequently go into permanent exile. If Dryden had ever hoped that Clarendon might become an influential friend and patron, that hope now was vanishing. All five members of the Cabal, moreover, were to come into Dryden's life, for good or ill: Clifford, now a Treasury commissioner but soon to be Lord Treasurer, would contribute something to his financial well-being; Ashley he would forever anathematize as Achitophel and Buckingham as Zimri; Arlington, later Lord Chamberlain, would pass judgment on the acting of his plays; and Lauderdale would contribute to his translations. The shifting winds of political life in 1667, of course, gave little indication of the roles to be played by these men in the years ahead, nor could Dryden, in this busy summer, have foreseen what the whirligig of time and the revolutions of Fortune's wheel would bring.

In fact, the unpredictability of events and the sudden changes of fortune to which life is subject were brought home to him in two events of the summer. One was as bizarre and perhaps as exciting as any of the fictional events he ever put into a heroic play. As

Pepys tells it, on the evening of July 28, Sir Henry Bellases and Tom Porter, warm friends, entered upon a causeless and silly quarrel in the house of Sir Robert Carr—an "emblem of the general complexion of this whole kingdom at present." They began to fight (both apparently in their cups), but were parted; whereupon Tom Porter left the house and encountered Dryden, and told him of the whole affair and of his determination to fight Sir Henry at once. For "he knew, if he did not, they should be friends tomorrow, and then the blow [which Sir Henry had given him] would rest upon him." He then asked Dryden to lend him his link boy to report upon Bellases' movements. Waiting at the coffeehouse in Covent Garden, they were notified that Sir Henry's coach was approaching. Whereupon Porter went out, stopped the coach, got Sir Henry out, and they fought a duel, their acquaintances in attendance. Both were wounded. Sir Henry, in Pepys's account, "called to Tom Porter, and kissed him and bade him shift for himself; 'for,' says he, 'Tom, thou hast hurt me; but I will make shift to stand upon my legs till thou mayest withdraw, and the world not take notice of you, for I would not have thee troubled for what thou has done.' And so whether he did fly or no I cannot tell." Within ten days Sir Henry had died of his wound.

Dryden, of course, was only an innocent bystander in this affair. A few days later he saw death under a different aspect. Abraham Cowley, "the darling" of his youth—as Dryden later was to refer to him—had spent most of the years since the Restoration at his Sabine farm in Chertsey. Now he was dead, in his fiftieth year, but his fame lived on, even now enhanced by his ode "To the Royal Society," prefixed to Sprat's *History*. On August 3 his funeral attracted, according to Evelyn, all the wits of the town, lords, bishops, and the clergy. That Dryden was among them seems likely; and he probably followed the procession to Westminster Abbey for interment of Cowley in the corner where thirty-three years later Dryden himself would be laid. The passing of Cowley removed a poet whom Dryden had followed at Westminster School and from whose verse he had learned much.

The remainder of the summer, however, held other things than death. With *Sir Martin Mar-All* a success, he could turn some of his energies to the collaboration with Davenant on *The Tempest*. At the same time, the success of his plays induced him to prepare the manuscripts for publication. On August 7, Herringman registered *The Wild Gallant*, which presumably had been acted in revised form during the summer,[18] and the *Essay of Dramatic Poesy*. About this time or shortly thereafter *The Indian Emperour* was in press and was to be published in the early autumn.

By the middle of August the bare state of the King's exchequer was beginning to elicit great concern among a number of people. On August 3, Pepys had reported to the commissioners of the Treasury the serious news of the navy debt—£950,000. Retrenchment—as well as ready money—was needed. On August 20, Sir William Coventry suggested to Pepys and his colleague Sir William Penn that they should lend the King money, and within ten days Penn had lent £500, and Pepys, £300. At the same time some Parliament-men, to be called "Undertakers," among whom were Lord Vaughan and Sir Robert Howard, undertook to raise money from other persons. Pressure was brought to bear, as Pepys makes plain, in his notation of August 24: "This day comes a letter from the Duke of York to the Board, to invite us, which is as much as to fright us, into the lending the King money; which is a poor thing, a most dishonourable, and shows in what a case we are at the end of the war to our neighbours. And the King do now declare publickly to give 10 per cent to all lenders." Such a high rate of interest, he reports, causes some to think that even "the Dutch will send over money, and lend it upon our publick faith, the Act of Parliament."

One lender was Dryden, and the steps by which he found the money and made the loan are curiously interesting. Sir Robert Howard, we recall, had in the preceding year prevailed upon the Treasury to make a payment on Elizabeth Dryden's grant. Now he may have pointed out to his brother-in-law and his sister some of the advantages, even beyond the promised return, that might accrue to them if a loan could be made in this extremity. At any rate, he again put into motion the machinery of the Treasury, and on August 21 he laid before the Commissioners a move to confirm a warrant "on behalf of his sister the Lady Draydon for 3000 £, whereof part is paid."[19] Perhaps he pointed out to them that a payment would benefit everyone: Elizabeth would receive something on an old account, the commissioners would get credit for it, and the King would get the money—surely a case of shrewd bookkeeping. Whatever arguments he used, he was successful. On September 16 an order appears to pay her £500 and three days later (September 19) the warrant for that amount was approved.[20] Within a month the entire £500 was transferred by Dryden to the King; and letters of

Privy Seal were issued on October 16, confirming the loan.²¹ No
mere poet could achieve such legerdemain unaided.

In the midst of these negotiations the revision of *The Tempest*
continued. More than two years later, when he wrote a preface to
the published play, Dryden gives only a bare hint of his contribution,
reserving the major part of the credit—or discredit—for Davenant.
The creation of the man who had never seen a woman (as a counterpart to Miranda) came from Davenant: "this excellent contrivance
he was pleased to communicate to me and to desire my assistance in
it." Dryden was so pleased with it, he says, that he never "writ any
thing with more delight." Perhaps then he was chiefly responsible
for this "improvement" on Shakespeare. Yet his writing "received
daily [Davenant's] amendments." Indeed their individual styles so
merged that identification of their respective scenes can hardly be
made with any assurance. On November 7, the new *Tempest* opened
to a full house at Davenant's theater. Pepys reports that the King
and court were there. The play struck him as "most innocent," lacking some wit, but, even so, above the ordinary play. Not worthy of
note were the tricky contrivances, but he did find a "curious" piece of
music "in an echo of half sentences, the echo repeating the former
half, while the man goes on to the latter; which is mighty pretty."
On the same day, Lady Elizabeth and her father were directed by the
Treasury Commissioners to appear the following Monday about the
original grant of £8,000, out of which had come hers of £3,000.

Before *The Tempest* was acted, *The Indian Emperour* must have
been in print, for Dryden dated the dedication on October 12. Its
popularity with the court circle makes understandable his addressing
it to one of the most beautiful and important ladies of that group—
Anne, Duchess of Buccleuch and Monmouth. The popularity of
heroic plays, he points out, has resulted from the approbation they
have received at court: "the most eminent persons for wit and
honour in the royal circle having so far owned them, that they have
judged no way so fit as verse to entertain a noble audience, or to
express a noble passion." He further testifies to the favor accorded
him by the Duchess and begs her to take the play under her protection. "Offsprings of this nature are like to be so numerous with
me, that I must be forced to send some of them abroad; only this is
like to be more fortunate than his brothers, because I have landed
him on a hospitable shore." Fulsome and extravagant in praise of
Anne and her husband, James Fitzroy, the King's natural son created
Duke of Monmouth, this dedication, to our more squeamish age, al-

most passes the bounds of propriety; it is the first of many which Dryden will write in excessive flattery of rank and titles. To blame him for acting as a man of his time is as impertinent as to blame his century for its being different from ours. Yet in this dedication, as indeed in most of those written during his career, he never loses sight of the fact that he is a poet urging the claims of poetry. In the midst of perhaps the most outrageous sentence in his tribute, the poet appears:

To receive the blessings and prayers of mankind, you need only to be seen together: we are ready to conclude that you are a pair of angels, sent below to make virtue amiable in your persons, or to sit to poets, when they would pleasantly instruct the age, by drawing goodness in the most perfect and alluring shape of nature.

In the play itself, he tells the Duchess, he has not wholly followed the truth of history, but has "taken the liberty of a poet to add, alter, or diminish, as I thought might best conduce to the beautifying of my work: it being not the business of the poet to represent historical truth, but probability."[22] Some of the ideas implied here he had already made public, and fuller treatment of others was soon to be forthcoming.

By October 28, when Pepys had his copy, *The Indian Emperour* was public property. Apparently delighted with Dryden's tribute to them in the dedication, the Duke and Duchess of Monmouth began to make plans for an amateur performance of it. By the end of the year preparations were well in hand and the ladies and gentlemen of the court were declaiming Dryden's rolling couplets. That average playgoer, Samuel Pepys, saw the court applaud it on January 13, but was himself dissatisfied. The following week, King, Queen, and court attended another performance at the Theatre Royal, where they doubtless saw it acted properly. A week later still, Charles's "play," *The Maiden Queen,* already acted at the Theatre Royal on January 4, was given at court.[23]

The new year thus began auspiciously. Dryden's reputation had increased without interruption, and his public success was matched by his personal well-being. His financial affairs were prospering and his family life, dim as it is to us, seems to have been happy. His first son was now more than a year old; his second would be born within three months; and he would be named John.[24] Family responsibilities no doubt became more exacting and constant from this time forward. As can be seen in the works of these months, for ideas Dryden drew constantly, and often heavily, upon his reading. Yet he usually attempted to make over his sources rather than to transfer materials bodily.   In the preparation for the writing of both the *Essay of Dramatic Poesy* and *Sir Martin Mar-All* Dryden had very thoroughly read the plays of the two Corneilles, Molière, and Quinault.   In the last two he had already found materials for *Sir Martin;* in Thomas Corneille, who had relied much upon Spanish novels for plots, he now found some hints for another comedy, upon which he was beginning to work.[25]   It was to be called *An Evening's Love,* or *The Mock Astrologer;* the second title and some of the incidents he found in Corneille's *Le Feint Astrologue.*   At the same time Sir Robert Howard was completing a job of play-doctoring, apparently taking over and making his own without much essential contribution an old play of Ford's, the manuscript of which had become available to him.[26]   This play, *The Duke of Lerma,* was ready for acting in February at the Theatre Royal.   At the other theater, Davenant was rehearsing a revival of an old play by Thomas Tomkis called *Albumazar,* and perhaps because he knew Dryden was writing about an astrologer, asked him to contribute a prologue.   Howard's *Duke of Lerma* was first acted on February 20, 1667/68.   Pepys arrived early to take his place among the courtiers and the King; and whether he misinterpreted Howard's play, or listened to gossip in the playhouse, cannot be determined: he viewed it as "designed to reproach our king and his mistresses that I was troubled for it, and expected it should be interrupted; but it ended all well, which solved all."   The next day, February 21, *Albumazar* was acted at the Duke's Theatre, preceded by Dryden's prologue.[27]   Though Dryden erroneously supposes that Jonson took his Subtle (in *The Alchemist*), from Tomkis' *Albumazar,* his point is not invalidated by this error.   Jonson, he says, stole what he needed, but in the process of transference became himself an alchemist of sorts by transmuting others' lead to his gold, and reigns like "an unrighteous sovereign," ruling well what he "unjustly gains."   Not so the authors of this age, who

> . . . make whole plays, and yet scarce write one word;
> Who, in this anarchy of wit, rob all,
> And what's their plunder, their possession call;
> Who, like bold padders, scorn by night to prey;
> But rob by sunshine in the face of day:
> Nay scarce the common ceremony use
> Of "Stand, sir, and deliver up your muse;"
> But knock the poet down, and, with a grace,

Mount Pegasus before the owner's face . . .
They strip the living, and these rob the dead. . . .
Such men in poetry may claim some part:
They have the license, tho' they want the art;
And might, where theft was praised, for Laureats stand,
Poets, not of the head, but of the hand.

This is all especially pertinent, since the astrologer in *Albumazar* praises theft, and mention is made of Sparta, where thievery is held lawful. *There* such poets could be laureates indeed by virtue not of thought but of the ability to use a pen. His strictures point directly to Howard and to his play acted on the preceding day. Although Dryden himself was never disturbed about taking materials from whatever source he found them, his attack here is upon wholesale robbery that transfers intact and passes off the old material as new. This in his eyes was reprehensible. The boldness of Dryden's attack and the scorn which he employs to drive home his disapproval are noteworthy. To Howard alone, in these early weeks of 1667/68, did his words apply; for he was close enough to his brother-in-law and to the theater to have known long before February 20 that *The Duke of Lerma* was none of Howard's.[28] Why he should have launched this public attack on Sir Robert is still not clear. It may have been the result of private disagreement about drama. Some of their points of difference had already been made public by Howard; others emerge from this prologue, and still others from the *Essay of Dramatic Poesy,* now probably in press.

Before its appearance, however, another event of greater significance happened. After a few days' illness Davenant died on April 7, and was buried two days later. His death left vacant the post of Poet Laureate. To find an appropriate candidate to succeed Sir William required no very long debate on the part of the King and his advisers in such matters. Dryden's accomplishments and his reputation, plus his political loyalty, singled him out at once. Within four days of Davenant's funeral, a warrant for a grant to John Dryden of the office of Poet Laureate was recorded in the state papers; the Privy Seal would be issued sometime later.[29] The post carried a salary of £200 per year; to it would, within a few years, be joined the position of Historiographer Royal, which had been allowed to lapse for some time after the death of James Howell. Dryden no doubt found the new honor exhilarating and the promise of an increased and regular income greatly satisfying. But the difficulties he was already encountering in getting money out of the Treasury on Elizabeth's account might have tempered somewhat his satisfaction at being on the King's payroll.

The death of Davenant had wide ramifications in the world of the Restoration theater. His accomplishments were common property, and none knew better how well he had managed the Duke's Theatre than Killigrew and the members of his company at the Theatre Royal. They had not met very successfully the competition offered them by Davenant, though they had the advantage of a larger and more sumptuous building. Now upon the death of Sir William the control was kept by his widow, but the practical direction was allotted to Betterton and Harris, two of the most distinguished actors of the company, and both shareholders. In their capable hands the fortunes of the company would hardly diminish. And there was talk of a new building to enable them to draw larger audiences and to develop further their already great proficiency in producing elaborate musical plays. At this juncture the King's company, aware that Dryden was the only regular, and frequent, contributor to their repertoire, took steps to meet the expected competition from the new management of the other theater. Sometime in May they proposed that Dryden should join them as an exclusive writer, who would give them all of his output. Their expected preemption of his plays of course carried a *quid pro quo:* they agreed to give him a share and a quarter of the total of twelve and three-fourth shares of the acting company. This arrangement put him on equal terms with the three leading actors of the company: Hart, Mohun, and Lacy.[30] In return he contracted to deliver three plays a year. The proposal he must have found very attractive, for it promised, in the first place, to add enormously to his income and probably to bring with it both a voice in the direction of the company and a measure of prestige. On the basis of his output during the past year, he would have had no reason to suppose that he could not write three plays a year. Yet in no single year did he discharge this part of his contract; he did, however, share in the receipts of the company to the extent (no doubt inflated) of three or four hundred pounds a year, as the complaint against him in 1678 bitterly asserts. Whatever he was paid, the company had its bargain: all of his plays for the next decade—until the virtual dissolution of the company under Killigrew's chicanery and mismanagement—went to the Theatre Royal.[31]

The cup of honors accorded Dryden almost overflowed before

the summer was past. The respect in which he was held by King and court was never higher. In early June, Charles wrote to his Archbishop of Canterbury requesting that the new poet laureate should be recognized by a Lambeth degree. Accordingly, on June 17, Gilbert Sheldon sealed a dispensation for Dryden to be awarded an honorary M.A. degree. Headed "Dispensatio Joanni Dryden, pro gradu Artium Magistri," the citation testifies to his "vitae probitas, bonarum literarum scientia, morumque integritas, vel ipsius domini Regis testimonio perspectae sunt. . . ."[32] Perhaps the honor thus given him amounted to little, but it served as one more indication of the King's regard for him at this time, and of his position as a major figure in letters.

During these weeks, the *Essay of Dramatic Poesy* was published, though the precise date is difficult to fix. The public replies it evoked suggest that May or June may have marked its appearance; for Howard's *Duke of Lerma* was registered by Herringman on June 24; at its publication it contained the preface taking issue with some of the ideas discussed in the *Essay*. Furthermore, the second edition of the *Indian Emperour* (with its "Defence of an Essay"), Shadwell's *Sullen Lovers,* and a *Letter from a Gentleman* (an attack on Dryden) were in print either in August or early September.

Since its composition at Charlton during his retreat from the plague, the *Essay* had lain among his "loose papers" (as he says) unpublished, but not, we can assume, unheeded. As a perceptive critic of the work of others, Dryden could not have been unaware of the quality of the essay or of the fact that nothing quite like it had yet appeared in English. Distinct from the literary criticism written by his great predecessors, which had been fragmentary and limited (like Daniel's), conventional (like Sidney's), or random, unorganized jottings (like Jonson's), the *Essay* was the first sustained piece of practical criticism written by an English dramatist on his craft. Presumably it might have been sent to the printer at any time during the past two and a half years; why its publication was delayed for such a time neither he nor anyone else has explained. If explanation were needed, it might be sought in the dedication (only recently written), in the materials of the *Essay* itself, and in the details of his career since 1665. Many years afterwards, in late 1692 when he dedicated to the Earl of Dorset another essay (as he had dedicated the *Essay*) he recalls that he had presented him his first critical work, "when I was . . . in the rudiments of my poetry, without name or reputation in the world, having rather the ambition of a writer, than the skill; when I was drawing the outlines of an art, without any living master to instruct me in it. . . ."[33] This may be unduly modest, or in his old age Dryden may have been remembering that he had written the *Essay* before his reputation had been made. We can hardly take exception to the further statement that he was "drawing the outlines of an art" without a living master to instruct him. The *Essay* was a speculative adventure into the discovery of ways to write drama; and in 1665 he had not yet learned. For this reason, reticence and even a certain diffidence may be allowed him for not publishing a discourse on the writing of drama until he had sufficiently demonstrated a practical ability to succeed in the only proving ground known to the playwright—the theater. By the summer of 1668 he had progressed in his practice far enough to make his theories relevant and important. Earlier publication might have seemed presumptuous.

The dedication to Buckhurst (later Dorset) provides a key to Dryden's thinking about drama, his purposes in writing the *Essay,* and something of its origins. He confesses that he finds "many things in [it] which I do not now approve; my judgment being [not] a little altered since the writing of it; but whether for better or worse, I know not: neither indeed is it much material, in an Essay *where all I have said is problematical*" [italics mine]. He adverts to the matter of rhyme, which he says he has here seemed to favor; but he has laid the "practice of it aside" because he now finds it "troublesome and slow."[34] His opinion of its usefulness, however, remains unaltered, for he is not convinced by those who argue against it because they have not tried it or have written badly in it. Buckhurst's own practice (in Act IV of *Pompey*) he cites as a good argument for it, and he adjures the young nobleman to write more.

By this tribute he leads up to a statement which relates his *Essay* to the larger controversy that has continued since he first publicly mentioned it to Orrery in 1664. He uses the dedication of *The Rival Ladies* as his justification for some of the points of view in the *Essay.*

In treating this subject, [he writes], I sometimes dissent from the opinion of better wits, . . . not so much to combat their opinions, as to defend my own, which were first made public.

The dialogue form in which he casts his discourse gives him the proper vehicle for his purpose of surveying all of the relevant and current ideas on the making of plays.

Sometimes, like a scholar in a fencing-school, I put forth myself, and show my own ill play, on purpose to be better taught. Sometimes I stand desperately to my arms, like the foot when deserted by their horse; not in hope to overcome, but only to yield on more honorable terms, And yet, my Lord, this war of opinions, you well know, has fallen out among the writers of all ages, and *sometimes betwixt friends* [italics mine]. Only it has been prosecuted by some like pedants, with violence of words, and managed by others like gentlemen, with candour and civility.

Even Tully, he points out, had a controversy with his "dear Atticus"; and "in one of his Dialogues makes him sustain the part of an enemy in philosophy, who, in his letters, is his confidant of state, and made privy to the most weighty affairs of the Roman Senate." As in this instance, so, he seems to say, the public disagreements respecting drama in no way impair the friendship between Howard and him. Both had their convictions, and were not loath to express them, Howard often with violence and arrogance (as he so frequently demonstrated in parliamentary debate), and Dryden with quieter arrogance and a rapier wit. Their friendly personal relations despite the apparent enmity in the "critical war," survived—as far as any evidence shows—the public washing of critical linen. At the close of his dedication Dryden restates his purpose, in the event that anyone should misunderstand:

I will give your Lordship the relation of a dispute betwixt some of our wits upon this subject, in which they did not only speak of plays in verse, but mingled, in the freedom of discourse, some things of the ancient, many of the modern ways of writing; comparing those with these, and the wits of our nation with those of others: 'tis true, they differed in their opinions, as 'tis probable they would; neither do I take upon me to reconcile but to relate them. . . .[35]

Although the dedication was written very close to the time of publication and therefore refers to a situation in 1668, the materials of the *Essay* had their origin in ideas which had been explored in 1664 and 1665, and not only by those whom Dryden called "wits." Sprat's answer to Sorbière's *Relation* suggests that both the Frenchman and his English antagonist, writing before the plays in rhyme had reached the stage in any number, were talking about the revived Elizabethan plays, which were generally those written in blank verse.[36]

Some of the points of dissension and disagreement, then, were to be seen in areas quite outside the precincts of the wits. All of these Dryden gathered into a dialogue which gave him the scope and the speakers to relate, but not to reconcile, varying points of view. It becomes a speculative discourse on the most pertinent questions being raised with respect to drama. Following the traditional form of dialogue, he gives his speakers names; and as the grand manipulator he not only gives them ideas, shrewd and simple, crucial and trivial, but also arranges them artistically to emphasize the speculative and tentative nature of the discourse. Attempts to identify the speakers— Neander, Eugenius, Lisideius, and Crites—with living persons have tended to disregard Dryden's stated purpose and to obscure the exploratory technique which becomes evident if we regard them only as literary mouthpieces for divergent points of view.[37]

Although Dryden was inclined to minimize the originality of his ideas (it was "a little discourse in dialogue, for the most part borrowed from the observations of others"), the *Essay* remains the consummate expression of a free-ranging mind. He did indeed lay under heavy contribution his predecessors in the republic of letters: Aristotle, Horace, Cicero, Tacitus, Terence, Quintilian, Plautus, Juvenal, Scaliger, Jonson, and Corneille among others provide examples, points of view, and critical support. Yet, as Professor Huntley points out, "it is Horace and Quintilian who are his true masters; and drama as rhetoric, in the sense of persuading, influencing, or having a particular audience by means of language, is his main concern. . . ."[38] If the question of rhyme bulks large, it only reflects the point of largest contemporary controversy; other matters were perhaps of more importance: the relative quality of the ancient versus the modern drama, the unities as an aid, not a prescription, in writing plays, the achievement of French and English drama. More immediate smaller problems of the practicing playwright, like relations, liaison of scenes, decorum of the stage, character portrayal, appropriate language adapted to character—all received perceptive treatment. In such a discourse with such an announced purpose no final conclusions could be reached, and no laws were intended to be laid down. Unanswered, because unanswerable, was the question, "What is the best way to write a play?" For nearly thirty more years he experimented, but, as he no doubt would have known early, the answer eluded him, as it has all others.

In the meantime Sir Robert Howard, already brought to unfavorable public notice by the thinly-veiled charges of literary theft in Dryden's prologue to *Albumazar,* was to suffer another attack through the comic ridicule by a new playwright for the Duke's Theatre, Thomas Shadwell. On May 2, *The Sullen Lovers, or The Impertinents* was first acted, and in its initial run scored a *succès de scandale* unmatched at the time. At once the court and town identified Sir Robert with Shadwell's character Sir Positive At-All, "a foolish knight, that pretends to understand everything in the world, and will suffer no man to understand anything in his company; so foolish Positive, that he will never be convinced of an Error, though never so grosse." Although Pepys saw it on the first day he seems not to have found Howard shadowed under Sir Positive At-All until his attendance the second and third nights, when the gossip reached his ears. By May 8, he marvels how the play "does take . . . everybody's talk being of that, and telling more stories of him of the like nature that it is now the town and country talk, and they say, is most exactly true." Sir Robert, as the town knew, had in Parliament earned the reputation of a know-it-all, and his similar reputation among the theatrical wits Shadwell explicates. Sir Positive is a playwright who undertakes to inform his companions of his superiority, not only in writing plays but in criticizing them. He is made to say (Act III) to Emilia: "I am an Ass, an Idiot, a Blockhead, and a Rascal, if I don't understand Drammatique Poetry of all things in the World; why this is the only thing I am esteem'd for in England" —to which impertinence she later replies, "would it not distract one to see Gentlemen of 5000£ a year write Playes, and as Poets venture their Reputations against a sum of Money, they venture theirs against Nothing?" Elsewhere Sir Positive charges a rascally clerk with crying down his latest play. For satisfaction to his honor, he demands that the offender sign a certificate testifying, among other things, that the noble knight "is no purloiner of other mens work, the general fame and opinion notwithstanding, and that he is a Poet, Mathematician, Divine, Statesman, Lawyer, Physitian, Geographer, Musician, and indeed a *Unus in Omnibus* through all Arts and Sciences."

It is hardly surprising that Howard, when in June he gave *The Duke of Lerma* to Herringman to publish, should make a public reply to these attacks on his character and abilities. Acting with more discretion than might have been expected by a town thoroughly apprised of his putative weaknesses, Howard answered Dryden, but refused to dignify Shadwell's attack. That he was irked by the charges of theft levelled at him is shown by his reference to them early in his preface: "Some were pleased to believe little of it mine." He recites a circumstantial story of an unnamed gentleman who brought the manuscript to the King's company, which thereupon asked him to read it to determine its fitness for the stage. Upon their urging, he altered it. Not again will he trouble the town with a play, for this, because of the pressure of other business, is his valedictory; nor will he again venture into "the Civil wars of censure." The remainder of the apparently hastily written piece deals with an attempted rebuttal of some of Dryden's ideas in the *Essay of Dramatic Poesy,* but by no means of all, for he admits that he is "extremely well pleased with most of the propositions laid down in the *Essay.*"[39]

Herringman published for both Dryden and Howard, and, on June 24, he registered *The Duke of Lerma* and *Sir Martin Mar-All.* At the same time, or soon after, he began to arrange for a second edition of *The Indian Emperour.* A shrewd businessman, Herringman could see profit also in Shadwell's play, which had enjoyed a long run only weeks before. Thus, in the late summer all four manuscripts were being edited and prepared for publication in the same stationer's shop. It seems inescapable that the three authors were aware of the progress of the works of the others. No contemporary notice enables us to fix the dates of their publication, but upon the testimony of Pepys, the order would appear to be as follows: *The Duke of Lerma, Sir Martin Mar-All, The Sullen Lovers, The Indian Emperour.* By September 20, Pepys had purchased one of the copies of *The Indian Emperour* which included Dryden's *Defence of an Essay,* his answer to Howard's preface. And he also had a copy of *A Letter to a Gentleman,* which he thought "mighty silly, in behalf of Howard."

Although a newcomer to the theater, Shadwell, with the success of his first play still fresh, felt no reluctance to intrude himself, though warily, into the controversy.[40] The dedication of *The Sullen Lovers* to Newcastle, dated September 1, includes comments on both the brothers-in-law. Shadwell picks up and repeats a favorite tag of Dryden's, "I am so far from valuing myself . . . upon this Play, that . . .", compliments himself on keeping the three unities, especially that of time, the decorum of the characters, and on the linking of scenes ("accompted a great Beauty" among the French). He praises Ben Jonson ("whom . . . all Dramatick Poets ought to imitate"), and reprehends Dryden for suggesting (as he thinks) that Jonson "wrote his best plays without Wit." All of these ideas come straight from the *Essay.* But he also alludes to Howard's preface: "Perhaps you may think me as impertinent as any one I represent; that, having so many faults of my own, shou'd take the liberty to judge of others . . . I must confess it very ungenerous to accuse those that modestly confess their own Errors; but positive Men, that justify all their faults, are Common Enemies, that no man ought to spare. . . ."

These are comparatively mild comments, but they serve notice to the public that Shadwell, the beginning playwright, is *au courant.* Not so mild is the tract entitled *A Letter from a Gentleman to the Honourable Ed. Howard Esq. occasioned by the civiliz'd Epistle of Mr. Dryden's before his Second Edition of his Indian Emperour.* This fourteen-page tract, signed "R. F.," achieves a certain factitious importance because it is the first sustained attack on Dryden and the genesis of certain allegations and gossip that were to be repeated *ad nauseam* for many years.   He sneeringly refers to Dryden as "The Squire" and implies that actually he had no real claim to gentility.   The reason for his taking up the cudgels on Howard's behalf, he says, is that the knight "could not so well make a Return in a Billingsgate style."   "R. F." rebuts Dryden's earlier charge that *The Duke of Lerma* was stolen, by asserting that the poet laureate was hardly one to level such an accusation, since he claims the right of theft by custom, witness *The Maiden Queen,* most of *The Mock Astrologer,* and *The Indian Emperour.*   If Howard wrote verses that made little sense, Dryden too was vulnerable; he quotes, "And follow Fate, that does too fast pursue," a line that in future served many third-rate antagonists of Dryden as a convenient club.   The Squire further had been meant for the clergy but had been diverted— to the great loss of the Church—from taking orders.   But of course the most heinous offense, as seen by "R. F.," was that he "had been employed [as a "puny statesman"] under his father, a zealous committee-man and Sir Gilbert Pickering, a crafty councellor in the late times." Adopting Dryden's own phrase describing Howard, "R. F." concludes that "the Corruption of a Statesman is the generation of a poet laureate."   The tradition of attack on Dryden's work and his character begins here; it was not to end even with his death.[41]

When Dryden addressed himself to writing *A Defence,* he must have been irritated in the extreme; for Sir Robert, in some anger and in seeming haste, had innocently (or perhaps willfully) misread Dryden's intention in the *Essay,* and in the choice and discussion of separate propositions perverted its original meaning.   Further, his careless composition had left some of his own objections obscure in the extreme, and he had left himself wide open to Dryden's playful, but often cutting, wit.   Since the answer was to be a defense of his own propositions advanced in the *Essay,* Dryden of necessity was bound to their reconsideration rather than to the introduction of new ideas.   As a result, the *Defence* appears to be a series of repetitions, yet the elaboration enriches the points already made in the earlier work.

As a beginning, he sets the time and circumstance of his aware-ness of Howard's remarks—the appearance of *The Duke of Lerma* while he was correcting copy for the second edition of *The Indian Emperour*. The author of the former, "a noble and most ingenious person" has done him "the favour to make some observations and animadversions upon my Dramatic Essay." He expresses a mock fear that "so good a cause as mine may suffer by my ill manage-ment, or weak defence"; but he must take the glove when it is thrown down, even though he is "only a champion by succession, and no more able to defend the right of Aristotle and Horace, than an infant Dimock to maintain the title of a king." He sees his concernment in this controversy as so small that he could be content to be driven from his notions, "especially by one who has the reputation of understand-ing all things." Shadwell's character of Sir Positive is levied upon here, as he is to be later; Dryden continues to work the vein of de-traction by alluding slyly to the old charge of literary theft: "he gives me the compellation of 'The Author of *a Dramatic Essay*'; which is a little discourse in dialogue, for the most part borrowed from the observation of others; therefore, that I may not be wanting to him in civility, I return his Compliment by Calling him 'The Author of *The Duke of Lerma*.'" He proceeds to a re-examination of the question of rhyme, pointing out, amid numerous digressions, that the question whether rhyme is "natural or not in plays . . . is not demonstrable." He will not make himself ridiculous by trying to decide whether "prose or verse be nearest to ordinary conversation," or to agree with Howard that, "a play will still be supposed to be a composition of several persons speaking ex tempore." Dryden in-sists, on the contrary, that a play is the "work of the poet, imitating or representing the conversation of several persons." Howard, he says, does not speak to the question, and the world may suspect he is the same man who in Parliament had "maintained a contradiction *in terminis,* in the face of three hundred persons."[42] Moving from the consideration of rhyme, Dryden takes up *seriatim* the other ob-jections voiced by Sir Robert: the choice of words (and Dryden pokes fun at his mistranslation of Latin phrases), differences between tragedy and comedy, the imitation of nature as the foundation of drama, and the treatment of the unities. Among other examples of Howard's wrongheadedness which he resents is the inference that Dryden attempts to lay down laws for drama. At considerable length he cites his own words in the dedication, the address to the reader, and in the *Essay* itself to prove that the whole "discourse was sceptical, according to that way of reasoning which was used by Socrates, Plato, and all the Academics of old, which Tully and the best of the Ancients followed, and which is imitated by the modest inquisitions of the Royal Society." Anyone who has taken the trouble to read "that trifle," he thinks, will agree that he was not being magisterial. "The truth is, if I had been naturally guilty of so much vanity as to dictate my opinions; yet I do not find the character of a positive or self-conceited person is of such advantage to any in this age, that I should labour to be publicly admitted of that error."

The Defence remains an excellent example of literary rebuttal, and the whole arsenal of debating technique Dryden rifles to annihilate his antagonist. Even the close may be viewed as part of the traditional form: "But I lay my observation at his feet, as I do my pen, which I have often employed willingly in his deserved Commendations, and now most unwillingly against his judgment. For his person and parts, I honour them as much as any man living, and have had so many particular obligations to him, that I should be very ungrateful, if I did not acknowledge them to the world." It was indeed a matter of *prior laesit*: he had not first taken up arms; but he will be the first to lay them down. This paper scuffle was at an end. Howard would not again serve as his opponent, but others, in growing numbers, would take his place.

Premier Dramatist of the Age
1669-1673

WHILE DRYDEN was busy with literary affairs, Lady Elizabeth pertinaciously and with some success besieged the Treasury. Her petition for payment was read before the Commissioners on June 2 and promise was entered to consider her request when money should be available. Within the next month, she petitioned for £657 14s. 4d. Ten days later Sir Robert Long, who, we recall, had succeeded in getting the early first payment for her in 1666, reported to the Commissioners, who were to investigate the basis of her grant and of her father's. On August 12 and 13 one warrant was issued for £500 and another for £523 10s. 1d.; but not until August 11, 1669, was she to receive the requested £657 14s. 4d. With that warrant her grant was at last paid.[1]

At the beginning of 1669, Dryden might, like Pepys, have surveyed the past year and found it good. Honors and enhanced literary reputation had come to him, and a measure of financial well-being, which he and his family had not known before. It was clearly time to establish permanent living arrangements as soon as a proper house should be found. Their two sons were growing up and were presently to be joined by another, the last. Erasmus-Henry, whom Lady Elizabeth was always to call Harry, was born on May 2.[2] In the meantime a house was found on the north side of Longacre, where the family was to remain until all the sons were grown. Dryden left it for Gerrard Street in 1686.[3]

Nearly six years had passed since Dryden wrote his first play for the Theatre Royal. The memory of its failure seems to have induced in him no great desire to spend time in preparing it for publication. Now he turned to it again, and after writing a very short preface, gave it to Herringman, who published it about the middle of

May. Without knowledge of the original text, and in the absence of any statement from him, we can only assume that it appeared in print as it was acted.⁴ Though its biographical import is slight, *The Wild Gallant* is interesting as the kind of pastiche he managed to put together in his first attempt. In addition to the as yet unidentified plot which he was able to use as his groundwork, he levied upon his Elizabethan predecessors for character and incident. Some of the characters are humors from Jonson: Justice Trice, Bibber, the tailor and his wife, and Lord Nonsuch; others are skillful improvements of the gay ladies and blades in the Beaumont and Fletcher comedies. Mr. Loveby and Lady Constance foreshadow the later witty couple of the comedy of manners. But much of the action, the disguises, and the tricks suggest its origin and its relationship to an earlier theater more than an earnest of what was to come.⁵

During the early months of 1669, he began to block out a new play, *Tyrannic Love,* which was to be his most ambitious and significant drama up to this time. He admits that he wrote it in seven weeks. In early April he had progressed far enough to lay out, in close consultation with members of his company, plans for scenic exploitation of his material dealing with the conflict between a pagan tyrant, Maximin, and a Christian Princess, St. Catherine. The company possessed in its scene-room a number of painted canvases accumulated in the past five or six years; and some of them could be utilized, such as the Indian Cave scene already used over and over in the productions of *The Indian Queen* and *The Indian Emperour.* But for the elaborate mounting they had in mind a fresh scene of some magnificence was needed. So in late April or early May, Dryden went to visit Isaac Fuller, a painter. Accompanied by a joiner of the theater, for expert and practical opinion concerning measurements, clearances, and so on, he laid before Fuller (who was ill in bed) the requirements for the scene. Tentative agreements were reached, to become permanent within a week when Fuller visited the theater for a final conference. The company urged speedy delivery of the scene, within a fortnight if possible, so that the play could be presented during Easter and Trinity terms to catch the patronage of visitors in town for the law courts. Fuller began work about May 12, but, whether because of the size or of the elaborateness of set, he was unable to complete the contract in two weeks: it required six, and was not delivered to the company until about June 23. The company chose to regard the delay as breach of agreement and refused Fuller his money. In the subsequent law

suit brought in June, 1670, against the painter, many details are rehearsed in both Bill and Answer that provide insights into this area
of Dryden's life. The company alleges that they have lost £500
because of Fuller's tardiness. Furthermore, Fuller has so botched
the job that the play "was disparaged and lost its reputation." Indeed, the King had appointed a time for its acting, and members of
the court were eager to see it produced; the lengthening delay
exasperated them so much that harsh words were passed on the
company. Having already paid him £40 for a second-rate scene,
they hope Fuller will recompense them for their loss. Instead,
Fuller entered countersuit to recover £335 10s. for his work on the
Elysium scene, and was awarded judgment against Hart and Mohun,
the principals for the company. Not only did they not lose patronage,
says Fuller, they gained handsomely partly because of the quality of
his scene: *Tyrannic Love,* he says, was acted fourteen days together
"and brought in £100 per day, whereas the ordinary play produced
only £40 or 50 per day."[6]

The cost of the scene was enormous by the standards of the
time, but if it helped to fill the theater for fourteen days running,
it might have been worth the price. The extraordinary receipts—as
alleged by Fuller—meant that the income for the shareholders was
temporarily inflated, and Dryden, holding one and a quarter shares,
found his profits enlarged beyond anything he had yet known since
he became a shareholder. At any rate the success of *Tyrannic Love*
justified the action of the company in taking Dryden in on equal
terms with Hart, Mohun, and Wintershall. The popularity of the
play in its first run no doubt explains the early registration of it by
Herringman within two weeks—on July 14. Publication, however,
was delayed for more than a year.

Now Dryden seems to have entered a period of comparative in-
activity. For the eighteen months between June, 1669, and the end
of 1670, there is only *The Conquest of Granada.* Coming after at
least three very active years, this slackening poses a problem not
easily solved. One of the most obvious explanations is that he was
tired and needed a period of freedom and refreshment to supply a
literary reservoir on which he had made heavy demands. Yet by
this time he was a professional writer devoting his life to his craft,
and writing was his life. Lack of production, to be sure, can be no
sure indication of idleness; it may be more nearly an indication of
literary replenishment, and a period of assessment and of stock-taking.
Up to the writing of *Tyrannic Love,* Dryden had, in a sense, worked

out an apprenticeship, almost the canonical seven years of learning his art. This play may be seen as the end of his first period, the dividing line between experiment in a variety of ways, and the hope and expectation of moving onto higher and more important ground.

On this higher ground dwelt the epic. There have been many directive signs that point to his continuing fascination with the noblest poem within the reach of ambitious poets. The names of Virgil and Homer had always been on the tip of his pen, and he seldom missed an opportunity either to praise them or to employ them for illustrations of epic achievement. Virgil was his master, as he often made plain, and it was to Virgil that he returned time and again when he needed to cite the ultimate of art and strength in poetry. *Annus Mirabilis* was composed in the shadow of ancient precept and practice in heroic poetry. Though Dryden ranges over the whole field of the ancients for the *Essay,* his concern is with drama, not epic; yet even so, Virgil and Homer serve him for illustrative purposes: Virgil is cited for the proper conduct of verse and for truth as the foundation of his poetry. "This is that which makes Virgil be preferred before the rest of poets." His interest in the epic received powerful reinforcement with the appearance of Milton's *Paradise Lost*; and though Dryden makes no direct reference to it at this time, his later comments on it, and on Milton, demonstrate conclusively that its first issue (in 1667) made a great impression upon him. *Tyrannic Love,* coming soon after Milton's poem, seems to reflect, in passages dealing with the exercise of free will and necessity, parts of *Paradise Lost* and probably marks the beginning of Dryden's study of the modern epic. His hope and dream of writing one was to come to naught, but it continued to be an active goal until 1676, when he seems finally to have relinquished all plans for the long poem.

At the birth of his third child in May, Dryden's family was complete. The added responsibility and the future financial obligations which now became a charge to him he could in 1669 face with equanimity. His wife's success in procuring the payment of her early grant from the King's Treasury, the continuing success of his plays, his augmented income from his share in the Theatre Royal, and his income from Blakesley, plus the £200 salary from the post of poet laureate, provided an income almost beyond the most sanguine hopes of a professional writer in his time. Yet some of it was at best only a temporary contribution; and his salary as poet laureate was to prove most uncertain. For although appointed in April of the preceding year, he had not yet received a penny, nor would he find the Treasury sufficiently solvent to enable a payment to be made for more than another year.   Now that money was available and they were at last in a permanent residence, he and his wife seem to have begun purchasing some necessary silver at the goldsmith's, Blanchard, which would remain his banking connection for many years.   On Christmas Eve, 1668, they bought (and charged) a sugar box and six spoons for £10 0s. 6d. and had them engraved for an additional 3s. 6d.; in the following month, six salts at £2 15s. 2d.   In May, after the birth of Erasmus-Henry, they bought two tumblers and six more spoons at £6 11s.; later, a small locket for £1 and a ring for £1 5s. 6d. (gifts for the baby?).   Powder boxes (at £4 3s. 9d.) and a "Basson" for £15 16s. 6d. followed in March of 1670.[7]

Dryden's return to the heroic play in *Tyrannic Love* and his growing interest in the epic and the related heroic poem turned his thoughts and his energies, during the end of 1669 and most of 1670, toward a study of both forms.   In a sense they were one for Dryden and his time; for in theory and in practice the epic and the heroic had at times merged.   Epic imagination and grandeur were being translated into prose in the romances, both Italian and French, as well as in verse.   Tasso, Spenser, and now Milton, drawing upon the glories of antiquity, had employed "for modern purposes and in a modern language the grand style of which the example had been set by the classical authors."[8]   Wherever he looked, Dryden found this modern modification of epic form, whether in La Calprenède, de Scudéry, or other writers of prose heroic romance, or in poetic imitations.   The origin of his heroic plays is here, and his purpose is now to translate into romantic structure the elevation, the grandeur of the epic idea.   To this problem he addressed himself; and the result of his months of study and writing in 1670 was to be *The Conquest of Granada*.   Because of his dedication to the heroic idea, and the largeness of concept, the play was not to be contained within the normal framework of five acts: it required ten acts, or two parts. and the grandeur was to be matched by elaborateness of mounting, the details for which Dryden was probably arranging in November.

During the summer, Dryden received another mark of the King's favor by his appointment as historiographer royal.   When he had been made laureate there was no suggestion that he was wanted as an official interpreter of official acts of government, even though the office was then vacant by the recent death of Howell.   But the aftermath of the Dutch War seems to have changed the attitude of the King's advisers to this neglected position; and on February 1, 1668/69, Evelyn wrote a long letter to his friend Clifford, retailing the news from Holland that the English were being treated with great contumely and suggesting that an able pen should be employed to write a "true history" of the war. Evelyn's pen was to be employed eventually, but at the moment he wishes Clifford to "move my Lord Arlington, and with him to provoke his Majesty to impose this province upon some sober and well-instructed person, who dignified with the Character of his Royal Historiographer, might be obliged to serve and defend his Majesty's honour, and that of the public with his pen; a thing so carefully and industriously observed by the French king and other great potentates." If his proposal should be well received, Evelyn is willing to suggest a man who will be satisfied with a "very modest subsistence."[9] This suggestion brought no immediate result, but Clifford apparently returned to the proposal sometime later. He may have advised the King to combine the position with that of the laureateship, since Dryden already had demonstrated not only his loyalty but also his skill in writing. He might also have pointed out that it would be cheaper this way since it would not be necessary to increase the laureate's salary. At any rate, in July, Dryden was constituted Poet Laureate and Historiographer Royal; and on August 18, letters patent were issued under the great seal. The salary remained at £200.[10] It is not clear whether he was expected to write anything in justification of the last war; perhaps he was merely being held in readiness for the next.

Of immediate importance, however, was the publication of *Tyrannic Love,* in November.[11] Emboldened by his dedication of *The Indian Emperour* to the Duchess of Monmouth, Dryden addressed this play to the Duke; the reception of his earlier dedication he says, "has encouraged me to double my presumption." He reminds the Duke that it is dangerous to "admit a poet into your family," for he can never after "be free from the chiming of ill verses, perpetually sounding in your ears, and more troublesome than the neighbourhood of steeples." The fulsome tribute to Monmouth's youth, beauty, and courage—"so goodly a fabrick was never framed by an Almighty Architect for a vulgar guest"—was to be ironically repeated a dozen years later when Monmouth became Absalom. It was not alone in praise of Monmouth that Dryden writes the dedication; he for the first time sends up a trial balloon regarding an epic which already is taking shape in his thought. "Instead of an heroick play, you might justly expect an heroick poem, filled with the past glories of your ancestors, and the future certainties of your own.   Heaven has already taken care to form you for an hero.   You have all the advantages of mind and body, and an illustrious birth, conspiring to render you an extraordinary person.   The Achilles and the Rinaldo are present in you, even above their originals; you only want a Homer, or a Tasso, to make you equal to them."[12]   Though Dryden seems to be aiming at the Duke, his main target is higher than the bastard son: it is the father and the "uncle," the Duke of York. The plan for a poem obviously is quite nebulous, but already he sees it as celebrating the Stuarts, already he is preparing the way for acceptance by the King.   Monmouth, we can be certain, would be no major figure in such a poem; his father and uncle would be. But as a favorite son of Charles, Monmouth could be used as a conduit to the King.   *The Conquest of Granada,* now completed and awaiting performance, celebrates not the Stuarts but heroic virtue. If his plans for the epic should begin to mature hereafter, he will need to bespeak the interest of the principals involved.   This he will do when he comes to dedicate the great heroic play to the Duke of York.   Within a year two very important figures are, then, publicly addressed in terms of their heroic nature, and a poem to celebrate them is proposed.   Only one more step needs to be taken.   When the time is ripe, that step will be taken, and the King's promise of support—for what it is worth—will be obtained.

The dedication to *Tyrannic Love* looks ahead; the preface looks to the play, which Nell Gwyn in the epilogue is made to call a "godly out-of-fashion play"—

> A play, which, if you dare but twice sit out,
> You'll all be slander'd, and be thought devout.

At some length and with considerable care, Dryden explains and justifies his play, which in only a very limited sense can be called heroic.   At the center stands, not an heroic figure like the earlier Montezuma or the later Almanzor, but the Christian St. Catherine and the heathen tyrant Maximin.   The play is about religion and irreligion, and—as far as dramatic proprieties allow—about the basis of the Christian religion and the force of faith, as exemplified in the figure of St. Catherine.   Without being specific about the origin of the idea or his personal interest, Dryden hints at a novelty in the subject.   "I was moved to write this play by many reasons; amongst others the commands of some persons of honour, for whom I have a most particular respect, were daily sounding in my ears, that

it would be of good example to undertake a poem of this nature."
The "persons of honour" remain unidentifiable, yet we should no
doubt be safe in suggesting that they were not members of Charles's
court, who were hardly noted for a deep enough interest in religion
to urge the poet to write a play "of good example." His own inclination, he says, was "not wanting to second their desires," for pleasure
is not the "only end of poesy"; precepts and examples of piety might
also be included. Indeed, "to leave that employment altogether to
the clergy were to forget that religion was first taught in verse, which
the laziness or dulness of succeeding priesthood turned afterwards
into prose." He is not intent upon comparing the use of drama with
that of Divinity; he is only maintaining that "patterns of piety . . .
may be of excellent use to second the precepts of our religion."

Professor Bredvold has traced the course of religious controversy
as it was carried on between the Anglican divines and the Catholic
controversialists during this decade. The Catholic technique was to
strike at reason as a guide to faith and to substitute the certitude of
an infallible Church. The Anglican appeal was based upon a
"power of the individual reason to interpret scripture."[13] For the
Anglicans, Scripture contained the necessary rules for salvation which
could be apprehended by the exercise of reason. If the Catholic
controversialists could demonstrate the unreliability of scriptural
texts—as they were in process of doing—they hoped to induce doubt
and then rejection: the alternative would be acceptance of interpretation by an infallible authority.

Dryden's exploitation of a religious theme—the opposition of the
Christian Catherine to the pagan Maximin—does not beyond doubt
place him on the side of the Anglican divines in the current controversy, but he works in enough Christian doctrine, some with more
than a tinge of the Anglican, to suggest that within the limits of his
dramatic form he might have been presenting a pattern of piety
"equally removed from the extremes of superstition and prophane-
ness," to "second the precepts of our religion."

When confronted by Maximin, St. Catherine advances the claims
of reason to account for her "settled mind, enlightened from above":

> But where our reason with our faith does go,
> We're both above enlightened, and below.
> But reason with your fond religion fights,
> For many gods are many infinities:
> This to your first philosophers was known,
> Who, under various names, adored but one.

By the force of reason, she has no trouble converting the heathen philosopher Apollonius, who has been appointed by his emperor to combat her ideas. The defeat of the philosopher is paralleled, for dramatic purposes, by Maximin's rebuff in love, given him by the fair Christian captive. As a last resort to move her stubborn heart, Maximin calls upon his necromancer Nigrinus, who, through an elaborate scene of conjuration, produces Nakar and Damilcar; and Damilcar calls up the sleeping Catherine. This is the Paradise scene. As she rises on her bed, a song of love is followed by a Dance of Spirits, who are at once dispersed by the descent of the angel Amariel, with a flaming sword. Damilcar begs for mercy, confesses he is one of the "changelings and fools of heaven," who, shut out of heaven, "roam in discontent about," "spotted all without and dusky all within." Amariel breaks the spell put upon the saint and dismisses the evil spirit with the threat of chaining him underground, "all swoln and bloated like a dungeon toad." The scene of Paradise, the guardian angel with the flaming sword protecting the woman, the frustration of evil, the swoln toad associated with this "fool of heaven" —all may remind us of *Paradise Lost*. Though temporarily saved by her guardian angel, she is doomed at the hands of the tyrant. In IV, i, she talks with Berenice, Maximin's wife, who also is condemned and who fears the prospect of death. The interchange between them serves both the dramatic and a religious purpose:

ST. CATHERINE: The will of heaven, judged by a private breast,
Is often what's our private interest;
And therefore those, who would that will obey,
Without their interest must their duty weigh.
. . . .
Were there no sting in death, for me to die,
Would not be conquest, but stupidity;
But if vain honour can confirm the soul,
And sense of shame the fear of death control,
How much more then should faith uphold the mind,
Which, showing death, shows future life behind?

BERENICE: Of death's contempt heroic proofs you give;
But, Madam, let my weaker virtue live.
Your faith may bid you your own life resign;
But not when yours must be involved with mine.
. . . .

ST. CATHERINE: Heaven does in this my greatest trial make,
When I, for it, the care of you forsake.

. . . .

Thus with short plummets heaven's deep will we
sound,
That vast abyss where human wit is drowned!

. . . .

Faith's necessary rules are plain and few;
We many, and those needless, rules pursue.
Faith from our hearts into our heads we drive,
And make religion all contemplative.
You on heaven's will may witty glosses feign;
But that which I must practice here is plain:
If the All-Great decree her life to spare,
He will the means, without my crime, prepare.[14]

St. Catherine speaks Anglican doctrine. In a scene between Maximin
and Porphyrius, Dryden emphasizes another aspect of Anglican doctrine—passive obedience. One of the most controverted points in
political philosophy revolved about the question "whether subjects
have the right to resist their rulers—of course for supposedly good
reasons, usually concerned with the maintenance of sound Christian
doctrine—or whether they owe a duty of passive obedience such
that resistance is in all cases wrong."[15] Dryden, in this scene, approaches passive obedience in reverse—not what the Anglican
positively believes, but what the dissenters and the Catholics must
adhere to:

MAXIMIN: 'Tis said, but I am loth to think it true,
That my late orders were contemned by you:
That Berenice from her guards you freed.

PORPHYRIUS: I did it, and I glory in the deed.

MAXIMIN: How, glory my commands to disobey!

PORPHYRIUS: When those commands would your renown betray.

MAXIMIN: Who should be judge of that renown you name,
But I?

PORPHYRIUS: Yes, I, and all who love your fame.

MAXIMIN: Porphyrius, your replies are insolent.

PORPHYRIUS: Sir, they are just, and for your service meant.
                If for religion you our lives will take,
                You do not the offenders find, but make.
                All faiths are to their own believers just;
                For none believe, because they will, but must.
                Faith is a force from which there's no defence;
                Because the reason it does first convince:
                And reason conscience into fetters brings;
                And conscience is without the power of kings.

MAXIMIN: Then conscience is a greater prince than I,
                At whose each erring call a king may die!
                Who conscience leaves to its own free command,
                Puts the worst weapon in a rebel's hand.

PORPHYRIUS: Its empire, therefore, sir, should bounded be,
                And, but in acts of its religion, free:
                Those who ask civil power and conscience too,
                Their monarch to his own destruction woo.
                With needful arms let him secure his place;
                Then, that wild beast he safely may release.

Thus Dryden isolates the causes of civil disorders, as England and the continent had known them in the past century. The exercise of the unfettered conscience in civil—as well as in religious—matters by determined religious minorities had led to rebellion against constituted civil authority. Dryden had seen a king beheaded because he had not secured his peace with "needful arms." This tendency toward rebellion he was to reprehend more severely, and with telling particularity, a dozen years later.[16]

Beyond *Tyrannic Love,* Dryden's only other publication of 1670 was *The Tempest,* which he regarded as more Davenant's than his own. It appeared in February, with a preface dated December 1, 1669. He generously gives his collaborator most of the credit for this revision of Shakespeare, reserving to himself the pleasure of having assisted Sir William and of testifying to his skill and to his imagination.[17]

While Dryden studied for his epic and undertook the writing of *The Conquest of Granada,* subterranean events occurred which in one way or another would touch him as a man and as a poet. The King, unable to procure sufficient money supplies from a suspicious and often hostile Parliament, launched upon a fateful course of negotiation with Louis XIV.   The King's prorogation of Parliament from December 11 to February 14, 1669/70, coincided with the drafting of a secret treaty with Louis.   Urged by Louis, Charles apparently was preparing to declare his adherence to Catholicism—for a price.   He asked £200,000 down payment plus an annual subsidy of £800,000 (later reduced to £300,000), with armed assistance, should a declaration of Catholicism cause a rebellion in England. Such substantial payment would free him from the stern paymaster, the Parliament.   The announcement would precede a declaration of war against Holland, which could readily be provoked by an "incident."   By May all was in readiness, and Charles, accompanied only by Clifford and Arlington of the Cabal, journeyed to Dover to meet his sister, Madame, Duchess of Orleans.   Here was signed a secret treaty by Charles and only these two Catholic or crypto-Catholic members of the Cabal.[18]   It was determined to negotiate later a bogus treaty, identical except for the declaration of Catholicism.   When Parliament finally convened on October 24, it proved unexpectedly generous in money supplies, and a concord was established between the King and the two houses.   In December, all members of the Cabal (including, of course, the three Protestant members) signed the bogus treaty.   Now certain of his finances, Charles (in the following March), upon the petition of the houses against the growth of Popery, sacrificed the Catholics.   He appeased Parliament by a proclamation requiring all Jesuits and Romish priests to leave England by May 1, and directing the judges to enforce the laws against recusants.   The third Dutch War was in embryo, and the tortuous course of Charles's domestic and foreign diplomacy was begun.   Whether it was to please the fools (to paraphrase Dryden's later comment), it managed to "puzzle all the wise."

While the false treaty of Dover was being made ready for official signing in December, Dryden completed *The Conquest*.   Since the first performance of Part I occurred during the last half of December, it would be reasonable to assume that it was ready for rehearsals in November, and probably the writing was finished well before this time; for in the epilogue to the first part, he says that he was prepared but the women were away.   Nell Gwyn had dropped out of the company after *Tyrannic Love* by the King's command: On May 20, 1670, she gave birth to the Duke of St. Albans.   Both Mrs. James and Mrs. Davis were away for the same kind of illness. There would of course be other reasons for delay, among them the many problems of production for both Parts in succession.   No record of particular scenes or effects for the Theatre Royal presentation is available, but perhaps new painted scenes would have been prepared by either Robert Angus (Aggas) or Samuel Towers, both of whom painted scenery for the company for some years.[19] There were, however, special spectacular scenes for the acting at court several months later. These were done by Robert Streeter, Serjeaunt Painter to the King (who had bought the position from Sir Robert Howard in 1662/63). Evelyn saw the court performance of Part I on February 10, 1670/71, and called it the "famous play." He commented particularly on the "very glorious scenes and perspectives, the work of Mr. Streeter, who well understands it." The next day Part II was given. The date of first acting of Part I at the Theatre Royal is uncertain. Lady Mary Bertie writing to her niece, Katherine Noel, on January 2, 1670/71, reports:

There is lately come out a new play writ by Mr. Dreydon who made the *Indian Emperour*. It is caled the *Conquest of Grenada*. My brother Norreys tooke a box and carryed my Lady Rochester and his mistresse and all us to, and on Tuestay wee are to goe see the second part of it which is then the first time acted.[20]

It would seem reasonable to suppose that she refers to a very recent performance though perhaps not that of the first day.

Contemporary notices of the play leave little doubt that it scored an immediate success. Not all comment at the time, however, was complimentary; perhaps more was unfavorable than laudatory: it made partisans on both sides, and most found difficulty in maintaining a neutral position on its merit or lack of merit. And posterity seems to have experienced the same difficulty.

While *The Conquest of Granada* made friends and enemies, the offices of government were trying to implement the promises made in Dryden's appointments of the previous two years. On January 11 a warrant was issued directing the Board of the Green Cloth to deliver a butt or pipe of canary (in kind or in money) to the laureate and historiographer, together with all arrears in salary that had accumulated since Davenant's death, nearly three years before. And on January 27 came a money warrant for £500 "in full of what is grown due on his pension of £200." A warrant, however, was not money in hand, as Dryden had long since learned; but within the month the Exchequer managed to pay his long overdue salary.[21] At the same time, the Exchequer's good faith was shown in an order, dated February 17, to repay the loan which Dryden had made to the King in 1667. But the order became nonoperative, and the money

came to him two years later, and then only by the personal interven-
tion of Lord Clifford, Chancellor of the Exchequer.[22]   Since Dryden
had not received any salary until this month, the payment of two and
a half years' accumulation would hardly be viewed as an act of grace.
The uncertainty of payment, and finally the total stop, were to bring
serious financial stress in the years ahead and to force him to the
galling role of beggar—an unhappy and almost insupportable position
for a man of pride.

Before February 13, when it was advertised, *The Mock Astrologer*
was in print, appropriately dedicated to the Duke of Newcastle, who
had been Dryden's collaborator in *Sir Martin Mar-All.*   The joint
effort goes unmentioned in the dedicatory epistle, Dryden preferring
to emphasize the loyalty of Newcastle to the interests of the royal
cause and the great sacrifices which it had entailed.   Since the
learned Duchess had already published a life of the Duke, Dryden
is able to make cross references to it and pay becoming tribute to
the wife as well.   More important, however, is the preface, written
in all likelihood during the weeks when *The Conquest of Granada*
was being made ready for production.   His original intention,
(abandoned because of the pressure of time) to follow up some of
the comparative critical ideas first suggested in the *Essay of Dramatic
Poesy,* notably Ben Jonson's pre-eminence in humor and in "contrivance of comedy," and the precedence of the Restoration heroic
play to certain plays of Shakespeare and Fletcher, he defers, says
Dryden, until the publication of *The Conquest of Granada,* "where
the discourse will be more proper."   Now he takes up comedy as it is
at present written and as it may be compared with Jonson's, and he
attempts to answer some of the criticism directed at him during the
past two years.   His own earlier castigation of Howard and others
has boomeranged, and he finds himself the object of attack from
numerous quarters.   Many of the attacks have been oral, but some
have appeared in print, such as those of "R. F." and Shadwell; and
soon Edward Howard will add his to the growing voice of faultfinding.   The preface becomes a justification, then, of his practice in
comedy and an answer to charges of literary theft.

He places no value on a reputation gained in comedy, for he
thinks it, "in its own nature, inferior to all sorts of dramatic writing."
Low comedy he finds particularly displeasing since it requires "much
of conversation with the vulgar and much of ill nature in the observation of their follies."   His disgust "proceeds not so much from my
judgment as from my temper."   For he admits to a "sullenness of

humour," which prevents his liking any comedy equally with tragedy. The kind of farce recently presented—that copied from the French— becomes anathema to him, and even *The Mock Astrologer* "would rise up in judgment" against him if he attempted to defend it. He admits that he cannot write humor; indeed Jonson "was the only man of all ages and nations, who has performed it well." Contrary to charges levelled at him by Shadwell and others, he asserts that he is no enemy to Jonson, but that he does not blindly admire him. "For why," he asks, "should he only be exempted from those frailties, from which Homer and Virgil are not free? Or why should there be any *ipse dixit* in our poetry, any more than there is in our philosophy? I admire and applaud him where I ought." In the analysis that follows he sharply distinguishes between wit and the imitation of folly; in the latter Jonson was excellent; his wit, however, was not extraordinary. Relying heavily upon Quintilian's *de movendo risu*, Dryden shows a preference for the mixed way of comedy— "that which is neither all wit, nor all humour, but the result of both." He would have more humor than he finds in Fletcher, and more love and wit than he finds in Jonson; fewer tricks than in Jonson, and less adventure than in Fletcher.

In justifying his own practice in comedy, Dryden examines with care two charges that have been made against him, notably by Shadwell in the prefaces to *The Royal Shepherdess* and *The Humorists*: that he makes debauched persons (like Wildblood and the Astrologer in this play) his protagonists and leaves them happy at the end against the law of comedy, which is to reward virtue and punish vice; and that he steals all of his plays. Those who make the first charge have not distinguished "betwixt the rules of tragedy and comedy." It is tragedy, both in its theory and practice, "that punishes vice and rewards virtue: tragedy [thus] fulfils one great part of its institution, which is by example to instruct." But not so comedy: its aim is to make folly ridiculous and to induce laughter. Delight is the first aim and perhaps the only one; instruction, if admitted at all, is purely secondary. The second charge—of theft—he answers directly: "It is true, that wherever I have liked any story in a romance, novel, or foreign play, I have made no difficulty, nor ever shall, to take the foundation of it, to build it up, and to make it proper for the English stage." In tracing openly the descent of the present play, he declares what he has retained, changed, and discarded. His practice in this finds justification in that of greater poets: Terence, Virgil, Tasso ("whom I reverence next to Virgil"), Shakespeare, Fletcher, Jonson

—all have purloined from others. What is the work of the poet? The story is the least important; the craft of the fashioner, the most: "The employment of a poet is like that of a curious gunsmith, or watchmaker: the iron or silver is not his own, but they are the least part of that which gives the value; the price lies wholly in the workmanship."[23]

Twelve days after the appearance of this preface, Herringman entered *The Conquest of Granada* in the *Stationers' Register*. Though Dryden answered one group of his critics in the preface to *The Mock Astrologer,* he was creating other groups of future attackers, both by his ambitious heroic play in ten acts and by the inclusion, at the end of Part II, of a provocative epilogue, which was taken to be an attack upon Jonson in particular and the Elizabethan dramatists in general. In reality, Dryden is intent upon doing something quite different: he is praising the taste of the new age of the Restoration and citing the difficulties encountered by the new dramatist in pleasing a more highly educated, more "refined," and more censorious theatergoing audience than that in Elizabethan times. He asserts that those who have best succeeded on the stage have always "conformed their genius to their age." In Jonson's time, men were dull; conversation was low; comedy, coarse; and love, mean. The lot of the playwright was easy:

> Fame was cheap, and the first comer sped;
> And they have kept it since, by being dead.

Were they to write now, when critics weigh every word and every line, none of them could succeed, not even Jonson. If love and honor, wit and conversation now surpass those of the preceding generation, the new age is to be praised, not the poet alone. Language has been refined, and now ladies and gentlemen speak more wit in their conversation than early poets were able to write. The corollary is plain: this modern playwright either writes "short of you," and imitates badly, or his writing is not worse than that of the Elizabethans. As will be seen, these comments in the epilogue parallel to some degree what he has said in his preface devoted to comedy, and they adumbrate the proposed essay mentioned in the opening lines of that preface.

As the months passed and Dryden's position became more firmly established, he began to make acquaintances outside of purely literary coteries. As far as can be known, he had only slight contact with the court circles or the persons who frequented them. A dedication addressed to a Duchess or a Duke of Monmouth betokens only a bid for favor, not a sign of personal acquaintanceship; but he was certainly meeting those persons who had interest in literature or pretensions to cultivation, along with many acknowledged or self-appointed wits of the "polite" world.   Men of title and fortune he could hobnob with, but never could he join them on terms of equality; yet his learning, his wit, and his flow of good talk no doubt admitted him to circles for which his background and temperament ill-fitted him.   Among others to whose company he had been admitted was the Earl of Rochester, whose scandalous behavior at last became a reproach to King and court, and whose capricious patronage of poets brought in its train envy, backbiting, and hatred.   But in 1671 he and Dryden were on friendly terms.

During the spring months of this year Dryden wrote one of his most successful plays.   In form tragicomic, the new play was called *Marriage à la Mode,* its title coming from the comic plot, which contributes the chief value to the play.   Having confessed his inability to write humors and having pointed out the contribution of his own age to polite and polished conversation, Dryden now took special care to demonstrate his skill in providing comedy that depends upon wit and gaiety, not humor, to produce laughter.   He further develops the witty couples of *The Mock Astrologer,* and it is the comic interchange of the two pairs, Doralice-Rhodophil, Palamede-Melantha, that makes the comedy.   Spun out of his own imagination, the sparkling wit and repartee imitates, he would have said, contemporary examples; and it completely justifies his contention in the epilogue, noticed above.   His practice, in this instance at least, fully underwrites his theory.[24]   And in Melantha, the female fop, Dryden has contributed one of the best comic characters of the age and one of the best of the type in the whole range of English drama.   That the play was completed, or nearly so, by the end of July seems certain, for in the later dedication to Rochester he recalls that that nobleman had looked it over in manuscript, had made some "amendment," and had recommended it to the King while he was at Windsor.   This was in June and July, 1671.[25]   The play was acted sometime later this year.

The attacks on the laureate continued, as might be expected, in consequence of the success of *The Conquest of Granada.*   In July, Dryden's brother-in-law, Edward Howard, published his *Six Days Adventure, or the New Utopia,* containing a preface highly critical of Dryden's ideas.   For the moment, he seems to have supplanted his brother Robert as a family gadfly.   But a more important and durable attack upon Dryden and the whole heroic species was being made ready for public performance—*The Rehearsal*. First put together as a burlesque nearly ten years before, with Sir Robert Howard as the protagonist under the name of Bilboa, it had languished without performance. After the reopening of the theaters and upon the subsequent development of the heroic play, more and more appealing targets presented themselves; and by the time *The Conquest* had taken its place as the supreme example of the species, the time was adjudged to be right for completing it. Howard, however, had bowed out of dramatic affairs for more remunerative activity in the government, and a new hero was to be sought in his place. Bilboa gave way to Bayes—perhaps a composite figure of the writer of heroic plays, but with large ingredients of Dryden in its make-up. Likewise, the authorship was composite: Buckingham, Martin Clifford, Sprat, and perhaps Butler.[26] All of Dryden's heroic plays are given attention, as well as two of his comedies. It was (and is) a rollicking farce, and its ridicule and sharp satire on some of the extravagances of heroic plays (and of drama in general) performed a therapeutic if not a reforming function. That the contemporary playgoer may have viewed it as a generalized statement rather than a specific attack on Dryden (though of course the name Bayes was to stick to him for the remainder of his life) is apparent from the observation of Evelyn, who saw it during the initial run, on December 14: to him it was "a ridiculous farce and rhapsody . . . buffooning all plays."

It is hard to believe that *The Rehearsal* came as a surprise to Dryden. He could very well have followed it through all phases of its preparation and performance. It was acted at the Theatre Royal by the company in which he was one of the main shareholders. In the leading parts were Lacy, Wintershall, and Cartwright—all of them shareholders. Wintershall and Cartwright had recently acted in both *The Conquest* and *Marriage à la Mode*. Thus, with his theater colleagues acting in the burlesque, his own latest play part of their current acting season, and his own and their financial health tied up in production, it would be almost miraculous if Dryden did not follow the fortunes of *The Rehearsal*. As a "witty" man he must have been too sensible to resent his share in the composite portrait; and the box office returns could have mollified any injury he may have felt.

In October, Sir Robert Howard was given the post of Secretary of the Treasury to succeed Sir George Downing. A friend in that sensitive position might very well look after the interests of the laureate, or so he must have thought, for a month later he inquired about payment of the loan for £500, a warrant for which had already been drawn. The secret plans of Clifford and the King, however, militated against immediate payment. For among the plans leading to war with the Dutch was the Stop of the Exchequer, a device apparently broached by Clifford to ensure sufficient revenues for the commencement of the new venture in continental politics. The Exchequer had been closed on January 2, with the immediate effect that all taxes as they came in became available to the government; and the payment of loans, annuities, and other claims on the money supply was suspended. In March, Evelyn looking back remembered that his good friend Clifford had hinted that the King would "shut up the Exchequer," an event that Evelyn viewed with the greatest misgiving, for not only did it ruin widows, orphans (and other pensioners) but it took away public confidence. Never, he says, did the King's affairs prosper afterwards. The movement toward war on Holland accelerated, and step by step the King began to carry out the provisions of the secret treaty with Louis. The great stake was Catholicism. Unlike the second war declared by Parliament for the aid of mercantile interests, and therefore assured of considerable popular support, the third Dutch War found little support, since the reasons for it were wrapped in the enigma which was Charles's devious policy.

The Stop of the Exchequer affected Dryden's chance of collecting the money due or overdue him, but in the same month another event, which was to cause him more immediate distress, occurred. On the evening of January 25, 1671/72, the Theatre Royal burned to the ground. The fire, which began under the stairs at the rear of the building, spread rapidly, soon got out of control, and consumed most of the theater and all of the stock of scenery and costumes. Fanned by a strong wind, it moved to nearby houses in Drury Lane. To stop its spread, the firefighters, having learned lessons in the great fire of 1666, blew up contiguous buildings; but before it was under final control, the fire had burned out between fifty and sixty houses, in addition to the theater.[27] For the company it was sheer disaster. The only bright spot in the situation was the availability of Lisle's Tennis Court, which the rival theater had vacated some weeks before in order to occupy their large and sumptuous new building in Dorset Garden. To this the company moved, without costumes or scenery: after nine years, they were back where they had started—in a tennis court. This, to be sure, was discouraging enough; but added to their difficulties was the increased competition of the Duke's company in a new and larger building. Within a month, however, they had renovated Lisle's and had borrowed enough finery from the courtiers to open, without much scenery, on February 26. Dryden not having a new play ready, they began with Fletcher's *Wit without Money,* a painfully apt title for the King's Comedians at this juncture.[28] But Dryden did write a special prologue for the opening night which reflects the melancholy and discouraged state of the company:

> Our stage does human chance present to view,
> But ne'er before was seen so sadly true:
> You are changed too, and your pretense to see
> Is but a nobler name for charity.
> Your own provisions furnish out our feasts,
> While you the founders make yourselves the guests.

He adverts to the comments of the pious folk, who could always see the hand of divine judgment:

> You cherished it [wit] and now its fall you mourn,
> Which blind unmannered zealots make their scorn,
> Who think that fire a judgment on the stage,
> Which spared not temples in its furious rage.

There is, however, some hope. As the new London is taking shape, after the Great Fire, with many new, magnificent buildings, so new theaters may rise from the old. But his heart seems not to be in it as he closes:

> But we with golden hopes are vainly fed,
> Talk high, and entertain you in a shed:
> Your presence here, for which we humbly sue,
> Will grace old theaters, and build up new.[29]

The company was slow to recover from the disaster: it required time to assemble enough money to enable the shareholders to proceed with plans for rebuilding. More than a year and a half would pass before articles of agreement between company and entrepreneurs could be settled. Meanwhile the wretched state continued, and in prologue after prologue Dryden bewails the difficulties under which they labor. In a prologue to a revival of Carlell's *Arviragus and Philicia* he writes:

With sickly actors and an old house too,
We're match'd with glorious theatres and new,
And with our alehouse scenes, and clothes bare worn,
Can neither raise old plays, nor new adorn.
If all these ills could not undo us quite,
A brisk French troop is grown your dear delight,
Who with broad bloody bills call you each day,
To laugh and break your buttons at their play.[30]

In the circumstances, they were fighting almost a losing battle. Killigrew and his company tried all sorts of plays and all kinds of devices to meet the combination of French troupes and the new Duke's Theatre. A favorite was the all-female cast, the women in men's dress apparently titillating the audience. Again Dryden did yeoman service in writing saucy epilogues and prologues for such performances; but the fortunes of the Theatre Royal showed little improvement, nor would it do so until a new theater was ready.

Charles's War meantime came into being. On March 15, 1671/72, the King issued his Declaration of Indulgence, which was to serve as a test of his dispensing power and at the same time to secure the position of the Catholics. To veil his intent, it also applied to all Dissenters and in effect suspended the execution of all penal laws against both groups, assuring them against interference as long as they celebrated their religious duties in private. The Declaration was a "kind of trial flight of the grand religious revolution that had been planned by Charles."[31] In the same week the arranged provocative incident took place when Admiral Holmes was ordered to intercept the Dutch Smyrna fleet off the Isle of Wight, and in the ensuing fight captured several ships, suffering some damage to his own. It was enough: on March 17 war was declared on the States General. In May occurred the great naval battle of Sole Bay. It was marked by gallantry on both sides—and claimed as a victory by both. The English lost many ships and at least twenty-five hundred men, of whom one was the Earl of Sandwich. The inconclusiveness of this action and the lethargy which followed produced a feeling of indifference among the populace. Hatred of the Dutch was being replaced by hatred for the French, whose fleet made a very bad showing at Sole Bay.

Since his appointment as historiographer two years before, Dryden had had no occasion to write anything on behalf of the King. The occasion now was at hand, for the government needed an intensification of propaganda to try to make an unwanted war palatable, if not popular. Probably at the instance of Clifford, whose voluntary retirement was imminent because of his refusal to take the Anglican sacraments as required by the Test Act, Dryden wrote—in a month— a propaganda drama designed to whip up feelings against the Dutch. He called it *Amboyna,* the title derived from the massacre of the English factory at Amboyna in the East Indies in 1624. His usually ready invention was pushed to the limit; neither he, nor apparently anyone else, thought the play of any consequence. When he came to dedicate it, in the following year, to Clifford, he confesses that the subject was barren, the persons low, and the writing not "heightened with many labored scenes." Posterity has agreed with him, for it has never considered the play seriously.[32]

The speed with which Dryden turned out this propaganda (not a "potboiler," as it is often called) may be explained by his complete lack of interest in fomenting popular feeling against the enemy and by the fact that he was engaged upon another play, *The Assignation, or Love in a Nunnery.* This was his first attempt since the theater had burned to provide the company with something that might "take." The desperate need to draw audiences to their makeshift stage at Lisle's might well have produced strain between Dryden and the company. For he had not kept his contract to deliver three plays a year, and at this point a new play was almost a necessity. While suffering the anxieties and stresses which beset the whole company in these months of adaptation to changed conditions, Dryden turned part of his energies to other concerns. He had written, during the preceding winter, the essay "Of Heroic Plays" and the "Defence of the Epilogue," both of which were incorporated in the first edition of *The Conquest of Granada,* which was advertised for sale on February 7. Along with these he now wrote a dedication to the Duke of York.

Dryden's absorption in the theory of the epic and his tentative proposals to the Duke of Monmouth in *Tyrannic Love* for an epic poem have already been noted. Now he comes closer to Augustus in the dedication to his Royal Highness. "Heroick poesy," he begins, "has always been sacred to Princes and to Heroes. Thus Virgil inscribed his *Aeneid* to Augustus Caesar; and of later ages, Tasso and Ariosto dedicated their poems to the house of Este." "It is only justice," he continues, "that poets should employ heroic verse to celebrate those who have been the patterns of their imitation." This consideration has impelled him to dedicate to York "these faint representations of your worth and valour in heroic poetry." He proceeds to recount the valor of the Duke in military and naval engagements from Cromwell's time to the present. Nor is virtue and concernment for the honor of England his possession alone: it is sharèd by a brother, "the most excellent of kings."

In your two persons are eminent the characters which Homer has given us of heroick Virtue, the commanding part in Agamemnon, and the executive in Achilles. And I doubt not, from both your actions, but to have abundant matter to fill the annals of a glorious reign; and to perform the part of a just historian to my Royal Master, without intermixing with it any thing of the poet.[33]

Again, it is the epic to celebrate the Stuarts which he has much on his mind. His concluding phrase should be clearly seen as meaning that the abundance of heroic actions of the Stuart line will relieve him, as poet, of feigning actions that had no basis in history. From Homer and Tasso comes the figure of Almanzor, not a tame or perfect hero but one of "over boiling courage." If Almanzor should be found to fail in any point of honor, he deviates from the Duke, who is the pattern of it.

The essay "Of Heroic Plays" is both an answer to the attacks made upon *The Conquest of Granada* and a reasoned statement about heroic poetry, particularly as it may be adapted to the stage. Whether heroic verse may be used in serious plays is, he says, no longer a matter of dispute, for it is in possession of the stage. Indeed, as he has already maintained in several places, the only case—and not a very good one—against it amounts to no more than that is not so near conversation as prose. Serious plays should not imitate conversation too closely; images and action should be raised beyond life, else "the foundation of poetry would be destroyed." Moving from the vehicle to the material, he finds the origin of the heroic play in the heroic poem; from Ariosto, he takes the idea that it should be "an imitation, in little, of an heroick poem; and consequently, that love and valour ought to be the subject of it." And since all poets have agreed that the heroic poem remains the "most instructive way of writing in verse, and, withal, the highest pattern of human life," he will need no other argument to justify his choice "in this imitation." Having made clear the antecedents of the heroic play, Dryden descends to a defense of his heroic figure Almanzor. He comes from Homer's Achilles, Tasso's Rinaldo, and La Calprenède's Artaban—an unexceptionable pedigree. From these heroes Almanzor inherits a fiery temper, impatience of injury, insolence, and unexampled prowess. His extravagance of speech can also be paralleled in the ancient heroes, as well as in Jonson's Cethegus, whose rhodomontades are more irrational than Almanzor's. Here as in some of his earlier essays Dryden addresses himself to the proper work of the poet; that there is a life beyond life where poetry must dwell he has no doubts.

The case with the "Defence of the Epilogue" is considerably different, even though it is likewise an answer provoked by the exceptions taken by his detractors. His "bold epilogue" had seemed to be a denigration of his Elizabethan predecessors, yet there is nothing lacking in his veneration for the past. "I would ascribe to dead authors their just praise in those things wherein they have excelled us; and in those wherein we contend with them for the pre-eminence, I would acknowledge our advantages to the age, and claim no victory for our wit." He hopes that he will not be charged with arrogance if he inquires into their errors. For we live, he says, "in an age so sceptical that as it determines little, so it takes nothing from antiquity on trust; and I profess to have no other ambition in this Essay, than that poetry may not go backward, when all other arts and sciences are advancing." His present purpose he makes clear—to show that language, wit, and conversation in his age are improved. Dryden was well aware of the differences in these respects between his and the former age. From the vantage point of 1672 he sees in the earlier dramatists improprieties, antiquated words, puns, solecisms, ill-placing of words, extreme Latinism, redundancies, double comparisons (and other examples of "false English") and general meanness of expression. He illustrates by quoting from his great predecessors and by citing specific plays and scenes. Improvement of language has occurred, as well as refinement of wit and conversation —an effect of a polite and polished court. As he had said in his epilogue: the age he would praise, not the individual poet. Dryden closes with a peroration that summarizes, and explicates, all that he had maintained in the epilogue and in this skillful essay in comparative criticism:

Let us therefore, admire the beauties and the heights of Shakespeare, without falling after him into a carelessness, and (as I may call it) a lethargy of thought, for whole scenes together. Let us imitate, as we are able, the quickness and easiness of Fletcher, without proposing him as a pattern to us, either in the redundancy of his matter, or the incorrectness of his language. Let us admire his wit and sharpness of conceit; but let us at the same time acknowledge that it was seldom so fixed, and made proper to his character, as that the same things might not be spoken by any person in the play. . . . Let us ascribe to Jonson the height and accuracy of judgment, in the ordering of his plots, his choice of characters, and maintaining what he had chosen, to the end. But let us not think him a perfect pattern of imitation, except it be in humour. . . . To conclude all; let us render to our predecessors what is their due, without confining ourselves to a servile imitation of all they writ; and without assuming to ourselves the title of better poets, let us ascribe to the gallantry and civility of our age the advantage which we have above them.

The need to defend himself against the growing chorus of attacks, his extreme busyness in preparing the essays and the play for publication and undertaking to provide propaganda for the government in *Amboyna,* and the discouragement following the destruction of the Theatre Royal must all have induced in Dryden considerable perturbation of mind. Whether such a combination of distractions during the summer affected his work we can only surmise. At any rate he was preparing another "mixed" play of serious and comic plots, after the pattern of *Marriage à la Mode* and *The Maiden Queen.* Finally ready in the autumn, *The Assignation* was acted in November. For part of his comic plot he relied rather heavily upon Calderón's *Con Quien Vengo Vengo.*[34] But the play was a failure—the only one since he wrote his first play a decade before. The combination of discordant materials might have been accepted by his critical audience if the comic characters (the witty couples particularly) had exhibited any of the sparkle, any of the gaiety which their earlier counterparts had possessed in abundance. In comparison *The Assignation* is a lackluster performance. Dryden was further irritated, during the summer, by the huge success at the Duke's in July, of Ravenscroft's adaptation from Molière's *Le Bourgeois Gentilhomme,* which was entitled *The Citizen Turn'd Gentleman.* Usually too generous to be displeased by the success of another, Dryden must have had other reasons for casting aspersions on Ravenscroft's play when he devoted part of the prologue of *The Assignation* to it. Part of his feeling was induced by the fact that in two recently published critiques he had tried to point out that farce was much too prevalent on the stage and that it was distinctly second-rate as comedy; and that the comedy of wit, reflecting the more polished conversation and manners of the time was vastly superior. Yet *The Citizen Turn'd Gentleman* drew crowds to the rival theater by virtue of its farce and to the discomfiture of the struggling company in Lisle's Tennis Court. In the prologue of his play, Dryden pays his compliments:

He who made this, observ'd what farces hit,
And durst not disoblige you now with wit.
But, gentlemen, you overdo the mode;
You must have fools out of the common road.
Th' unnatural strain'd buffoon is only faking;
No fop can please you now of God's own making.

.   .   .   .

You must have Mamamouchi, such a fop
As would appear a monster in a shop:
He'll fill your pit and boxes to the brim,
Where, ramm'd in crowds, you see yourselves in him.
Sure there's some spell our poet never knew,
In *hullababilah da,* and *chu, chu, chu.*
But *marabokah sahem* most did touch you;
That is: "O how we love the Mamamouchi!"
Grimace and habit sent you pleas'd away:
You damn'd the poet, and cried up the play.

Benito, the fool in Dryden's play (who speaks the prologue), admits that he was created by the poet as a kind of answer to the other fools in farce, especially Mamamouchi, and hopes he's fool enough to please. When Ravenscroft's next play, *The Careless Lovers,* appeared, in the following March, the author replied in kind, pointing out that *The Assignation* was so thoroughly damned that even the players were ashamed to play their parts. But no rancor continued between them: months later in his "Epistle to the Reader" included in the published play, Ravenscroft says his prologue was written in reply to Dryden's "before the *Assignation. . . . Laesit prius.* But Devils of Wit are not very dangerous, and so we both sleep in whole Skins."[35]

The Epic Dream
1673-1676

Dryden's latest failure and his complaints about the kind of comedy now finding favor on the stage emphasize both the unsatisfactory condition of the company to which he was attached and the realities of his personal situation. At the beginning of 1673, the King's players had for nearly a year been at loose ends in the inadequate tennis court, attempting to compete on unequal terms with the Duke's company, shrewdly managed by Betterton and Harris and occupying a magnificent new theater which far surpassed even the old Theatre Royal. There seems to be no doubt that the recovery of Dryden's group from the effects of the fire had been very slow and incomplete. Helpless to prevent it, they watched their patronage dwindle, and the continuation of the war reduced even further their clientele. Even the King and court seem to have found attendance somewhat melancholy, and to make up for the gaiety he missed there, Charles imported troupes of French and Italian players to enliven the atmosphere of his court.[1] Dryden himself was faced for almost the first time with a group of younger playwrights who were able to write comedy even better than he could. Etherege, Shadwell, Ravenscroft, and Wycherley were all demonstrating their ability to produce comedy that pleased the audiences of these years. Dryden might continue to deplore the presence of farce and the lack of wit; the unpleasant fact for him was that their plays were popular. To add to his discomfiture, attacks upon him and his work began to appear in ever greater numbers; the new year was hardly well under way before the first of many appeared. Had he not already committed himself to an epic poem, the events of 1673 alone would have served to alienate his affections for the theater and to make him long for a more retired literary life.

Nor did the actions in the larger theater of England bring any comfort. Charles's War with the Dutch had been moving into a deadlock, and expenses had been mounting month by month in the face of a virtually bare Treasury. Talk of making peace was beginning to be heard, and Charles was forced to go to Parliament with a request for money. An eighteen months' supply (at £70,000 per month) was voted—with a string attached. The point at issue was the King's dispensing power, as shown in his Declaration of Indulgence of the preceding year and in the suspension of the penal laws against dissenters and recusants. Parliament's determination that it would wield such power was supported by its ability to withhold funds unless Charles could be forced into compromise. Desperately in need of funds for the ill-starred adventure against Holland, Charles capitulated, and on March 8 he cancelled the Declaration of Indulgence. Thoroughly disenchanted with the war and aware that the Declaration had been chiefly for the benefit of Catholics, the London populace received the news of Parliament's victory with rejoicing. As if to underscore not only its sense of power but its Protestantism, the Commons passed the Test Act aimed to drive from positions of public trust under the King all persons who refused to take the oaths of allegiance and supremacy and the sacraments according to the Church of England. "Its strength lay in its intolerance and exclusiveness, a fact which came to be appreciated by English Catholics and Dissenters; because, in place of the shifting sands of latitude and compromise, it substituted the rock of rigid dogma, and transformed a Reformation doctrine from a spiritual conviction into a national safeguard."[2] The effects of the Act soon became manifest: The Duke of York, unable to take the sacraments, gave up his command in the navy; and Clifford, for the same reason, left his post as Lord Treasurer. By midsummer, a number had found it necessary to leave service under the Crown. Dryden was not affected, for he could take the sacraments; and on at least one occasion he vouched for a friend as having taken them.

The Treasury may have been bare, but Dryden discovered that it had money enough to pay his salary. On March 10, he was granted payment for a full year.[3] Was Sir Robert Howard, who in this month moved from his position as Secretary of the Treasury to that of Auditor of the Exchequer, looking out for his interests?

As long as both Howard and Clifford held positions in this office, Dryden seems to have been assured of special consideration; for before Clifford departed, in late June or July, he made a successful attempt to pay back Dryden's old loan to the King, with interest.

Financial matters, however, were not to be Dryden's chief difficulty during these months. We have already noticed Ravenscroft's retaliation in the prologue to *The Careless Lover* to Dryden's comments on the earlier *Citizen Turn'd Gentleman*. But not all the paper battles of the year were to end so pleasantly as this innocuous scuffle. For the most part the controversies about the drama had been conducted by those primarily on the creative side; only occasionally did an outsider (like "R. F.") intrude himself into the quarrels of the literary fraternity. Now a change becomes evident as a number of men, not only in London but in the university towns, broke into print with remarks and reflections, answers and animadversions. Their tracts are characterized largely by dullness and tediousness, the worrying to death of one or two anonymous, unremembered ideas. The authors' lack of writing ability was matched by an almost total absence of critical acumen. Not always was Dryden an object of their attention, but he was ridiculed more often than any other figure of the time. A series of tracts in 1672 dealing in general with the humors and conversation of the Town mentioned Dryden on occasion, though they were not primarily aiming at him or at his work. Hardly had 1673 got under way, however, when he became the central figure of a new series, usually referred to as the "Censure of the Rota," or the "Athenian Virtuosi." It began in Oxford with a tract called *The Censure of the Rota on Mr. Driden's Conquest of Granada,* apparently by one Richard Leigh. In this tract of twenty-one pages, the Athenian Virtuosi, meeting in a coffeehouse, devote their critical session not only to a castigation of *The Conquest* but also to a number of Dryden's other plays and his poems as well. The carping criticism to which his work is here subjected finds a ready second in the next tract, with the ironic title *The Friendly Vindication of Mr. Dryden.* Published within a few weeks in Cambridge, it furthers the attack of the first pamphlet. A genuine vindication of Dryden, however, was attempted by the authors of the two other publications in the series: *Mr. Dreyden Vindicated,* and *A Description of the Academy of the Athenian Virtuosi.* The author of the first, supposedly Charles Blount, makes a sincere but somewhat feeble effort at defending Dryden. The anonymous author of *A Description* does rather better. Some of his descriptions have almost a Swiftian tone.[4]

All of these small pieces came out before May, since Dryden, in the dedication to *The Assignation,* took occasion to allude to them. He finds his attackers "two wretched scribblers, who desire nothing more than to be answered." Yet even strangers have taken up the cudgels for him and have defended him in stronger terms than the "contemptible pedant" could use against him. The man from Cambridge is "only like Fungoso in the play, who follows the fashion at a distance, and adores the Fastidious Brisk of Oxford." Thus in the spring he answers the two pedants; another Cambridge pedant will attack him later, but that one he will not answer.

While the Rota tracts were appearing, Dryden was writing dedications to *Marriage à la Mode* and *The Assignation,* both in print by May 29. Appropriately enough, he addressed them to two of the wits of the town and court—John Wilmot, Earl of Rochester and Sir Charles Sedley. Amid the customary effusiveness and flattery with which Dryden consistently filled his dedications, the two addresses are noteworthy for giving a vague but interesting insight into the associations he had formed during the past months. Rochester's wit and conversation, he says, have been a model to him and to other comic writers of the age. Though of the court, Rochester has not been like the common run of courtiers, for he has not forgotten "ties of friendship or the practice of generosity." He then launches upon a generalized attack on the chicanery and venality of many associated with the court. "In my little experience of a court (which I confess I desire not to improve,) I have found in it much of interest, and more of detraction; few men there have that assurance of a friend, as not to be made ridiculous by him when they are absent." As he warms to his attack, he becomes bold in the extreme, when one considers the surface passions in this violent age when men were beaten and sometimes done to death for imagined affronts less overt than Dryden's direct allegations made here:

There are a middling sort of courtiers, who become happy by their want of wit; but they supply that by an excess of malice to those who have it. And there is no such persecution as that of fools; they never can be considerable enough to be talked of themselves, so that they are safe only in their obscurity, and grow mischievous to witty men by the great diligence of their envy, and by being always present to represent and aggravate their faults . . . they are forced to live on the offals of their wit whom they decry. . . . These are the men who make it their business to chace wit from the knowledge of princes, lest it should disgrace their ignorance. . . .

Rochester, by the favor of the King and by his own parts, has been able to preserve himself in "so dangerous a course," but his recognition of the hazards, Dryden goes on, has brought him some pity for lesser men, "who being of an inferiour wit and quality to you, are yet persecuted for being that in little which your Lordship is in great." Perhaps thus darkly he may refer to the sneers, public and private, of the would-be wits of court and town on the writers of the age. That it is a personal complaint becomes clear in his next sentence: "For the quarrel of those people extends itself to any thing of sense; and if I may be so vain to own it amongst the rest of the poets, has sometimes reached to the very borders of it, even to me: so that if our general good fortune had not raised up your Lordship to defend us, I know not whether any thing had been more ridiculous in court than writers." The attack so masked leaves in question the identity of the men who depreciate him and others, but it may be that he refers among others to the Duke of Buckingham, whose *Rehearsal* had lately pilloried Dryden. This conjecture is supported by a letter Dryden wrote sometime later to Rochester, who from the country had sent him a complimentary note thanking the poet for this dedication. In it Dryden asks Rochester not "to omitt the occasion of laughing at the Great Duke of B—— who is so oneasy to [him] self by pursueing the honour of Lieutenant Generall which flyes him, that he can enjoy nothing he possesses . . . he is so unfit to command an Army, that he is the onely Man in the three Nations who does not know it." More satiric remarks are ended by the thought, "These observations would easily run into lampoon, if I had not forsworn that dangerous part of wit. . . ."[5]

Dryden's strictures introduce a new note and a new bitterness. Heretofore he has had no occasion to complain in print, perhaps because his nearly unbroken series of successes had not yet exposed him to the envious comment of small, proud men whose pretensions far exceeded their performance. Now, however, his very pre-eminence begins to make him an easy target for the barbs of the illustrious obscure who obtain a moment's attention by depreciation of excellence they cannot reach, and of those men of parts who find it a happy frolic to ridicule upstart poets who need to be kept in their places. Another group he reserves for special comment—"those people who have the liberality of Kings in their disposing; and who, dishonouring the bounty of their master, suffer such to be in necessity, who endeavour at least to please him; and for whose entertainment he has generously provided, if the fruits of his royal favour were not often stopped in other hands." Since Dryden's salary as laureate and historiographer is not in question, his references to the "liberality of Kings" and the "fruits of his royal favour" which are "stopped in other hands" possibly are connected with his attempt to push forward his project for the epic, though now temporarily at a standstill. He will press ahead in his effort to obtain royal support, not through Rochester, however, but the Earl of Mulgrave. His present expectation of Rochester's continuing patronage will be disappointed; and with a kind of prescience he seems almost to be certain that the unstable and changeable Rochester will desert him. For at the end of his dedication, he writes a revealing passage: "Your Lordship has but another step to make, and from the patron of wit you may become its tyrant, and oppress our little reputations with more ease than you now protect them. But these, my Lord, are designs which I am sure you harbor not. . . ." Two years later he may have reflected on his powers of prophecy.

His thoughts were seemingly much taken up with the wits and with the pretenders, for in the dedication of *The Assignation* to Sir Charles Sedley, written at the same time, he distinguishes between the true wits and the pretenders. Sedley he likens to Tibullus for his poetry, as well as for candor, wealth, and way of living. He recalls to Sedley that the present concourse of wits (the true kind) resembles those of ancient times, when the poets enjoyed "much happiness in the conversation and friendship of one another." They pursued "innocent and unoffensive pleasures; that which one of the ancients called—*eruditam voluptatem.*" With Sedley and others he has enjoyed literary gatherings—those "genial nights, where our discourse is neither too serious nor too light, but always pleasant, and for the most part instructive; the raillery neither too sharp upon the present, nor too censorious on the absent, and the cups only such as will raise the conversation of the night, without disturbing the business of the morrow."[6]

He has often been amused to read the description of the wits, as given by the pedants who know nothing about this rarefied atmosphere denied to them. They "paint lewdness, atheism, folly, ill-reasoning, and all manner of extravagancies amongst us, for want of understanding what we are." Such wits he has never seen in Sedley's company; for the "wits they describe are the fops we banish; for blasphemy and atheism . . . are subjects . . . worn so threadbare,

that people who have sense avoid them, for fear of being suspected
to have none." But attacks upon men of wit often occur because
the pretenders have a "picque to some one amongst us, and then they
immediately interest heaven in their quarrel." This happens to be a
"usual trick in courts, when one designs the ruin of his enemy, to
disguise his malice with some concernment of the King's, and to
revenge his own cause with pretense of vindicating the honour of
his master."

There seems little doubt that Dryden had raised up enemies at
court, and perhaps the chief was Buckingham, who as a member of
the Cabal occupied a position of power and influence. But Dryden
also had friends at court, and he paid tribute to one—Baron Clifford, in the dedication to *Amboyna*.[7] As Lord Treasurer, Clifford
was ultimately responsible for the favorable treatment Dryden had
received from the Treasury, even during the days when that institution
seemed almost bare of funds. On June 17, as probably one of his
last official acts before giving up his office, Clifford gave peremptory
orders that Dryden should be repaid—with interest—the loan which
the poet had made years before to the King. The order for payment
of the £500, made out on February 17, 1670/71, had lain dormant
since. Now Clifford wrote a note to Sir Robert Long: "Let this
order and ye interest due upon it be paid forthwith out of any money
that comes to your hands of his Mat^{es} customs. Wallingford House
June ye 17th 1673. Clifford." A notation on the order, in Latin,
states that "this day" (June 19) the £500, with £60 interest has
been paid.[8] This example of Clifford's friendly attention to Dryden's
interests serves as background to the dedication, which was probably
written within the next few weeks—certainly after Clifford's retirement from his post. It is with a knowledge of his sincerity that we
can read Dryden's address to Clifford which otherwise might be set
down as only one more example of the poet's extravagance in such
dedications. A sense of gratitude suffuses it, as well it might. He
alludes to the "many favours, . . . conferred on me by your Lordship these many years, which I may call more properly one continued act of your generosity and goodness." He waxes almost lyrical about Clifford's conduct of the Treasury, his equitable distribution of the King's favor so that "Justice herself could not have held
the scales more even." In conclusion he has the grace to apologize
for *Amboyna*, which "will scarcely bear a serious perusal," but "I
had not satisfied myself in staying longer, and could never have paid
the debt with a much better play." Had he postponed his address, it

would have come too late: Clifford hanged himself with his cravat on August 18.

With these three dedications to *Marriage à la Mode, The Assignation,* and *Amboyna* in the early summer of 1673, and with occasional prologues and epilogues, Dryden's literary work came to a virtual standstill; nothing of consequence would be published for three more years. But he was not inactive in theatrical matters, since the affairs of his company were very much his concern. When the actors went to Oxford he sent along a special prologue and epilogue. In his letter to Rochester he was induced to say that of their success he "will judge how easy 'tis to passe any thing upon an University; and how grosse flattery the learned will endure." The prologue of course might be read as gross flattery of the college audience; but the epilogue provides a running account of the severe kind of competition which the hapless comedians are subjected to in London: the French players came first, followed by a troupe of Italians (to entertain that court which Dryden was complaining about). But these troupes were only temporary rivals; the real competition, it is obvious, came from the rival company. Betterton, who well knew how to arrange and combine music, dancing, singing, and novel use of machines into exciting spectacle, was exploiting to the limit the advantage he enjoyed in the large and well-equipped Dorset Garden Theatre. Dryden complains of the "wicked engines," and the scenes of "magic" and legerdemain in place of "wit." Mechanical genius has been substituted for poetical; Fletcher and Jonson are despised and out of fashion. The great hit of the summer is the mechanized *Macbeth,* "the *Simon Magus* of the town." Though briskly and amusingly narrated, the epilogue betrays the fear of the King's Company: with their "staple authors," they will find it hard to compete against the operatic devices at the other theater. Even then—as they no doubt knew—Betterton was preparing to mount even more elaborate entertainments.

Though Dryden had temporarily absented himself from the realm of the heroic play, the species was far from inactive. In March, a comparative newcomer to the theater, Elkanah Settle, found himself catapulted to a sudden popularity when his *Empress of Morocco,* through a series of fortuitous circumstances, was given a performance at court. The influence of the Earl of Norwich and the speaking of a prologue by Rochester, plus rather elaborate costuming and scenes, contributed to its success, which was repeated at Dorset Garden in July.[9] Such acceptance proved heady wine to the young playwright,

and when the play was handsomely published in the autumn with
the novelty of five engravings of scenes from the play and a frontispiece of the façade of the Duke's Theatre, it made printing history.
Settle's pride knew no bounds; his boasting about his mediocre play
made certain a later attack, in which Dryden has been supposed to
have participated.[10]   He was himself attacked by one Joseph Arrowsmith in a burlesque comedy like *The Rehearsal,* called *The Reformation,* an amusing scoff at the heroic play, with Dryden as the Tutor
subjected to ridicule more intelligent than that of the Rota pamphlets.
The Tutor, baited by Antonio and Pisauro, gives his recipe for
success.   Using tags from Dryden's various discourses on the heroic
play and on comedy, Arrowsmith unmistakably identifies the Tutor
with the poet.   "Tragedy I say's my Masterpiece," the Tutor begins:

TUTOR: I take a subject, as suppose the Siege of Candy, or the conquest of Flaunders, and by the way Sir let it always be some
warlike action; you can't imagine what a grace a Drum and
Trumpet give a play.   Then Sir I take you some three or
four dozen Kings, but most commonly two or three serve
my turn . . .

You must alwayes have two ladies in love with one man,
or two men in love with one woman; if you make them the
Father and the Son, or two Brothers, or two Friends twill
do the better.   There you know is opportunity for love and
honour and fighting, and all that.

PEDRO: Very well Sir.

TUTOR: Then Sir you must have a Hero that shall fight with all the
world; yes, i'gad, and beat them too, and half the gods into
the bargain if occasion serves.

The Tutor goes into many more details, and he points out that
though his genius does not lead him to comedy, he can still out-write
the other comic playwrights: all he needs is a few scenes from French
plays, a little bawdy, brisk *double-entendres,* a little love and some
honor (keeping the characters alive who would be killed off in
tragedy), and the play is a success.   Then he divulges to his friends
what he calls the Great Arcanum:

When I have writ a play, I pick some Lady out of general
acquaintance, or favourite at the Court, that would be
thought a wit, and send it in pretence for to submit it to her

judgment. This she takes for such a favour—and raises
her esteem so much—she talks of nothing else but Mr. such
a ones new play, and picks out the best on't to repeat, so
half the town by this means is engag'd to clap before they
come.[11]

As the weeks passed, Dryden perhaps continued reading and
study on the epic poem, for which he still awaited the proper encouragement from Charles—an encouragement that was not un-
connected with more substantial support. But public events he was
perforce aware of, and several events of the autumn months were
to have unexpected and in many ways incalculable effect on his
future. The Duke of York, whose first wife, Anne Hyde, had died
in 1671, was eager to marry again, and he looked to Louis XIV to
find him an acceptable Catholic princess. Louis found Mary of
Modena, a member of the Italian family of Este, and by September
negotiations had progressed to a final stage. On the thirtieth of that
month a contract was signed and the marriage completed by proxy.
Unaware of all this the Commons argued about the possibility of an
alliance, but insisted that the Duke should find his bride in the
Protestant fold. Secrecy, indeed, was becoming epidemic, as the
winding course of Stuart policy baffled more and more people. On
November 9, Charles summarily dismissed his Lord Chancellor, the
Earl of Shaftesbury, the last Protestant in high office. A few days
earlier, on Guy Fawkes Day, there had been a great Pope burning,
which included an effigy of a Frenchman who could be shot at by the
mob of Londoners. Shaftesbury, suspicious of the provisions of the
Treaty of Dover, went into opposition, with far-reaching effects on
Charles, on England, and on Dryden. The Dutch War was drawing
to an end without honor, and tensions built up over long months
were finding outlets in wild rumors, attacks, lampoons, and libels.
Sir Nicholas Armourer, writing to Sir Joseph Williamson on September 23, reports that "heare is 1000 coffee-house reports and libells
sans numbers."[12] Despite Parliament, the Duke of York proceeded
with his plans to espouse Mary of Modena, and the ceremony took
place in London on November 21. Those who were wont to deplore the inroads already made by Catholics could now view with
real alarm the situation presented to them by the Duke's marriage.
Both the heir apparent, unless Charles should by some miracle beget
a legitimate child, and his Duchess, were communicants of the
Catholic faith. Divisions would soon take place, and opposition to

a feared Catholic dynasty would harden.   Dryden though quite
unaware of the future turn of Fortune's wheel would find himself
in the literary vortex of the constitutional struggle that was even now
beginning.

At the moment, however, he was deep in the affairs of the
Theatre Royal.   The new building was far along, and would within a
relatively few months be ready for the opening.   On December 17,
the shareholders of the acting company met to sign agreements with
the building investors.   Since the final cost of the new house could
not then be determined, a contingent agreement was arrived at.   If
the theater should cost the same as the old theater (£2,400), they
would pay the entrepreneurs at the old rate of £3 10s. for every
acting day.   But if the building cost should be more, they would pay
proportionately more per acting day.   As it turned out, the cost was
nearly £4,000, so that they were obligated to pay £5 14s. per
day.[13]   Other demands for money became pressing, for in order to
provide new costumes and properties, new scenes and a scene house
to keep them would be of paramount importance.   Apparently only
one method of raising money was open to them—assessments on the
shareholders.   Meetings and discussions on the touchy subject must
have gone on all winter.   But decisions had to be reached, for the
theater was nearing completion.   Finally on March 20, 1673/74,
only six days before the grand opening, it was agreed that each share
should be assessed at £160 to help defray the extraordinary expenses.   Along with Hart, Mohun, and Lacy, Dryden was liable for
a contribution of £200.   One interesting item in the agreement
which Dryden may have used when he came to the breaking point
with the company was the proviso that if, within three years of the
date, any shareholder gave three months' notice of his intention to
retire, he would be reimbursed for his contribution at the rate of
£1 13s. 4d. per acting day, or £10 per week.

Although the new house was a vast improvement over the
tennis court, it was no match for the Duke's Theatre, which had cost
more than twice as much to build.   The position of the company
vis-à-vis Betterton's seems not to have improved so much as had
been hoped.   One reason was that the latter had acquired much
experience in staging operatic entertainments in their well-equipped
house.   For some months they had been planning a very ambitious
program, as we learn from a letter written on August 22, 1673, to
Sir Joseph Williamson by James Vernon:

And now that I am among players I ought not to omitt to acquaint your Excellency that the Duke's House are preparing an Opera and great machines. They will have dansers out of France, and St. Andre comes over with them, who is to have a pension of the King, and a patent of master of the compositions for ballets; further the King hath granted them what boys of his Chappell they shall have occasion for to sing.

Although this opera, *Psyche,* was to be delayed for a year, the Duke's Theatre would be ready with the operatic *Tempest* at about the time the new house of Dryden's company was occupied. The course of these preparations is exceedingly uncertain, and one can only conjecture about the steps taken by the Theatre Royal to counter the formidable threat of the new operatic rage. Knowing of the other theater's plan for *The Tempest,* the company may have brought pressure to bear on Dryden to provide a competing opera; and they may not have given him much time to do it. Immersed in Milton and his studies for the epic, he took what was close to his thoughts and converted parts of *Paradise Lost* into an operatic entertainment, which he called *The State of Innocence.* This he accomplished in one month's time, as he admitted three years later when it was published. Though we may decry his bad taste or even his effrontery in daring to "debase" a noble poem which he admired beyond almost any other in his experience, we must understand, if possible, the referential frame in which this project was placed. From his view and that of his contemporaries there was nothing sacrosanct about Milton or anybody else. Shakespeare and the other Elizabethans were being constantly "improved" for the contemporary taste. The operatic *Macbeth* had been the popular success of the preceding year; and now *The Tempest* was being prepared on an even grander scale. The theme for these operas was not the prime consideration, but rather the episodes and characters that could be properly fashioned to take advantage of both the mechanical devices available and the talents of varying groups of performing artists. Thus, instrumental and vocal music, dancing, elaborate scenes in perspective, spirits and other supernatural or mythological characters, sound and visual effects of various kinds, machinery to lower gods and goddesses and angels from heaven, and platforms that could raise or lower evil spirits beneath the stage—these were the details of this kind of semi-opera. A text for the regular actors was necessary, for they carried most of the play; the "operatic" part was performed by the professional artists.

For Dryden's need, *Paradise Lost* contained nearly all of these elements in solution, and probably it was his recognition of its adaptability that moved him to undertake it. Heaven, Chaos, Hell, and Paradise (the company already had an expensive painting for this scene) provided opportunity for scenic splendor; astral spirits, both debased and pure, were present in great number; the heavenly messengers winging their course between Heaven and Paradise were ready-made for operatic exploitation. Eve and Adam and Satan, the Tree of Knowledge, the temptation scene—all were grist for the opera mill. And the contemporaneity of the subject was obvious to Dryden, who may then have known that the publication of the second edition of *Paradise Lost* was imminent. Whether Aubrey's story that Dryden waited upon Milton to seek permission to use the poem and was told that he might "tag" his verses is true or not signifies little in this connection, though it may testify to Dryden's sense of courtesy toward the great blind poet already nearing death. The emphasis should be placed where it belongs: *The State of Innocence* was designed as a semi-opera to be acted probably upon the opening of the new house. Its failure to achieve production may perhaps be referred to a decision within the company, already burdened with debt. There is little doubt that Dryden's opera would have cost a small fortune to mount; and money was the scarcest commodity in the Theatre Royal when the new theater was occupied in March.[14] It was not acted; instead Fletcher's *Beggar's Bush* (an ironic if somewhat mordant title for the occasion) opened the new house. Dryden contributed a special prologue and epilogue. A month later, on April 17, *The State of Innocence* was entered in the *Stationers' Register.*

Dryden, in the special prologue and epilogue, exhibits no great happiness at being in the new theater at last; it seems a disappointment to the poet and, he thinks, to the customers; the old problems have not magically disappeared:

> A plain-built house, after so long a stay,
> Will send you half-unsatisfied away;
> When, fall'n from your expected pomp, you find
> A bare convenience only is design'd.
> You, who each day can theaters behold,
> Like Nero's palace, shining all with gold,
> Our mean ungilded stage will scorn, we fear,
> And, for the homely room, disdain the cheer.

"Plain-built," "bare convenience," "homely"—it was all of these, as the company realized. Dryden goes on:

> For fame and honor we no longer strive,
> We yield [to the Duke's] in both, and only beg
>   to live:
> Unable to support their vast expense,
> Who build and treat with such magnificence.

The apologies are softened somewhat by the recognition that Charles II had exercised his influence to prevent the company from over-extending itself in the construction of their theater:

> Yet if some pride with want may be allow'd,
> We in our plainness may be justly proud:
> Our royal master will'd it should be so;
> Whate'er he's pleas'd to own, can need no show:
> That sacred name gives ornament and grace,
> And, like his stamp, makes basest metals pass.

Though this attempts to pluck comfort out of the necessity, chagrin and disappointment are written here. Continuing his contention that the theater is "good enough," Dryden nevertheless returns to the perennial complaint:

> 'T were folly now a stately pile to raise,
> To build a playhouse while you throw down plays,
> Whilst scenes, machines, and empty operas reign,
> And for the pencil you the pen disdain.
> While troops of famish'd Frenchmen hither drive,
> And laugh at those upon whose alms they live:
> Old English authors vanish, and give place
> To these new conqu'rors of the Norman race.

He again refers not only to the French competition but also to that of the Duke's:

> I would not prophesy our house's fate:
> But while vain shows and scenes you over-rate,
> Tis to be fear'd—
> That as a fire the former house o'erthrew,
> Machines and tempests will destroy the new.[15]

In the epilogue, he says that though the prologue spoke what is sadly true, yet the house *is* new, and he attempts, without much conviction, to list some of the advantages enjoyed by the new theater. He promises that if they cannot please, they will find better men who will; already they are preparing a "troop of frisking monsieurs" to follow soon, for they are "sure cards at time of need,"—doubtless an ironic reference to the sorry French performance as allies during the Dutch War, only formally ended by treaty in February.

In view of his stillborn opera was there perhaps some bitterness in his reference to the training of the French group destined to present an opera four days later? The details of the arrangements for the presentation of an opera at the Theatre Royal so soon after the opening are obscure, but the main outlines can be followed. Robert Cambert, the French composer, had come to England in the preceding year, perhaps at the urging of his pupil, Lewis Grabu, master of the King's Violins. These two founded the Royal Academy of Music, and Cambert set the music for an operatic piece (written by his friend Perrin) called *Ariane, ou le mariage de Bacchus.* The Killigrew company, determined to present opera, approached Grabu to make arrangements for *Ariane* to be given within the first week of the opening of the new playhouse. Grabu, no doubt, agreed to supply the music and the dancers, a group of French dancing masters who seem to have been resident in England. They were not, as is often said, a French troupe. Grabu, through his official position, was able to borrow—three days before the performance—"such of the Scenes remayning in the Theatre at Whitehall." He was expected to return them within fourteen days.[16] The six dancers were to have ten shillings a day when they danced and five shillings whether they danced or not. Clothes were made for them, and for two months they rehearsed for the opera. The agreement apparently extended beyond the original run, for in May—after much quibbling with respect to their employment—they were ordered to "observe and perform" Killigrew's commands. So the company presented its opera, without contribution by Dryden, in competition with *The Tempest,* which was probably remodeled from the Davenant-Dryden version of 1667 by Thomas Betterton and lavishly mounted by the Duke's company.[17]

Dryden seems now to have reached a kind of impasse in his career. Except for the abortive opera, he had written little since the summer of 1672, when *The Assignation* was completed. Yet his seeming sloth covered an intensive study of epic and dramatic theory and practice, the results of which would be made public in various ways during the next five years. One thing appears certain:

he had temporarily lost his taste for drama, as well he might after the failure of his latest comedy and the fiasco of the opera. Between the summer of 1672 and the summer of 1677 (when he finished writing *All for Love*) he produced only the opera and the modified heroic play *Aureng-Zebe*. Had he taken his contract with the Theatre Royal seriously, he should have turned out fifteen plays. The obvious defection emphasizes the fact that his thoughts were absorbed with matters that he considered at the time more important; and it also lends justification to the complaint of his colleagues in the early months of 1678. The alienation between them may well have begun about the time of the opening of the new Theatre Royal.

Dryden's interest in Milton and in the epic received further reinforcement in the summer, when *Paradise Lost,* the second edition in twelve books, appeared about the beginning of July. Though he may not have been pleased with Marvell's verses attached to it, particularly the couplet referring to him as the Town-Bayes, he found in the poem a greatness which he may already have seen in 1667. The carping of Marvell against the poet laureate contrasts ironically with Dryden's generous and enthusiastic comments upon Milton and *Paradise Lost.* The appearance of this great poem almost coincided with an upsurge of critical interest in the epic in France. Two works with which Dryden became intimately acquainted in the next few months were René Rapin's *Réflexions sur la poétique d'Aristote et sur les ouvrages des poètes anciens et modernes,* and Boileau's *D'art poétique* and also his translation of Longinus, both of which were included in *Oeuvres diverses du Sieur D—— avec le Traité du Sublime ou du Merveilleux dans le Discours.* Thomas Rymer had already seen the significance of Rapin's work, and had completed enough of a translation to have it licensed by L'Estrange on June 26. Dryden was probably reading both Rapin and Boileau in the late months of 1674 or early in 1675. Of even more immediate importance to him and his interests was Le Bossu's *Le poëme épique,* published in Paris in 1675 and soon discovered by Dryden, who was to call Bossu "the best of the modern critics."[18]

Of leisure Dryden had an abundance, since his voluntary retirement from the theater. In the summer he provided a special prologue and epilogue for the company for its summer season at Oxford, but as far as is known nothing else can be assigned to this period. He found, perhaps, opportunity for social life: on June 27 he called on Evelyn, a friend from the early days of the Royal Society. To Evelyn the visit was worth recording: "Mr. Dryden, the famous poet and now laureate, came to give me a visit. It was the anniversary of my marriage."

But his chief concern must have been to get on with the epic. There is no indication that his tentative proposals made publicly elicited any interest in the people who were to be celebrated. Since the death of Clifford his court connections to the King must have been meager. Perhaps he had hoped, almost against his better judgment, that Rochester might provide a conduit to the kingly presence, through which favor might descend to him. If he had really entertained such hope, it was rudely dashed when in the autumn Rochester used his influence to have John Crowne, not John Dryden, write a masque for presentation in Whitehall by the court ladies and gentlemen.[19] Although the course of events leading to Crowne's selection remains unclear, it is, however, clear that Dryden, the laureate, was bypassed in favor of a comparative newcomer to the profession. His dependence upon Rochester was at an end; in fact, within a few months the noble Earl attacked him in a satire, *The Allusion to the Tenth Satire of Horace,* and thereby placed himself in the group of those courtiers whom Dryden had so thoroughly anathematized in the dedication of *Marriage à la Mode* to Rochester in early 1673.

In this extremity Dryden turned to the Earl of Mulgrave as the instrument to further his project of the epic, or at least we are led to believe so by his next public statement, the dedication to *Aureng-Zebe.* Here we find Dryden's most complete account of his theme, his plan, and part of the negotiations to enlist the support of the King and his brother. Since it reviews Dryden's concerns of these months, the dedication may best be considered at this point.[20]

He writes a bold and subtly phrased beginning:

It is a severe reflection which Montagne has made on Princes, that we ought not, in reason, to have any expectations from them; and that it is kindness enough, if they leave us in possession of our own. The boldness of the censure shews the free spirit of the author; and the subjects of England may justly congratulate to themselves that both the nature of our government, and the clemency of our King, secure us from any such complaint. I in particular, who subsist wholly by his bounty, am obliged to give posterity a far other account of my Royal Master than what Montagne has left of his.

Such a contrast—and such praise of Charles—is designed to take some of the sting out of his later reprimand, though mildly expressed, of the King's dereliction of duty toward poetry and poets in his neglect of tangible encouragement to the projected epic. The "accusations" cited from Montaigne he believes would be "more reasonable if they had been placed on inferior persons [i.e., courtiers]; for in all courts there are too many who make it their business to ruin wit." He then proceeds to give what he calls the "character of a courtier without wit." "Malice secures them in their fortune," he points out, but they have a speciousness that recommends them to princes, and "diligence in waiting is their gilding of the pill; for that looks like love, though it is only interest." Too often the man of real wit waits attendance on these people, but the "nauseousness of such company is enough to disgust a reasonable man; when he sees he can hardly approach greatness but as a moated castle—he must first pass through the mud and filth with which it is encompassed." Often they assume an honesty which is not theirs, and they use their power mischievously. "They fawn and crouch to men of parts, whom they can not ruin . . . but to those who are under them and whom they can crush with ease, they shew themselves in their natural antipathy: there they treat wit like the common enemy." Such as he describes are those who stand between the poet and "greatness." In much the same tenor he had complained to Rochester earlier and had pinned his hopes on his intercession. If by the time this was written —in January (?), 1675/76—Rochester's *Allusion* was circulating, we may imagine that the generalized portrait might have directly pointed to him.[21] Whether it did or not, Dryden moves toward a sharp contrast when he describes Mulgrave's worth and courage and loyalty, a tribute that follows Dryden's usual pattern of compliment and flattery.

By such degrees he reaches the meat of his discourse. He would be content in a retired life, like Epicurus and his "better Master Cowley," for he desires only a humbler "station in the Temple of Virtue, than to be set on the pinnacle of it." It is not worth our pains, he says, to consider "so vain a creature as man; [I have] fool enough at home without looking for it abroad; and am a sufficient theatre to myself of ridiculous actions, without expecting company either in a court, a town, or a playhouse." On this account he is weary with "drawing the deformities of life" in the theater, where many of his predecessors have excelled him in all kinds of plays and "some of my contemporaries, even in my own partial judgment, have outdone me in comedy." After expressing the hope that he may make amends "for many ill plays" by the composition of an epic poem, Dryden recalls to Mulgrave that he has "long been acquainted with my design." Just how long defies an accurate answer. "The

subject," he continues, "is great, the story English, and neither too
far distant from the present age, nor too near approaching it." The
reason why Dryden chooses to recall these facts to Mulgrave soon
becomes clear:

> Such it is in my opinion, that I could not have wished a nobler
> occasion to do honour by it to my king, my country, and my friends;
> most of our ancient nobility being concerned in the action.   And your
> Lordship has one particular reason to promote this undertaking, because
> *you were the first who gave me the opportunity of discoursing it to his
> Majesty, and his Royal Highness* [italics mine]; they were then pleased
> both to commend the design, and to encourage it by their commands. . . .

Perhaps Dryden had reminded the royal brothers of the many
heroic actions of their family that might be proper materials for
heroic verse: from the learned grandfather, brought from Scotland
to become king on the death of Elizabeth; through the growing
"epic" struggle with Parliament, the "Martyrdom" of King Charles I,
the war and conflict between Royalists and Parliament, the trials and
exile of Prince Charles to the glorious Restoration and the return of
the Golden Age.   There were plenty of materials that Dryden could
easily have put into his design, and some of them he had already
partially exploited in his early poems.   The King and the Duke
might well encourage such a plan by their commands; were they
also prepared to encourage it by something more tangible?   Apparently not, for Dryden complains that

> . . . the unsettledness of my condition [i.e., lack of money] has hitherto
> put a stop to my thoughts concerning it.   As I am no successor to Homer
> in his wit, so neither do I desire to be in his poverty.   I can make no
> rhapsodies, nor go a begging at the Grecian doors, while I sing the
> praises of their ancestors.   The times of Virgil please me better, because
> he had an Augustus for his patron; and to draw the allegory nearer you,
> I am sure I shall not want a Maecenas with him.

He pleads, then, for the necessary financial aid to go on with the
work that had in effect divorced him from the theater.   Mulgrave,
because of his initial representations to the King, should continue
his good offices: "It is for your Lordship to stir up that remembrance
in his Majesty, which his many avocations of business have caused
him, I fear, to lay aside; and, as himself and his royal brother are
the heroes of the poem, to represent to them the images of their
warlike predecessors. . . .   For my own part, I am satisfied to have
offered the design; and it may be to the advantage of my reputation
to have it refused me."[22]

Although this was written very early in 1676, it seems obvious that the lack of encouragement made public here had forced him to interrupt whatever plans he had made for the large poem and to return to the drama in the spring and summer months of 1675. No doubt financial distress helped to force him to the stage again; from that source he had received no income for more than two years expect for the unknown amounts received from Herringman for the copy of the plays published in 1673. His salary as laureate, fortunately, was being paid, not by the quarter but by yearly grants of £200. During the months between grants he must have suffered real deprivations. Perhaps one reason his salary had not fallen into arrears was the careful management of finances under Danby, who had taken Clifford's place as one of the King's closest advisers, and under whose guidance was promoted a policy of Anglicanism and loyalty to the Crown, which provided the nucleus for a Tory party now in formation. The opposition too found cohesion under the leadership of Shaftesbury, and the Whig Party began to emerge, with strength among the county gentry and the city dissenters. Their determination to subordinate the King to the Parliament had already shown itself, and it was to receive intensification in the following months. Charles used his proroguing power again and again; and in November, faced with an irreconcilable and adamant Parliament, he prorogued the body that had convened the previous month. It was to remain uncalled for the extreme period of fifteen months. In the interval, government by council and advisers obtained. As the months passed and the elected Parliament was not reconvened, gossip, rumors, libels grew. Fears multiplied that great and unwelcome changes were afoot; and anti-Catholic and anti-French feelings increased. Factions were forming for the great constitutional struggle that came closer by the month; and Dryden, like countless others, was being forced to take a stand. It is perhaps too much to imagine that in the summer and autumn he could even partially foresee the course of events. Yet whether he was aware or not, he was inexorably being drawn, as a person and poet and as a loyal supporter of kingship, into the vortex of the developing conflict.

While these events were in embryo, Dryden's new play was taking shape. As we might expect, it took the form of the heroic play, but not precisely after the old models. The "heroics" are muted somewhat, the extravagant rhodomontades of the earlier plays virtually absent. The couplet he retains, but so modified from that of *The Conquest of Granada* that it approaches blank verse in suppleness. The chiming of the rhyme is toned down, so that in sections the effect is actually that of blank verse—an experiment in a freer couplet than he had ever before written. But he keeps the heroic postures and the twin heroic themes of love and honor. Such modification of the old pattern may doubtless be attributed to numerous influences at work: the attacks upon him and his early heroic plays in dramatic burlesques and prose pamphlets; the impact made upon him by his close study of Milton's epic and other poems that were within the limits of heroic or epic form and intent; his absorption in the French critical treatises of 1674 and 1675; a probable reacquaintance with his great English predecessors in drama; and his own personal desire for a new direction after his lengthy absence from drama.[23]

Aureng-Zebe was acted on November 17. Apparently it enjoyed a successful initial run: royalty attended on the opening night and again on November 20.[24] In the prologue he admits to having "another taste of wit" and that he grows weary of his "long-loved Mistress Rhyme." He is willing to "damn this laborious trifle of a play," though it is not worse than his others.

> But spite of all his pride, a secret shame
> Invades his breast at Shakespeare's sacred name.
> Aw'd when he hears his godlike Romans rage,
> He, in just despair, would quit the stage.

Perhaps *All for Love,* his next play, is already taking shape in his thoughts as an answer to the challenge which continually faced him as he somewhat reluctantly admitted the difficulty of competing with the "greater dead." The King's company at this juncture needed more than one success like *Aureng-Zebe* to give them health. Their failure to present opera which could take some of the patronage away from the other playhouse is pointed up by the unintelligent course they took to combat that popularity. Duffett's series of burlesques (*The Empress of Morocco, The Mock Tempest, Psyche Debauch'd*) provided no satisfactory answer to the successful *Tempest* and *Psyche* at Betterton's theater. These inter-playhouse rivalries were probably in mind when Dryden wrote in the prologue:

> There needs no care to put a playhouse down,
> 'Tis the most desart place of all the town:
> We and our neighbors, to speak proudly, are,
> Like monarchs, ruin'd with expensive war.

It was not this alone, however, that was ruining the Theatre Royal: it was the financial crises created by the impecuniousness and venality of Killigrew. He had pawned his own shares in the enterprise and had borrowed money against those that were being held as security for other obligations; and soon after this time he was to turn over for debt all of his acting and building shares—as well as his patent. Hart and Mohun had become its managers. The tangled affairs of Killigrew exercised a depressing effect upon the whole company; after the agreement of March, 1673/74 (at the opening of the new theater), expected profits did not appear. And by 1675, the important actors of the company threatened to cease acting altogether, as they did for a short time three months after the presentation of *Aureng-Zebe*. They were brought back by express command of the King. Upon the instance of Killigrew his son Charles acted as mediator in this latest contretemps, and on May 1, 1676, a new agreement was drawn up and signed by all of the major shareholders, except Dryden. It is not clear whether his failure to sign means that he was no longer a shareholder or that he refused to accept the less favorable terms of the new agreement and was holding out for an eventual settlement under the terms of the original agreement. The latter would appear more reasonable in view of the complaint of the actors against him in 1678, when he seems still to be a shareholder.[25] At any rate, for more than another year bickering continued, and relations between the poet and the company probably moved from one crisis to another.

After *Aureng-Zebe* Dryden appears to have written little. Only an epilogue to Sir George Etherege's *The Man of Mode,* acted on March 11, can be assigned to the early months of 1675/76. It was now that Rochester's satire on him was making the rounds, the background of which is extremely vague. Whether Rochester's enmity arose because of Dryden's friendship with Mulgrave and the subsequent position of patron assumed by that nobleman, or whether Rochester felt that Dryden should be humbled is not known. Though *The Allusion to the Tenth Satire of Horace* is quite malicious and abusive, Rochester has grace enough to admit that the laureate's plays have pleased the town and that his excellences more abound than his faults. But he repeats the by now well-worn charges of Dryden's depreciation of Jonson, Shakespeare, and Beaumont and Fletcher. Once the would-be wits and the wits got hold of an idea they often showed a lamentable lack of judgment by worrying it to an unimpressive death.

Personal and family matters of which we have little or no knowledge doubtless encroached upon his time and thoughts during the many months when he appears to have done little writing. Although the Treasury had been unusually solicitous of him, the arrears on his salary now began; a payment due at Christmas, 1675, was paid six months late. Never in the future, during Charles's reign, was he to receive full payment. In June he in all likelihood spent some time at his old home in Northamptonshire, for on June 14, 1676, his mother died. She had survived her husband for twenty-two years. Her will, proved in the following year, mentions nine of her children. To her "beloved son John Dryden" she bequeathed a silver tankard marked "I. D." and a "goold ring which was my wedding ring." The latter was directed to be passed on to his son Charles. Elizabeth and Frances were named sole executors and Erasmus the overseer.[26] With his mother's death the home at Titchmarsh was broken up, but many relations remained with whom he visited during many summers and with whom he corresponded during the winters.

Critical Theories and Tragedy
1676-1678

AFTER HIS RETURN from Northamptonshire in the summer of 1676, Dryden devoted the remainder of the year to preparing *The State of Innocence* for publication (in early February, 1676/77) and to the writing of the essay which accompanied it, called the *Author's Apology for Heroic Poetry and Poetic Licence*.[1] Although he seems now to have shelved the epic, his studies for it had not been forgotten. The *Apology*, accompanying his operatic adaptation of *Paradise Lost*, properly enough discusses theories and problems of this noblest type of poetry. Nor did he miss the opportunity to give his unacted opera the best introduction he found at hand: he dedicated it to the Duchess of York, whom the Duke had brought from Italy for his bride three years before, and whose family (Dryden reminds her) had been the patrons of both Ariosto and Tasso. In extravagance and fulsomeness, Dryden never surpassed this address to the Duchess, which Dr. Johnson said was "written in a strain of flattery which disgraces genius, and which it is wonderful that any man that knew the meaning of his own words could use without self-detestation."[2]

The *Apology*, however, is far different: it is a reasoned defense against the misuse of reason employed by the little critics of his time to depreciate what he sees as the great beauties of epic poetry. He begins with a tribute to Milton:

I cannot, without injury to the deceased author of *Paradise Lost*, but acknowledge, that this poem has received its entire foundation, part of the design, and many of the ornaments from him. . . . I should be sorry, for my own sake, that any one should take the pains to compare them together, the original being undoubtedly one of the greatest, most noble, and most sublime poems, which either this age or nation has produced.

Milton, he says, like his great predecessors has suffered at the hands of those critics who seem to believe that the nature of criticism is "principally to find fault." On the contrary, as instituted by Aristotle, by criticism "was meant a standard of judging well; the chiefest part of which is, to observe those excellencies which should delight a reasonable reader." If the large design and conduct of the poem, along with the thoughts and language proceed from genius, the poet is to be praised, despite small lapses of the pen, from which even Homer and Virgil were not exempt. Support for this point is found in Longinus, whom he paraphrases from Boileau's translation.[3] Despite the "hypercritics of English poetry," heroic poetry has ever been "esteemed, and ever will be, the greatest work of human nature." It was so considered by the best of the Greek and Roman writers as well as by the succeeding Italian and French, among whom he regards Boileau and Rapin the greatest critics of his age. Exalted language, he points out, must be a concomitant of great poetry and must be enumerated among the beauties of the epic. "Are all the flights of Heroic Poetry to be concluded bombast, unnatural, and mere madness" because they happen to transgress the criticaster's sense of what is reasonable? Not all is fustian that is so labelled by these men, yet there are limits to be set, both by the writer and the critic, who must understand the limits. Bold figures, hyperboles, metaphors, in short, the *materia poetica,* are the lifeblood of great poetry before which reason is baffled. So it is too when one considers the use of chimeras, fairies, pigmies, and other "fantasies"; but the poet is not to be limited by that kind of reason which would deny latitude in their use. So Dryden writes a defense, based upon his own judgment and upon his cited critic's for the imagining—for poetic fictions—of "immaterial substances." The *Apology,* as Ker has said, "is comprehensive, a claim for poetical freedom, a protest in the name of Reason and Common Sense against a narrow and trivial misuse of Common Sense to the detriment of imagination."[4]

The publication in February, 1676/77, of *The State of Innocence* seems to have written finis to his plans for the epic, but not to his interest in epic form. No doubt the reasons for his abandonment of the plan are complex and beyond our interpretation until new sources of information are forthcoming. It may be assumed that the King's lack of tangible encouragement was a factor, but this could not have been the determining bar to Dryden's completion of a poem that must by this time have been under way.   The explanation may eventually be found in his recognition of his own limitations.   Milton—as Dryden so well recognized—had written in *Paradise Lost* the greatest poem yet produced in England.   To attempt even to equal, much less to surpass, such an achievement he may wisely have concluded was beyond his poetic powers.   Indeed he suggests as much in his address to Mulgrave in *Aureng-Zebe,* when he remarks that it may be to his advantage to be refused the needed financial support to prosecute his planned chronicle of the Stuarts.   Nothing he had written thus far had really demonstrated his capacity for the kind of sustained poetic invention demanded by the epic form, nor was he in future to demonstrate it.   His own critical requirements, enunciated some years later, were so severe that they actually disqualified him— as perhaps he was aware.   Addressing Dorset in the *Discourse Concerning the Original and Progress of Satire* in 1692, he included a section dealing with the epic, in which he cited the specifications for the epic poet:

. . . if any of so happy a genius be now living, or any future age can produce a man, who being conversant in the philosophy of Plato, as it is now accommodated to Christian use, for (as Virgil gives us to under- stand by his example) that is the only proper, of all others, for an epic poem; who, to his natural endowments, of a large invention, a ripe judgment, and a strong memory, has joined the knowledge of the liberal arts and sciences, and particularly moral philosophy, the mathematics, geography, and history, and with all these qualifications is born a poet; knows, and can practice the variety of numbers, and is master of the language in which he writes—if such a man . . . be now arisen, or shall arise, I am vain enough to think that I have proposed a model to him.

About a week after *The State of Innocence* appeared in print, a money warrant for £200 was granted him on his pension—a full year's payment which was not immediately paid; for several months later he is pleading for even a half year's payment which would have paid the arrears only until Christmas, 1676.   But the good will of the King, despite the difficulties of the Treasury, was being demonstrated by his grant of another annuity of £100 to be added to the original grant.[5]   Perhaps Charles belatedly made the gesture in response to Dryden's requests for aid to further the epic; if so, it was now too late.   Had the original grant been paid currently, Dryden no doubt would have welcomed the additional promise; but arrears were to continue on both.   It might not have consoled him, however, to reflect that his total grant of £300 a year as poet laureate and historiographer now equalled the salary of some of the King's musicians.

In the spring months he devoted himself to the writing of a new play, *All for Love,* on which he lavished more care than on many, if not all, of his heroic plays. His return to the drama in *Aureng-Zebe* had been marked by a change, both in tone and in verse. Now the new play continued the process of further departure from the conventions of the old type, as if to implement the dissatisfaction, indeed the "shame" he expressed in the prologue to *Aureng-Zebe,* at Shakespeare's "sacred name." Not only did he determine to put himself in competition with his predecessors, but with the best of them. Shakespeare became his model, and he chose for purposes of imitation the one play whose theme intrigued him and whose treatment by Shakespeare he considered somewhat unsatisfactory. In the story of Antony and Cleopatra he found all of the ingredients which could serve him well for his purposes: to use the same sources for the same material, but to impose upon them a dramatic form dictated both by the best of the "classic" theorists and by the taste of the generation of playgoers for whom he was writing. If this was indeed the "bow of Ulysses," he was not loath to try his hand at it.

While work went ahead on the new play Dryden found that the affairs of the King's company became increasingly more involved and unsatisfactory. The Duke's Theatre, however, was prospering, and now preparing to mount another opera, this one by Charles Davenant and called *Circe.* For some months Betterton and Harris (and no doubt Davenant, who at twenty-one was just now coming into his inheritance of the shares left by his father) had been collecting properties and scenes for this new performance. Perhaps Dryden now began to look toward the Duke's, preparatory to a complete break with a company that was inevitably going to ruin. At any rate, when *Circe* was acted in May, it was accompanied by a prologue from the poet laureate. Whether his small contribution helped the production or not, the accounts of the Duke's Theatre for May suggest beyond much doubt that *Circe* scored a great success at the box office.[6] Exasperation against Dryden among the King's company must have increased the tensions already existent between playwright and actors. It was one thing for their colleague to contribute an epilogue for his friend Etherege when *The Man of Mode* was acted at the Duke's; it was another matter for him to give a laureate's accolade to the virtual head of the rival theater. To the mounting difficulties of Dryden's company, there seemed no end. Charles Killigrew had not much better luck than his father. In this very month (or shortly before) he had been forced to discharge the musicians attached to the Theatre Royal; and the repertory he had been able to present with his aging actors had been undistinguished. Before many months had passed, some of the actors were walking out of the theater in their costumes and "embezzling" them.[7] By July the shareholders successfully petitioned the King for self-government. It was the last stand; debts mounted as bills for properties and costumes remained unpaid. So, as Dryden saw the end in sight, he prudently looked to the Duke's Theatre for the future.

Progress on *All for Love* continued throughout the spring and early summer, and by July it was completed, but was probably not yet ready to turn over to the company. Dryden's concerns during these weeks we catch a glimpse of in a letter he wrote to Lord Latimer, the son of Danby. Eager to go to Northamptonshire for a holiday, Dryden wrote Latimer in an attempt to use the young man to influence his father to write the necessary order for payment of £100 on his overdue salary. He points out that "the Kings Comedy lyes in the sudds till you please to send me into Northamptonshyre: it will be almost such another piece of businesse as [Durfey's] the fond Husband, for such the King will have it, who is parcell poet with me in the plott; one of the designes being a story he was pleasd formerly to tell me; and therefore I hope he will keep the jeast in countenance by laughing at it."[8] The comedy, in which the King is "parcell poet," was no doubt *The Kind Keeper,* acted a few months after *All for Love.* He reminds the young man that the "other part of my businesse depends upon the King's memory and your father's kindnesse, who has promised my Lord Mulgrave, that I shall not fare the worse for Mr Mayes persecuting me." Dryden's request perhaps has reference to the additional grant of £100 on his salary which may have been held up by the activities of Baptist May, the King's Keeper of the Privy Purse. If so, his appeal was successful, for the letters patent were issued on July 31. Part of the reason for the success may be the request that Latimer seek his father's permission for Dryden's dedication to him of *All for Love,* which he hopes will be acted in Michaelmas term.

Whether through the auspices of Latimer or not, Dryden went to the country and was established there not later than August 20, when his friend Wycherley informed Mulgrave that there was no "poetical news" in town because Dryden was in Northamptonshire.[9] He established himself, not at Titchmarsh, where he no longer had a family home, but at the house of his second cousin, Thomas Elmes, at Lilford, near Oundle.   Here, entertained for a time by local gossip and by the learned discourse of a young relative who "talkes nothing all day long . . . in French & Italian to show his breeding," he settled down to prepare *All for Love* for acting and to finish the comedy.[10]   Rymer sent him a copy of his *Tragedies of the Last Age Considered,* which was just off the press; and he at the moment thought it the "best piece of criticism in the English tongue; perhaps in any other of the modern."   About Rymer he was to have second thoughts; nor was he completely in accord with all of Rymer's critical dicta in this book, though he is glad that Rymer spared him the kind of severe strictures he used on Shakespeare and Fletcher. The narrow dogmatism of Rymer's critique, despite this temporary approval, proved antipathetic to Dryden's more liberal approach, and it was perhaps during this sojourn or soon after that he jotted down the remarks that survive as "Heads of An Answer" to Rymer. By September or October he was probably back in London, for he brought back *All for Love,* which he expected to be acted by the company before the autumn was over.

The closing months of the year were occupied by the mounting and acting of his tragedy, which since it was written *con amore* he must have devoted much attention to, and by completing *The Kind Keeper.*   On December 12, *All for Love* was presented at the Theatre Royal.[11]   No contemporary evidence records its success or failure, and the play was never acted—according to the accounts printed by Nicoll—before royalty.   The quality of the play (in the eyes of posterity at least) might be expected to provoke some kind of contemporary comment or, at the very least, to be accorded the favor of performance before the King.   The lack of such evidence strongly suggests that the company had done a very poor job with Dryden's masterpiece, scarcely surprising in view of the rapid disintegration taking place.   Dryden's defection from the group within the next ten or twelve weeks, as evidenced by his giving the Duke's Theatre the right to *The Kind Keeper,* underlines his final break with the King's company and provides a reason for their complaint against him very soon thereafter.   The association formed eleven years before was now irretrievably broken.

As the year ended, libels, lampoons, and various kinds of attacks upon men of letters and upon the wits continued.   In prologues and

epilogues to many of the plays acted in 1676 and 1677 their presence
and what would appear their increasing incidence were noted.   Circulating in manuscript, the attacks made the rounds of coffeehouses,
and copies were made for wider circulation.   One such, a "Litany"
of nineteen stanzas, achieved a certain popularity in the closing weeks
of the year; and another of much more importance, "A Trial of the
Poets for the Bays," perhaps by Rochester and his group of friends at
Woodstock, had surveyed the particular claims of the contemporary
poets.   Dryden had survived these pasquils without much damage.[12]
But as the political tensions of the next few months became intensified, so too did the acerbity and the frequency of anonymous attacks.

Always sensitive to the political events of the time, Dryden followed the crucial conflict of 1677 with more than common interest.
When Parliament met in February after the unprecedented holiday
of fifteen months, Shaftesbury spoke for its dissolution on the ground
that the long recess had automatically dissolved it, and that the
election of a new Parliament was indicated.   For his pains, he was
committed to the Tower, where he remained for a year.[13]   The
Parliament, much concerned with Louis' success in arms against
Holland, urged the King to take some kind of active measures to
help the Dutch.   Charles countered with requests for money, but
resisted the demands of his Parliament.   Louis' need to keep English
soldiers out of Europe led him to a campaign of bribery of parliamentary leaders.   In return for his largess, they refused funds for
the military, but were willing to underwrite a naval program.   In
July Charles recessed Parliament.   Between this month and the beginning of the fateful new year, many events were on foot.   In
October the betrothal of William and Princess Mary was announced
—an alliance favored by the King because it would perhaps allay
suspicions of his pro-French policy and particularly the fear of his
design to impose Catholicism on his people.   It also had the effect
of giving notice to Louis that he would need to continue courting his
English dependent.   Following a policy of playing for time, Charles
negotiated in late December—through his emissary Lawrence Hyde
—a treaty with Holland, which provided that unless France and
Spain should accept certain territorial adjustments, England would
lend military support to Holland.   This he never ratified, for it already had served notice to Louis, whose unexpected bribery of
English lawmakers gave Danby a chance for counter-bribery of
members in order to get a majority for the King's policies.   When
Parliament finally convened again in late January, chicanery, double

talk, and double dealing became epidemic; and Dryden, though denied access to documents easily available to later historians, followed events as well as he could and with growing concern.

Having already secured Danby's permission to dedicate to him *All for Love,* Dryden used his opportunity not only to laud Danby and his statesmanship but also to write a personal testament on government in general and the present government in particular. The play was registered on January 31, 1677/78, but it seems reasonable to suppose that the dedication was written in February or March, after the new Parliament was in session; for his comments on the affairs of that body could not have been made earlier. The play with the dedication was advertised for sale in the *London Gazette* of March 21.

Dryden began his tribute to Danby by pointing out a natural tie that exists between poets and statesmen; "though ours be much the inferior part, it comes at least within the verge of alliance. Nor are we unprofitable members of the commonwealth, when we animate others to those virtues which we copy and describe from you." Those who work toward the subversion of governments find it to their interest to discourage poets and historians, "for the best which can happen to them is to be forgotten." But those who by their prudent management seek to preserve their country have reason "to cherish the chroniclers of their actions . . . for such records are their undoubted titles to the love and reverence of afterages." Of such is Danby, who has brought order out of confusion in the King's Treasury and who, in spite of determined enemies, has earned the praises of the King and the prayers of private persons to whom he has brought aid and comfort. Warming to his subject, Dryden finds the "disposition of Princes to their people" in the choice of ministers, "who, like the animal spirits betwixt the soul and body, participate somewhat of both natures, and make the communication that is betwixt them." The choice of Danby was made by a just and moderate King who rules according to the laws and "makes us happy by assuming over us no other sovereignty than that wherein our welfare and liberty consists." Moderation, he points out, is "An establishment of greatness; but there is a steadiness of temper which is likewise requisite in a minister of state: so equal a mixture of both Virtues, that he may stand like an isthmus betwixt the two encroaching seas of arbitrary power and lawless anarchy." Obviously, not all of Dryden's friends or family would have agreed with him about Charles's just and moderate nature or about Danby's fitness to serve

as a great minister of state. But as Dryden now understood Danby's
policy of Anglicanism and the support of Protestant Holland against
the power of Catholic France, he agreed with what may be called
Tory policy in 1677/78. The opposition, led by Shaftesbury, out-
wardly approved the policy because they were left no choice; they
too were anti-Catholic and anti-French. But they could frustrate
Tory policy by refusing funds for enough substantial support to Holland to effect the temporary royal policy. The Whigs were after
larger game, for they were intent upon whittling away the few prerogatives left to kingship. This struggle Dryden saw clearly, and he
took his position against the usurpation of power by the Parliament.
To serve as an isthmus between these two seas would be "difficult
to any but an extraordinary genius, to stand at the line, and to divide
the limits; to pay what is due to the great representative of the nation,
and *neither to enhance nor to yield up the undoubted prerogatives of
the crown* [italics mine]."

Dryden here moved politically along lines laid down by many
political theorists of the century. He made a frontal attack upon
the great central struggle of his age between royal prerogative and
parliamentary encroachment upon it. And he left no doubt upon
which side he would fight or about his opinion of the present leaders
and their motives. To find this place in the middle, but to acknowledge the powers reserved to both extremes and yet to eschew total
commitment to one or the other, he believed to be the virtue of the
English. In a stirring statement of English political principles, he
explicated the essential elements in the current struggle and provided
a clear-cut exposition of his personal credo. No people in the world
are capable of such virtues except the English,

who have the happiness to be born under so equal and so well-poised a
government—a government which has all the advantages of liberty beyond
a commonwealth, and all the marks of kingly sovereignty without the
danger of a tyranny. Both my nature, as I am an Englishman, and my
reason, as I am a man, have bred in me a loathing of that specious name
of a Republick; that mock-appearance of a liberty, where all who have
not part in the government are slaves; and slaves they are of viler note
than such are the subjects to an absolute dominion. For no Christian
Monarchy is so absolute, but it is circumscribed with laws; but when the
executive power is in the lawmakers, there is no farther check upon them,
and the people must suffer without a remedy, because they are oppressed
by their representatives. If I must serve, the number of my masters, who
were born my equals, would but add to the ignominy of my bondage.

The nature of this government is suited "both to the situation of our country and the temper of the natives": an "island more proper for commerce and defence than for extending its dominions on the continent." He saw little enhancement in such adventures, for there was small chance of winning a land-war. He appeared to counsel a contrary policy to that of Danby by suggesting that England is better designed for defense; and "the consent of a people is easily obtained to contribute to that power which must protect it. *Felices nimium bona si sua norint, Anglicanae.*" Yet was he not advancing the idea of a wise moderation, which reinforces his concept of government?

In spite of the oratory of the Whig opposition that spoke largely and in general terms of liberty and conscience, Dryden saw political trickery afoot. There were malcontents who would persuade the people "that they would be happier by a change":

It was indeed the policy of their old Forefather, when himself was fallen from the station of glory, to seduce mankind into the same rebellion with him, by telling him he might be freer than he was; that is, more free than his nature would allow, or (if I may so say) than God could make him. We have already all the liberty which freeborn subjects can enjoy; and all beyond it is licence. But if it be liberty of conscience which they pretend, the moderation of our Church is such, that its practice extends not to the severity of persecution; and its discipline is withal so easy, that it allows more freedom to dissenters, than any of the sects would allow to it.

Some men arrogate to themselves the right to attempt "innovations in church and state." "Who made them," he asks, "the trustees, or (to speak a little nearer their own language) the keepers of the liberty of England?" If they have been "called" to such work, they should demonstrate their election by producing miracles. Here Dryden boldly attacks the leader of the Whigs, the Earl of Shaftesbury, in a passage that contains the germ of his character of Achitophel more than three years later, yet even now he shrewdly assessed not only his character but his purpose and his techniques:

He who has often changed his party, and always has made his interest the rule of it, gives little evidence of his sincerity for the publick good; it is manifest he changes but for himself, and takes the people for tools to work his fortune. Yet the experience of all ages might let him know, that they who trouble the waters first, have seldom the benefit of the fishing; as they who began the late rebellion enjoyed not the fruit of their undertaking, but were crushed themselves by the usurpation of their own instrument.

These were prophetic words, not arrived at through a special sense of prevision but through Dryden's special sense of the workings of history. It is not enough, he says, for such men to answer "that they only intend a reformation of the government, but not the subversion of it: on such pretenses all insurrections have been founded." And the current technique of those who talk and write against this established government he understood: "Every remonstrance of private men has the seed of treason in it; and discourses which are couched in ambiguous terms are the more dangerous, because they do all the mischief of open sedition, yet are safe from the punishment of the laws." If one be a true Englishman, he concludes, one must "be fired with indignation, and revenge himself as he can on the disturbers of his country."

The political arena was, as the Marquis of Halifax called it, "an active and an angry world." As Dryden and many others were soon to be aware, it was also a vastly complicated one. But here Dryden's statement of principles and his shrewd interpretation of the developing conflicts demonstrate a penetrating insight which would lose none of its edge in the coming months. Already Shaftesbury's probable course was partly charted in Dryden's mind, and it remained only for the evolving events to justify his worst fears. Already the figure of a Satanic Achitophel ready to pervert others to his own use has been sketched; the unfolding events of the immediate future would give particular and detailed substance to it. And already the wrath of a righteously aroused loyal poet is enlisted to wreak a devastating revenge upon the "disturber" of a nation.

The preface to *All for Love* is not so remarkable a document as the dedication, or as informative as we might wish. Only a relatively small portion of it is devoted to the play; the remainder is taken up with a general attack upon the small critics of the day and with a severe castigation of the Earl of Rochester, whom he here repaid for the *Allusion to the Tenth Satire of Horace*. The theme of the play has been treated by the greatest wits of the nation, he says, and so variously that "their example has given me the confidence to try myself in this bow of Ulysses amongst the crowd of suitors." His concept of the hero was Aristotelian: the characters of Antony and Cleopatra he drew as favorably as the sources (Plutarch, Appian, and Dion Cassius) would allow. They are not of perfect virtue, so that room is left for the working of pity and fear. In construction the drama is strictly unified; all episodes conduce to the furthering of the main design, all disruptive sub-actions are rigidly excluded. It is more regular, with regard to the three unities "than perhaps the English theatre requires." One fault in the contrivance he finds in the person of Octavia, whose appearance in Alexandria to confront Cleopatra tends to divert pity from the main character, yet the possibilities inherent in the clash of two proud women were appealing enough to excuse such an error. His critics have not urged this against him but have been content with minor cavils. His observation of the peccadilloes of the French playwrights provides a background for comments on their "nicety of manners" in character portrayal and their "civility" which neutralizes character to such an extent that there is little left for the critics to blame or to praise. An easy transition brings him to the English condemners—hardly critics—who have "too narrow souls to judge of poetry." Among them he finds the witty men of quality, those who are not "contented with what Fortune has done for them, and sit down quietly with their estates, but they must call their wits in question and needlessly expose their nakedness to publick view." For they have no necessity of poverty to force them to scribble; but the case of the poor poet is hard: if he fails, he starves; and if he succeeds, some "malicious satire is prepared to level" him for daring to please without permission of the great. Their eagerness to defame others arises from their ambition to be thought poets, but they have entirely missed the lesson of Maecenas, who became a poet at second-hand by his great liberality as patron to Virgil and Horace. The contemporary rich care not for "such expensive ways to fame"; on the contrary they refuse to serve as patrons and yet take every opportunity even to persecute Horace. And in particular, the author of the *Allusion,* whose lack of understanding and ignorance become a reproach to Horace, who could have taught him better than to call Shadwell "hasty" or Wycherley "slow."

Dryden closes the preface with a tribute to the "divine Shakespeare," whose style he has attempted to imitate, and for this reason has written in blank verse. Nor has he servilely copied his predecessor, for language changes. Despite this fact, however, "it is almost a miracle that much of his language remains so pure" and that he has performed so much that he "has left no praise for any who come after him." Indeed the force of Shakespeare's genius has enabled him by his imitation to excel himself.

In the interval of three months between the first acting of *All for Love* and its publication, Dryden brought to completion the "king's comedy," *The Kind Keeper,* and allied himself with Nat Lee, his fellow playwright at the Theatre Royal, to begin a play on

Oedipus. As we have seen, the final break with his colleagues at the Theatre Royal came at this time. The complaint about him in a petition to the Lord Chamberlain signed by Charles Killigrew, Hart, Burt, Goodman, and Mohun did not alter his determination to cast his fortune with the Duke's Theatre. Though undated, it may safely be assigned on internal evidence to the weeks following the performance of *All for Love* and before the acting of *The Kind Keeper* at the Duke's Theatre on March 11, 1677/78.[14] The assertion that Dryden had received as much as three or four hundred pounds a year for his share and a quarter of stock we may doubt; but we cannot doubt the truth of their statement that he had scarcely delivered one play a year, despite his agreement to provide three. If they omitted the unacted *State of Innocence* in their calculations, he had in ten years delivered nine plays to the company. In equity they had a legitimate complaint against him; and it is easy to understand their grievance against their chief playwright on his desertion at this juncture in their sad state. It is equally understandable why the poet, with his official salary in arrears and with a steadily diminishing return from a disorganized and bankrupt company, should look to the prosperous rival company for the future.

Dryden's first appearance at the Duke's playhouse, however, was not auspicious. *The Kind Keeper* (or *Mr. Limberham* as it is usually called) apparently had the making of a hit, but after the third day it was banned by royal order. Little is known of the causes of this ban, and that little comes from Dryden himself in the dedication to the play more than a year and a half later, where he guardedly alludes to them. In the revision for the press he says he has taken "becoming care that those things which offended on the stage might be either altered or omitted in the press; for their authority is and shall be ever sacred to me, (as much absent as present, and in all alterations of their fortune,) who for those reasons have stopped its farther appearance on the theatre; and whatsoever hindrance it has been to me in point of profit, many of my friends can bear me witness that I have not once murmured against that decree." Since the "crying sin of keeping" was one of the most popular sins among certain classes in London, we may believe the playwright's assertion that "no one character has been drawn from any single man"; there were more than enough to pose for a composite portrait. Those Royal Keepers, Charles and James, were normally not sensitive about their mistresses; but in early 1678, when James was discarding Arabella Churchill for Catherine Sedley, the satire against "keeping," whether directed toward royalty or not, may have struck too close to the throne, especially in view of the fact that James's popularity was at a very low ebb. Nothing short of a royal command and royal displeasure could have swept it off the boards. The King apparently had not kept "the jeast in countenance by laughing at it."[15]

The forced removal of *The Kind Keeper* helped to intensify Dryden's accumulating strains. Disagreements, disappointments, and frustrations seem to have jaundiced his view of life, and the reflection of his mood is found in the prologues and epilogues to his own plays and in those he wrote for Lee's *Mithridates* and Shadwell's *A True Widow.* In these, bitter and ironic verses abound, directed against the fops, the fools, the knaves, the keepers and their punks, the carping critics of the pit. He is particularly bitter about the low state to which drama has fallen, and almost, it appears, angry with himself for truckling to tastes which he deplores. Baffling in the extreme are his relations with Shadwell. Having written, presumably as a gesture of friendly feeling, a prologue to Shadwell's *A True Widow,* Dryden before many months passed turned upon his new colleague among the playwrights in the Duke's Theatre and annihilated him in what may be regarded as the best lampoon of the period—*Macflecknoe.* Though the date of this excoriating piece of invective has been determined, all attempts to explain the reasons for it have failed.[16] Until this time, the relations between the two men, so far as we can now see, had not been unfriendly and certainly not strained enough to justify the severity of Dryden's satire. Some personal disagreement, perhaps even an ingrained antipathy born of political antagonisms, may have offered the initial provocation to Dryden. Never before, to our knowledge, had he used that "dangerous part of wit" which he had called lampoon. Whatever the cause, the result of *Macflecknoe* was significant and far-reaching. Beyond the personal bitterness created (hereafter they were rogue and fool to each other), it helped to exacerbate the party conflicts of 1681-83, and stigmatized Shadwell forever as the high priest of dullness.

As the summer passed, Dryden and Lee were probably working on their joint effort, *Oedipus,* supposed on indirect evidence to have been performed in January, 1678/79. In the intervening months Dryden with the mood of revision upon him looked again to Shakespeare and found in *Troilus and Cressida* a baffling play that intrigued him; and he saw in it an opportunity to try again the "bow of

Ulysses," to pit himself for the last time against an excellence that he could approach but never quite meet.   But before this attempt was very far along, events about him began to assume a fearful aspect; and before the year was out, the worst fears of which he had written in the address to Danby took shape.   In August, Titus Oates and Ezeral Tonge stepped upon the stage of history to enact a plot compounded of tragedy and comedy, and of such ramifications in dramatic invention as to surpass any fictional piece that all the playwrights of the time together could hardly have devised.

The Angry World
1678-1681

THE SUCCESS of Titus Oates in foisting upon the nation the Popish Plot should be viewed against the seventeenth-century background, as Dryden saw it. It was an age of plots, oaths, vows, and tests: they were woven into the fabric of everyday life, and hardly a person in England escaped being touched by them. Hearsay and rumor as often as not passed as truth; and barefaced lies and personal enmity sent many innocent old women to the fire and many a hungry, small-time felon to the scaffold. Nor were the underprivileged alone the victims of perjurers and informers: courtiers and politicians and even a king went to their deaths in an age when religious conviction and observance often bore no relationship to personal integrity or probity. Laws were made and enforced to protect and maintain property; human beings were expendable. Nothing indeed was more calculated to produce immediate reaction than tales of the Scarlet Woman or the Whore of Rome; and there was never wanting the manipulator of mass psychology to create the climate necessary to uncritical acceptance of the most fantastic and farfetched allegation —a heritage which the twentieth century, with vastly increased mechanical means, has refined to a satanic subtlety.

In this heated climate of temperament and predilection, Oates and Tonge drew up and presented to Danby an indictment of forty-three articles, detailing an amazing plot. Almost beyond belief, it was at first not taken seriously enough for action; but on September 28, Oates and Tonge made their legal depositions before Justice Sir Edmondbury Godfrey. On the same day, the two conspirators were examined by King and Council. Shrewd, self-confident, unprincipled, Oates warmed to his task of revelation, and unfolded, with circumstantial detail, the fantastic story. According to him, Pope Innocent XI had given to the Jesuits control of Roman Catholic interest in England to overthrow the government, to kill Charles, and to establish a Catholic state with James Duke of York at its head, under the supervision of the Jesuits. Louis XIV, the Pope, and many of their co-religionists in England were in league with the Jesuits to bring about the desired end. As Oates's chimera of details grew, obvious questions about his sources were asked. To these Oates had ready answers: pretending to a conversion, he had wormed his way into the Society of Jesus in 1677, and had been sent to Spain (where he alleged he received a doctorate at Salamanca University); there he ferreted out the secrets of the plot. Although the King was highly skeptical, his council, swept along by Oates's plausibility, reacted according to expectations. With a receptive audience the plot burgeoned and within a few days became public property.

Like an uncontrolled fire, the revelations of Oates gathered speed and swept the city, accumulating ever new and more elaborate details of treachery and treason. On October 12, Sir Edmondbury Godfrey, before whom the plotters had made their oaths a fortnight before, disappeared. Five days later his body was found on Primrose Hill, pierced by his own sword. Vaulting terror ensued. Rumors and hearsay multiplied, and to many it was crystal clear that the Justice had been murdered by the Catholics, since he was privy to their designs, as contained in the allegations of Oates and Tonge. The inquest brought in a verdict of willful murder, and the reward of £500 for the discovery of the murderer opened up a new and lucrative business for conscienceless informers. Parliament, having been prorogued on September 21, reassembled four days after the discovery of Godfrey's body and proceeded at once to appoint committees to examine witnesses, of which there were not wanting a great number to add hireling voices to a confusion compounded by the week. The discovery of the indiscreet letters of Father Coleman, secretary to the Duke of York, to Louis XIV's confessor suggesting a grand plan to establish Catholicism in England, though written several years before, provided all the confirmatory "evidence" desired. Led by their parliamentary representatives, who gave every indication of complete belief in the plot, the populace accepted the testimony of paid informers as the truth; and it was extremely difficult for even the most skeptical of men to escape the almost universal frenzy.

The Opposition—or the Whigs as they were now becoming

known—took Oates as their own: they insisted that he be installed in Whitehall, and they voted him a pension of £ 1,200. As the Earl of Shaftesbury and others indefatigably gathered more and more evidence, the parliamentary majority, throughout the autumn, were busy with their legislative answer to what they considered a massive threat. A new Test Act was passed, and a bill to disable Catholics from sitting in either House. Sent to the Tower for treason were Catholic lords, committed on the testimony of informers; and sent to their deaths were Father Coleman and other priests in the Duke of York's establishment. As the weeks wore on, Danby came under fire, and the Commons, before the end of the year, found sufficient matter to impeach him. Though the Lords refused to commit Danby, Charles sent him to the Tower to protect him; there he was to remain for five years. In the meantime Charles prorogued and then dissolved the Parliament that had sat for eighteen years; a new one was to be elected in February, 1678/79, and to assemble on March 6.

In the Parliament, Dryden had friends and relatives. Sir Robert Howard in the Commons was counted with the Opposition and served on numerous committees. Sir Robert's elder brother Charles, second Earl of Berkshire, sat among the Lords and was one of the Catholics disabled by the bill against the Catholic Lords. Mulgrave and Vaughan in the Lords supported the royal side. Through these sources Dryden no doubt was apprised of events from the point of view of men in the midst of parliamentary debates and maneuvers. Though there is little reason to doubt that he followed the unfolding course of affairs with close attention, he had as yet no occasion to publish anything upon Oates or upon the plot. Having already published an attack upon Shaftesbury, the leader of the Opposition, and a tribute to Danby, now the target of that Opposition, caution now may have been the better part of wisdom. Not for another year was he to make any substantial statement in derogation of the plot or its promulgators.

During these weeks Dryden and Lee completed *Oedipus,* which was acted at the Duke's Theatre probably in the late autumn or early winter.[1] According to his own statement in the *Vindication of the Duke of Guise* (1683), Dryden wrote the first and third acts and "drew the scenery of the whole play." As put together by these two accomplished playwrights, *Oedipus* became almost a travesty of Sophoclean tragedy. Their "necessary" changes include a free re-working of character and concept, and the inclusion of scenes designed to tease the jaded appetites of the audience of 1678. In Act II, thunder resounds, and "prodigies" ("the perfect figures of a man and a woman") appear against the sky. Later a cloud that veiled the figures "draws" and shows them crowned, with the names "Oedipus" and "Jocasta" written above them in characters of gold. In the next act occurs the often-used incantation scene, which Dryden and Lee had both employed with theatrical effect in their earlier plays. Here Tiresias calls up the ghost of Laius, who "rises in his chariot as he was slain." The end of the play is filled with violence and death, most of which takes place in view of the audience. The characters in the subplot—Eurydice, Creon, Adrastus—are all slain within a half-dozen lines; Jocasta appears "stabbed in many places of her bosom, her hair dishevelled, her children slain upon the bed." The blind Oedipus plunges to his death from a window, to the accompaniment of thunder. Though we may deplore such melodramatic effects, the audience of the time found them satisfying: the play had a spectacular run of ten days.[2]

Copy must have been turned over to the publisher soon after the initial run of *Oedipus,* for it was in print and advertised in the *London Gazette* for March 10-13. It did not appear, however, under the imprint of Herringman, who had published for Dryden since 1659, but under that of R. Bentley and M. Magnes, noted as publishers of prose romances. The business association with Herringman thus came to an end, for reasons unknown. Dryden also gave Bentley and Magnes *The Kind Keeper,* which was to appear in the autumn. Almost coincidentally with the appearance of that play, Dryden broke this new relationship and entrusted *Troilus and Cressida* to Jacob Tonson. From this time forward Tonson remained his publisher. The sudden withdrawal from whatever arrangement he had made with Bentley and Magnes is a subject only for speculation. There is only one comment from Dryden that might point to a good reason for discontinuing his connection with them. In the dedication to *The Kind Keeper* he says that "it was printed in my absence from the town this summer [1679] much against my expectation, otherwise I would have overlooked the press." Had he been present, he might have excised more of the objectionable language of the play than he had taken out before releasing his copy. However that may be, Bentley and Magnes never published for him again.

In the months between the acting and publishing of *Oedipus* Dryden pressed forward with *Troilus and Cressida,* which was probably produced in the late winter or early spring.[3] His approach to this Shakespearean play was quite different from that to *Antony and Cleopatra*. He was now not intent upon imitating his predecessor's style and creating a new play from the same sources. On the contrary, he now undertook "to correct" a play in which he discerned much potential value obscured by faulty construction and by a style "so pestered with figurative expressions, that it is as affected as it is obscure." Dryden's bafflement in attempting to understand Shakespeare's play has been shared by generation after generation since his time: the twentieth century (no less than the seventeenth) has found it a "problem." He began by "new modelling" the plot, trying to give it a coherence of action that he found lacking: "I made, with no small trouble, an order and connexion of all the scenes, removing them from the places where they were inartificially set." In many places he made sweeping revisions, sometimes transferring the Shakespearean material from several acts and scenes and condensing it to impose a unity which he found lacking in the original. Act V of Dryden's play, except for one scene, is an entirely original creation demanded by his continual rearrangements and alterations of character. From first to last, he makes use of Shakespeare's basic materials, yet reducing, condensing, reorganizing in order to leave room for his own contribution of new scenes and speeches. In shearing away the long speeches of Shakespeare's characters, Dryden often imitates the figurative language of the original, but in a plainer style that erases the obscurity, and creates his own figurative language that is immediately perspicuous to his audience. Steeped in Latin though he was, Dryden found it necessary to eliminate from the speeches of Ulysses, Agamemnon, Hector, Troilus, and Thersites the large number of Latin words which no longer conveyed meaning to his audience; *tortive, conflux, convive, maculation, abruption, recordation, deceptious, propend, prenominate,* among a host more, are missing in Dryden's version. Though his evident care in remaking the old play resulted in a better braced drama—structurally superior to Shakespeare's—and in a less difficult poetic language, Dryden's achievement—as he well knew—fell short. Both the depth and the imaginative stretch of the original were beyond him; and to have extracted from posterity a highly favorable comparison with Shakespeare for the second time would have been an unmatched accomplishment.

During the following weeks Dryden composed the longest essay in criticism that he had undertaken since his reply to Howard in the *Defence of An Essay* in 1668. He entitled his new piece "The Grounds of Criticism in Tragedy" and perhaps intended it for

separate publication, since it was entered in the *Stationers' Register*
by title on June 18. Instead, he incorporated it in the prefatory material to the play when it was published in the autumn of 1679.

Meanwhile, the political scene had worsened. The general election in February returned relatively few members upon whom
Charles could count for support, and the newly revised Council contained most of the old members of the opposition, including Shaftesbury. The intent of the Whigs (a word that for many now replaced
"Presbyterian" as an epithet of abuse) soon became clear. In view
of the disclosures of the plot and James's position as a Catholic
prince, and the frenzy and passion of the populace against all things
savoring of Rome, they proposed that James's right to the throne be
sacrificed. All the King needed to do was to declare that he had gone
through a marriage with Lucy Walters, the mother of the Duke of
Monmouth, and thus he would by a stroke of a pen legitimatize that
young man who was being promoted by the Whigs as a Protestant
substitute for James. It was an ingenious plan, but Charles, meeting
with his council on March 3, 1678/79, produced a signed declaration
asserting that he had never married anyone but his consort. He thus
effected a compromise to satisfy the Duke of York, on condition that
the Duke leave the country until passions against him should subside.
But the new Parliament, which convened three days later, was in no
mood for such compromises. The Commons began to debate the
whole problem of Exclusion and by May 15 the first of the Exclusion
bills was introduced to disenable the Duke of York from inheriting
the Crown. It passed by a vote of 207 to 128, and Charles, to gain
time for the supreme test that would come, prorogued Parliament on
May 27 and thereby prevented further action for the time being.
But to combat successfully the power of the Commons, he perforce
acquiesced in the execution of men he knew to be innocent of complicity in the Popish Plot. In the meantime, the King announced that
he had granted Danby a full pardon, in spite of impeachment proceedings against him; and before a month had passed, Danby was in
the Tower for safety against the fury of the Commons. Dryden had
called him the isthmus between the powers of monarchy and anarchy;
now the buffer between the two was removed, and Charles, armed
chiefly with the remnants of his kingly prerogatives, particularly his
power to prorogue and dismiss Parliaments, faced a hostile Parliament.

In the course of the rapidly changing political conflict, it is not
possible to chart Dryden's personal involvement. That he followed

—as indeed did most men—the unfolding developments is certain,
and during the summer and autumn more and more allusions to
events of the moment may be found in his published work.   Indeed,
one could not have been unaware of the constant seething of opinion,
for as Luttrell recorded in July "many libells and seditious books
fly about."[4]   The epilogue to *Troilus* ends with a topical comment.
Thersites, speaking the epilogue, says:

> I could rail on, but 'twere a task as vain
> As preaching truth at Rome, or wit in Spain:
> Yet to huff out our play was worth my trying;
> John Lilburne scap'd his judges by defying:
> If guilty, yet I'm sure o' th' Church's blessing,
> By suffering for the plot, without confessing.

In a prologue written in September for Lee's *Caesar Borgia* he
complained that the poet wastes his "life and blood to please others,"
yet he can be condemned to starve; for the lack of patronage at the
theater, the result of alarms and excursions and the "hum and buzz"
of daily gossip, was becoming damaging.   All your entertainment,
he tells the audience, is fed

> By villains in our own dull island bred:
> Would you return to us, we dare engage
> To show you better rogues upon the stage.

These, however, merely glance obliquely at the political scene: the
prologue he contributed to Nahum Tate's *Loyal General,* acted toward the end of the year, is entirely devoted to it.   If there remain,
he says, a few who can take pleasure in what reasonable men should
write, to "them alone we dedicate this night":

> The rest may satisfy their curious itch
> With city gazettes, or some factious speech,
> Or whate'er libel, for the public good,
> Stirs up the Shrovetide crew to fire and blood.
>
> .   .   .   .
>
> The plays that take on our corrupted stage,
> Methinks, resemble the distracted age;
> Noise, madness, all unreasonable things,
> That strike at sense, as rebels do at kings!
> The style of forty-one our poets write,
> And you are grown to judge like forty-eight.
>
> .   .   .   .

They talk of fevers that infect the brains,
But nonsense is the new disease that reigns.

.   .   .   .

We must lie down, and, after all our cost,
Keep holiday, like watermen in frost;
Whilst you turn players on the world's great stage,
And act yourselves the farce of your own age.

Dryden was not the only man who began to note the resemblance of
the present explosive situation to the conditions that enabled the
Long Parliament, in 1641, to take over executive powers and to
dispense with the King. He could recall his own words written two
years before to Danby: "What right can be pretended by these men
to attempt innovation in church or state?" The opening attack upon
the Succession might have seemed to him to make timely and
pertinent his earlier comment that it is not "enough for them to
answer, that they only intend reformation of the government, not the
subversion of it: on such pretense all insurrections have been
founded."

During part of the summer, Dryden escaped from the madness
in London by a visit to the country, where he combined work and
relaxation. Two of his plays were yet unpublished, and both required dedications: *The Kind Keeper* and *Troilus and Cressida*. As
we shall see, the dedication to the first was not written until his
return to town in early autumn; *Troilus* he dedicated to Robert
Spencer, Earl of Sunderland. Sunderland was distantly connected
with Dryden through his sister, who was the wife of Dryden's
brother-in-law Thomas Howard. Born in 1641, the son of Dorothy
Sidney (Waller's "Sacharissa"), Sunderland was now Secretary of
State, having purchased the post for £6,000 from Sir Joseph
Williamson in February, 1678/79. Well-educated and brilliant, he
was to prove as unprincipled in politics as he was brilliant. At the
moment he was a supporter of the King; and shortly he would make
one of a triumvirate (with Hyde and Godolphin) known as the
"Chits," through whom Charles managed to govern during the
intervals when Parliament was in prorogation or in dissolution. He
was therefore a powerful figure, and Dryden may have supposed
that a word spoken to him about a matter close to his own heart
might result in some tangible encouragement. In this he proved much
mistaken, for Sunderland was too far immersed in intrigue (and in
gambling at basset) to pay much attention to the laureate's proposals.

In the dedication Dryden approached Sunderland diffidently, admitting that "I never could shake off the rustick bashfulness which hangs upon my nature; but valuing myself as little as I am worth, have been afraid to render even the common duties of respect to those who are in power. The ceremonious visits, which are generally paid on such occasions, are not my talent." He proceeded to demonstrate the talent for flattery which is so consistent an ingredient in his (and others') dedicatory epistles. Especially in this dedication we can see that his extravagance served as prelude to a proposal which needed as much powerful aid as could be found. It is no less than the establishment of an English academy, but only after "the quiet of the nation . . . be secured, and a mutual trust betwixt prince and people be renewed"; then will this "great and good man . . . have leisure for the ornaments of peace, and make our language as much indebted to his care, as the French is to the memory of their famous Richelieu." Having been a member of the committee of the Royal Society in 1664 to consider the improvement of the English language, Dryden was well aware of the difficulties involved. And in the intervening fifteen years he became, through his constant practice in writing and his reading of other tongues, more and more alive to the shifting meanings of English words and phrases and to the constant change which English was undergoing in his own time. When he considered his own language against the changeless elegance of the Roman and Greek—and even the French—he found it lacking in definition, in statements of propriety against which "measures of elegance can be taken."

We have already noted Dryden's continuous interest in such matters, contained in one kind of comment or another in nearly everything he had written since 1669. In this decade he had addressed himself to the many facets of propriety in language. But he knew that his solitary concern was not enough—"one Vaugelas [French grammarian, author of *Remarques sur la langue française*] [is not] sufficient for such a work; it was the employment of the whole [French] Academy for many years; for the perfect knowledge of a tongue was never attained by any single person." A cooperative enterprise, he sees, is needed, in which "the court, the college, and the town must be joined." For English "is a composition of the dead and living tongues" and to encompass an adequate study of it "there is required a perfect knowledge not only of the Greek and Latin, but of the old German, the French, and the Italian." He reminded Sunderland of how barbarously the English write and speak, and he admitted his own problem: "I am often put to a stand in considering whether what I write be the idiom of the tongue, or false grammar, and nonsense couched beneath that specious name of *Anglicism*; and have no other way to clear my doubts but by translating my English into Latin and thereby trying what sense the words will bear in a more stable language." To be able to write with a "certainty of words and a purity of phrase" is his fervent and urgent desire. For it is a mortification to reflect that although Italian has varied hardly at all from the times of Boccaccio and Petrarch, the "English of Chaucer, their contemporary, is not to be understood without the help of an old Dictionary." One drawback to English he will revert to later in life, for it posed a continuous challenge to him as he attempted to inject variety into the couplet form: "We are full of monosyllables, and those clogged with consonants; and our pronunciation is effeminate: all which are enemies to a sounding language." To supply the poverty of English, he goes on, "we have trafficked with our neighbor nations, by which means we abound in words, as Amsterdam does in religions; but to order them, and make them useful after their admission, is the difficulty."[5]

Dryden included in the dedication a remark on the "Grounds of Criticism in Tragedy," which he tells Sunderland is only preliminary to the main object—"the words and thoughts that are suitable to tragedy"—which he has had neither the leisure nor the encouragement yet to write. This promise he never subsequently fulfilled, because within a short time he was gathered up in the contemporary political and religious controversies, and to tragedy he was to give little thought for another decade. "The Grounds of Criticism" is largely derivative and formal and therefore lacks much of the distinctive and characteristic touch that we have come to associate with Dryden's comment on poetry. He relied heavily upon Boileau's translation of Longinus, quoting verbatim or paraphrasing at length, as well as upon Rapin, Bossu, and Rymer. Beginning with Aristotle's definition of tragedy, Dryden moved along the lines laid down by his French critics into a discussion of the moral basis of tragedy, the plot, the manners, the characters (particularly that of the tragic hero), decorum, the treatment of the passions. Since Shakespeare was much in his mind, he often cited him for illustrations of many practices in dramatic writing. It is here that his admiration and enthusiasm for Shakespeare shine through even the most serious arraignment that Dryden can bring himself to write. For example, he asserted that though Shakespeare thoroughly distinguished his characters and understood rightly the passions, yet he had his failings:

> I will not say of so great a poet, that he distinguished not the blown puffy style, from true sublimity; but I may venture to maintain, that the fury of his fancy often transported him beyond the bounds of judgment, either in coining of new words and phrases, or racking words which were in use into the violence of a catachresis . . . I would [not] explode the use of metaphors from passion . . . but to use them at every word, to say nothing without a metaphor, a simile, an image, or description is, I doubt, to smell a little too strongly of the buskin.

To demonstrate the excess of figurative expression Dryden quotes the "mobbled queen" passage from *Hamlet* (though he believes it not to be Shakespeare's): "What a pudder is here kept in raising the expression of trifling thoughts! Would not a man have thought that the poet had been bound 'prentice to a wheelwright for his first rant?" He admits that Shakespeare does not often write thus; and he proceeds to do justice to that "divine poet" by instancing the moving scene of Richard II's deposition: "refrain from pity," he says, "if you can." He further avers that if Shakespeare "were stripped of all the bombast in his passions, and dressed in the most vulgar words, we should find the beauties of his thoughts remaining, if his embroideries were burnt down, there would still be silver at the bottom of the melting pot." With all his faults Shakespeare remained the incomparable: "we who ape his sounding words have nothing of his thought, but are all outside; there is not so much as a dwarf within our giant's clothes." It is a happy despair he feels; the pleasure denied him in his imitating Shakespeare only at a distance is compensated to him by the generosity of his praise of that genius.

Troilus was published in November by Tonson, Dryden's new publisher. About the same time *The Kind Keeper* appeared,[6] with a dedication to John, Lord Vaughan, who had been one of the group of bright young men with whom Dryden had discussed literature in 1665, and who had contributed congratulatory verses to Dryden, included in the first edition of *The Conquest of Granada*. After the expected flattery of Vaughan's learning and his lament that only a few noblemen are friends to learning, Dryden explains that the play, acted while Vaughan was in Jamaica, was "intended for an honest satire against our crying sin of *keeping*." Though he alludes to its early demise, he contents himself by saying that the "crime for which it suffered was that which was objected against the Satires of

Juvenal, and the Epigrams of Catullus—that it expressed too much of the vice which it decried." He hints that a royal order stopped it and that in deference to the wishes of those whose "authority is and shall be ever sacred to me" he has not "once murmured against that decree." The unexpected printing of it by Bentley and Magnes while he was vacationing in the country prevented him from reading proof. Had he done so, he would "have been yet more careful that neither my friends should have had the least occasion of unkindness against me, nor my enemies of upbraiding me." And despite what some town critics have said, he takes special care to deny that the satire in the play was directed against any particular person.

The "great plot of the nation," as Dryden alluded to it in his address to Vaughan, had almost run its preliminary course, and though plots and rumors of more plots were to make their appearance in the succeeding months, the grand design of the Whigs under Shaftesbury's leadership was of public record. Dryden's early awareness of the probable course of the opposition testifies not to his prescience but to his knowledge of history and of men. Although his position as historiographer might have demanded a defense of the King, he had as yet not written anything known to us that could be viewed as an official apologia. The situation was so fluid and so shifting that no real focus could be found upon which a reasoned defense might be written. Monmouth, seduced by dreams of greatness, was being advanced by the Whigs as the Protestant answer to the threat of a Catholic successor. Charles, bedevilled by the problems of a bastard son and a Romish brother, bought a temporary quiet by exiling them both in the early autumn. When Parliament again assembled in October, he promptly prorogued it and continued the policy of preventing a meeting for a full year in order to save the Succession. He dismissed Shaftesbury from the Council, and appointed a group more subservient to the royal policy.

Yet Dryden remained a poet and a playwright: despite the distractions of the political scene, his work was writing. During the late months of autumn and throughout the winter he was busy with two projects—a translation of Ovid's *Epistles* and a new play, *The Spanish Friar*. The origin of the edition of Ovid in an English translation remains obscure. Although Dryden's interest in Ovid's poetry was of long standing, it can hardly be supposed that he promoted an edition which would include the contributions of at least sixteen persons and perhaps more.[7] Nor is it likely that he would have agreed to serve either as collector of the contributions or as editor. Rather, it appears to have been a bookseller's venture promoted by the shrewd and energetic Jacob Tonson, who no doubt asked Dryden to write a preface in order to give it a certain cachet. He also contributed two of the translations—that of "Canace to Macareus" and "Dido to Aeneas," and one in collaboration with the Earl of Mulgrave, "Helen to Paris." Copy for the volume must have been in the hands of the printer before the end of the year, for it was advertised for sale on the following February 6, in the *Protestant (Domestick) Intelligence.* The play, which Dryden was to label a "Protestant play," was acted first on March 8. But before he had completed either of these tasks, Dryden suffered a physical attack baffling to him and his contemporaries and still without adequate explanation.

The "Rose Alley" attack upon Dryden took place on Thursday night, December 18, when he was on his way home to Longacre, apparently from Will's coffeehouse. Set upon by three men, he was beaten severely before they escaped, unidentified. How extensive were his injuries is still not certain, but it may be assumed, in spite of rather highly colored news stories in the journals, that he was at the very least badly shaken up. On the next day, *Mercurius Domesticus* carried the story of the assault; and in the next issue of *True Domestick Intelligence* (Tuesday, December 23), it was stated that he was so severely beaten "that 'tis thought he will hardly recover it." Rumor and hearsay were at work, and Dryden during the days of his recovery doubtless heard numerous theories expounded as he tried to discover the identity of either the actual culprits or their principal. He met with no success, however, and on Friday, the day after Christmas, he (or someone close to him) offered—in the columns of the *Domestick Intelligence*—for information leading to the identity of his assailants a reward of £50, deposited with his goldsmith, Mr. Blanchard. To facilitate a confession from one of the three rogues, immunity to the informer was offered: if he should "be one of the actors he shall have the fifty pounds, without letting his name be known, or receiving the least trouble by any prosecution." The reward was set high enough to tempt the avarice or the poverty of the attackers; and though, in the absence of evidence, it is always assumed that no informer came forward, the contrary may be true.[8]

In the background of every attempt to explain the attack has been the appearance in mid-November of a long satire which was going the usual rounds in manuscript, called the *Essay upon Satire.* Speculation about its authorship seems to have been keen at the time.   On November 27, John Verney wrote to Sir Ralph Verney that "there is a satyr come out against the men of the town, wherein two of your friends, Rochester and the Chancellor, are paid off, but 'tis very long and thought to be by Dryden."[9]   On November 21, Rochester himself was writing to Henry Savile: "I have sent you herewith a Libel, in which my own share is not the least; the King having perus'd it, is no ways disatisf'd with his: the Author is apparently Mr. ———; his Patron, my——having a Panejerick in the midst. . . ."[10]   It is understandable that some contemporary gossip would connect Dryden with this satire, and even his most urgent disclaimers might have had little force at the time.   Within two years, however, Mulgrave admitted his authorship and absolved Dryden of any complicity in it.   Yet though Mulgrave cleared Dryden's name then, the Rose Alley attack had already been made.   There is no certainty that the libel provoked the attack; and Rochester's putative responsibility for it can no longer be entertained.   It may prove indeed that the basis for the assault had no connection with literary men, but with politicians, and particularly with Shaftesbury.   He had already once been verbally attacked by Dryden, and the appearance of both *The Kind Keeper* (in which "the fumbling lecher" has been identified with him), and the *Essay upon Satire* (in which his physical deformities were laughed at) within a week or two of each other could have provided him a sufficient reason for revenge.   But in the absence of any evidence, it is best to label the Rose Alley affair "unsolved."

At the turn of the year, Dryden, smarting from at least the physical effects of his beating, could well have agreed with the Marquis of Halifax, who wrote to his brother early in January: "Our world here is so over-run with the politicks, the fools' heads so heated, and the knaves so busy, that a wasp's nest is a quieter place to sleep in than this town is to live in. . . .   I dream of the country, as men do of small beer when they are in a fever."[11]

Dryden's real contribution to the volume of Ovid's *Epistles* was not his own translations, which amounted to 617 lines, but that part of the preface dealing with his theories of translation.[12]   This was his first critical essay on an art which would employ his best talents for many years and on which a part of his poetic reputation still rests. All translation, he says, may "be reduced to these three heads":

First, that of metaphrase, or turning an author word by word, and line by line, from one language to another.   Thus, or near this manner, was Horace his Art of Poetry translated by Ben Jonson.   The second way is that of paraphrase, or translation with latitude, where the author is to be kept in view by the translator, so as never to be lost. . . . Such is Mr. Waller's translation of Virgil's fourth AEneid. The third way is that of imitation, where the translator (if now he has not lost that name) assumes the liberty not only to vary from the words and sense, but to forsake them both, as he sees occasion. . . . Such is Mr. Cowley's practice in turning two odes of Pindar, and one of Horace, into English.

Citing Horace, *nec verbum verbo curabis reddere fidus Interpres* (and using the Earl of Roscommon's as yet unpublished version of Horace's *Ars Poetica*),[13] he rejects metaphrase as too pedantic, for Latin "a most severe and commodious language, often expresses that in one word, which either the barbarity or the narrowness of modern tongues cannot supply in more." The verbal copier is beset by many difficulties from which he cannot extricate himself: to consider "the thought of his author, and his words, and to find out the counterpart to each in another language; and besides this, he is to confine himself to the compass of numbers and the slavery of rhymes." Not even Jonson could avoid obscurity in his literal rendering of the *Ars Poetica*. Imitation he finds at the other extreme, and as used by Cowley and Denham, "an endeavour of a later poet to write like one who has written before him on the same subject" and to set "him as a pattern," and "to write, as he supposes that the author would have done, had he lived in our age, and in our country." Such a method he realizes has grave drawbacks, the more serious when it is practiced by lesser poets than Cowley. And he will allow him only that privilege with respect to Pindar—"so wild and ungovernable a poet cannot be translated literally; his genius is too strong to bear a chain, and Samson-like he shakes it off."

These are the extremes, both of which Dryden rejects for the middle way of paraphrase. But he sets up qualifications for the successful translator that were met by few if any of his colleagues in the project to which his remarks serve as introduction: "No man is capable of translating poetry, who besides a genius to that art, is not a master both of his author's language and of his own. Nor must we understand the language only of the poet, but his particular turn of thoughts and expression, which are the characters that distinguish, and as it were individuate, him from all other writers." In the process the translator must "conform our genius" to the author's and preserve his thought if the language will sustain it or "vary the dress"; but the thought must be preserved. The "outward ornament, of the words" may be changed, indeed must be, for what is "beautiful in one [tongue], is often barbarous, nay some-times nonsense in another." A certain freedom of expression is necessarily to be allowed the translator; the sense of the author is, however, to be held "sacred and inviolable." If "the fancy of Ovid be luxuriant, it is his character to be so; and if I retrench it, he is no longer Ovid." The principles laid down in this preface were to guide Dryden in his later translations: he never relinquished his belief that the main task of the translator remained the transference of the sense and the "character" of the original author, regardless of the change in the "outward ornament of words."

When *The Spanish Friar* took the boards at the Duke's Theatre on March 8, 1679/80, the cast included the best actors available in London at the time: Elizabeth Barry, Thomas Betterton and his wife, Underhill, and Leigh. The combination of superb acting and a text that exploited some of the great questions of the moment, such as Succession, legitimacy, a rebellious *mobile,* loyalty to the Crown, provided material for a great popular success, which according to Downes brought "vast Profit to the Company." Even after the passions of the moment were long dead, the play was revived with success far into the eighteenth century and remained one of Dryden's most popular plays. Its success justified Dryden's remark in the dedication that he thought the play surpassed any of his other tragi-comedies. The comic plot, built around a situation which involves the attempt of Lorenzo to cohabit with the pretty young Elvira (who turns out to be his sister), wife to the elderly miser Gomez, through the pimping services of Friar Dominic, gives the play both its title and its claim to be a Protestant play. Protestant it is only in the sense that anti-Catholic bias is writ large in the character of Dominic, whose lust, perversion of priestly office, and greed are held up for ridicule and for a symbol of the flagrancies of the Roman Catholic religion. Dryden seems to cater to the passions of the moment and to ally himself with the very people whom he reprobates upon every occasion during the next few years. Such a seeming contradiction may be resolved if we think of Dryden here as a showman never reluctant to please an audience, not as an ecclesiastic or a polemicist in the theater. The Friar is a comic character placed in a con-ventional comic plot of the age. By the same token, Dryden's ob-servations on some of the lively questions and controversies of the time may be seen as features built into the texture of his serious dramatic plot, and not primarily short treatises on political theory. In a time seething with plots, Dryden, as we might expect, does not let slip the chance to exploit the current interest for a comic scene. Gomez, charged with plotting against the state (so that he may be removed as a barrier to Lorenzo's courting of his wife), answers his accusers: "I never durst be in a plot: why, how can you in conscience suspect a rich citizen of so much wit as to make a plotter?   There are none but poor rogues, and those that can't live without it, that are in plots."   This cuts both ways, and the sardonic quality of it would not have been lost on the audience at the Duke's Theatre in 1680. When the King and the Tories saw *The Spanish Friar* in the week of March 8, they perhaps found many sentiments of the stage king and queen and courtiers which they could approve, and the Whigs, many that might appear to be critical of their current practice.[14] Who, in 1680, could have resisted applying the following ideas to the contemporary scene:

> Mercy is good, a very good dull virtue;
> But kings mistake its timing and are mild,
> Where manly courage bids them be severe:
> Better be cruel once, than anxious ever.

and:

> The rabble gather round the man of news,
> And listen with their mouths;
> Some tell, some hear, some judge of news, some make it;
> And he, who lies most loud, is most believed.

and of the city mob:

> You do not know the virtues of your city,
> What pushing force they have; some popular chief,
> More noisy than the rest, but cries Halloo,
> And, in a trice, the bellowing herd come out;
> The gates are barred, the ways are barricadoed,
> And *one and all's* the word; true cocks of the game,
> That never ask for what or whom they fight;
> But turn them out, and show them but a foe,
> Cry—Liberty! and that's a cause of quarrel.

And the dialogue between Bertran and Leonora:

> BERTRAN: If princes not protect their ministers,
>   What man will dare to serve them?
>
> LEONORA: None will dare

> To serve them ill when they are left to laws;
> But when a counsellor, to save himself,
> Would lay miscarriages upon his prince,
> Exposing him to public rage and hate;
> Oh, 'tis an act as infamously base,
> As, should a common soldier skulk behind,
> And thrust his general in the front of war:
> It shows, he only served himself before,
> And had no sense of honor, country, king,
> But centered on himself, and used his master
> As guardians do their words, with shows of care,
> But with intent to sell the public safety,
> And pocket up his prince.

and finally:

> RAYMOND: What treason is it to redeem my King,
>   And to reform the state?
>
> TORRISMOND: That's a stale cheat,
>   The primitive rebel, Lucifer, first us'd it,
>   And was the first reformer of the skies.

There exists no complete record of the performances of *The Spanish Friar* during the months following its initial production in March. Yet because of its relation to the movements of the time, it might be imagined that Betterton and his group would have revived it often, not for its political or religious biases, but for its potential earning power at the box office. As late as November 1, Ann Montague could write to Lady Hatton, "I was to see the new play, The Spanish Frier, and there was all the world, but the Court is a letell dull yet."[15] With this play Dryden became, in a sense, committed to an immediate and almost total concern with the political scene. Hardly any new work was undertaken which did not bear more or less directly on contemporary problems: with the exception of the Life of Plutarch (1683), his contribution to *Sylvae* (1685), and *A Song for St. Cecilia's Day* (1687), his energies, until after the Revolution of 1688, were devoted to a principle in which he thoroughly believed, and which, *mutatis mutandis,* prevailed because of the English talent for compromise. Beginning with 1680 it is almost as if Dryden laid aside his role of poet and assumed that of historiographer royal.

Political Commitment

1681

THE SIGNS of Dryden's mounting interest in the Popish Plot and its aftermath are evident in nearly everything he published during the late months of 1679 and the whole of 1680. In his translation of Ovid's *Dido to Aeneas,* for example, he intrudes a couplet for which no justification can be found in the original, but which makes pointed comment upon the first attempt at Exclusion:

> What people is so void of common sense,
> To vote succession from a native prince?[1]

His extended comment in *The Spanish Friar* was reinforced by the epilogue, which he accepted from a friend, Robert Wolseley, and which was devoted entirely to the clergy and their unholy role. When the players repaired to Oxford for their summer season at the university, Dryden contributed a special prologue for his friend Nat Lee's *Sophonisba.* In this, for the learned audience, he specifically points out that there exists another villain besides that of Rome:

> But 'tis the talent of our English nation,
> Still to be plotting some new reformation;
> And few years hence, if Anarchy goes on,
> Jack Presbyter shall here erect his throne,
> Knock out a tub with preaching once a day,
> And every prayer be longer than a play.
> Then all your heathen wits shall go to pot,
> For disbelieving of a Popish plot.

The dire effects of such an event would reduce the players to the status of vagabonds, as of old:

> Nor should we scape the sentence, to depart,
> Ev'n in our first original, a cart.

But for the university, the result would be even more serious:

> Religion, learning, wit, would be suppress'd,
> Rags of the whore, and trappings of the beast.
> Scot, Suarez, Tom of Aquin, must go down,
> As chief supporters of the triple crown;
> And Aristotle's for destruction ripe;
> Some say, he call'd the soul an organ pipe,
> Which by some little help of derivation,
> Shall then be prov'd a pipe of inspiration.

Dryden's casual shots at the Popish Plot in prologue and epilogue were reinforced, as we have seen, by numerous references in *The Spanish Friar*. /As the summer of 1680 began, Dryden had as yet written nothing—as far as is known—in support of the Crown or as historiographer./ Yet the plot by this time was nearly two years old, and the intervening months had been filled with oaths, counterplots, perjuries, arrests, trials, informations, recantations, and executions. It is inconceivable that he who had made such an unequivocal attack upon Shaftesbury and the Whigs before the plot and its aftermath should not have written for the King during the months of greatest strain. Shaftesbury and the Whig Party had mobilized a number of the literary fraternity, including Settle and Shadwell, and were supervising with great acumen both the kinds of tracts produced and the timing of their release. The royal managers, on the contrary, relied for the most part on L'Estrange and upon loyal volunteers. Yet considering Dryden's position as historiographer, his publicly-announced position as an antagonist of subverters of government, and his known antipathy to dissent and its political connections, there seems little reason to doubt that he was drawing his pen for the royal cause under the cloak of anonymity, as was the contemporary fashion in party controversy. Because of this practice he has set his editors and biographers a task of the greatest difficulty to identify his contributions to the mass of pamphlet literature. When Dryden published *Absalom and Achitophel* and *The Medal* without his name prefixed, the public found no difficulty in accurately and immediately identifying the author; but the case was entirely different when he published a prose pamphlet: only in a few instances was his hand detected and commented upon.[2]

As Dryden began to assume a more active role in political and religious controversy, his personal situation could not have been a very easy one. Certainly his financial affairs must in 1680 have been worsening, for the condition of the King's Treasury was even more desperate than usual. Laurence Hyde, the new Chancellor, had worked a minor miracle to keep any kind of order in the King's money affairs. Writing to Henry Sidney some months later, Hyde remarked, "I can assure you that the Privy Purse, and one body nearer than that too, have been sufferers this last year. . . . This is not a condition for those who have any share in the administration of the King's revenue to brag of. . . ."[3] /Dryden was one of the sufferers, for his salary had fallen into serious arrears, which became more grave with every passing quarter./ In January he received a quarterly payment of £75, which had been authorized in the preceding month for a quarter's salary due nearly two years before. In June a similar warrant was issued, and by the end of the year another of £50 is recorded, to pay him for the Christmas quarter of 1678. The loss of payments from his former connection with the Theatre Royal he must have felt keenly. But if the King could not maintain his poet laureate's salary, he seems to have been willing enough to help him in other ways. Dryden's oldest son was now in his fourteenth year and no doubt upon the petition of Dryden, Charles gave him a King's Scholarship to Westminster, which the boy now entered for a three-year period under his father's old master, Richard Busby.[4]

An assessment of Dryden's position in the summer of 1680 must take into account a number of divergent, complicated, and often apparently irreconcilable facts. Descended from two county families of fixed "puritan" (but not "dissenting") convictions, Dryden in his adult life thus far adhered to the Church of England. By marriage with Elizabeth Howard he allied himself to a large, important family that for the most part had maintained both its Roman Catholicism and its devotion to Charles I and to his son. The religious convictions of Elizabeth and her immediate family are not entirely clear. Sir Robert Howard maintained his connection with the Church of England, though his eldest brother, Charles, the second Earl of Berkshire, was a devoted Catholic and several years before had been privy to some of the designs of Father Coleman. That Jesuit plotter had been brought to trial and executed in December, 1678, and the second Earl of Berkshire had died in Paris in March, 1679. Not until the end of 1680 would Berkshire's early letters to Coleman be known through publication. They were to show only that Berkshire was a good Roman Catholic, and a loyal subject, who dissociated himself from the more rabid of his faith and from their ill-timed design to establish their religion by force or stratagem in England as the predominant religion.[5] Evidence about Dryden's wife's religion is lacking; but because of his later change to Rome, it has often been assumed that Elizabeth was already a communicant and exercised her influence upon him. No proof of her affiliation has ever been brought forward; indeed, so little is known of her that it would be unsafe to express any opinion about her during these years.

With respect to Dryden's political leanings somewhat more can be said. His hatred of commonwealth principles and of the mob was of long duration and deep-seated. At the Restoration he was vigorous in his criticism of the political activities of the various sects, who he thought had used their religion as a cloak for political action and who had justified their excesses in this sphere by their self-conscious assurance that they were of the elect. The "Saints" he had always excoriated. From dissenters in the matter of faith, they had become rebels in matters of state and subverters of an established royal government. Their demand for freedom of conscience in religion had developed into a freedom of action in politics, and once power was in their hands, they had not scrupled to kill a king. The principle which Dryden saw at work here among the dissenters was precisely the same as he, and many others, saw in the political actions of the Jesuits—the release of the subject from responsibility for adhering to an oath of allegiance to a king whose religion differed from theirs and freedom to follow the individual spirit in other exigencies. That Dryden was a royalist admits of no doubt, but his devotion to Charles II as king did not necessarily include devotion to him as a person. Arbitrary power in the king he would not accept as necessary within the framework of the English system. He was no Hobbesian. He believed in the proper exercise of the divided powers as they had developed over the past century: the king, the parliament of hereditary and elected representatives, and the people. In this chain, the king by hereditary right, represented the executive power with certain prerogatives; and acting both as complement to Parliament and a check to it, he served as the sole representative of all the people of his realm. He ruled by law, not by fear. The legislative function was performed by the Parliament, a body that should provide an informal balance to the monarch who could indeed veto their acts, but who nevertheless must depend upon them for many things; for they held—as Charles discovered—a most powerful weapon in their legal right to manage the revenue and the voting of money supplies. The "people," in Dryden's view, were those qualified by ownership of property to enable them by law to exercise their franchise. He was no libertarian, no democrat, no believer in the virtues of the common man. To Dryden, as to most gentlemen of the century, the comman man was too common to qualify for a voice in government. Thus far in theory; but Dryden was not simpleton enough to expect an ideal system of government to work ideally, since it must be managed by men who were all too human. He realized the power exercised by special interests; he knew how the franchise operated and how members of the Commons were elected; he knew the limitations and the prejudices of men sitting in the Lords by hereditary right. He also knew that unchecked power tended to corrupt and that it could change a king into a tyrant, and a parliament into a many-headed beast, when either usurped the rights and functions of the other. The "late troubled times" had come about, he firmly believed, because of the usurpation by Parliament of the privileges and the function of the king. The vacuum caused by the loss of this function had necessarily to be filled by a substitute king; it was filled, only temporarily by a multiple-headed legislative body which proved incapable of rule; ultimately it fell to Cromwell, supported by the power of the New Model Army. Tyrannical government resulted because certain of the checks on arbitrary power were absent: the hereditary House of Lords and a popularly elected Commons. The death of the dictator and the decline of military power produced another crisis, this one settled by the return of a hereditary king. Under such conditions as he saw in operation during his younger days, he was convinced no stable government could endure.

Now in 1680 he found some of the same forces in operation out of which had come the anarchy forty years earlier. Nor was Dryden alone in the belief that '81 was '41 all over again. The idea fast became a commonplace of these months. Yet a new ingredient, not of importance in 1641, was present: the Roman Catholic prince and the machinations of his co-religionists. These complicated immeasurably the total situation and gave an almost complete cover to those who for reasons of their own were intent upon destroying monarchy in its present form; and it gave them an instrument which they played with consummate skill. By the use and manipulation of paid informers and suborned testimony to convict and execute many persons innocent of treason, and by the carefully managed and contrived Pope burnings of 1679, 1680, and 1681 to inflame the

London mob against papists in general and the Duke in particular, as well as by the parliamentary maneuvers of Test Act, attainder, and impeachment, the Whig Party under Shaftesbury's competent hand moved from triumph to triumph. Final victory was denied them only because they were pitted against a political intelligence, deeper, shrewder, and no less unprincipled than theirs, but hitherto hidden under the character of a lazy, lustful, merry monarch— Charles II.

The center of attack by the Whigs was the principle of succession to the Crown. "The exclusion of James was to be the touchstone of English politics for two years, and the lines on which parties were to be divided by it showed themselves at once."[6]   Charles at the outset made it plain that he would never sacrifice his brother's right to succeed him, in the absence of a legitimate heir, and he held steadfast to his resolve. To the Whig demand that he declare Monmouth his legitimate son, he publicly announced that Catherine his Queen had been his only wife. After the reading of the Exclusion bill for the first time in May, 1679, Charles prorogued and then dissolved the Parliament; for months government managed to operate through the Council and the King. Exclusion became the topic of interest and of furious debate throughout the country; for the elections for the now dissolved Parliament had been built upon it as the chief issue. In the never-ending pamphlet war, writers concentrated upon Exclusion. In the spate of tracts on this topic, one, appearing in July, was addressed to the King and was entitled *Great and Weighty Considerations Relating to the D, or Successor of the Crown.* Written as "By a True Patriot" and in a style suggestive of Dryden's, the tract of eight pages takes to task the Parliament for its unlawful assumption of power in proposing the Exclusion bill, and attempts to demonstrate that, from Biblical times to the present, rulers and people of different religious beliefs have been able to coexist. The author argues with some cogency these two points: that the oath of allegiance binds the subject to maintain the right of the presumptive heir; and that a Popish successor, such as the Duke of York, can hardly hope to subvert a strong Protestant country, for he "can neither make any new Statutes in favour of Popery, nor yet alter the present Government, without the consent of Parliament." Indeed, he finds it "timorous and foolish" of anyone to believe that an English king, "though the most zealous of Papists," is capable of effecting such a change, for the King "can hardly move or stir but with a concentrick motion, to both Houses of Parliament."[7]   A number of the arguments and even the illustrations cited are the same as those used by Dryden a year later in *His Majesties Declaration Defended* and in *The Vindication of the Duke of Guise* (1683). *The Great and Weighty Considerations* was answered by a Whig tract entitled *A Word Without Doors concerning the Bill for Succession*. The anonymous author writes, on page three: "And here I might conclude: But because a late *Pentionary* Pen has publickly Arraign'd the Wisdom, Loyalty, and Justice of the Honourable House of Commons, on the account of this Bill, I will *ex Abundanti* add a word or two more to that particular. Whereupon he pluckt a Paper out of his Pocket, Entitled *Great and Weighty Considerations relating to the Duke and Successor of the Crown*." Was Dryden that "*Pentionary* Pen"? That he may have been is suggested by a comment contained in a letter written by Christopher Philipson to one "D. F." (Daniel Fleming?) on November 27: "I shall buy that History of Dryden's, and if you would have it sent down I shall send it by the carrier."[8] This "History," which in the idiom of the times would be an "account," has never been identified. If it does not refer to the tract on the Succession, it must then point to another anonymous contribution by Dryden to the controversy of the time.

Following what seems to have become an annual custom, Dryden left London for a summer holiday in the country. Though it is impossible to follow his movements, we may assume that he spent some time in Northamptonshire to visit relatives and to look to his small estate and its management by his tenant. It is certain that in August he was visiting in Staffordshire at the home of Sir Charles Wolseley, whose son Robert had only recently contributed the epilogue to *The Spanish Friar*.[9] It may be that while in that county he also took the occasion to pay his respects to his cousin Frances, who had married Ralph Sneyd and was living at Keel Hall. Perhaps also he spent some time at Trentham, the seat of the Leveson-Gowers, a visit that he recalls ten years later in the dedication of *Amphitryon* to Sir William Leveson-Gower. It is possible that, according to his custom, the retirement to the country was to read and to write, away from the distractions of his immediate household and the confusions in the city. This sojourn in 1680 may have been longer than was customary; for on December 14, he executed a power of attorney to George Ward to receive his salary at the Exchequer.[10] Since a grant of £50 (for the Christmas quarter of 1678) on his salary was made on December 16, it seems probable that Sir Robert Howard had informed him that such grant would be made and that—in the poet's absence—he should empower someone to receive it for him. Hence, the power of attorney to Ward, who was then a solicitor in the Treasury (and no doubt a friend of Howard's), and who was to become Attorney-General in 1693.

If we can with some reason postulate an extended stay in the country, we can also determine by Dryden's later publications some of the subjects to which he devoted his time. We can be sure that he was preparing no play for performance in Michaelmas or Christmas term, but we can be almost certain that he was reading widely and thinking deeply about the crucial questions confronting the country and him. Among them must be reckoned the move for Exclusion, the role of Roman Catholic and Jesuit (and at the moment he separated the two), the tendencies of the dissenters in political affairs, the activity of Shaftesbury and his party, the historical background against which political and religious controversies were unfolding, the situation involving kingship, the meaning of oaths and loyalty, the position of the subject. To find a way through such mazes required unusual endowments of knowledge, historical perspective, sharpness of intellect, psychological penetration, and tempered judgment. Not many men of the time possessed such endowments, but Dryden was assuredly among them.

In the absence of a statement by Dryden himself, it becomes an impossible task to call the roll of the works he was reading for what we now know to be some of his greatest work; for there can be little doubt that these months marked the actual beginning of *Absalom and Achitophel* and the background reading and thinking for much of his published work for the next three or four years: *The Medal, Religio Laici, The Duke of Guise* and its *Vindication, The History of the League* (and its important Postscript), and the occasional prologues and epilogues of these years. His interest in French history of the late sixteenth century, dating at least from *Astraea Redux* (1660), he revived through Davila's *History of the Civil Wars in France,* the second edition of which had been issued in 1678. The parallels between the Holy League in France and the Covenanters in England were matters of common knowledge, and Dryden repeatedly cited the parallels to demonstrate the similarity between the Whig principles of 1681 and those of the Catholics in France nearly a century before. Dryden also studied—or refreshed his knowledge of—the principles of the reformers and their followers: Calvin, Luther, Theodore Beza, Mezeray, George Buchanan, and among contemporaries, Marvell, Milton, a host of anonymous dissenters, Lord Herbert, George

Cranmer. And he read much Church history and controversial literature of his time. His subsequent references suggest an acquaintance
with a long line of prominent writers from Athanasius and Arius to
such more recent men as Mariana, Bellarmine, Emmanuel Sa, Molina,
Santarel, Simancha Sleidan, and Maimbourg, on the continent, to
the English Hooker, Doleman, Campion, Hugh Cressy, and Parsons,
and even Martin Marprelate.[11]

As summer moved into autumn, Dryden would follow, during
Charles's fourth Parliament, which met on October 21, the most
serious and determined attempt yet made on the Succession. On
November 2, the Exclusion bill was voted, and on the fourth it was
introduced. The "turbulence [was] almost unexampled," writes Sir
John Pollock, "even in the hot times that had passed." The King
had for some time been willing to entertain a compromise that would
leave the Duke in possession of the title of king but which would
shear away the power; and Halifax had proposed that James, as an
expedient, might be exiled for five years. The Commons rejected
all proposals, saying in effect that once a popish king had the title,
he would not be behind-hand in seizing the power. Said one, "you
shall have the Protestant religion. . . , but you must have a popish
king who shall command your armies and your navies, make your
bishops and judges." Amid violence and threats the arguments proceeded; and on November 11 the bill was passed; four days later
it went to the House of Lords. At the debate here, sat the King,
who heard and watched as his son Monmouth, Shaftesbury, and the
other Whigs urged the exclusion of James. Halifax, chief of the
King's supporters, spoke to the question fifteen or sixteen times and
carried "the day by his inexhaustible powers of wit, sarcasm, and
eloquence. At nine o'clock in the evening, after a debate of six
hours, the bill was thrown out by sixty-three votes to thirty." In
succeeding meetings the fury of the Opposition was expressed in
votes against many who stood by the King. Shaftesbury and his
party even went so far as to begin to prepare a bill for establishing
a Protestant association to govern the country, with Monmouth as
the head. On January 10, 1680/81, with no warning, Charles
prorogued and then dissolved Parliament, with the provision that
the next Parliament should meet at Oxford—away from the London
mob—on March 21.[12]

Dryden may well have been in London during the late winter.
The Duke's company had accepted a play from a youngster named
Charles Saunders, and Dryden agreed to write an epilogue, to help

it along. Sometime in February, Saunder's *Tamerlane the Great*
was acted.[13] In the following month Dryden's *Spanish Friar* appeared with a dedication—devoted oddly enough at this time to a
discussion of playwriting—addressed to Lord Houghton, later to
become Marquis of Clare. He admits to Houghton that it sounded
more like a preface than a dedication, and indeed it lacks almost all
the marks of Dryden's usual performances of this kind. Hardly a
week later, a considerable portion of the court and town were beginning to flood into Oxford for the meeting of Parliament.

In a remarkable era, this meeting was more striking than any
that had preceded. The newly-elected Whig members, with armed
retainers obviously prepared for trouble, rode into Oxford during
the week of March 14, and the royal party, while perhaps not so
accoutered, joined them in the university city. Along with the
official groups came a troupe of hangers-on who in ordinary times
would not have attended such a meeting. But these were not
ordinary times, and a recognition of the extraordinary nature of the
proceedings could be seen at every hand. Perhaps in anticipation of
a long session arrangements had been made for the entertainment
of the members. The players, down from London, brought Saunder's
Tamerlane and a special epilogue from Dryden. On Saturday,
March 19, both were presented. Dryden took the offered opportunity
to write in serious vein on the eve of the crucial meeting; for he—as
well as all men—realized that Exclusion would be the main business
of the Parliament. In measured tones and with exemplary moderation, Dryden speaks directly to the members. He points out that
"crowded Oxford represents mankind" and that "Great Britain seems
confined within the walls." Indeed the world appears to watch as
Oxford becomes the public theatre:

> And you both audience are and actors here.
> The gazing world on the new scene attend,
> Admire the turns, and wish a prosp'rous end.
> This place, the seat of peace, the quiet cell
> Where arts remov'd from noisy business dwell,
> Should calm your wills, unite the jarring parts,
> And with a kind contagion seize your hearts:
> O may its genius like soft music move
> And tune you all to concord and to love
>
> .   .   .   .
>
> From hence you may look back on civil rage

And view the ruins of the former age.
Here a new world its glories may unfold
And here be sav'd the remnants of the old.[14]

Moderate and unexceptionable sentiments these were, but they were designed for the ears of more moderate men than those assembled in Oxford to debate Exclusion.

Moderation was thrown to the winds. Oxford was crowded not only with members but with all kinds of retainers. Of particular interest were those of what Roger North termed "the Tongue and Pen Managery." These he describes at length as the "Writers, Talkers, and Disposers of News and Libels, by Directions of wiser Heads than their own." They insinuated themselves in places frequented by members and there argued, ridiculed, bantered the loyal side, and "by Dexterity of Courtship, Flattering, Wheadling, Lying, and Reviling" tried to win proselytes to their Whiggish cause. Money flowed freely from men who had no estates and little more than a precarious existence in town; and as North comments, "they serve none for nothing, rien pour rien." In their service they had a "magazine provided of Ammunition, Libels, Lampoons, Satyrs, Pictures and Sing-songs." Some were "adopted to deceive men of Fortune and Education, well-penned, and perhaps in Heroic Verse; others for the Rabble, and drunken, scottish Clubs, in Ballad Doggerel, with witty Pictures affixed." One of the most popular raree-shows represented the King, "with his box of Parliament Motions at his Back, and the Saints pulling him down into a Ditch." Another represented the Duke of York, or "Mac-Ninny . . . where he was expressed Half Jesuit, and Half Devil." And L'Estrange, the chief pamphlet writer for the Tories, was represented as a dog called Towzer, running from a Whip.[15] In this atmosphere, the Parliament met on Monday, March 21. The Commons refused any compromise, and Charles likewise refused to yield or to be intimidated on the matter of the Succession. Shaftesbury's plan—as always—was to force the abandonment of James and the recognition of Monmouth as heir to the throne. By Saturday, the twenty-sixth, Exclusion was voted, and the first reading of it was to be on Monday, the twenty-eighth. The King took his place on Monday, summoned the Commons to attend, and forthwith had his Lord Chancellor announce the dissolution of the week-old Parliament. "The Dissolution scattered the opposition as a gust of wind the leaves of a tree in autumn." Shaftesbury tried in vain to hold his forces together; instead they fled as rapidly as they could find transportation, which had become scarce and expensive within the hour. The Whigs had lost their trump card by the coolness and shrewdness of their political master. Deprived of their parliamentary forum, they could not now effectively operate, and whatever plots or rebellions they could hatch would need to be done without a show of legality.[16]

To pursue his advantage, Charles took his case to the country in *His Majesties Declaration to all His Loving Subjects, Touching the Causes & Reasons that Moved Him to Dissolve the Two Last Parliaments.* Dated April 8, it was soon after in print and was commanded to be read from all the pulpits in the country. In his justification, the King pointed out that he had asked the Parliament to consider and to act upon a number of important issues, which included the preservation of the Succession in its legal course of descent. He was met with remonstrances, not answers; by arbitrary orders to take his subjects into custody; and by "strange illegal votes, declaring divers eminent persons to be enemies to the King and kingdom, without any order or process of law, any hearing of their defence, or any proof so much as offered against them."[17] The effect of taking his case directly to his people was to incline opinion toward him and to bring a flood of loyal addresses, expressing "abhorrence of those members who had acted in such a manner as to bring the nation to the brink of armed conflict." The alarmed opposition marshalled its writers for replies, and within a month at least three replies and attacks appeared. Luttrell on May 19 recorded that two treasonable and seditious pamphlets were lately in print and that several persons had been apprehended for questioning.[18] The title of one was *An Answer to His Majesties Late Declaration;* another, about the same time, was called *A Just and Modest Vindication of the Proceedings of the Two Last Parliaments*; a third, *A Letter from a Person of Quality to his Friend: Concerning the King's Late Declaration.* The last was answered in *His Majesty's Declaration Defended,* which according to *The Observator* was in circulation by June 22.[19]

Since Dryden has been advanced as the most likely author of this tract, it deserves examination. For it establishes, as we find, a procedure in controversy which later becomes a mark of Dryden's authorship. He begins with a general statement of the origin of the reasons why *A Letter from a Person of Quality* was written, with an attempt to ferret out the author or authors. After the preliminary generalities, he moves to a careful scrutiny of particular passages, quoting them verbatim and refuting them by the weapons in his debater's arsenal: irony, close dissection of equivocations, ridicule of elementary errors in grammar, lively exposure of false logic, consummate scorn, and an infectious humor and raciness that permeates the whole piece. And what is more, Dryden rehearses in this tract some of the same ideas which were to appear five months later in *Absalom and Achitophel.*

Upon the publication of the King's Declaration, Dryden says, the chiefs of the Whig Party determined that it must be answered and that at once "five several Pens of their Cabal were set to work; and the product of each having been examin'd, a certain person of Quality appears to have carried the majority of Votes, and to be chosen like a new Matthias, to succeed in the place of their deceas'd Judas [Marvell]." He launches at once into rebuttal of specific points made by the Whig author. To the expressed fear that a House of Commons might be so packed in future as to make the English Papists by law, Dryden retorts: "This supposition . . . is to lay a most scandalous imputation upon the Gentry of *England*; besides, what it tacitly insinuates, that the House of Peers and his Majesty, (without whom it could not pass into a Law) would suffer it. Yet without such Artifices . . . the Fanatique cause could not possibly subsist: fear of Popery and Arbitrary power must be kept up; or the St. *Georges* of their side, would have no Dragon to encounter."

To expect Charles to assume arbitrary power strikes him as preposterous; the Opposition can never persuade a reasonable man "that a King, who in his younger years, when he had all the Temptations of power to pursue such a Design, yet attempted it not, should now, in the maturity of his Judgment, and when he sees the manifest aversion of his Subjects to admit of such a change, undertake a work of so much difficulty, destructive to the Monarchy, and ruinous to Himself, if it succeeded not; and if it succeeded, not capable of making him so truly Great as he is by Law already." The allegations that arbitrary power is the "aim of the King" fall down, Dryden thinks, in a maze of contradictions. For one thing, the Parliament has plainly attempted, and successfully, to whittle down the royal prerogatives guaranteed by custom and by law, and is continuing to do so by controlling the money supplies and so making the Monarch a "Minor at no less than fifty years of age." It is evident, he thinks, that the King's temper is averse to more power and that "the notion of an absolute power in the Prince is wholly unpracticable, not only in this Age, but for aught any wise man can foresee, at any time hereafter."

In noting the charge that the King and his Council have sought to stifle the investigations of the Popish Plot and subsequently dissolved four parliaments in order to obscure the facts and the ultimate reality, Dryden strikes at what he considers the real political purposes behind the plot in a masterly analysis that is reminiscent of his more condensed, but equally penetrating poetic analysis, in *Absalom and Achitophel*:

The Popish Plot has nothing to do with the Dissolution of Four Parliaments. But the Use which has been made of it by the House of Commons to Dis-inherit the Duke, to deny the King Supplies, and to make some Votes, which the King declares to be illegal, are the real and plain occasions of dissolving those Parliaments. 'Tis only affirm'd . . . that the King or his Ministers have ever been desirous to stifle the Plot. . . . To what end has his Majesty so often offer'd the Popish Lords to be brought to their Trial, but that their innocence or guilt, and consequently, that of the whole party might be made manifest? Or why, after the execution of the Lord Stafford, did the House of Commons stop at the other Lords, and not proceed to try them in their turns? . . . If it were for want of Witnesses, which is all that can be said, the case is deplorable on the part of the accused; who can neither be bail'd, because impeach'd in Parliament, nor admitted to be tryed, for fear they should be acquitted for want of evidence. I do not doubt but his Majesty . . . is desirous (for what good man is not?) that his care and trouble might be over. But I am much deceiv'd, if the Anti-monarchical Party be of the same opinion; or that they desire the Plot should be either wholly discover'd, or fully ended. For 'tis evidently their Interest to keep it on foot, as long as possibly they can; and to give it hot water, as often as 'tis dying; for while they are in possession of this Jewel, they make themselves masters of the people. For this very reason I have often said, even from the beginning of the Discovery, that the Presbyterians would never let it go out of their hands, but manage it to the last inch upon a Save-all. And that if ever they had tryed one Lord, they would value themselves upon that Conquest, as long as ever it would last with the Populace: but whatever came on't, be sure to leave a Nest Egg in the *Tower*. . . . I am apt to think, that his Majesty saw at least as great a danger arising to him from the discontented spirits of the popular Faction, as from the Papists . . . ever since the beginning of the Plot, they have been lopping off from the Crown whatever part of the Prerogative they could reach. . . .[20]

With respect to Monmouth and the Protestant succession his attitude is somewhat different from what it was to be in his later poetic treatment. He doubts that the Whig leaders were seriously advancing the claims of Monmouth:

Whether his nomination to succeed would, at the bottom be pleasing to the Heads of [the] Cabal, I somewhat doubt. To keep him fast to them by some remote hopes of it, may be no ill Policy. To have him in a readiness to head an Army, in case it should please God the King should die before the Duke, is the design; and then perhaps he has reason to expect more from a Chance-Game, than from the real desires of his party to exalt him to a Throne. But 'tis neither to be imagined, that a Prince of his Spirit, after the gaining of a Crown, would be managed by those who helped him to it, let his ingagements and promises be never so strong before, neither that he would be confin'd in the narrow compass of a Curtail'd Mungril Monarchy, half Commonwealth. Conquerers are not easily to be curbed.[21]

Monmouth's pretended friends, furthermore, probably do not even plan that much for him, but their "mutual necessities" keep them together, joined by all the "several Fanatic Books." If their design is finally successful, Dryden foresees unceasing strife among the groups because of their conflicting interests. "Every sect of High Shooes would then be uppermost; and not one of them endure the toleration of another." As Dryden had reminded Danby three years earlier, those who first trouble the waters seldom have the advantage of the fishing. What, he asks, will become, in such an unholy association, of "those Speculative Wits, who drew the plan of this New Government?" "For their comfort," he points out ironically, "the Saints will then account them Atheists, and discard them." And what of Monmouth, the supposed Protestant successor? "If he be not wholly governed by the prevailing party, will first be declared no Protestant; and next, no Successor."

A change that has occurred in the political climate may be found in the concluding paragraphs. Picking up a phrase from his antagonist, he points out that only angry men are the pillars of the party, men who have been disobliged at court. Where, he asks, "are the principles of Virtue, Honour, and Religion, which they would persuade the World, have animated their endeavours for the publick?" The knavery of their leaders must be known throughout to the anti-monarchical party:

But the Nation begins to awaken: [the] party is mouldring away, and as it falls out, in all dishonest Combinations, are suspecting each other so very fast, that every man is shifting for himself, by a separate Treaty. . . . My adversary, wisely fears no change of government from any, but the Papists. Now I am of a better heart, for I fear it neither from Papists nor Presbyterians. Whether Democracy will agree with Jesuitical principles in England I am not certain; but I can easily prove to him, that no Government but a Common-wealth is accommodated to the systems of Church-worship invented by John Calvin.[22]

This defense, though it may not have exercised much influence at the time and in the midst of the great volume of tracts that were appearing, nevertheless indicates the fundamental views which Dryden was now taking, and his careful assessment of the developing situation. The summer months were to prove momentous, and both sides were bracing themselves for the showdown. The "violent paper scuffle," as Luttrell called it, proceeded apace; and every day saw the appearance of new libels and tracts against the King, the Duke, and the Succession. The Whig efforts were gradually frustrated, as Dryden saw, but a menacing force still existed. Steps, however, were even then being taken to combat it through the medium of legal processes. Since they were not now granted pardons in advance of their testimony, the paid informers no longer had evidence to sell. The Council and King inquired diligently into the details of the Whig machinations and uncovered enough new evidence to put Lord Howard of Escrick into the Tower on a charge of high treason, and to take into custody the Earl of Shaftesbury. After intensive examination, he too was sent to the Tower on July 2, and his papers were impounded.

It was one thing, however, to imprison those high persons, and quite another to bring the law to bear upon them because of the power still held by the Whig sheriffs to pack juries, which monotonously found no True Bill, but returned an *ignoramus* to almost every case. Lord Howard was not brought to trial because of the fear that he would be freed. During July and August the case against Shaftesbury was building up. Using a leaf from his book, the Tories collected "evidence" from the same witnesses whom he had earlier suborned. Shaftesbury, faced with the certainty of being brought to trial (though he could be sure that a factious jury empanelled by the Whig sheriffs would bring in an *ignoramus*),[23] moved for a compromise. He promised that if released he would retire to his estates or go abroad, perhaps to Carolina. But Charles, acting against the advice of Halifax, who counselled acceptance of the offer, refused to compromise.[24]

Attacks and Counterattacks
1681-1682

T HE ARREST of Shaftesbury was the signal for a determined royal attack upon the Opposition. Within a fortnight Luttrell records that partisans of both sides were publicly announcing their affiliations by wearing red and blue ribbons in their hats—red for the Duke of York, blue for Monmouth.[1] During the summer and early autumn the Crown built up a case against Shaftesbury, the bill of indictment of treason to be based upon an article passed in 25 Edward III for intention to rebel and to seek the death of the King.[2] Though no overt act had yet been committed, papers found among Shaftesbury's belongings outlined the plans for a Protestant association, dedicated by oaths against Popery, and the succession of the Duke.[3] Eventually the trial was scheduled before the London Grand Jury for November 24.

While the political pot boiled, Dryden's thoughts must have been almost completely centered upon *Absalom and Achitophel*. His interest in political matters, no doubt already incorporated in his early drafts of his poem, may be seen in the prologues and epilogues he contributed to the plays of other writers during the early autumn. To welcome the King and Queen at a performance of John Banks's *The Unhappy Favorite,* he wrote a special prologue and epilogue, in both of which the current situation is fully exploited. In the prologue he writes:

> Tell me, you powers, why should vain man pursue,
> With endless toil, each object that is new
> And for the seeming substance leave the true?
> Why should he quit for hopes his certain good,
> And loathe the manna of his daily food?

Must England still the scene of changes be,
Toss'd and tempestuous, like our ambient sea?
Must still our weather and our wills agree?
Without our blood our liberties we have:
Who that is free would fight to be a slave?
Or, what can wars to aftertimes assure,
Of which our present age is not secure?

.   .   .   .

Our land's an Eden, and the main's our fence,
While we preserve our state of innocence:
That lost, then beasts their brutal force employ,
And first their lord, and then themselves destroy.
What civil broils have cost we know too well;
O let it be enough that once we fell,
And every heart conspire with every tongue,
Still to have such a king, and this king long.

The epilogue bewails the low state of the drama and stage, particularly the Theatre Royal, where Banks's play was acted. Never did men live more on Providence, he says, than the players, not even courts or courtiers "living on the rents/ Of the three last ungiving parliaments." The times are out of joint:

'Tis not our want of wit that keeps us poor;
For then the printer's press would suffer more.
Their pamphleteers each day their venom spit;
They thrive by treason, and we starve by wit.

When the first play of Thomas Southerne, called *The Loyal Brother,* was accepted by Betterton's company, and acted sometime in October or very early November,[4] Dryden contributed both prologue and epilogue. Properly enough, the prologue, introducing a play with rather obvious political overtones, is devoted entirely to an attack upon the Whigs and their machinations: Poets, he says,

. . . like lawful monarchs, rul'd the stage
Till critics, like damn'd Whigs, debauch'd our age.
Mark how they jump: critics would regulate
Our theatres, and Whigs reform our state:
Both pretend love, and both, (plague rot 'em) hate.
The critic humbly seems advice to bring;
The fawning Whig petitions to the king:

But one's advice into a satire slides;
T'other's petition a remonstrance hides;

.   .   .   .

The critic all our troops of friends discards;
Just so the Whig would fain pull down the guards.
Guards are illegal, that drive foes away,
As watchful shepherds, that fright beasts of prey.
Kings, who disband such needful aids as these,
Are safe—as long as e'er their subjects please:
And that would be till next Queen Bess's night.

He then describes the procession during the celebration of a Pope
burning on Queen Bess's night, and points out that after the effigy
has been committed to the bonfire:

He burns; now all true hearts your triumphs ring:
And next (for fashion) cry: "God save the king!"
A needful cry in midst of such alarms,
When forty thousand men are up in arms.

.   .   .   .

Five praying saints are by an act allow'd;
But not the whole Church-militant in crowd.
Yet, should Heav'n all the true petitions drain
Of Presbyterians who would kings maintain,
Of forty thousand, five would scarce remain.

These occasional attacks, designed for presentation to a mixed
and shifting theater audience, were but pinpricks at best. Dryden's
real attack upon the Whigs, long in preparation, was timed perfectly
in its publication to achieve a maximum effect. It appeared anony-
mously about November 9, only a week before the next Pope burning on November 17, and a fortnight before the trial of Shaftesbury
for treason.[5] Within a week Tonson had given a copy to his friend
Luttrell, who wrote on it the date, November 17, and added "An
excellent poem agt ye Duke of Monmouth, Earl of Shaftesbury &
that party & in vindication of the King & his friends."[6] Many others
were also getting copies, and some were broadcasting their comments. On November 19, Richard Mulys wrote to the Duke of
Ormond: "I also here send you Mr. Dryden's poem Absolom and
Achitophel wherein is honourable mention of my Lord Lieutenant
and also of my late Lord. This piece was writ as I am credibly
informed at the instance of our great Minister, Mr. Seymour, but

that is a secret to yourself."[7]   It is thus clear that there was never
any doubt about the authorship; the stamp of Dryden's genius was
too obvious to be missed.   Nor so far as we can judge did the contemporary readers find any difficulty unveiling either the meaning
or the persons shadowed under the Biblical names.   The practice
of using such names in poems, political tracts, and sermons had become such a commonplace of the century that readers were habituated
to it and knowledgeable in the application of them to contemporary
figures.   Particularly frequent had been the use of the Absalom and
Achitophel story; and for Dryden, at least, Charles II had been David
as early as 1660.   Quite consciously Dryden used well-worn names,
assured that readers would immediately recognize the public figures.
In the use of the story of deluded Absalom and the wicked counselor
Achitophel, Dryden showed no "originality"; that was shown in the
treatment he gave it.[8]

Introductory to the poem Dryden wrote an address "To the
Reader," which is an integral part of the poem, explaining the limitations that he put upon himself and suggesting the artistic incomplete-
ness forced upon it by the unforeseeable ending of the actual conflict.   "It is not my intention," he says, "to make an apology for my
poem; some will think it needs no excuse, and others will receive
none."   For he recognizes that whoever "draws his pen for one party
must expect to make enemies of the other.   For wit, and fool, are
consequents of Whig and Tory; and every man is a knave or an ass
to the contrary side."   This apparent conciliatory approach conceals
the rapier, which appears at once.   He admits that "There is a
treasury of merits in the fanatick church, as well as in the papist,
and a pennyworth to be had of saintship, honesty, and poetry, for
the lewd, the factious, and the blockheads; but the longest chapter
in Deuteronomy has not curses enough for an Anti-Birmingham
[Whig]."   Dryden had enough self-esteem in his make-up—and
enough critical acumen—to know the quality of his poem and to
take pride in it.   Despite the prejudices of the opposite party which
"will render their judgment of less authority against me," he writes,
"yet if a poem have a genius, it will force its own reception in the
world."   In good verse, he goes on, there is a sweetness

which tickles even while it hurts, and no man can be heartily angry with
him who pleases him against his will. The commendation of adversaries
is the greatest triumph of a writer because it never comes unless extorted.
But I can be satisfied on more easy terms. If I happen to please the
more moderate sort, I shall be sure of an honest party, and in all proba-

bility, of the best judges; for the least concerned are commonly the least corrupt: and I confess I have laid in for those, by rebating the satire (where justice would allow it) from carrying too sharp an edge.   They who can criticize so weakly as to imagine I have done my worst may be convinced, at their own cost, that I can write severely with more ease than I can gently.   I have but laughed at some men's follies, when I could have declaimed against their vices; and other men's virtues I have commended as freely as I have taxed their crimes.

He sustains the ironic tone by suggesting that if the reader be malicious he might charge the author with affecting "to be thought more impartial than I am."   Yet if people are not to be judged by their professions, he says, "God forgive you Commonwealths-men for professing so plausibly for the government."   Nor can he be taxed for not putting his name to the poem, for the Whig writers always remain in craven anonymity, even though "they have the advantage of a jury to secure them."   "If you like not my poem," he says with tongue in cheek, "the fault may possibly be in my writing (though it is hard for an author to judge against himself); but more probably it is in your morals, which can not bear the truth of it."

Dryden's desire to appeal to moderate opinion, not to extremists on right or left, is made manifest when he comments on the treatment of Monmouth in the poem:

The violent on both sides will condemn the Character of Absalom, as either too favourably or too hardly drawn; but they are not the violent whom I desire to please.   The fault on the right hand is to extenuate, palliate, and indulge; and to confess freely, I have endeavoured to commit it.   Beside the respect I owe his birth, I have a greater for his heroick virtues; and David himself could not be more tender of the young man's life, than I would be of his reputation.   But since the most excellent natures are always the most easy, and as being such, are the soonest perverted by ill counsels, especially when baited with fame and glory, it is no more a wonder that he withstood not the temptations of Achitophel, than it was for Adam not to have resisted the two devils, the serpent, and the woman.   The conclusion of the story I purposely forebore to prosecute, because I could not obtain from myself to shew Absalom unfortunate.

Dryden's compromise with his poetic license is further illustrated by his final comments on both Monmouth and Shaftesbury.   "Were I the inventor, who am only the historian, I should certainly conclude the piece with the reconcilement of Absalom to David; and who knows but this may come to pass?   Things were not brought to an extremity where I left the story; there seems yet to be room left for a composure; hereafter, there may only be for pity."   In order to understand fully Dryden's poetic achievement, it is important to recognize that his artistic conscience is at work here. His poem, cast as a miniature epic, and containing an epic gravity along with certain Miltonic accents and verbal devices, began *in medias res,* and it ended there. For his sense of being an historian, or recorder, of the contemporary situation prevented him from pursuing it to a satisfactory fictional ending. As for Absalom, so for Achitophel—within the limits of the poem—there is no end. Yet he has a hope for Achitophel—which carries a sharp edge. He is content "To be accused of a good-natured errour, and to hope with Origen that the devil himself may at last be saved: for which reason, in this poem, he is neither brought to set his house in order, nor to dispose of his person afterwards, as he in wisdom shall think fit." The Biblical Achitophel hanged himself.

Absalom and Achitophel defies classification into any known type of poem. Though usually labelled "satire," because many of the quotable sections of it are found in the satiric portraits of the chief figures among the Whig Opposition, the poem is not a satire. Though it contains a brilliant historical summary of events of the century, it is not historical. Epic dignity and epic tags are present, but one can scarcely label it epic. Political actions and beliefs are described and approved or condemned, yet it is not essentially a political poem. Philosophic comment abounds, yet it is not philosophic. Professor A. W. Verrall perhaps came close to a satisfying definition when he suggested that it is "best to call it an 'epyllion,' or epic in miniature comprising satiric elements."[9] Yet even this leaves out of account a good deal of the most powerful material in the poem. However viewed or however labelled, *Absalom and Achitophel* has exercised a perennial fascination and has evoked, since the passions of the moment subsided, an almost universal chorus of praise. But the praise has not always been showered upon the same things, and this fact may provide testimony to its greatness.

In structure the poem is a model of simplicity, despite its obviously labyrinthine subject matter. Dryden tells no connected story, in the usual meaning of the word, but exposes a changing situation, or rather "fixes" it at a moment in time when no man can predict its end. Carefully organized, the materials are strung on a horizontal line, each division complete in itself but yoked to another, either integrally or "artificially," by short transitional paragraphs. The poem is made up of about eighteen divisions or "movements." The introductory section of forty-two lines describes the promiscuity of Charles II, the lack of legitimate offspring, and the "numerous progeny" carrying the bend sinister, of whom Absalom was the most attractive. Following this comes a historical summary of the troubles of the century, the Popish Plot and its aftermath in the rise of factions, a brilliant section on Achitophel, the temptation scene between Achitophel and Absalom, comment on Absalom's fall, the organization of the disparate factions to destroy the government and advance Absalom, a catalog of portraits of the chief manipulators, Absalom's deluded, ambitious courting of the people, and the author's comment on Absalom's progress and its purpose. At this point in the poem (11. 759-810) Dryden comes forward with his own political credo, most of the details of which we have already traced in his work from 1677 onwards. After this section there is a short transition to the gallery of portraits of the King's friends and supporters in the worst of times, with Dryden's comment on their loyal actions and advice; and after another short link, a long section in which the King speaks directly to his people, justifying the royal position and actions. The poem closes with a six-line prophecy of Charles's triumph.

The first twenty couplets of the poem foreshadow the irony and the humor with which the poem abounds, and if laughter be therapeutic, Dryden included enough basis for it to exercise a healing effect upon the body politic; and though we may not actually believe that the people "after three years of madness . . . read *Absalom and Achitophel* and laughed themselves out of their own follies,"[10] we may believe that some kind of balance might have been restored to them. Who except the most dour fanatic would have resisted laughing at Dryden's thumbnail description of his countrymen—

> The Jews, a headstrong, moody, murm'ring race,
> As ever tried th' extent and stretch of grace;
> God's pamper'd people, whom, debauch'd with ease,
> No king could govern, nor no God could please;
> (God's they had tried of every shape and size,
> That god-smiths could produce, or priests devise).

Or at the famous portrait of Zimri (Buckingham)—

> A man so various, that he seem'd to be
> Not one, but all mankind's epitome:
> Stiff in opinions, always in the wrong;
> Was everything by starts, and nothing long;

> But, in the course of one revolving moon.
> Was chymist, fiddler, statesman, and buffoon:
> Then all for women, painting, rhyming, drinking,
> Besides ten thousand freaks that died in thinking.

Or at Shimei (Bethel)—

> whose youth did early promise bring
> Of zeal to God and hatred to his king,
> Did wisely from expensive sins refrain,
> And never broke the Sabbath, but for gain;
> Nor ever was he known an oath to vent,
> Or curse, unless against the government.

That Dryden's real purpose, as he wrote in the address "To the Reader," was to appeal to the moderates and not to the extremists may be seen in many passages. In the rapid, succinct, penetrating account of the course of political action in his own lifetime, we see this feeling for moderation at work:

> They who, when Saul [Cromwell] was dead, without a blow,
> Made foolish Ishbosheth [Richard Cromwell] the crown
>   forego;
> Who banish'd David did from Hebron bring
> And with a general shout proclaim'd him king:
> These very Jews, who, at their very best,
> Their humour more than loyalty express'd,
> Now wonder'd why so long they had obey'd
> An idol monarch, which their hands had made;
> Thought they might ruin him they could create,
> Or melt him to that golden calf, a State.
> But these were random bolts; no form'd design,
> Nor interest made the factious crowd to join:
> The sober part of Israel, free from stain,
> Well knew the value of a peaceful reign;
> And, looking backward with a wise affright,
> Saw seams of wounds, dishonest to the sight:
> In contemplation of whose ugly scars
> They curs'd the memory of civil wars.
> The moderate sort of men, thus qualified,
> Inclin'd the balance to the better side;
> And David's mildness manag'd it so well,
> The bad found no occasion to rebel.

But when to sin our bias'd nature leans,
The careful Devil is still at hand with means;
And providently pimps for ill desires,
The Good Old Cause reviv'd, a plot requires:
Plots, true or false, are necessary things,
To raise up commonwealths, and ruin kings.

His analysis of the formation of the Opposition, under Shaftesbury's blandishments, seems to represent an honest and sincere attempt to understand the complexity of motive which had combined to subvert the Monarchy:

The best, (and of the princes some were such,)
Who thought the pow'r of monarchy too much;
Mistaken men, and patriots in their hearts;
Not wicked, but seduc'd by impious arts.
By these the springs of property were bent,
And wound so high, they crack'd the government.
The next for interest sought t' embroil the State,
To sell their duty at a dearer rate;
And make their Jewish markets of the throne,
Pretending public good, to serve their own.
Others thought kings an useless heavy load,
Who cost too much, and did too little good.
These were for laying honest David by,
On principles of pure good husbandry.
With them join'd all th' haranguers of the throng,
That thought to get preferment by the tongue.
Who follow next a double danger bring,
Not only hating David, but the king:
The Solymaean rout, well vers'd of old
In godly faction, and in treason bold;

.   .   .   .

Hot Levites headed these; who, pulled before
From the ark, which in the Judges' days they bore,
Resumed their cant, and with a zealous cry
Pursued their old beloved Theocracy:
When Sanhedrin and priest enslaved the nation,
And justified their spoils by inspiration.

.   .   .   .

But far more numerous was the herd of such,
Who think too little, and who talk too much.

We are more concerned, however, with Dryden's statement of his own political position:

> What shall we think! Can people give away,
> Both for themselves and sons, their native sway?
> Then they are left defenseless to the sword
> Of each unbounded, arbitrary lord:
> And laws are vain, by which we right enjoy,
> If kings unquestioned can those laws destroy.
> Yet if the crowd be judge of fit and just,
> And kings are only officers in trust,
>
> .   .   .   .
>
> Then kings are slaves to those whom they command,
> And tenants to their people's pleasure stand.
> Add, that the power for property allowed
> Is mischievously seated in the crowd;
> For who can be secure of private right,
> If sovereign sway may be dissolved by might?
> Nor is the people's judgment always true:
> The most may err as grossly as the few;
>
> .   .   .   .
>
> Nor only crowds, but Sanhedrins may be
> Infected with this public lunacy,
> And share the madness of rebellious times,
> To murther monarchs for imagin'd crimes.

If Parliaments may take and give at will, he points out, then not only kings but government itself must eventually fall into chaos. And therefore, he asks, what prudent man would shake a throne?

> All other errors but disturb a state,
> But innovation is the blow of fate.
> If ancient fabrics nod, and threat to fall,
> To patch the flaws, and buttress up the wall,
> Thus far 'tis duty: but here fix the mark;
> For all beyond it is to touch our ark.
> To change foundations, cast the frame anew,
> Is work for rebels, who base ends pursue,
> At once divine and human laws control,
> And mend the parts by ruin of the whole.
> The tamp'ring world is subject to this curse,
> To physic their disease into a worse.

Such a conservative position comes close to that of the Trimmer only in that it takes a stand between the extremes of royal tyranny unrestrained and parliamentary irresponsibility unchecked. What is missing is a kind of political expediency which may justify the highest motives of a politician intent on maintaining equilibrium in the state, but which may not be operative in a subject faced with the necessity of finding satisfactory general principles of government in which he can believe. Dryden was no Trimmer: he had taken his stand on an hereditary Monarchy bound by law and by a Parliament of the two houses; and looking back with a "wise affright," he had rejected the commonwealth principle of a supreme Parliament. So far as can be determined he never changed.

Both the timing of the poem and the attack it contained on Shaftesbury and the rebellious, if not treasonable, course of the factions, Dryden well knew might be calculated to enrage those who were arrayed against the Monarchy. Yet even he could have been surprised, and perhaps a bit pleased, at the storm which immediately broke about his head. In truth, the extent and virulence of the attacks upon him during the next twelve months are unparalleled in the history of English letters up to his time, and there have been few parallels since.[11] Within the week Shaftesbury's trial resulted in the refusal of the jury to find a True Bill, and the release of the Earl was the signal for wild rejoicing among his adherents. Almost at once the Whig writers mobilized for their onslaught on the poet laureate. The difficulty, indeed the impossibility, of answering Dryden's poem soon became clear, but that offered no bar to the exercise of party animosity. The favorite, and almost the sole, method of rebuttal took the form of attacks on Dryden, his alleged changeableness, from support of Cromwell to support of Charles, on his verse, and on his wife; on almost anything in fact but the poem itself. Some of the allegations about his character, his private life, and his wife, made in the anger and the frustrations of the hour, have unhappily forced themselves into such a commanding position that Dryden's reputation has suffered almost irreparable harm. Their persistence into our own day and their acceptance, without the check of corroborative evidence, is to be decried. Contemporary tributes to his poetic powers and himself as a person, on the contrary, have received very little attention.

On December 10 the first of the attacks, *Towzer the Second,* appeared. In rapid succession four more were going the rounds of the city before the end of the month: *Poetical Reflections on Absalom* and *Achitophel* (December 14), *A Panegyrick on the Author of Absalom and Achitophel* (December 19), *A Whip for the Fools Back* (December 24), and probably *An Elegy on the Usurper O. C. by the Author of Absalom and Achitophel*. The last is a reprint of "Heroique Stanzas," with a postscript of some twenty lines, in which Dryden is made to say:

> The Printing of these Rhimes afflicts me more
> Than all the Drubs I in Rose-Alley bore,
> This shows my nauseous Mercenary Pen
> Would praise the vilest and the worst of men.
>
> . . . .
>
> This may prevent the pay for which I write;
> For I for pay against my Conscience fight.
>
> . . . .
>
> Villains I praise, and Patriots accuse,
> My railing and my fawning Talents use;
> Just as they pay I flatter or abuse.
>
> . . . .
>
> He who writes on, and Cudgels can difie,
> And knowing hee'l be beaten still writes on, am I.

In *A Panegyrick* much the same statements are made regarding his presumed change of loyalties in 1660:

> Thou cans't make Treason Glory, Murderers Heroes live;
> And even to Regicides cans't God-heads give.
>
> . . . .
>
> A bagpipe Drone to the old Priestcraft cant:
> Who once did consecrated Daggers Chant,
> And England's great Ravilliac sung before;
> Now tunes his Pipe to Davids Righteous Lore.
>
> . . . .
>
> Is there not mighty sound and mighty sence
> In great Iscariots thirty clinking Pence!
>
> . . . .
>
> Write on, and more than winds or Frenzy Range,
> Keep still thy old prerogative to change.

By mid-January at least two other long and insulting libels attacked Dryden: *A Key (With the Whip)* and *Azaria and Hushai*. The first by a non-conformist parson (Christopher Nesse?) is long and tedious. A sample of the parson's poetic style and his good manners may be seen in an extract:

Oh thou Incongruous Fool, what parallel
That's Congruous 'twixt these *two* canst thou tell
        [Absalom and Monmouth]

.   .   .   .

Oh lump of Impudence, where canst thou find
That 'ere pride budded thus in Monmouth's mind?
Was 'ere he hammering and hatching out,
For two full years any Rebellious Rout?
As did thy Absalom

.   .   .   .

Thy venom'd Quill spares neither Earl nor Duke,
Nor Queen nor King, in thy pernicious Book.

Azaria and Hushai, perhaps by Samuel Pordage,[12] attempts, under
Hebrew names, to offset Dryden's criticism of the Whig leaders; and
Dryden is abused under the name of Shimei, who, in *Absalom and
Achitophel,* was Slingsly Bethel, the Whig Sheriff of London. Azaria
and Hushai were Monmouth and Shaftesbury:

  [He could] The bad make good, good bad, and bad make
     worse,
  Bless in heroics and in Satires curse.
  Shimei to Zobed's [Cromwell's] praise could turn his Muse,
  And princely Azaria could abuse
  Zimri, we know, he had no cause to praise
  Because he dubb'd him with the name of Bayes:
  Revenge on him did bitter venom shed,
  Because he tore the laurel from his head.

  .   .   .   .

  Tell me, Apollo, for I can't divine
  Why wives he curs'd, and prais'd the concubine;
  Unless it were that he had led his life
  With a teeming matron, ere she was a wife;
  Or that it best with her dear Muse did suit,
  Who was for hire a very prostitute.

The aspersion upon his wife, here for the first time used in print, was
to become a standard item of personal attack from now on. His
enemies never wearied of repeating it, along with other unsubstantiated details of his personal life.

    Although Dryden by choice found himself in the midst of the
political conflict and continued in his own way to do battle with

the Opposition, it can hardly be assumed that he was an important spokesman for the King or for the Tories. It was L'Estrange, "Towzer the first," fighting day in and day out in *The Observator,* who was the chief Tory publicist. Even so, there were not wanting people at the time who considered Dryden of importance in the ultimate defeat of the Whig controversialists. The author of *The Laurel* (1685), for example, thought him second only to L'Estrange in this role.[13]   That he was serviceable to the King hardly admits of doubt, yet effective counterattack depended not upon his occasional pieces, as powerful as they were, but upon the close, constant fighting that the professional publicist like L'Estrange could contribute. What the King thought of Dryden's blows in his behalf can only be deduced from what he did and did not do for his laureate. In his constant state of near bankruptcy, he did not pay the poet's salary in full, nor was he able to catch up the arrears that had grown larger by the year. But under Laurence Hyde's management of the Treasury, Dryden was receiving, usually in semiannual payments, about half his salary, or £150 per year. This could hardly have been sufficient to provide more than the bare necessities in a period of creeping inflation. The King, however, seems to have been gracious enough to Dryden when his influence became a substitute for money. He had provided Dryden's eldest son a King's Scholarship at Westminster School; and we can be sure that upon the petition of the poet, he appointed, within a few months of this time, the second son, John, to a King's Scholarship, which he took up probably in the summer.[14] The youngest son, Erasmus-Henry, was approaching his thirteenth year, and with two boys already at Westminster on scholarships it was perhaps too much to ask that the third be accorded the same honor. Consequently, Dryden petitioned the King to nominate the youngest boy to a place at the Charterhouse. On February 28, Charles recommended to the Governors of the foundation that "Erasmus Henry Dryden" be elected and admitted one of the children of that foundation "on the first Vacancy."[15] Since the regulations of the Charterhouse provided for the education of children of poor people, it must have been a blow to the laureate's pride to ask for such a favor, the more so since it denied a place to another boy, whose father promptly complained of the preferential treatment given Dryden.[16] But time was pressing, for Erasmus-Henry would need to be admitted before his fourteenth birthday, on May 2, 1682/83, else he would have been superannuated and denied admission. The King's recommendation was effective, and the boy went to the Charterhouse on February 5, 1683, only three months before his birthday.

In the meantime, after the first group of attacks had come out against Dryden, the Whig writers enjoyed a respite of several weeks, to be followed by a further intensification of their campaign of hate against him. About January 14, however, appeared a different kind of book, which seems to have enlisted Dryden's interest at once. It was an English translation of Father Richard Simon's *Histoire Critique de Vieux Testament* by a young man named Henry Dickinson.[17] It may be that Dryden made the acquaintance of Dickinson, for the translation and Dryden's *Absalom* were in Tonson's hands about the same time. Simon's *Histoire* was an erudite work, subjecting the Biblical texts to searching analysis. By showing corruption in the texts upon which Protestant religious faith was largely based, Simon, following the tactics of the Catholic counter-reformation, hoped to undermine the authority of Scripture as the sole basis for faith. After first inducing skepticism into the Protestant mind, it would be only a further step to propose an acceptance of the infallible Church that could interpret Scripture by virtue of a long oral and written tradition. Dickinson's translation caused little stir in the London of 1682, only a few copies having been sold (as we learn by a suit brought in Chancery by Dickinson against Tonson); but it quickened Dryden's interest in the large problems of religion in his own time, to which—as we have seen—he had for some years been attracted. Simon's book, indeed, appears to have served as a fluxing agent for *Religio Laici,* which was to be in preparation during the summer and early autumn.

But in February or early March occurred an event that angered Dryden beyond anything that the Whigs had yet perpetrated. They struck off a medal, engraved by George Bower, in celebration of Shaftesbury's release on November 24. On one side was a bust of the Earl, and on the other, a view of London, the Bridge, and the Tower, behind which rose the sun to dispel the clouds: on the margin was the word *Laetamur.* Many copies were in general circulation and were worn by those who wished to declare their continuing allegiance to Shaftesbury. Dryden went to work at once, and in a very short time wrote *The Medal, A Satire Against Sedition.* By March 16, it was printed and in circulation.[18] Coming so soon after *Absalom and Achitophel* and provoked by a trivial event, *The Medal* has generally lain in the shadow of the far greater poem. Yet it has many merits, and provides a more complete characterization of

Shaftesbury and a more deadly and merciless attack than the earlier. As might be expected, there is repetition of political ideas from *Absalom and Achitophel,* but it has a value of its own unrelated to that poem.

Of special interest is the prose "Epistle To the Whigs," prefixed to the satire. Dryden asks to whom he can with more justice dedicate the poem, which, like the medal itself, is a representation of their hero "drawn at length, which you admire and prize so much in little." He ironically suggests that one side of the medal could have been omitted: "the head would be seen to more advantage, if it were placed on a Spike of the Tower, a little nearer to the sun, which would then break out to better purpose." Such sentiments were hardly calculated to assuage the anger which the Whigs were still nursing from the treatment accorded them in *Absalom.* Dryden, however, was in no mood to show the Whigs any quarter; and he proceeded with the attack: "Never was there practised such a piece of notorious impudence in the face of an established government. I believe when he is dead, you will wear him in thumb-rings, as the Turks did Scanderbeg; as if there were Virtue in his bones to preserve you against monarchy." He rallies them on their daily meetings in factious clubs to vilify the government and to traduce the King. They complain that the King has lost the love and confidence of the people, and by the very urging of it, they try to make him lose them. Again Dryden repeats his firmly-held beliefs:

All good subjects abhor the thought of arbitrary power, whether it be in one or many; if you were the patriots you would seem, you would not at this rate incense the multitude to assume it. . . . Give us leave to enjoy the government and the benefit of laws under which we were born, and which we desire to transmit to our posterity. You are not the trustees of the publick liberty. . . .

The Whig practices are, he sees, not new; he traces them from Calvin, Beza, through Buchanan and Milton into the present time. The Solemn League and Covenant of 1643, and the new Association of 1682, come directly from the Holy League of the French Guisards. Davila has informed him of the conflict in France: "there were the same pretences for reformation and loyalty, the same aspersions of the King, and the same grounds of a rebellion." Both Calvin and Buchanan had "set the people above the magistrate," and this he asserts is the fundamental tenet of the Whigs. In closing his "Epistle" he makes much fun of the frenetic Whig efforts of the past three months to reply to *Absalom*: his advice to them on how to answer him rubbed the wound raw:

Rail at me abundantly, and not to break a custom, do it without wit; by this method you will gain a considerable point, which is wholly to wave [*sic*] the answer of my arguments. . . . If God has not blessed you with the talent of rhyming, make use of my poor stock and welcome: let your verses run upon my feet; and for the utmost refuge of notorious blockheads, reduced to the last extremity of sense, turn my own lines upon me, and in utter despair of your own satire, make me satirize myself.

No more comfort was to be given them in the poem itself. In contrast to his intention in *Absalom and Achitophel*, Dryden here shows no desire to palliate, to extenuate, to be moderate: the latest example of the incorrigibility of Shaftesbury's party left him little choice but to attack with the utmost severity. The medal itself he again describes and says of the artistry,

> Five days he sate for every cast and look
> Four more than God to finish Adam took.
> But who can tell what essence Angels are,
> Or how long Heav'n was making Lucifer?

Dryden never tired of emphasizing the satanic quality of Shaftesbury, yet in *The Medal* he celebrates more thoroughly his opportunism, his ambition for power:

> A Martial hero first with early care,
> Blown, like a pigmy by the winds, to war.
> A beardless chief, a rebel, ere a man:
> (So young his hatred to his prince began)
> Next this, (how wildly will ambition steer!)
> A vermin wriggling in th' usurper's ear.
> Bart'ring his venal wit for sums of gold,
> He cast himself into the saintlike mold.

But only so long as godliness brought gain did Shaftesbury maintain his pose. "His open lewdness he could ne'er disguise./ There split the saint; for hypocritic zeal/ Allows no sins but those it can conceal." From treachery to treason Dryden follows his career, until at last he regards him as a "pander to the people's hearts" whose "blandishments a loyal land have whored/ And broke the bonds she plighted to her Lord." And all for what? To be finally undone by his canting friends, whose God and his "will never long agree."

Dryden predicts, as he has before, that Shaftesbury's muddying of the waters will prevent him from enjoying the fishing. The swelling poisons of the sects

> Shall burst its bag; and fighting out their way
> The various venoms on each other prey,
> The presbyter, puff'd up with spiritual pride,
> Shall on the necks of the lewd nobles ride,
> His brethern damn, the civil pow'r defy,
> And parcel out republic prelacy.
> But short shall be his reign: his rigid yoke
> And tyrant pow'r will puny sects provoke;
> And frogs and toads, and all the tadpole train,
> Will croak to Heav'n for help from this devouring crane.

The result of all will be chaos again, and again monarchy will be called back to establish peace and tranquillity.

The Medal replaced to some extent *Absalom and Achitophel* as the main object of Whig attacks on Dryden. Within a few days of the appearance of his poem, replies began to be published, the first called *The Mushroom,* to be followed within a fortnight by *The Medal Revers'd.* Attacking Dryden had become by this time a thriving business, and hardly a fortnight passed without a new assault, to all of which the poet laureate paid little attention. About May 15, Thomas Shadwell published *The Medal of John Bayes,* an angry, bitter, and sometimes obscene lampoon, containing a number of allegations about Dryden's life not previously made in attacks of this kind. Having suffered under the lash of Dryden's satire, Shadwell had a personal as well as a party reason for repaying him. Some of the statements of biographical interest are innocuous enough, and matters of common knowledge, such as his habitual resort to Will's coffeehouse, where he was surrounded by young literary men to whom he handed down certain *obiter dicta.*

Repeated too are some of the early aspersions regarding his employment in the government of Cromwell, his plagiarism, his diffident and phlegmatic nature (which can be found in Dryden's own comments on himself). New and previously unused ingredients are not many, and some may be suspect. A story in "The Epistle to the Tories" (prefixed to the verses), to illustrate Dryden's stupidity may serve as a sample:

You may know he is no concealer of himself, by a story which he tells of himself, *VIZ.* That (when he came first to Town) being a young raw fellow of seven and Twenty, as he call'd himself when he told the story, he frequenting but one Coffeehouse, the Woman (it seems finding him out) put Coffee upon him for Chocolate, and made him pay three pence a dish for two years together: till at length, by what providence I know not, he discovered the Cheat.

Dryden, we know, came to London when he was about fourteen, and his years at Westminster no doubt left him knowledgeable enough about city life not to be imposed upon by a waitress in a coffeehouse. To enforce the stigma of stupidity—which must have been rather difficult in view of *Absalom* and *The Medal*—Shadwell finds the age of twenty-seven serviceable, for later he uses it again to suggest that late age as the closing of Dryden's fontanel, "which may," he says, "be the reason he has had such a devilish soft place there ever since." Such anecdotes were, of course, grist for the mill of party controversy; and we may feel sure that neither Shadwell nor any of his perceptive readers thought of Dryden as anything but dangerously brilliant. Otherwise, there would have been little need to attack him. Other statements in this lampoon, however, have a show of truth: that Ann Reeves, a minor actress, was his mistress for a time, that he early shared lodgings with Sir Robert Howard, that the Duchess of Monmouth served as Dryden's early patron and that through her influence his plays became popular at court. For such, there is some corroborative evidence; but along with them are some obvious distortions and innuendos that occur nowhere else in the literature of the age and that are not susceptible to proof or disproof.[19]

Amid this welter of attack and vilification Dryden busied himself with other work, some of which savored little of party controversy, such as *Religio Laici.* Soon after he had completed *The Medal,* he was approached by Lee, who claimed his earlier promise of a collaborative play after the success of *Oedipus.* Accordingly, they began to write *The Duke of Guise,* a subject of interest to him since 1660 (when he says he actually had planned such a play), and now of particular importance because of the parallels he had already pointed out between the history of Henry IV in France and his conflict with the Liguers, Charles I in England with the Solemn League and Covenant, and now at the moment, the threatened repetition of it through Shaftesbury's New Association. It was to be a political tract in dramatic form. The collaborators pushed forward on it with great speed, Dryden writing the first scene of Act I, the whole of Act IV, and the first half of Act V. According to Dryden's later vindication of the play, it was completed before midsummer and was then ready to be acted. Rumor, however, had gone abroad that "some great persons were represented or personated," and the play was complained of to Arlington, the Lord Chamberlain, who commanded about July 18 that it be brought before him for review. Dryden, armed with Davila's *History*, appeared to defend controverted sections, particularly the first scene of Act IV, in which the Duke of Guise returns to Paris without permission. A parallel had been found by the Whigs in the Duke of Monmouth's return to London, after Charles had sent him into temporary exile.[20] Dryden could show Arlington the source in Davila for the sections objected to; and he left the history of the French troubles with him for a comparison between play and history. In the meantime the play was proscribed. Gossip went the rounds that not only Monmouth but the King himself was personated, in the figure of Henry III, and that the King, though displeased with Monmouth, would not allow others "to abuse him."[21] After two months the Lord Chamberlain released the play and gave orders to allow its performance, the King perhaps having decided that as an attack upon the Whig position, the play contained positive value to him, despite the presence of parallels, adventitious or deliberate. The King could afford to be liberal in this matter, for the tide of affairs had turned in his favor during the summer with the election of two Tory sheriffs in the city, Dudley North and Peter Rich. The hold of the Whigs on judicial proceedings was thereby broken; and hereafter any packing of London juries would be done in the King's interest. Furthermore, the steady success of the royal campaign to call in city charters for "remodeling" made it certain that the London charter itself would soon be changed: the end of Achitophel's influence came into clear view.[22]

While the King and Arlington decided the fate of the *Duke of Guise* and while *Religio Laici* was being written, Dryden had personal and family matters to concern himself with. His two older boys were having trouble at school. In a letter to Busby, written perhaps in late summer or early autumn, Dryden rehearses enough of the situation to give us an insight into one facet of the fatherly concern for his sons. Charles had been dismissed from school because of two minor misdemeanors, in one of which he seems to have been the innocent victim of a mistake. Having thoroughly investigated the occasion, Dryden was ready to withdraw the boy from school, but was restrained by his obligations to his school and to his old master. But even these loyalties did not prevent him from penning a criticism of the handling of the case.   The second son, John, had apparently only recently entered school as King's Scholar, and the letter suggests that he was there partly through the influence of his father's old friend John Dolben, Bishop of Rochester and Governor of the school.   He has found that John might have had "the first place" had Busby not opposed him for that honor, and the boy—so thinks his father—no doubt deserved it, because of his performance at the Election.   And Charles being but sixth in his class (according to Busby) may not stand a very good chance of being elected to the University.   Dryden wonders whether he should not go to Cambridge at once by Busby's consent.   The result of his complaint is not known by any document, but the affair must have been amicably settled, for Charles continued in school and was duly elected in the following year to Trinity College, Cambridge.[23]   In this brief glimpse of his domestic life, we find no hint of the atheist, the traducer, and the treacherous monster painted in the Whig pamphlets.

Religious Incertitude
1682-1683

The succession of libels against Dryden's character and reputation continued with unabated fury. In numbers and in virulence they attempted, by discrediting the man, to save the inconvenience of answering his charges. They have much in common, beyond their chorus of hate: they are generally dull, repetitious, and unconscionably long. Written in a shambling couplet form, they only rarely rise above common doggerel, and then only in single lines or couplets. Their collective ineffectiveness during these months of greatest strain resulted not only from the fact that the political ground beneath the Whig position was progressively being undermined by forces quite different from those exercised by the writers of lampoon and pasquil, but also from the serious flaws in the tracts themselves. They failed for "want of commonsense." Now, when the height of madness had passed, and sobering second thoughts were to be the rule rather than the exception, the tract writers proceeded as if nothing had changed in the past three years. In 1679 almost any rumor, falsehood, or wild charge found acceptance among otherwise reasonable people. But not in 1682. The Whigs were writing too much about too little, and many of their complaints against Dryden were controverted by the public record available for all men to consult. Only the most factious, the most unprincipled, could have accepted some of the preposterous allegations levelled at Dryden. He recognized that animosities engendered by party controversy led men to say in public what they knew in their hearts to be false. In his *Vindication of the Duke of Guise* he tends to exculpate his antagonists for this very practice.

The autumn of 1682 found Dryden engaged on numerous ventures, some of which were not of his own making. On October 4, his lampoon of four years earlier on Shadwell appeared, apparently without his prior knowledge or consent, under the imprint of "D. Green," who has never been identified.[1] Its appearance at this time intensified the animosity between the two poets and before another month had passed, Dryden added more insult to the already badly injured Shadwell. The popularity of *Absalom and Achitophel* had been so great that a continuation of it seemed a reasonably good business venture. The astute Tonson apparently proposed a second part to bring the account up-to-date. Dryden, already engaged on *Religio Laici* and the negotiations for the *Duke of Guise,* declined, but suggested that Nahum Tate undertake it. When it appeared about November 10, it contained a section of two hundred lines (ll. 309-510), always, with good reason, attributed to Dryden.[2] The first hundred lines are taken up with satiric portraits of minor figures who had found no place in the original poem; the next hundred lines are devoted to Og and Doeg, the two prominent Whig poets, Settle and Shadwell. The incisive, devastating verses on Og and Doeg, full of rollicking good humor, Dryden never surpassed. To render them innocuous, to enforce their impotence as poets was his design; and he succeeded brilliantly. Both are "fools that crutch their feeble sense on verse." Settle is treated first:

> Doeg, tho' without knowing how or why,
> Made still a blund'ring kind of melody;
> Spurr'd boldly on, and dash'd thro' thick and thin,
> Thro' sense and nonsense, never out nor in;
> Free from all meaning, whether good or bad,
> And, in one word, heroically mad. . . .

Settle's stupidity receives full treatment; and what Dryden regards as his treason is treated lightly; for, incapable of thought, Settle cannot be blamed overmuch, because he acts only by instinct.

> Let him be gallows-free by my consent,
> And nothing suffer, since he nothing meant;
> Hanging supposes human soul and reason,
> This animal's below committing treason.

The ineffectiveness of his poetry, Dryden is sure, will reduce him to the lowest level of the writing fraternity (as in fact happened):

> The height of his ambition is, we know,
> But to be master of a puppet show:

> On that one stage his works may yet appear,
> And a month's harvest keeps him all the year.

In Shadwell's portrait Dryden repeats some of the familiar points already made in *Macflecknoe,* but enough new elaboration is added to make it a powerful portrait in its own right, without reference to the longer attack. He begins:

> Now stop your noses, readers, all and some,
> For here's a tun of midnight work to come,
> Og, from a treason-tavern rolling home.
> Round as a globe, and liquor'd ev'ry chink,
> Goodly and great he sails behind his link.
> With all this bulk there's nothing lost in Og,
> For ev'ry inch that is not fool is rogue:
> A monstrous mass of foul corrupted matter,
> As all the devils had spew'd to make the batter.
> When wine has given him courage to blaspheme,
> He curses God, but God before curs'd him. . . .

The opening section of *Macflecknoe,* which rehearses Shadwell's dullness, finds repetition here, in a somewhat different idiom:

> But tho' Heav'n made him poor, (with rev'rence speaking,)
> He never was a poet of God's making.
> The midwife laid her hand on his thick skull,
> With this prophetic blessing: *Be thou dull*:
> Drink, swear, and roar, forbear no lewd delight
> Fit for thy bulk, do anything but write:
>
> .　　.　　.　　.　　.　　.　　.　　.　　.
>
> Eat opium, mingle arsenic in thy drink,
> Still thou mayst live, avoiding pen and ink.
> I see, I see, 'tis counsel given in vain,
> For treason botch'd in rhyme will be thy bane;
> Rhyme is the rock on which thou art to wreck,
> 'Tis fatal to thy fame and to thy neck.

The brand of dullness and nonsense fastened upon the luckless Shadwell earlier Dryden takes pains to fix more securely, pointing out that even if he had used his pen to support the King, instead of traducing him, the result would have been satire. Looking back perhaps to the personal attack on him in Shadwell's *Medal of John Bayes,* Dryden merely says,

> I will not rake the dunghill of thy crimes,
> For who would read thy life that reads thy rhymes?

And he ends with the execration;

> But of King David's foes be this the doom,
> May all be like the young man Absalom;
> And for my foes may this their blessing be,
> To talk like Doeg, and to write like thee.

Dryden's sharp but good-natured execution of Shadwell's reputation left little more to be said at the moment, but it opened the way for another attack by Shadwell as soon as *The Duke of Guise* was acted, about three weeks later.

By this time *Religio Laici* was in print and was issued by Tonson about November 28.[3] That it was merely a casual poem of the moment called forth by Dickinson's translation of Father Simon's work on the Old Testament is refuted by Dryden's evident interest in the problems of religion and religious belief extending over many years.[4] Without doubt Simon's book focussed Dryden's thought on the ecclesiastical controversies at a time when he was intimately associated with the political manifestations of belief and dogma. Professor Bredvold has shown that Dryden was acquainted by long study and reading with "the problems of religious and philosophical certitude," and that the poem became his expression of "a mode of thought with which he had been long familiar," i.e., skepticism.[5] And, as we have seen, he had for years been aware of the controversies concerned with the principle of authority in religion. *Religio Laici* investigates some of the bases of religious belief, and through a series of propositions, with attendant objections, becomes essentially an assertion of the fideistic position against the proponents of reason. Concomitantly it recognizes that the private spirit, eccentric and unstable, must at length bow to some kind of official ecclesiastical interpretation and organization armed with tradition and authority. As a communicant of the Church of England, Dryden was adhering in his poem to many of the official positions maintained by the divines. The dilemma he faced arose when he sought the authoritative organization qualified to speak for the private spirit. The Protestant faith in England since the Reformation had been under continuous process of fragmentation; and the multitude of sects each spoke solely for themselves and reprehended every other. Over them the Church by established law exercised neither an ecclesiastical control nor a suasive influence: for obvious reasons, they were anathema to the Church. And the Church itself harbored such a variety of diverse opinion that it did not and could not speak with one voice on every item of controverted dogma. Dryden's desire now for an omniscient Church competent to pronounce on doubtful points of Scripture helps to point the way to his eventual conversion to Roman Catholicism.[6] Yet he is not willing here, nor was he ever to be content, to accept the political role, as separate from the fideistic, of the Catholic Church.

There seems little doubt that a powerful catalyst for *Religio Laici* was the political actions and affiliations of the Protestant sects during the preceding three years of civil controversy. This may be most clearly seen in the preface with which Dryden introduced his poem to the reader. He admits that he has received help in writing his poem from some of the works "of our own reverend divines of the Church of England," and he is willing to submit his opinions to "my mother Church, accounting them no further mine, then as they are authorized, or at least uncondemned by her." Here, as in the poem, he dismisses those who would prove religion by reason: they "do but weaken the cause which they endeavour to support; it is to take away the pillars from our faith, and to prop it only with a twig." Reason, he says, has only one thing to do: to allow man to see that God has revealed himself in the Scriptures. All beyond is the work of faith. But, as he knows, to assert that Scripture is the "canon of our faith," raises at once two enemies against him: the Papists because they have reserved the "right of what they have [of Scripture] delivered, under the pretence of infallibility," and the fanatics because they "have assumed what amounts to an infallibility in the private spirit." The latter have distorted texts not necessary to salvation "to the damnable uses of sedition, disturbance and destruction of the civil government." The Catholics, he thinks, are less dangerous to the state because their number is small and the penal laws are still in force. Yet he recognizes that most Protestants may believe in an uninterrupted plot of their clergy since the Reformation to regain "their fat possessions." His chief complaint against the "Jesuited Papists" is their almost universal opinion that "their infallible master has a right over Kings, not only in spirituals, but temporals." He calls the roll of Catholic writers who have expressed the belief that "the Pope can depose and give away the right of any Sovereign Prince, *si vel paulum deflexerit,* if he shall never so little warp." The other extreme—the fanatics—he attacks with even more vigor. He points out that since the Bible has been translated into English, the sects have used it "as if their business was not to be saved, but to be damned by its contents." Out of Hooker and Lord Herbert, Dryden traces the factious career of the sectaries, who "were born with teeth, foul-mouth and scurrilous from their infancy." And from Maimbourg (though "an adversary to our religion"), in the *History of Calvinism,* he cites evidence that where Calvinism "was planted and embraced, rebellion, civil war, and misery attended it." The doctrine of king-killing, espoused by only the worst party of the Roman Catholics, has been embraced and maintained "by the whole body of nonconformists and republicans."

In the poem he explores four current religious creeds: Deism, Roman Catholicism, Dissent, and Anglicanism. The first three he rejects. The principles of natural worship, or Deism, with its fundamental reliance on reason, was to him entirely unsatisfactory. Reason, he says, could hardly have produced a faith, else the ancients would have found it; reason indeed remained ineffectual until revealed religion "taught it." It is, essentially, revelation, and not the exercise of reason that has produced a faith. Reason, in short, was not sure enough for a guide. What, then, was? The Scriptures. They contain all that is necessary to salvation. This refrain runs through his poem and of course is the position of the Dissenters and of Anglican clergymen. But what of the much-mooted unreliability of the scriptural texts? Some of them may be corrupt, he admits, but one need not base his salvation upon those controverted texts: all the needful texts for salvation are plain. If some still distrust this surest of guides, they must fall back upon Church tradition, which has sometimes been used, especially by its priestly interpreters, to obfuscate. If some persons distrust and object to Church tradition, oral and written, they must retreat into the exercise of the private spirit. Put into every "vulgar hand," the Bible then becomes an arsenal from which men take the dangerous weapons of ignorant interpretations and vehement disagreement.

Having dismissed these three positions, Dryden proceeds to a somewhat anticlimactic, yet positive statement: points not clearly understood can be left alone; belief depends not on the will or on reason, but on faith in the clear and plain texts; if, after hearing what "our Church" says, we find our reason running another way, it is better to curb that reason than to disturb the public peace. His personal belief seems grounded upon Scripture and only those texts of Scripture necessary to salvation. Yet he is not entirely happy, for the dilemma tends to be compounded: even though his private spirit be learned, he still finds himself uncomfortably close to the schismatics, for whom he has never a good word, and far closer than he may at the moment suspect to the Papists, many of whose practices and beliefs he abhors.   From this point his road for the next three years will lead, we may suspect not without travail of spirit, into the Roman Catholic faith.   From occasional comments of Dryden in subsequent years, one may hazard a surmise that had the Church of England spoken more clearly and with a single voice, Dryden would have found the Church of his youth and middle years sufficiently satisfying for his later life.   But then perhaps it would not have been the Church of England.

Within two or three days after *Religio Laici* made its appearance, the *Duke of Guise,* earlier released by the Lord Chamberlain with a clean political bill, was performed by the United Company at the Theatre Royal.   Dryden's old company had come to an inglorious end during the spring and summer, and by the middle of November the joint company began to act.   Dryden's colleagues of earlier days had nearly all died or were in retirement.   The new company, even with two houses on which to pay rent to building investors, was to enjoy relative prosperity under the direction of Betterton.[7]   *The Duke of Guise,* about December 1, was probably the first new play put on by the combined companies, and its success seems to have resulted from the presence of many Whigs to damn it, and of the Tories to applaud it.[8]   Hardly more than seven weeks later it was in print (February 13), with a dedication written by Dryden (though also signed by Lee) to Laurence Hyde, the Earl of Rochester.   Here Dryden points out that the play had been absolved by the Lord Chamberlain of charges that it was a libel and a parallel of particular persons.   There was instead a parallel between the Holy League plotted by the house of Guise against Henry IV in France and that of the Covenant against Charles I of England and of the New Association of the Whigs.   The railing of the Opposition he thinks of little consequence since he believes that "the tide of their popularity is spent" and that the King's triumph over his enemies, though not yet complete, may be discerned.

Immediately the Whigs went to work to answer this latest attack. On January 13, 1682/83, a tract by Thomas Hunt had been registered, *A Defence of the Charter,* which was re-registered on March 12 as new material was included to answer Dryden and Lee. On February 27, an anonymous tract, *The True History of the Duke of Guise,* was registered and was in print by March 3. And a third by Shadwell, *Some Reflections Upon the Pretended Parallel in the Play Called The Duke of Guise,* appeared about the same time. Neither this tract nor Hunt's attacked the play *qua* play, but animadverted at length on the intentions of the authors and their politics and personalities, particularly Dryden's. In reply, Dryden wrote at once his longest excursus in personal and political controversy: *The Vindication of the Duke of Guise,* which runs to sixty quarto pages and is one of his most skillful essays in this kind. It was probably published soon after its registration on April 2. Point by point he answers the allegations made by the Whig writers: he did not "seduce" Lee to join him in writing the play (after they had finished the *Oedipus* he had promised Lee to do another play with him); though the town regarded the play as Dryden's, he will not "arrogate to [himself] the merits of [his] friend"; the Whigs decry the play as *dull* entertainment: "that is a dangerous word, I must confess, from one of the greatest masters in human nature of that faculty"; the play was admittedly a Parallel, but was limited to similarities between the Holy League in France and the Covenant in England, between the Guisards and the Whigs; that parallel did not extend to persons, despite what the Whigs assert. Monmouth is not a parallel of the Duke of Guise, for "one was manifestly the leader; the other, at the worst, is but misled. The designs of the one tended openly to usurpation; those of the other may yet be interpreted more fairly; and I hope from the natural candour and probity of his temper, that it will come to a perfect submission and reconcilement at last." He has not lost his hopes for Monmouth's salvation.

The Parallels urged by the Whigs, in which they labored to show Dryden not only a detractor of, but almost a traitorous enemy to, both King and the Duke of Monmouth, tended to dissolve before Dryden's searching analysis. In Davila's *History,* he reiterates, are the historical facts which he molded to the contemporary situation. With a parallel to Charles, "neither the French history nor our own could have supplied me," he writes, "nor Plutarch himself, were he now alive, could have found a Greek or Roman to have compared to him in that eminent virtue of his clemency." And he adds dryly, "even his [Charles's] enemies must acknowledge it to be superlative, because they live by it." Though particular scenes in the play are cited by the Whigs as exact parallels to recent events, they, he points out, can hardly be so. Some are taken *verbatim* out of Davila; one scene indeed was written in 1660, and therefore if it is a *parallel,* it must also be a *prophecy,* uttered twenty years before the event. Another scene dealing with a revolution (in Act IV) he admits taking from Luigi Pulci. To the charge that the play was designed to stir up the populace, Dryden retorts that "it is the business of factious men to stir up the populace; Sir Edmond on horseback, attended by a swinging Pope in effigy, and forty thousand true Protestants for his guard to execution, are a shew more proper for that design than a thousand stage-plays." On the contrary, the "business of the theatre is to expose vice and folly; to dissuade men by examples from one, and to shame them out of the other. And however you may pervert our good intentions, it was here particularly to reduce men to loyalty, by shewing the pernicious consequences of rebellion and popular insurrections."

As a political tract the *Vindication* maintains those principles which Dryden had long been enunciating. He asserts again the inalienable right of James to the throne; he asserts again that Parliament has limited powers that stop this side of dethroning a king. As often before, he maintains that the Whigs continuously advocate treason and that it is only Charles's clemency that has saved them; and he ventures, on his own, into prophecy: "No more enemies are to be bought off with places and preferments; the trial which has been made in two Kings' reigns will warn the family from so fruitless and dangerous an expedient." He is confident, as were most people in March, 1682/83, that the Whigs were defeated. Shaftesbury had fled to Holland, where he had died in January: "I have no quarrel," Dryden wrote, "to his memory . . . ; he is now before another Judge." With some confidence Dryden could conclude his tract by asserting that

their party moulders both in town and country; for I will not suspect that there are any of them left in Court. Deluded well-meaners come over out of honesty, and small offenders out of common discretion or fear. None will shortly remain with them but men of desperate fortunes, or enthusiasts; those who dare not ask pardon, because they have transgressed beyond it, and those who gain by confusion, as thieves do by fires; to whom forgiveness were as vain as a reprieve to condemned beggars, who must hang without it, or starve with it.

But the *Vindication* is more than a political tract; it is also a personal defense of Dryden's own long-established principles and of his character. His certainty that Shadwell was one of the authors of the *Reflections* led Dryden to answer him in detail and to expose again the fat poet's dullness, chicanery, and espousal of treasonable

principles and actions.   To the Reflector's charge that he has ar-
rogated to himself the whole of the play—to Lee's hurt—Dryden
replies with some heat.   He calls to witness the players at the theater
"that in all the rehearsals I never pretended to any one scene of
Mr. Lee's, but did him all imaginable right in his title to the greater
part of it."   In fact, he hints that far from blasting other mens' reputations he has on occasion even assisted the beginnings of some of the
very men who are so violent against him.   Particularly irritating is
the imputation repeated in *Reflections* from *The Medal of John
Bayes* that he has acted the part of an ingrate to the Duke and
Duchess of Monmouth, and has repaid their early kindnesses to him
by severe detraction.   He admits their favor, and that it was not
greater was not their unwillingness to grant, but his own backward-
ness in asking.   In view of our present knowledge of his financial
relations with the King's Treasury, we can easily believe the truth
and the sincerity of the justificatory passage which follows:

If I am a mercenary scribbler, the Lords Commissioners of the Treasury
best know. I am sure they have found me no importunate solicitor; for
I know myself I deserved little, and therefore have never desired much.
I return that slander with just disdain on my accusers: it is for men who
have ill consciences to suspect others; I am resolved to stand or fall with
the cause of my God, my King, and Country; never to trouble myself for
any railing aspersions which I have not deserved; and to leave it as a
portion to my children—that they had a father who durst do his duty,
and was neither covetous nor mercenary.

As little am I concerned at that imputation of my back-friends, that
I have confessed myself to be put on to write as I do. If they mean this
play in particular, that is notoriously proved against them to be false.
For the rest of my writings, my hatred of their practices and principles
was cause enough to expose them, as I have done, and will do more. I
do not think as they do, for if I did, I must think treason; but I must
in conscience write as I do, because I know, which is more than thinking,
that I write for a lawful established government, against anarchy, innovation, and sedition.

Other aspects of personal vilification Dryden affects not to be concerned with: the "noble name of Bays" is "a brat so like his father
that he cannot be mistaken for any other body."   Current names
applied to adherents of both parties and regularly used as counters
in this serious business of political controversy, Dryden recognizes
for what they are:

As for knave, and sychophant, and rascal, and impudent, and devil, and
old serpent, and a thousand such good-morrows, I take them to be only

names of parties; and could return murtherer, and cheat, and whig-napper, and sodomite; and in short, the goodly number of the seven deadly sins, with all their kindred and relations, which are names of parties too; but saints will be saints in spite of villany.

The running battle with Shadwell is drawing to a close. As the King more and more asserted his authority, and as the Opposition mouldered away after the death of Shaftesbury, Shadwell had little more to say; and Dryden found more formidable antagonists in an area beyond Shadwell's ken—religion.

The *Vindication* may be seen as an interlude—if a necessary one for his personal satisfaction—in the midst of work of a different kind. The one allusion to Plutarch in this piece suggests Dryden's main interest during the early months of 1683. He was engaged in a bookseller's venture—the publication of the entire Plutarch, trans-lated by a large number of gentlemen who were for the most part vocationally apart from the writers of the age. The origin of Tonson's plan is uncertain, as is Dryden's connection with it. But the details, as it worked out, are relatively clear: the several lives were parcelled out to some forty men, chosen by Tonson, "of known fame and abilities for style and ornament." The entire work was to be issued in five volumes, "as fast as they may be conveniently dis-patched from the press"; and all lives were to be translated from the Greek text—"the first attempt of doing it from the original."[9] Dryden agreed to write both a Life of Plutarch, for an introduction, and a dedication addressed to the Duke of Ormond. The first volume of the ambitious work, which finally included translations of forty men, was in print before May 2, when it was advertised in *The Observator*.

Both the dedication and the Life, frequently overlooked, are worth noting, for they show Dryden at his best in commenting upon men and events. His rare ability to infuse the breath of life into the derivative and otherwise sober materials of seventeenth-century com-mentators on the classics may be found in the Life of Plutarch. He not only illuminates the character of Plutarch and his importance among his peers in antiquity but also enlarges on the practical uses of history in its various branches. Rualdus, Vossius, and other editors and commentators are relied upon—and sufficiently acknowledged—for facts; but if Plutarch comes clear to the reader of 1683, the credit is to Dryden's discernment, his selection of detail, and his sprightly prose that by its tempo, its similitudes, and its allusive power speaks in an idiom unparalleled in its time.

Excerpted portions do little justice to the whole; they can merely suggest the variety and the tone of his work. "Like a true philosopher, Plutarch," he says, "minded things, not words," and consequently "strove not even to cultivate his mother tongue with any exactness." Nor during his life in Italy did he attempt to learn Latin, but only the names of things, "just as Adam (setting aside Divine illumination,) called the creatures by their proper names by first understanding their natures." Indeed Plutarch, he seems to believe, was much like his fellow countrymen, who wrote their Latin histories in Greek to show their contempt for Latin, "as Frenchmen now do of English, which they disdain to speak while they live among us." In referring to Plutarch's lack of dogmatism and his moderation, Dryden points out that in this he "opposed the two extremes of the Epicurean and Stoick sects . . . because they pretend too much to certainty in their dogmas, and to impose them with too great arrogance." Though he in temper inclined to skepticism himself, Dryden could still say: "The Pyrrhonians, or grosser sort of Skepticks, who bring all certainty in question, and startle even at the notions of common sense, appeared as absurd to him [Plutarch] on the other side; for there is a kind of positiveness in granting nothing to be more likely on one part than on another. . . ." His comments on Plutarch's religion remind us that Dryden is in the period of *Religio Laici,* and that his thoughts continue to be taken up with the problems which he surveyed in that poem. Plutarch's religion, he says, was heathen, though not polytheistic; for "I have ever thought that the wise men in all ages have not much differed in their opinions of religion; I mean as it is grounded on human reason: for reason, as far as it is right, must be the same in all men; and truth being but one, they must consequently think in the same train." He reflects that no doubt Socrates, Plato, and Plutarch postulated "One Supreme Intellectual Being, which we call God." He knows that Plutarch was no Christian, yet he finds no evidence that he ever spoke "with contumely of our religion like the other writers of his age, and those who succeeded him." Faith, arrived at through the Christian revelation, which is part of the poet's heritage, was denied to Plutarch:

But we need not wonder that a philosopher was not easy to embrace the divine mysteries of our faith. A modern God, as our Saviour was to him, was of hard digestion to a man, who probably despised the vanities and fabulous relations of all the old. Besides, a crucified Saviour of mankind; a doctrine attested by illiterate disciples; the author of it a Jew, whose nation at that time was despicable, and his doctrine but an innovation among that despised people, to which the learned of his own country gave no credit, and which the magistrates of his nation punished with an ignominous death; the scene of his miracles acted in an obscure corner of the world; his being from eternity, yet born in time; his resurrection and ascension; these, and many more particulars, might easily choke the faith of a philosopher, who believed no more than what he could deduce from the principles of nature; and that too with a doubtful academical assent, or rather an inclination to assent to probability, which he judged was wanting in this new religion. These circumstances considered, though they plead not an absolute invincible ignorance in his behalf, yet they amount at least to a degree of it; for either he thought them not worth weighing, or rejected them when weighed; and in both cases he must of necessity be ignorant, because he could not know without revelation, and the revelation was not to him.

When Dryden extends his particular comments to a generalized statement about history, its writers, and its uses, we find again the exercise of a moderation which he so greatly admires in Plutarch. History he calls "a school of wisdom," which so informs the understanding that the future, within limits, may be read in the history of the past, "if we have judgment enough but to draw the parallel." But he recognizes another limitation:

God, it is true, with his divine Providence overrules and guides all actions to the secret end he has ordained them; but in the way of human causes, a wise man may easily discern that there is a natural connection betwixt them; and though he cannot foresee accidents, or all things that possibly can come, he may apply examples, and by them foretell, that from the like counsels will probably succeed the like events.

Among writers of history he can find none in Britain to compare with those of other nations. Even though he could—in the preface to *Religio Laici*—anathematize George Buchanan, he finds him, by the purity of his Latin, and his learning, and "all other endowments belonging to an historian," among the greatest, "if he had not too much leaned to prejudice, and too manifestly declared himself a party of a cause, rather than a historian of it." Except for that, "our isle may justly boast in him a writer comparable to any of the moderns, and excelled by few of the ancients." Party differences seldom warped Dryden from an honest critical appraisal of literary worth and a generosity of statement in making it public.

The dedication of the *Lives* Dryden addressed to the Duke of Ormond, whom he had celebrated at some length in *Absalom and Achitophel* under the name of Barzillai. Among the most loyal of the King's supporters, Ormond was now seventy-three years of age, and his public service was virtually at an end. As Lord Lieutenant of Ireland for many years, he had served Charles with distinction and had survived attempts of the Whigs to destroy him. It was fitting that Dryden should use part of the dedication for comment on the contemporary political and religious situation, and it comes as no surprise to discover a restatement of his principles. His consistent refrain is skillfully introduced: from a graceful tribute to Ormond's administration of affairs in Ireland it becomes an easy step to point out that Ireland and England, rebellious in the reign of Charles I, had since taken separate paths. Ireland had truly repented, but England "had suffered a relapse. . . . The sons of guilty fathers there have made amends for the disloyalty of their families; but here the descendents of pardoned rebels have only waited their time to copy the wickedness of their parents, and if possible, to outdo it . . . they are still speculative traitors." He proceeds to an excoriation of the two large groups who to him were the real enemies of a settled government and of a peaceful life for Englishmen: the fanatics, who derive their authority from the Bible, and the "broad republicans," that is, the reformers of church and state. The fanatics "arrogate to themselves the right of disposing the temporal power according to their pleasure . . . so that the same reasons and scriptures which are urged by popes for the deposition of princes, are produced by sectaries for altering the succession." The Commonwealth men —those "broad republicans," Christians only in name—"are so wicked, that they conclude there is no sin." In this they contrast sharply with the sectaries, whose pride convinces them that they cannot sin. "Lewdness, rioting, cheating, and debauchery are . . . [the] work-a-day practice" of the republicans, and these men are the patrons of the sectaries. But both know each other: the republicans "are satisfied that the schismaticks are hypocrites, and the schismaticks are assured that the republicans are atheists." The chains that link them are their common principles of government: "both hold Kings to be creatures of their own making, and by inference to be at their own disposing."

"It is an age," he reminds Ormond, "which is only fit for satire, and the sharpest I have shall never be wanting to lance its villanies, and its ingratitude to the government." He had already lanced some of the villainies, and he would do more again. The constant iteration of his principles, in poetry, prose, and drama, should leave us in no doubt where Dryden stood. His position resulted not from any expectation of reward or from an opportunism epidemic in his time, but from a conservative turn of mind that sought moderation, a compromise for man's peace of mind. His reading of history warned him of ills to come unless proper choices were made. That he supported a ruling family who within five years would be discredited and driven out in no way invalidates his principles or his honesty.

Variety of Ways
1683-1685

ALTHOUGH the head of the Whig faction had died a natural death in exile, the body, like a decapitated snake, still showed signs of vigorous life. On June 12, 1683, the Rye House Plot was revealed. This was no Popish Plot, but a grand Protestant design to take direct action against Charles, James, and the members of their government on their return from Newmarket. Only a fortuitous fire, which led to their early departure, frustrated the plan to assassinate the whole group and to seize the government. The arrest of Ramsey and West and their subsequent testimony that involved, among others, Essex, Lord Russell, and Sidney, marked the beginning of the end. Yet Dryden's fears of the potency of faction were not, as this latest uprising demonstrated, entirely ungrounded. Because of the constant attack on him by the Whig writers, it might be supposed that they found him a dangerous antagonist. But even among the outcries of his enemies, some voices were beginning to be raised for him. "Sharp and noble Dryden," he was to T. Wood, the author of *Juvenalis Redivivus,* published in the summer; and in *Agathocles, The Sicilian Tyrant,* Thomas Hoy could pay tribute to the poet's genius in *Absalom and Achitophel.* Later in the year Charles Blount lent his voice to the chorus of praise in his *Religio Laici written in a letter to John Dryden.* During the week of the turmoil caused by the revelations of the Rye House, Evelyn records attending a dinner at the Earl of Sunderland's, where, among a large group of noble guests, Dryden found a place.[1] He still had friends, and some were in high station.

The threat posed by the incipient rebellion of the Rye House plotters moved the King to vigorous counterattack, one facet of which was "to command" his historiographer to turn into English Maimbourg's *History of the League*. Since Dryden for months had already exposed, in drama, and in verse and prose, the close parallels between the French League and the English Covenant and New Association, his contribution on this score might be supposed to have been sufficient. But probably the King desired a somewhat more authoritative account put formally before his people during the centenary year, 1684, of his grandfather's struggle against the House of Guise. At any rate, by August, Dryden was preparing to translate Maimbourg. To do a competent piece of work, however, he needed both leisure and release from financial distress, which had become deeper with the passage of every month. In his need for money he turned first to Sunderland, who may have promised his support. But perhaps he was too busy at the gaming tables, where (his mother complained in letters to Henry Sidney) he often lost as much as £5,000 in one evening. Failing to receive aid from Sunderland, Dryden wrote directly to Hyde, Earl of Rochester, the Lord Treasurer. Only six months earlier he had said that he was no importunate solicitor at the Treasury, and we can believe that he spoke truth. Now, however, he had a legitimate and thoroughly justifiable reason for asking, not for charity, but for some substantial payment on his salary, which for years had fallen deeper into arrears. In his request to Rochester he cites his "extreame wants, even almost to arresting, and my ill health, which cannot be repaird without immediate retireing into the Country." He pleads some merit for his services to the King, and says "I have three sonns growing to mans estate, I breed them all up to learning, beyond my fortune; but they are too hopefull to be neglected though I want." He asks for a half year's salary (£150), for a quarter's payment is only the "Jesuit's powder" to the disease. He reminds Rochester that the King and Duke look with favor upon him, and that the Earl is the conduit through which their favors pass. "Either in the Customes, or the Appeales of the Excise, or some other way; meanes cannot be wanting if you please to have the will."[2] He asks, that is, not for a position as collector of the customs—as has long been thought— but for a payment from these very certain sources of revenue.[3] He cannot go to the country—and it is now August—until he secures his family from want. Dryden's plea seems to have been partly successful, for on August 22 a warrant for only the "Jesuit's powder" (£75) was made out, but the money was not to be issued for more than another month; yet the promise of it must have allowed him to go to Northamptonshire to work on the translation of Maimbourg, and to recover his health.

At the same time, another project was on foot, in which Dryden had (or was to have) a share. Betterton, for nearly a year the manager of the United Company, arrived in Paris armed with a letter from Sunderland to the English ambassador, Lord Preston; this letter explained that Betterton had come at the King's command "to find persons capable of representing an opera in England." On August 25, Lord Preston reported to Sunderland that he was trying to help in this attempt.[4] Apparently finding it impossible to enlist the interest of French artists in the venture, Betterton met his old friend Lewis Grabu, who until 1675 had been Master of the King's Violins, and, as we recall, had successfully presented an opera at the Theatre Royal in early 1674.[5] Upon Grabu's return to France, Nicholas Staggins assumed his post; and Grabu left not only his position, but £675 in arrears on his salary.[6] We can only conjecture that upon Betterton's overtures to bring him to England for the purpose of composing operas, Grabu reminded him of the King's debt to him and insisted upon some guarantees. After Betterton assured him that the King would provide a pension and his personal protection, Grabu agreed to return. Manager and composer thus assured, it remained only to secure the librettist, or perhaps he had already been secured by virtue of his position as poet laureate. At any rate, Dryden within the next year was to work closely with these two to write a completely integrated operatic performance.

Of more immediate concern to Dryden during his sojourn in the country were the translation of Maimbourg and the preparation of material to be given Tonson for still another venture. The success of *Plutarch* may have suggested the launching of another collaborative volume, not a translation of one author, but a miscellany. Initial preparations must have been under way even before Dryden left town, and no doubt Tonson again made himself responsible for soliciting contributions from a number of persons, including Sedley, Mulgrave, Roscommon, Otway, Tate, Creech, Shadwell, and others. But Dryden was to be the chief contributor; and though we have no record of financial arrangements between poet and publisher we may assume that, in his great necessity, Dryden would have insisted upon a substantial payment. For his contribution amounted in all to twenty-six pieces, only eight of which, including *Macflecknoe, Absalom and Achitophel,* and *The Medal,* had already been printed. Among the remainder were many prologues and epilogues written years before but which had not yet been published. A few new poems seem to have been written for the occasion, though it is not possible to be certain. In this group may be tentatively placed the Fourth and Ninth Eclogues of Virgil, the Third Idyl of Theocritus, and the Nineteenth Elegy from Ovid's *Amores*. If these were really new, Dryden must have stolen time from the translation of Maimbourg to do them: both volumes were ready almost simultaneously. *The History of the League* was registered on April 2, and the *Miscellany Poems* on April 4; the latter was in print and advertised in *The Observator* on April 2; the former was advertised in the same paper for April 16, as being "in press." For some reason it was to be delayed until July 21, when it was publicly advertised to appear at the end of that week.[7]

This work, the translation of Maimbourg, which was to be Dryden's last defense of the King against his enemies, properly enough carried a dedication to Charles, and when Dryden wrote it, before April, the Rye House Plot on the King's life, and the aftermath of it, were clearly uppermost in his mind. The important members of the Council of Six were being gradually eliminated from the political scene: Lord Russell and Sidney had been executed, and Essex had committed suicide in the Tower. But some of the lesser figures had not been punished, nor were they ever to be. This latest example of Charles's clemency irritated Dryden, who was thoroughly convinced of the incorrigibility of the fanatics. He goes as far as he prudently can in reproving the King on this point. "Pardons," he says, "are grown dangerous to your safety, and *consequently to the welfare* of your *loyal subjects* [italics mine]." As one loyal subject who had constantly hazarded his public reputation, and perhaps even his person, by his vigorous attacks upon those persons who had not scrupled to attempt to kill a king, Dryden not unreasonably could feel that he is being exposed to a danger that might be obviated by sterner actions by the government. Frequent forgiveness, he is sure, merely provides encouragement to the enemies: "they have the sanctuary in their eye, before they attempt the crime." If the experiment of clemency, as he calls it, were new and if it had not been tried without effect, "your loyal subjects are generous enough to pity their countrymen, though offenders." But when such pity has demonstrably only resulted in worse offenses, then "it is time at length for self-preservation to cry out for justice, and to lay by mildness, when it ceases to be a virtue." This seems almost a *cri du cœur,* as strong a remonstrance as an outraged loyal subject can make.

Though miracles have seemed to preserve the King thus far, "who knows how long the miracle will continue?" He views the storm as not completely over, for it is still gusty and "there is a kind of sickness in the air." Dryden is perfectly aware of his presumption in thus lessoning the King, but "zeal and dutiful affection in an affair of this importance," he says, "will make every good subject a counsellor."

The dedication, of course, was an integral part of his assignment, but the "Postscript," paginated separately, was an afterthought that doubtless held up for sometime the final printing of the book. Here he goes over in far more elaborate detail much of the same material that he had already used in controverting the opponents of kingship. Nothing has changed, except his tone; no longer is there lightness of touch, no longer many squibs of flashing wit. His style is full of iron; and his virulent attack carries a seriousness not hitherto prominent. Only one answer, he sees, remains possible to the factions: the utmost severity. Yet as this postscript was being published, the Stuart revenge was nearing its completion; and the removal by execution and by exile of many of the aristocracy had finally drawn the teeth of the insurrection.

The late spring and early summer of 1684 saw Dryden engaged in the collaborative effort with Betterton and Grabu to create "something like an opera" in England. Most of his part of the work was completed before he went to the country, probably in August, on what appears to have been a holiday with his two older sons. But it was not all holiday, for he had set himself a rigid schedule for preparing new poems for a second miscellany, which Tonson intended to publish during the late winter. The record of this retirement from London and his immediate plans are contained in a letter sent to his publisher.[8] He had gone for his health, but soon after his arrival, contracted a "Hectique feavor," which kept him down for a fortnight; his son Jack caught it and for some time they were "deep in doctors, 'pothecaryes & Nurses." Plans for the new miscellany had been completed sometime before his leaving town, and it appears from his letter that he may be acting as its editor. Agreeing to leave out *Religio Laici*, since Tonson's desire is now to include only new poetry, Dryden says that he is determined to "have nothing but good, whomever we disoblige." He informs Tonson that he has already translated four Odes of Horace and proposes to contribute "another small translation of forty lines from Lucretius: the whole story of Nisus & Eurialus, both in the fifth, & the ninth of Virgils Eneids . . .

[and] forty lines more of Virgil in another place." As it turned out, his estimate was somewhat modest. As he proceeded into Lucretius he became interested in turning more of that poet into English than he had intended. Possibly with design he put himself into competition with Thomas Creech, who in the preceding year had published a translation of the whole of Lucretius. At any rate he found Lucretius engaging enough to do extracts from the first five books, totalling 762 lines. He included the four Odes of Horace, one inscribed to Roscommon on his returning to Ireland (where he was destined to die almost at the time this volume came from the press, in January, 1684/85) and one to Laurence Hyde, the Earl of Rochester. He also dipped into Theocritus, whose "inimitable tenderness" he much admired, to translate the 18th, 23rd, and 27th Idyls. With the certain exception of the Horatian Odes, all of these must have been written during the late summer and the early fall.[9]

His thoughts were also on the theater and his plays which Betterton had already scheduled for acting during the winter: revivals of both *All for Love* and *The Conquest of Granada,* and "the singing opera," which may have been *The Tempest.*[10] Upon his return to London, Dryden was at once caught up in the final details of both the miscellany volume and the completion of the opera: both were ready by the beginning of the new year. For the second miscellany, or *Sylvae,* which was advertised on January 1, 1685, in *The Observator,* Dryden had written a preface devoted to an extension of his theories of translation, as enunciated five years before in the foreword to Ovid's *Epistles,* and a series of appraisals of Virgil, Lucretius, Theocritus, and Horace from the point of view of the perceptive translator. Having been caught up in the whirligig of political controversy for nearly a half decade, Dryden returned now to what he loved best; and the sense of release he must have experienced can be felt by the reader as Dryden expatiates upon the merits and shortcomings of those classical poets whom he loved this side idolatry. The preface to *Sylvae* helps to establish Dryden's greatness in English criticism. Here are demonstrated his depth of feeling and his range of knowledge, his breadth of taste and balance of judgment, his enthusiasm and generosity, the unfailing precision and illumination of his similitudes, the sophistication of his analysis of the single poet, his perspicuous comparisons and contrasts that "individuate" one poet from another. Like his own spaniel, he ranges through the ample fields of great verse and never fails to spring his quarry.

The standards for the English translator that he had set up in

1680 he repeats in the beginning of his essay, the most crucial of which is absolute mastery of both languages. But it is not enough "to give his author's sense, in good English, in poetical expressions, and in musical numbers; . . . there yet remains a harder task; and it is a secret of which few translators have sufficiently thought." This he reveals as the maintaining of the character of the original author. It is the purpose of his subsequent analysis of the four poets whom he has translated to demonstrate his method of achieving this distinction. Virgil he finds a "succinct and grave majestick writer; one who weighed not only every thought, but every word and syllable." He crowds his sense into such narrow compass that the result is a highly figurative language that requires (almost) "a grammar apart to construe him." Yet Virgil's "numbers are perpetually varied to increase the delight of the reader; so that the same sounds are never repeated twice together." Not so Ovid, who makes one sort of music and who despite his "sweetness" has very little variety: "he is always as it were upon the hand-gallop, and his verse runs on carpet-ground." For Dryden, Virgil remains the standard of great poetry: "he is everywhere above conceits of epigrammatick wit, and gross hyperboles: he maintains majesty in the midst of plainness; he shines, but glares not; and is stately without ambition (which is the vice of Lucan)." To his shame he has not been able, he confesses, to translate any part of Virgil "so well, as to make him appear wholly like himself." Indeed those who have called Virgil "the torture of grammarians might also have called him the plague of translators; for he seems to have studied not to be translated." And since Virgil is "so very sparing of his words, and [leaves] so much to be imagined by the reader," Dryden is sure that he cannot be properly translated into any modern language. Yet Virgil offered him a constant challenge, and in the fullness of his age, ten years later, he accepted it.

In turning to Lucretius, Dryden finds his distinguishing characteristics to be a kind of noble pride and "positive assertion of his opinions." He holds an absolute command over his reader and uses a "magisterial authority" to instruct him. His genius is daring and masculine, and from a fiery temper proceed a loftiness of expression and a "perpetual torrent of his verse." Lucretius' need to instruct often overrode his necessity to delight, and he "was so much an atheist that he forgot sometimes to be a poet." In order to maintain the dogmatic character of his author Dryden admits that he was forced to lay aside his own "natural diffidence and skepticism." But the pains he has taken with Lucretius he finds justified by the result, which pleases him as much as his comparative failure with Virgil embarrasses him. To Theocritus he attributes a primacy in Eclogues, because of the tenderness of "his passions and the natural expression of them in words so becoming a pastoral. A simplicity shines through all he writes: he shows his Art and learning by disguising both." These shepherds of Theocritus are from the plains and the cottages and speak a language uncontaminated by learning. Realizing the impossibility of transferring the sweetness and the rustic language into English, he has not even attempted to do so, for Spenser had only a dubious success in the *Shepherds' Calendar*. Horace, in his Odes, (to which he tries to confine his comments) differs in style from all other poets by "the elegance of his words, and the numerousness of his verse. There is nothing so delicately turned in all the Roman language." And Dryden sees in Horace a man compacted of "jollity and good humour"; these he has tried to copy: Horace's other excellencies, he admits, are above his imitation. An association of thoughts leads him on to speak of imitation, particularly Cowley's Pindaric way, which "languishes in almost every hand but his." And yet with due respect to Cowley he finds the full development of Pindarics still lacking, particularly in lyrical verse and finer turns. Imitation, he says, is a "nice point, and there are few poets who deserve to be models in all they write." His generosity and fairness evoke high praise of Milton, whose politics he thoroughly disliked, but whose poetry he ever found great:

Milton's Paradise Lost is admirable; but am I therefore bound to maintain, that there are no flats amongst his elevations, when it is evident he creeps along sometimes, for above an hundred lines together? Cannot I admire the height of his invention, and the strength of his expression, without defending his antiquated words, and the perpetual harshness of their sound? It is as much commendation as a man can bear, to own him excellent; all beyond it is idolatry.

Even before the publication of *Sylvae,* the new opera, which "attempted a discovery beyond any former undertaker of our nation," had reached the rehearsal stage. Its ambitious scope, however, was narrowed, as Dryden later tells us, because of "some intervening accidents." Betterton, Grabu, and Dryden, proceeding under the encouragement of Charles, who had gone to some lengths to prepare for the importation of French opera, may have taken his interest as a royal command and as an earnest of his willingness to underwrite the cost. After what may have been a commitment by the King to Grabu, in order to attract the French composer to England, the group may reasonably have expected the continuation of his tangible support for the plan. Contemporary comment tends to support the view that the tremendous cost of the undertaking may have forced a change in plan. Edward Bedingfield writing on January 1, 1684/85, to the Countess of Rutland records that the company "advances 4000 £ on the opera" and that in consequence admission prices will be much higher than usual.[11] And contemporary verses suggest that "infallible Tom" made a blunder, and that perhaps as a result the members of the company had been subject to a forced contribution to make up some of the cost of the stunning scenes and devices which appear in the truncated version, as we know it under the title of *Albion and Albanius*. Using the original introduction, Dryden added two more acts to round out the allegorical presentation of Charles's triumph over Shaftesbury and the Whigs and his "second Restoration." It was rehearsed several times before the King, who found the music and the entire performance excellent.[12] The mounting of it, however, required much time, and before it was ready for public presentation, Charles died suddenly on February 6. The little plans of the comedians were all but forgotten in readjustments occasioned by the unexpected and devastating event of the King's death. Albion was dead; but Albanius lived to assume the throne which had been saved for him, partly by the efforts of the poet laureate and historiographer royal.

Convert to Rome

1685–1686

THE DEATH of Charles II affected Dryden deeply. From the day in 1660 when the King set his feet again on English soil Dryden had celebrated his virtues in prose and in verse. For eighteen years he had served as poet laureate to him, and for fifteen, as historiographer royal. During the years of greatest crisis in Charles's reign he had used his talents to support the royal position; and at the hazard of his person and his reputation he had, from principle, fought for monarchy against those whom he viewed as intent on establishing a commonwealth. In an age of materialistic self-seeking, Dryden's diffidence, and no doubt a devotion to belle-lettres, which is never calculated to bring wealth, prevented him from accumulating even the worldly substance that would allow him to move without embarrassment among companions of school and college years or among his wife's relatives. His rewards had been meager in the extreme. Not as well provided for as were many on the King's list, he was given a salary of £200 per year, graciously increased to £300 by Charles in 1677. Had it ever been regularly paid in full, and added to his earnings from his plays and the rents from his small estate, he might have been able to live on a scale somewhat above that of genteel poverty to which he was condemned, especially after he severed relations with the Theatre Royal in 1678. But as the years passed, arrears on his salary mounted; and by the time Charles died, they totalled £1,075. There can be little doubt that both he and his family suffered financial distress, which worsened as the years passed. Upon the accession of James in February, 1684/85, Dryden could hardly have expected better treatment in this respect than he had enjoyed, but it would have been only human for him to hope that the arrears on his salary might somehow be paid.

On February 14, Charles was carried to his grave under a velvet canopy, and mourning for him was mixed with speculation about the course to be taken by the new King, whose throne had been saved by a narrow margin. James's first announcement to his Council reassured most people of his good intentions, though they were unaware of his secret determination, supported by a stubborn will, to work for the toleration and the security of Catholicism in England. But his first words were to assure his people that he would endeavor "to preserve the government in Church and State as it is now by law established." Having a reputation for being a man of his word, James thus was able to begin well, and his early call for a new Parliament, since none had sat for four years, augured well for a period of internal quiet.

Dryden's first act was to pay his sincere tribute to Charles in a poetic memorial on his death, and in the same piece to welcome the new King. Hardly more than three weeks after Charles's funeral Tonson issued *Threnodia Augustalis,* a Pindaric ode in eighteen stanzas and the longest (516 lines) of Dryden's commemorative poems. But it is by no means his best. He reviews the last illness of the King, the apparent success of his doctors to save him, the relapse into death, the tearful farewell of his brother, his character, his patronage of arts and sciences, his triumph over faction, and the maintenance of "freedom," an English subject's sole prerogative. He reserves for James the praise due a loving brother and great friend and lauds him as a "monarch ripen'd for a throne," a warrior-hero who strikes fear into the hearts "of Gaul and Batavia," but who, above all, is a man of his word: "for him to promise is to make it fate."[1]

On April 23, St. George's Day, James and Mary were crowned, twenty-four years to the day from Charles's coronation. But for James, Dryden wrote no coronation poem. Changes in governmental personnel were of course inevitable, and the new King began by surrounding himself with Anglicans, like Rochester and Halifax, to lend credence to his expressed intention of maintaining the primacy of Anglican interest. Among the holders of places granted by Privy Seal relatively few changes were made. Dryden's patent, like all others, went through the process of renewal. On April 27, a royal warrant for a Great Seal was issued to constitute him poet laureate and historiographer royal, at the old salary of £200 and

£ 100, but without the butt of Canary, "that having not been allowed of late."[2] After the publication of the commemorative ode, Dryden and Betterton turned to *Albion and Albanius* to bring it, after the lapse of some months, on the stage. The intervening death of the King had not materially affected the allegory written before his death, and by an addition of between twenty and thirty lines at the end showing the apotheosis of Albion, Dryden made it proper to the changed conditions. It was finally ready for presentation on June 6 and began what might have been a distinguished run. But, on the eleventh, Monmouth landed in Dorsetshire to mobilize the peasants and others whom he could rally to his banner. *Albion and Albanius* was all but forgotten as the government moved to crush the rebellion: the musical allegory of the victory over faction gave way to the sterner realities of armed conflict to defeat this final threat to James. The end was at hand: Monmouth, captured within a month and his supporters cruelly and vindictively punished, was sent to the Tower on July 13, and to his execution two days later. Dryden could have reflected on his words written four years before: "there seems yet to be room left for a composure; hereafter there may only be for pity." Absalom, David, Achitophel—the main figures in his great poem were now dead. Threads with the past were being broken rapidly; and at fifty-four Dryden faced a period of change and uncertainties far deeper and more subtle than he could at this time hope to foresee.

Dryden's break with the Church of England and his going over to the Church of Rome cannot be specifically dated, but his final decisions were being made now in the summer and early autumn. His conversion was not a matter of expedience, entered into for ulterior motives of gain. It was a result of long thought and long study of the problems of faith. We have traced earlier his interest in the philosophical and ecclesiastical bases of faith, and likewise in the political connections that were inevitable in his time. In *Religio Laici* his survey of the larger issues which posed problems for him left him in a dilemma that could be resolved by only one step. The antirationalism that dismissed the position of the Deists as untenable (and this we noticed again in his Life of Plutarch) led him to a dependence upon Scripture and Christian revelation as the only secure grounds of faith. But he also saw clearly the results among Protestants of their private and unfettered interpretation of scriptural text: not merely a proliferating number of sects which could always find some text to justify their position, but also what was equally disturbing, the doctrines of civil disobedience—always justified by Scripture—which had produced the social and political chaos through which he lived as a youth. His angry feeling against the schismatics during the years between 1678 and 1682 was born in the earlier age; and his fear of the repetition of that chaos drove him to unrelenting battle against the destroyers of common quiet. To his conservative temper and cast of mind, the first fruits of individual scriptural interpretation, uncontrolled by any authoritative and un-doubted church authority, was innovation, which eventually led to destruction of an ordered political state and an ordered society. His own Church, as he came to realize, did not and could not speak with the authority that he wished: it was itself a schism, more parochial than the sects. As Professor Bredvold has said, "When he finally confessed to himself that the Anglican Church had renounced the necessary principle of authority, he went over to the Church which seemed to him still to possess it."[3]

The political background of Dryden's change can be ignored only at the risk of misunderstanding his eventual position. His hatred of the political action of the schismatics was matched by his hatred of similar manifestations among Catholics. But he came to dissociate the large body of Catholics from the Jesuits, in whom he found the same predilection for direct political action as he found in the Protestant sects: both groups could advocate the killing of a king if it would serve to impose their beliefs upon a people. He expressed himself more than once as convinced that danger to established Monarchy in England inhered in the fanatic Protestant sects rather than in the Catholics, whose numbers were minuscule among a large and highly prejudiced majority of Protestants of various shades of belief and conviction. Dryden was never fully convinced that the Popish Plot held any great danger, though he recognized a desire on the part of some Catholics to promote their religion in England; and he clearly preceived the political uses to which the plot was put by the Protestant left wing. But when the disclosures of the Rye House affair were made in 1683, his position seemed justified: the Protestant plot gave clear evidence of the lengths to which, for the second time in forty years, that body of men, manipu-lated by power-hungry leaders, was prepared to go.

Dryden's attitudes to the political basis of the Anglican Church are not so easily seen. In his early poems at the Restoration he had spoken of the destruction of the Anglican Church in the gen-eral holocaust of the rebellious times, and he viewed with approval its re-establishment upon the return of Charles. In *To My Lord*

Chancellor he had said that "wit and religion suffered banishment" along with the Prince, and his comments on Clarendon's role in promoting the Church's immediate rehabilitation are laudatory. He makes no mention of the Westminster Assembly or the Act of Uniformity. What his opinion was of the succession of political measures put into force against both Dissenters and Papists through penal laws of various kinds and the Test Acts we have no way of knowing. In *Absalom* he said that "priests of all religions are the same" and that the Anglican Church well understood the necessity of the "heathen priesthood" (no matter what the godhead) to espouse his cause "by whom they eat and drink." These random comments, to be sure, do not carry us very far. But after his break with the Anglican Church, he commented at large on the penal laws and the Test Acts, and though recognizing that not the Church but the politicians had promulgated them, he reprehended the divines for their approval and their acceptance of the fruits of these laws. But he was now among those discriminated against.

Another facet of his religious problem that has not often been examined is that of toleration. If skepticism was an informing element in Dryden's cast of mind and could lead him, as Professor Bredvold has shown, through the maze of thorny questions of a personal faith, it could also lead him to a toleration of a wide variety of personal belief—as long as it concerned the individual alone. He had said, we recall, that he "had ever believed that the wise men in all ages have not much differed in their opinions of religion; I mean as it is grounded on human reason." Socrates, Plato, and Plutarch doubtless believed in the one "Supreme Intellectual Being, which we call God." And he would grant the same concession to schismatics and Papists. He nowhere questioned their fundamental belief in a Saviour who is to be worshipped: his complaint against them consists almost wholly of what, as a conservative, he could not but deplore, that is, their pernicious doctrines of regicide and civil disobedience. If they will abjure such doctrines, if they will but keep separate the spiritual and the temporal, disturbance in the state will cease. In spiritual matters, he implies, a man may believe as much or as little as he wishes for his personal salvation; he may use Scripture as he pleases so long as it becomes no rule for another. What Dryden wrote during the Exclusion crises seems to bear the same implication. From the evidence of history and in the light of commonsense, he points out that neither a people nor a king is under any necessity to destroy the other who is of a different persuasion in religion: the two can live in harmony, if the spiritual and the temporal are kept discrete. The religious-political upheavals during his lifetime resulted from this failure of separation. He maintained that the succession of a Catholic king in England need pose no threat. If he tried to extirpate the Protestants, he could not succeed because of the checks and balances in the political organization. Yet he was well aware of the Catholic practice of interference in national politics, and if he relinquishes principle on this point, it was no doubt because he felt the Church was too weak to interfere successfully in England. Dryden's apparent move toward toleration, though not explicitly formulated, was in consonance with the slow processes of history during the century. When the settlement was reached in 1689, some measure of religious toleration found a place. And had Dryden been fully aware of the secret plans of James II, he could have cited his own words, written to assure him the throne, to forecast that Monarch's failure. As it turned out, his moderating words along with those of other conservative Catholics were not heeded; and the ruin visited upon them by the stubborn and intractable James, and by his feckless priestly advisers, helped to postpone complete toleration for a century and a half.

To many of his contemporaries, Dryden's change of religion inevitably represented only one more example in the career of a turncoat, of his veering with the wind of change for personal advantage. Yet Dryden saw more clearly than his contemporary detractors that such a move was fraught with inconvenience and even with danger. Public contumely he would expect, and perhaps even the loss of old friends. The first he received in full measure, but curiously enough he seems not to have forfeited the respect and attention of friends of years' standing. His enemies, as far as the record can inform us, were professional religionists, and secondary writers whose quarrel with him was not based so much on religious differences as on Dryden's position as the foremost poet of the age. No one knew more certainly than Dryden that the Catholic was a despised religion in England, and that the new religious community he now joined represented a very small fraction of the population. And since his conversion came so soon after the accession of James, it is hardly surprising that to many minds one became a sequent of the other, and to some, an acknowledgement of favors to come. This point of view must have appeared the ultimate irony to Dryden, who too well knew the hazard of a minor pension under a Stuart king.   Unhappily Dryden's reputation has long suffered from Macaulay's misinterpretations, which gained currency and belief for nearly a century through the repetition in the *Encyclopedia Britannica* and through Christie in the Globe edition of Dryden's poetry.[4] Macaulay's discovery of the reissue of Dryden's patent in 1685 in which his salary was listed as £200 and £100, induced him to decide that the extra £100 was in the nature of a bribe for changing faith.   Unfortunately, he did not search far enough to find the Privy Seal of 1677, which records the granting of the additional pension. On this failure rested for too many years the character assassination of Dryden in modern times.

Taken up, as seems probable, by the religious problems, the summer of 1685 found Dryden little occupied with poetry.   But by September he had agreed to write some commendatory verses for a small book of verse written by Anne Killigrew, daughter of Dr. Henry Killigrew, King James's Almoner, and a niece of Tom Killigrew.   The negotiations for Dryden's contribution are unknown, but it seems likely that the young lady's father was an old friend, who asked the poet for such a favor in memory of his daughter, who had died in June.   The book was licensed on September 30, and registered on October 2.   When it appeared in November, it carried Dryden's ode entitled "To the Pious Memory of the Accomplisht Young Lady Mrs Anne Killegrew."[5]   In the form of a Pindaric, the poem is divided into ten stanzas.   Conventional elegiac materials are combined with the utmost felicity.   Classical allusion, astrology, religion, Platonic idea, reminiscences of Milton and Donne mix with the usual praise of the young lady's birth, her family, her accomplishments in verse and painting, to produce one of the best examples of Dryden's supreme ability to weld disparate materials into distinguished verse and an excellent example of occasional poetry.   The usual elegiac laments of the survivor for the departed are metamorphosed into a stanza (IV) of personal, penitential acknowledgment of his profanation of the heavenly gift of poesy.   How far have we, he asks, "made prostitute and profligate the Muse/ Debas'd to each obscene and impious use."

> O wretched me!   Why were we hurried down
>   This lubric and adult'rate age,
> (Nay, added fat pollutions of our own,)
>   T'increase the steaming ordures of the stage?
> What can we say t' excuse our second fall?

Though we can read this stanza as a personal confession, we find no recantation: the atonement is to be for "this vestal," whose "Arethusian stream remains unsoil'd."

About the time the ode was being published Dryden became involved in a controversy to which he had no claim to be a party, except as a new proselyte to the Church of Rome. We can trace its beginnings only to October 2, when Samuel Pepys invited Evelyn to lunch, with the promise: "I have something to show you that I may not have another time." Upon arrival, Evelyn found another guest, Peter Houblon, a wealthy Huguenot merchant. To them Pepys displayed a document which was to become the center of an ever-widening controversy between Dryden and Stillingfleet, and which led the way to *The Hind and the Panther*. It was a copy of two papers of the late king, which King James (now about to make them public) had found in Charles's closet after his death. They purported to show that Charles had become reconciled to the Roman Catholic Church and had died a Catholic. To his friends Pepys related in detail the circumstances under which he had obtained his copies. Conversing with James one day, Pepys had made so bold as to ask whether Charles—as had been consistently rumored—had indeed been reconciled to Rome before his death. For answer, James took him to a closet in his apartment and extracted two papers "containing about a quarter of a sheet, on both sides written, in the late King's own hand, several arguments opposite to the doctrine of the Church of England."[6] Pepys asked for and was given copies of the papers. Pepys and his two friends were doubtless among the first to view them. Before the end of December, they were printed at the King's command, and to them was added a third paper by Anne Hyde, James's first wife, detailing the steps of her conversion to the Church of Rome in 1670.[7]

Appearing under the aegis of the King, the papers aroused concern among the Anglican clergy. On January 7, 1685/86, perhaps within a fortnight of their publication, Dr. Owen Wynne was writing from Whitehall to Sir William Trumbull:

You may have heard of and, it may be, seen the enclosed ere this: *a hundred* only were printed and given to the hand which ordered it. You will easily guess this is much valued by some men who run away with it as *the opinion* of the late King because found in his closet and handwriting, though it seems to be but that of some other d[elivere]d to the King.[8]

Warned of its imminent circulation, the Anglican clergy prepared an answer, so that by the time the papers were in print, a reply to the arguments was ready. It was written by Edward Stillingfleet, one of the ablest historians and controversialists in the Anglican Church.[9] In the meantime Dryden had formally accepted the discipline of the Roman Catholic Church. Evelyn reported on January 19, 1685/86, that the poet and his sons were said to attend mass. Very near this date, almost certainly in January, Stillingfleet's rebuttal to the King's Papers came out, entitled *An Answer to some Papers lately printed, concerning the Authority of the Catholick Church in Matters of Faith, and the Reformation of the Church of England.*[10] Bearing marks of rather hasty composition (which Dryden was later to make capital of), the tract voices the doubt of many Anglicans that the papers had actually been composed by Charles, questions their genuineness, and argues against the conclusions drawn from them. In the answer to the third paper, Stillingfleet draws upon all his resources in polemics to discredit the confessions of Anne Hyde and the reasons for her change of religion.

Whether Dryden undertook to answer it because of fundamental convictions or because it was part of his duty as historiographer, we cannot know. His role of defender of the papers against the *Answer* seems to have been generally known almost as soon as Stillingfleet's tract appeared. A hitherto neglected, but not unknown, manuscript open letter to Dryden offers ample evidence that Dryden was preparing an answer. Dated merely "Jan '85" (i.e., 1686), it is entitled "A Coppy of a Letter to Mr Dryden, occasioned by the Kings Papers."[11] The unidentified author begins: "Hearing, S^r, that the Laureat had undertaken the defence of his late M^ties papers, I could not be so wanting to myself, as not to desire that satisfaction from him, which I vainly expected in them. And w^thout doubt the powerfull Reasons of your own Conversion, being yet fresh in y^r Memory; to use them towards the enlightning my blindness will be an Easy Charity." In ironic and amusingly mocking tone, he continues:

the motives must be very strong that could turn a man so grounded & established in the Church of E and so far gon in the Protest Religion as Y^rself. For I differ much from those who think a poets head lies naturally to Theatric Devotion, or that his Purse inclines him to the winning-side. 'Tis therefore from Y^u, S^r I expect that information wch none yet has given me: & tis but but [*sic*] just Y^u should pay the first fruits of your Sptuall Endowmts to the King: and to be sure, every one is fond of haveing (if I may so speake) the maiden-head of so chast a pen in matters of Religion.

After a discussion of the main points of controversy in the King's Papers, (as the three documents came to be known) into which he draws much church history and also makes a reference to Stillingfleet's *Answer,* the author ends on a note of false apology: "Perhaps these low thoughts are oweing to my own Fogge; wch your Pen will dissipate with all the soundness & solidity of a Poet & all the moderation & calmness of a new Proselyte."

The appearance of Dryden's reply to Stillingfleet's tract was delayed until July, when it was issued by Henry Hills (who had printed the King's Papers).[12] Entitled *A Defence of the Papers written by the Late King of Blessed Memory and Duchess of York Against the Answer made to them,* it has curiously not in its entirety been given to Dryden: only the third part has been assigned to him. But there can be little doubt that he wrote all three parts.[13] *A Defence* is a superb example of Dryden's powers as a close reasoner and a skilled debater. He is quite aware not only of the identity of his antagonist but of the best methods to combat him. Conscious that he is a wrangler and engaging in a duel of wits, he more than once used a term from duelling to recall to Stillingfleet the limits he is setting on certain questions in debate. At one point, for example, he resists a temptation to attack frontally: "Parrying is my business, not thrusting now." But when the occasion comes, he thrusts with telling effect. Continually his rigorous exercise of logic in subjecting his opponent's language and intent to analysis reduces Stillingfleet's answers to nonsense and seems to make him almost an enemy of the faith he purports to uphold. Skillfully Dryden time and again avoids the trap of following his antagonist away from the question at issue, preferring always to do battle on his chosen ground. Had *A Defence* been recognized as Dryden's and studied as a document of importance to an understanding of his conversion, much of the uncertainty about his change of religion would have been settled long since. Suffice it to say here that Dryden's quarto of 126 pages completely supports the conclusions of Professor Bredvold, who unaccountably makes no mention of it.

To maintain his reputation as a controversialist, Stillingfleet was forced to reply, and within a few months he published the *Vindication of an Answer,* in which he quibbled over minor points, attempted to extricate himself from the untenable position to which Dryden had driven him, and having learned the identity of his antagonist, attacked the poet as a new proselyte to Rome. Dryden made no answer, for by that time he was at work on *The Hind and the Panther,* which contained a reply to Stillingfleet.

In the meantime, his services to James Stuart were being no better rewarded than those to Charles. Though his patent and his pensions had been officially renewed, they were not to be finally confirmed until February, 1686. Meanwhile, payments continued on the old basis. A payment on August 18, 1685, of £150 brought his paid-up account to September 29, 1681. This was the last payment on the old pension. The first on the new was made on February 20, 1685/86, for £150—a half-year payment to September 29, 1685. Nothing appears in the official record at this point to explain what was to happen to the £1,075 still owed him. Dryden was concerned about it; and through Sir Robert Howard he could have discovered that the Treasury tellers were examining all the pension accounts of Charles's reign to discover how large the total arrears were in fact. Once that task was completed, some official decisions about policy would be forthcoming. On July 7, 1686, Dryden received the news. Sir Robert Howard at the Treasury was directed by the Earl of Rochester, Lord Treasurer, to draw an order to his account for £358 6s. 8d.,

as remaining due him for the arrears of his said pensions computed to Christmas 1684 after making such a retrenchment thereout as was intended by his late Maty in his life time and is commanded by his present Maty in an order of Councill dated 16 Aprill 1686 to be generally observed and executed in cases of arrears of this nature.[14]

Dryden was given a settlement which erased two-thirds of the total amount due him. That it was a necessary retrenchment made it no more palatable, and he proceeded to appeal the decision. Perhaps on Howard's advice he postponed his formal protest until May 1687, when he sent a petition to the King, then holding court at Windsor,

praying his Mat^y to order the payment of the remaining part of his arrears upon his pension amounting to £716-13-9 besides the sume of £75 due from the Quarter from Christmas 1684 omitted in his present Patent.

At the Court at Windsor, May 24, 1687
Referre to Lords Com^s of the Treasury.[15]

His petition appears to have been denied.

Dryden and his wife were still living in the house in Longacre, where they had been for a number of years. Their three sons were in school, though each one completed or left his school in 1685 and

1686. Charles left Trinity College before taking a degree.[16] Presumably he returned home, where he found a place with Lord Middleton, one of the Secretaries of State.[17] John, a King's Scholar at Westminster, was elected to Christ Church in 1685, where he never matriculated. Perhaps he too made one of the Dryden household at this time. The youngest son, Erasmus-Henry on November 2, 1685, left the Charterhouse, having been elected to Oxford.[18] Yet he attended neither university; in 1690 he was in the English College at Rome. All of Dryden's sons—the oldest was now twenty—followed their father into the Roman Catholic Church.

During these months of late 1685 and the early months of 1686, the auspicious beginning of the new régime dissipated itself. Halifax, who had fought so valiantly to ensure the Succession, was dismissed from his office by James, for his rigid support of the Test Act. Rochester and other loyal Tories were daily losing ground. The large army, staffed with many Catholic officers, still remained in commission; and more and more James sought and took the imprudent advice of his most rabid and bigoted Catholic advisers, Father Petres, and Barillon, the French Ambassador, to the virtual exclusion of the more moderate counsels of the Papal Nuncio and the long-established, more conservative English Catholics.[19] When James demanded of the Parliament on November 9 not only money to keep his standing army but also the repeal of the Test Act, he met such a stubborn refusal that he finally prorogued it on November 20; no other Parliament met during his short reign. The suspicion that the King pressed for the repeal of the Test Act not merely to achieve toleration for Catholics but to put into key positions members of his own faith and thus help to bring about a Romanizing of England was widespread. The more moderate course of action to seek repeal only of the penal laws against Catholics, urged by the English Catholics, was not followed. During these months of deteriorating relations between the King and his people, Dryden wrote *The Hind and the Panther.*

For Church and King
1687–1688

T HAT DRYDEN'S conversion came as the result of a long and sincere quest for answers to his religious doubts seems clear. The *Omniscient Church,* which he had desiderated in *Religio Laici,* he has now found. "My doubts are done," he says in *The Hind and the Panther.* It would be difficult to cite any evidence in his published work hereafter to show that he ever regretted the step he had taken or that his commitment to the Roman Catholic faith was less than total. Writing a dozen years later to his young (Protestant) kinswoman, Mrs. Steward, he says: "I can neither take the Oaths, nor forsake my Religion, because I know not what Church to go to, if I leave the Catholique; they are all so divided amongst them selves in matters of faith, necessary to Salvation: & yet all assumeing the name of Protestants. May God be pleased to open your Eyes, as he has opend mine: Truth is but one; & they who have once heard of it, can plead no Excuse, if they do not embrace it."[1] Whatever reprehensions and accusations may be made on the change itself—and old habitudes die hard—no available evidence will sustain a charge either of insincerity or of personal self-seeking.

As he had devoted his full energies and talents to a defense of kingship against the attacks of the Whigs from 1680 through 1685, so now he devoted the same talents to a defense of his new religion. The tract against Stillingfleet's animadversion on the King's Papers was his first support of the Roman Catholic position in the series that ended two years later in the translated life of St. Xavier. The last months of 1686 and the early months of 1687 he devoted to *The Hind and the Panther,* his longest original poem, which included, among many other things, a confession of his faith and an exposition of his personal relationship to King and Church during the rapidly changing climate of 1686-87. He shared the fear of most conservative Catholics at James's injudicious actions and the irresponsible advice of his priestly advisers. On February 16, 1686/87, writing to Etherege in Germany, Dryden confesses that he has made his court to the King but once in seven months, and that Mulgrave (now Lord Chamberlain) and Sunderland seemed to have forgotten him. He hopes that James might emulate the idleness of Charles, for "my minde misgives me, that he will not much advance his affaires by Stirring."[2] Dryden at the same time was writing into his poem certain notes of warning regarding the probable outcome of James's actions. Yet it must be pointed out that whether through the excessive zeal of the proselyte, or a misplaced trust in James's reputation for truth, or a temporary—and inexplicable—suspension of long-held principles, Dryden put himself in the position of supporting the King's policies, even though he realized that some of his actions were extremely dangerous and illegal. Dryden's course almost paralleled—in reverse—that of many Anglicans who in these troubled months were to relinquish their cardinal belief in passive obedience by defying the King whom they had helped to put on the throne, and who after his destruction made their protest by refusing to take the oaths to the new joint Protestant sovereigns, William and Mary. By a different route, Dryden found himself on essentially the same political ground occupied by the Non-Jurors.

Before Dryden began his long poem he seems to have undertaken a translation of the first volume of the *Histoire des révolutions arrivées dans l'Europe en Matière de religion,* by Antoine Varillas, which had recently been published in Paris. Although Dryden's work was not to see print, there is every reason to believe that he had made a beginning on his translation. Tonson entered it in the *Stationers' Register* on April 29, 1686, under the English title translated literally from the French. Burnet thought Dryden had abandoned it because his own criticisms of Varillas had destroyed the Frenchman's credit as a historian. The reason, however, may lie elsewhere. The first volume of Varillas' work treated some of the heretical figures of the fourteenth century, including Wycliff and John Hus, and its relevance was therefore not so clear as that of other things that Dryden was concerned with. And Varillas, apparently not the most scrupulous of "historians," might have seemed to Dryden what he had called Buchanan—more of a party to a cause than a reliable recorder. More important to Dryden at the moment, was his poem, which like *Absalom and Achitophel,* treated in detail and at length conflicting points of view and in part attempted to "fix" a situation that changed from week to week. Though interrupted by illness, he pushed ahead on the poem as rapidly as possible, and by January 12, 1686/87, Tonson entered a caveat that "noe person enter the poem call'd *The Hinde and y*ᵉ *Panther.*" But it was not until April 11 that a license for its printing was secured from the Earl of Sunderland. In the meantime, however, James, on April 4, had issued the Declaration of Indulgence, which probably forced some changes in the body of the poem, as well as in the preface. It was not until May 27 that Tonson formally registered the poem. Copies of it were abroad about this time: a newsletter dated May 28 records that "Mr. Dryden is publishing a Poem called Ye Hinde and Ye Panther, by Wᶜʰ are meant ye Protestant and Papist."[3] By mid-July it was well known, and a burlesque answer to it by Montague and Prior, called *The Hind and the Panther Transvers'd,* was in circulation.[4]

The short preface Dryden attached to the poem includes only brief comment on the purposes which he had set himself, but that little is important. It was a time, he said, when "all men are engaged either on this side or that; and though conscience is the common word which is given by both, yet if a writer fall among enemies, and cannot give the marks of *their* conscience, he is knocked down, before the reasons of his own are heard." Such a plea for toleration must have proved fruitless, yet he puts it against the larger background of the King's recent Declaration of Indulgence, already, he says, accepted by many of the sects, who indeed should receive it thankfully and with due recognition that from such kindness is expected a return "in specie": "they should reciprocate it upon those of his [the King's] own persuasion." Changed conditions have mollified, though they have not changed, Dryden's earlier attitude to the incorrigible dissenters. He had now little choice but to embrace them, however gingerly, for he must have known the King's "kindness" to them was a political necessity to achieve liberty of conscience for "his own persuasion." In the poem already written, however, he found no necessity to blot the severe scorn of the "wolfish crew," and the tone of his reprehension is the same as he had always used. One of his original purposes when he projected the poem was to persuade the Church of England to remove the penal laws and the test, not we may think for benefit of dissenters but for the Catholics. As such it was a poem of special pleading. James's

exercise of his controverted dispensing power had obviated a portion
of Dryden's work. Lacking perhaps in his original plan also was the
defense of himself and of his change of faith, which he includes as
part of his reply to Stillingfleet's *Answer* to his defense of the King's
Papers and that of the Duchess. Finally he alludes to the two fables
included in Part III of the poem, indicating that he has drawn upon
a rich heritage of satire linked with the beast fable and that he has
merely "made use of the commonplaces of satire, whether true or
false, which are urged by the members of the one church against
the other." They are not his invention, he adds, but as old "as the
times of Boccace and Chaucer on the one side, and as those of the
Reformation on the other."

The Hind and the Panther is divided into three parts, each one
dealing with not always mutually exclusive aspects of the conflicts
of interests and differences in the beliefs of the two churches. In
general, Part I contains an introduction for the milk-white Hind,
now ranging along "in the kingdoms once her own"; a section on the
poet's confession of faith, along with his repeated abjuration of
reason; a roll-call of the factious sects—the "beasts of prey"; an
account of the origin and progress of the Church of England, some
of her beliefs and lack of church authority; and finally a meeting
between the Panther and the Hind, arranged by the former for "an
hour to talk." The stage is thus set for Part II, devoted at length to
varying doctrines of the two churches and especially to church
authority. Part III includes Dryden's defense of himself, animadversions on Stillingfleet and on the Latitudinarians in the Church of
England, the fable of the Martins and the Swallows and that of the
Doves, with the attack on Gilbert Burnet, the Buzzard.

In the account of the history of his former Church, in Part I,
Dryden introduces the doctrine of transubstantiation, one of the most
controverted differences between the doctrines of the two churches,
and one which underlay the Test Act of 1678, passed in order to
deny James his succession, though he had with difficulty been ex-
cepted from its application. The Hind remarks (ll. 410 ff.) that

> In doubtful points betwixt her diff'ring friends,
> When one for substance, one for sign contends,
> Their contradicting terms she strives to join

but without much success, for

> Her novices are taught that bread and wine
> Are but the Visible and outward sign,

Receiv'd by those who in communion join;
But th' inward grace, or the thing signified,
His blood and body, who to save us died:
The faithful this thing signified receive.
What is't those faithful then partake or leave?
For what is signified and understood,
Is, by her own confession, flesh and blood.
Then, by the same acknowledgment, we know
They take take the sign, and take the substance too.
The lit'ral sense is hard to flesh and blood.
But nonsense never can be understood.

Though "her wild belief on every wave is toss'd," she has been true to her king and has suffered because of her constancy. But Dryden finds weakness throughout the structure of her belief because of the lack of "innate authority" with respect to her own rebels, who using Scripture, which she admits she may mistakenly expound, reform again what was before reformed. After "all her winding ways" she slips aside "and leaves the private conscience for the guide." In Part II, when Dryden discusses in detail matters of church doctrine, he reverts to the attitudes toward transubstantiation and through the Hind says that the Test Act "has loos'd" the tongue of the Church of England and forced it to be equivocal on this point:

And, to explain what your forefathers meant
By real presence in the sacrament,
(After long fencing, push'd against a wall)
Your *salvo* comes, that he's not there at all:
There chang'd your faith, and what may change may fall.
Who can believe what varies every day,
Nor ever was, nor will be at a stay?

The Panther replies that

Tortures may force the tongue untruths to tell
And I ne'er owned myself infallible.

(ll. 603-11)

After the Hind remarks that "not only Jesuits can equivocate," the Panther admits that men may err, and taunts the Hind with that "wondrous wight Infallibility." In answer Dryden uses more than five hundred lines to exposit his attitude toward the Scriptures and the infallible interpretations given by his Church. Here, one may believe, are to be found the essential reasons for his change of religion. The "unfailing guide" resides, not in an infallible Pope, but in Pope and general councils, "both lawful, both combin'd." Doctrine on needful points as promulgated by these combined authorities, he thinks, has been so obvious, so clear that "no disputes about the doubtful text" have hitherto perplexed the "lab'ring world." Should any appear, new Councils must be called to make the meaning clear. The Anglicans, on the contrary, cannot presume to provide an unerring guide because they have set aside Pope, Councils, Church, and have allowed every man to be "his own presuming guide." This principle, he sees, has united every "jarring sect," and

> Where ev'ry private man may save a stake:
> Rul'd by the Scripture and his own advice,
> Each has a blind by-path to Paradise;
> Where, driving in a circle, slow or fast,
> Opposing sects are sure to meet at last.
>
> (ll. 695-99)

Yet where scriptural authority was cited by heretics in the early Councils, decisions were made not on recourse to Scripture alone but to the oral tradition, stemming from apostolic times. This unbroken tradition—from which emerged a faith before the written word appeared—provided authority for interpretation not found in Scripture alone. In the midst of the chaos of conflicting sects which recognized no one clear, accepted, and authoritative source of doctrine, Dryden turned to

> that Church [which] can only be
> The guide, which owns unfailing certainty.

This to him is the one Church "adorned with heavenly rays," which brings from antiquity the certain marks of majesty, to which neither the Church of England nor any of the sects can pretend:

> One in herself, not rent by schism, but sound,
> Entire, one solid shining diamond;
> Not sparkles shatter'd into sects like you:
> One is the Church, and must be to be true
> One central principle of unity.

Besides Unity, the other marks of majesty which he cites are Sanctity:

> None but she, th' insulting rage
> Of heretics oppos'd from age to age.

Still when the giant-brood invades her throne
She stoops from heav'n, and meets 'em halfway down,
And with paternal thunder vindicates her crown;

Catholicity:

The gospel-sound diffus'd from pole to pole,
When winds can carry, and where waves can roll;
The selfsame doctrine of the sacred page
Convey'd to ev'ry clime, in ev'ry age;

and Apostolicity:

A limpid stream drawn from the native source;
Succession lawful in a lineal course.[5]

The impassioned discourse of the Hind leaves the Panther mute.

The last division of the poem is the most diffuse, for it lacks the unifying elements of the first two. As he had said in the preface, it had "more of the nature of domestic conversation," especially in respect to the satire in the two fables, and in the sections dealing with his personal defense. Lest any reader should fail to understand the literary tradition his poem follows, Dryden uses the first fifteen lines of Part III to spell it out:

Much malice mingled with a little wit,
Perhaps, may censure this mysterious writ;
Because the Muse has peopled Caledon
With Panthers, Bears, and Wolves, and beasts unknown,
As if we were not stock'd with monsters of our own.
Let Æsop answer, who has set to view
Such kinds as Greece and Phrygia never knew;
And Mother Hubbard in her homely dress,
Has sharply blam'd a British Lioness,
That queen, whose feast the factious rabble keep,
Expos'd obscenely naked and asleep.
Led by those great examples, may not I
The wanted organs of their words supply?
If men transact like brutes, 'tis equal then
For brutes to claim the privilege of men.

But even with such a clear-cut statement, some found the theological discussions between two beasts ridiculous; and the bright burlesquers, Montague and Prior, thought it "monstrous . . . to make a *priest* of a *hind*, and a *parson* of a *panther* . . . disputing with all the

formalities of the school."[6] Dryden's defense of himself follows an
attack upon the "sons of latitude," whom he finds by "far the worst
of your [Panther's] pretended race."   Close to Calvinism, the
Latitudinarians—and he no doubt has in mind chiefly Stillingfleet
and Burnet—have intruded themselves "in your line" with material
gains in view, specifically "fat bishoprics."   The Panther replies that
"some sons of mine" have "sharply tax'd your converts" with following "you for miracles of bread."   To this charge of interest
Dryden addresses himself with vigor, putting into the Hind's discourse a ringing denial of the accusation of self-interest:

> Now for my converts, who, you say, unfed,
> Have follow'd me for miracles of bread;
> Judge not by hearsay, but observe at least,
> If since their change their loaves have been increas'd.
> The Lion buys no converts; if he did
> Beasts would be sold as fast as he could bid.
> Tax those of int'rest who conform for gain,
> Or stay the market of another reign:
> Your broad-way sons [Latitudinarians] would never
>   be too nice
> To close with Calvin, if he paid their price.
>   (ll. 1515-24)

My sons (that is, Dryden), she goes on, pay small attendance at the
Lion's (James's) court, do not rise with early crowds or flatter
late; they only wait silently and do not actively seek anything.   The
Hind waxes indignant that "with odious atheist names" the Panther's
sons label their foes.   An imprimatur, with a Chaplain's name, she
says, becomes sufficient license to defame.   This is a direct hit at
Stillingfleet's books.   After her outburst the Hind becomes more
quiet, and concludes this section by leaving vengeance to divine
powers:

> If joys hereafter must be purchas'd here
> With loss of all that mortals hold so dear,
> Then welcome infamy and public shame,
> And, last, a long farewell to worldly fame.
>
> .   .   .   .
>
> Down then, thou rebel, never more to rise,
> And what thou didst, and dost, so dearly prize
> That fame, that darling fame, make that thy sacrifice.

'Tis nothing thou hast giv'n, then add thy tears
For a long race of unrepenting years:
'Tis nothing yet, yet all thou hast to give.
Then add those *may-be* years thou hast to live:
Yet nothing still; then poor and naked come,
Thy father will receive his unthrift home,
And thy blest Savior's blood discharge the
    mighty sum.

(ll. 1575-91)

The Hind remarks that thus she disciplines a son whose "uncheck'd fury" would run to revenge, and turns to the Panther:

It now remains for you to school your child,
And ask why God's anointed he revil'd.
A king and princess dead!   Did Shimei worse?

The spotted dame, however, remained silent, glad that "none of all her fav'rite sons [were] expos'd."

To the Panther's wonder that "your converts come so slow," the Hind has a ready answer.   The reason is that her proselytes "are struck with awful dread" of the penal laws and the disabilities enforced by the Test.   Yet Dryden must have known that the temporary respite was the result of the King's illegal use of his dispensing power and that the best the Catholics can hope is "protracted punishment," since Parliament has been adamant in their determination not to repeal these laws.   In truth, his awareness of the dangers inherent in James's policy leads him to write a "timely warning" in the fable of the Martins and the Swallows—a tale told by the Panther upon the entreaty of the Hind, who desires him to tell what "sad mischance" befell those "pretty birds."   The Panther's introductory words may be read as significant of the poet's conservative attitude:

"Nay, no mischance," the salvage dame replied,
"But want of wit in their unerring guide,
And eager haste, and gaudy hopes, and giddy pride,
Yet wishing timely warning may prevail,
Make you the moral, and I'll tell the tale."

The fable relates the differences of opinion among the Swallows (Catholics) and the Martins (the priests) with respect to aims and procedures to ensure the health of their religion in such troublous times.   Priests of all religions are the same, Dryden had said, and

nothing in the conduct of the Catholic priests had led him to change
his feelings toward them. He thus describes the Martin:

> A church-begot, and church-believing bird;
> Of little body, but of lofty mind,
> Round-bellied, for a dignity design'd,
> And much a dunce, as Martins are by kind:
> Yet often quoted canon-laws, and code,
> And Fathers which he never understood;
> But little learning needs in noble blood.
>
> (ll. 1756-62)

At their head was Sir Martin (Father Petres), whose council of
precipitate action prevailed:

> His point thus gain'd, Sir Martin dated thence
> His pow'r, and from a priest became a prince.
> He order'd all things with a busy care,
> And cells and refectories did prepare,
> And large provisions laid of winter fare:
> But now and then let fall a word or two
> Of hope that Heav'n some miracle might show,
> And, for their sakes, the sun should backward go.
>
> (ll. 1821-28)

But Dryden was clear-sighted enough to know that the sun would
not "against the laws of nature upward climb." The result might
well be—as the fable clearly shows—disaster for the English
Catholics. He further seems to try to disassociate James from the
more outrageous aspects of the Jesuits' counsel. In this he was
clearly wrong. Yet when the Hind replies to the fable, the burden
of the argument centers upon the penal laws and the Test. A peaceful solution seems possible through compromise at this point. The
Test he points out is the weapon of the present age,

> Forg'd by your foes against your Sovereign Lord;
> Design'd to hew th' imperial cedar down,
> Defraud succession, and disheir the crown.
>
> (ll. 1997-99)

The effect has been to enlarge the atheists, whose lack of principle
allows them places in Parliament, and to disbar the members of the
King's religion; and it has also strengthened the sects, those foes
of the Church of England. The chief victims, as he views it, have

been Catholics.   The Panther is made to say that "conscience and interest" force her to maintain the existing injustice:

> The first commands me to maintain the crown,
> The last forbids to throw my barriers down.
> Our penal laws no sons of yours admit,
> Our Test excludes your tribe from benefit.
> These are my banks your ocean to withstand,
> Which proudly rising overlooks the land;
> And, once let in, with unresisted sway,
> Would sweep the pastors and their flocks away.
> Think not my judgment leads me to comply
> With laws unjust, but hard necessity:
> Imperious need, which cannot be withstood,
> Makes ill authentic, for a greater good.
>
> (ll. 2121-32)

The centrality of this issue is emphasized by the subsequent fable of the Doves and the Buzzard.   The role of Burnet (the Buzzard) in the intransigence of the Anglicans and their determined retention of these laws is spelled out in great detail.[7]   If Burnet in his later history of this period found it difficult to say a good word for Dryden, the reason may possibly be found in the incisive portrait of the Buzzard—"a theologue more by need than general bent," "more learn'd than honest, more a wit than learn'd," a man "by breeding sharp, by nature confident," "the most unlucky parasite alive."

The warning voiced in this poem, and issued in more official church quarters, failed completely to deter James and his advisers.[8] In the very weeks when Dryden's poem was making its first impression, James began his assault upon the stronghold of Anglican and Tory support—the University of Oxford.   Already, in April and May, James had brought pressure upon the vice-chancellor and senate of Cambridge to admit a Benedictine monk, Alben Francis, to a degree of Master of Arts.   They agreed to do so if he would take the necessary oaths; he refused, of course, saying that he had a special dispensation from the King.   James's hand-picked Court of High Commission eventually deprived the vice-chancellor of his position.[9]   But it was the Oxford colleges that felt the full force of James's policy and "by a series of arbitrary acts—James put three great Oxford colleges—Christ Church, University and Magdalen— under Romanist rule."[10]   In some quarters Dryden was mentioned as an active candidate for a college position. On June 30, a news-letter records that "a mandate is said to be gone down [to] Oxford for Mr. Dryden to go out Doctor of Divinity, and also that he will be made President of Magdalen College."[11] It was also thought that he might be designed for the Wardenship of All Souls. Nothing came of the proposals, if any were seriously considered, to make him a college head. Before the year was out, Dryden again lent his approval to the policy of James by permitting his son John to accept an appointment as fellow of Magdalen.[12] Such evidences of Dry-den's support of the illegal actions of the King gave his enemies ammunition for a new series of attacks upon him and his poetry, which beginning with Montague and Prior's *Hind and the Panther Transvers'd* in the summer of 1687 continued unabated for three years.[13]

As might be supposed, these fresh attacks concentrated largely upon Dryden the "turncoat." It was enough that he had removed himself from the communion of the Anglican Church and had embraced the discipline of the well-hated Roman Catholic faith. Al-most no effort was expended in assessing or in controverting Dryden's doctrinal arguments or in coming to grips with the central issue of Church authority. The writers of these tracts followed the examples of a half-dozen years earlier, and their purpose came to be identical: to assassinate the character of the aging poet. A Tom Brown could cheerfully assert that one clear and ready way to public notice and to quick and easy notoriety was to write a slashing satire upon the poet laureate. Not all, however, were actuated by this *pis-aller* of the second rate. Some, like one Mr. Fowke writing from Wiltshire to an unidentified friend, and already under deep prejudice, were some-what bemused and puzzled by Dryden's change, but not pleased. "The world," he wrote, "is ye most alterd [but?] Dryd^en of any man I know in it; from a declard patron of Atheism to a zealous C[h]ampion for Catholicism—from nothing to somthing (though next to nothing) is indeed a miracle, & as great as ever a Priest attempted. . . . I doubt not Mr Dryd. will be called to an act [ac-count] in good time, at his owne weapons."[14] The author of *The Revolter A Trage-Comedy acted between the Hind and Panther, and Religio Laici* saw him as "an ordained play-wright in the House of Prayer" writing a "rampant sermon . . . in Bully Rhime," a man angered and disaffected because his "native church/ Left his high Expectations in the Lurch." As the title of the tract suggests, the author emphasized the contradictions between the earlier Protestant

Religio Laici and the *Hind.* The charge that Dryden had sought and been denied a place in the Church again became a commonplace. But it was the assumed venality of his change that provided a convenient club with which to beat him. The author of *The Laureat Jack Squabbs History in a little drawn,* in reviewing the poet's course asserts that

> Gold is thy God, for a substantial summ,
> Then to the *Turk,* wou'dst run away from *Rome,*
> And Sing his Holy Expedition against Christendom;

and the anonymous writer of "An Inversion of Mr Drydens Answer to Sr George Etheredges Letter to the Earl of Middleton" was certain of the same self-interest:

> For now you are a Saint indeed
> For Holy Rhiming, holy Lying.
> A Saint in every thing but dying
> What if you sometimes fast and Pray
> Though gainst your Will I dare to say
> Gold can that Grievance take away.[15]

Indeed, the hunting was good during this open season on the laureate, and literary attacks competed with those on his religion. When Gerard Langbaine published his *Momus Triumphans: or the Plagiaries of the English Stage,* he found Dryden a particularly fruitful source for his avid citing of thefts in drama; and many of his citations of the authors and works which he found as sources must have caused some surprise to Dryden. But he had not the grace to say that Dryden often pointed the reader of his plays to the original authors and accounted his judicious use of them no plagiarism.

Although many severely criticized his religion, others were not inclined to let differences in religious opinion influence unduly their recognition of the poet. Among those were the Stewards of the Musical Society, which had begun in 1683 to celebrate with a musical feast St. Cecilia's Day, November 22. Forced to cancel the celebration in 1686, the stewards now came to Dryden to commission him to write a suitable song for the revival of the feast in 1687. The composer chosen to set Dryden's poem was Baptista Draghi, or "Signior Baptist," as he was popularly known, the organist at the Queen's Chapel. "The Song for St. Cecilia's Day," which Dryden wrote at this time may have been suggested to him

upon his reading of Spenser's *Faerie Queene*.[16]   Opposite the lines
(VII, vii, 12)

> When Phoebus self, that god of poets hight
> They say did sing the spousal hymn full clear
> That all the gods were ravisht with delight
> Of his celestial song, and musicks wondrous might.

Dryden wrote: "groundwork for a song on St. Cecilia's day."   Having already collaborated with Grabu on the music for *Albion*, Dryden knew, within limits, the effects that he could demand from the composer.   Draghi scored his music for a five-part chorus and for a string orchestra in five parts with the addition of flutes and trumpets in such passages as those in stanzas three and four.   Wind instruments were called for by Dryden's verse, and Draghi supplied them, for the first time in a Cecilian ode.[17]   The continuing experience gained in joint undertakings with composers served Dryden well as a preparation for his collaboration with Purcell in *King Arthur*.

While *The Hind and the Panther* continued to draw attacks, Dryden made preparations to move his family from Longacre to the newly laid-out Gerrard Street in Soho. Here early in 1688 he took up residence in the fifth house from the east end of the street, where he was to pass the remainder of his life.   The house was no doubt a considerable improvement over the place in Longacre.   For many years its assessed valuation ranged between £40 and £44, upon which he paid rates of 10s. and 13s. 4d. every half year.   Except for such aristocratic neighbors as the Countess of Macclesfield, the Countess of Suffolk, and Sir William Trumbull, Dryden had one of the largest assessments on the street.[18]   The tone of the neighborhood no doubt demanded a scale of living which the poet at this time could well enough afford; for his salary of £300 was being regularly paid.   The burden of heavy arrears under which he had suffered for years had disappeared, as we have seen, with the death of Charles II.

Almost coincidental with Dryden's changed family arrangements, with John intruded at Magdalen as a Papist fellow, Charles at home, and Erasmus-Henry preparing for a religious life and soon to go to Rome, the crisis in public affairs deepened.   The public events of the next half year and Dryden's personal course of action show with crystal clearness both his commitments and the dilemma in which he was placed.   It can hardly be supposed that his long-demonstrated

perspicuity had deserted him and that he now was unable to interpret
the meaning of events as they unrolled during these months. Having
already, in *The Hind and the Panther,* issued his own word of warning to James and his co-religionists, Dryden without question remained clear-sighted enough to read correctly the signs, multiplying
with every week, that the King and his flattering advisers had over-
reached themselves.[19] He could not have been unaware of movement of classes and sects to submerge many of their differences and
to unite upon a determined resistance to the Monarch's usurpation
of power. And from long experience of the London populace, he
knew better than most men that their violent prejudices against the
King were overmatched by their long hatred of his religion. The
re-publication of the Declaration of Indulgence, along with the King's
command that the bishops order all clergy of the Established Church
to read it from their pulpits, met the determined refusal of Archbishop Sancroft and his suffragans. They declared that Parliament,
not the King without Parliament, was the source of law and that the
King's suspension of statutes was therefore illegal. These churchmen
were high Tories, as was Dryden, and no less committed to their
Monarch. Like him, they had fought, in 1679 and 1680, to save the
succession for James, who now, provoked beyond measure, ordered
their arrest and prepared to put them on trial. On June 29, a great
throng gathered in the streets surrounding Westminster Hall, where
the case was argued. Two of the four judges, hand-picked by
James, instructed the jury in favor of the defendants; and on the
next day, the jury brought in a verdict of Not Guilty. The news
was received with great rejoicing, and at night bonfires in celebration
reflected the approval of the London populace.[20]

During these weeks Dryden continued to put his pen at the service
of his new religion despite the evidences on every hand of growing antagonisms. He was translating Bouhour's *Life of Saint Francis Xavier,*
which had been first published in Paris years before. What drew
him to the book in the first place and why he completed it during
the very time when James was bringing ruin upon all Catholics in
England remain unanswerable questions. Perhaps he saw in St.
Francis a dedicated spirit, the great missioner to Japan and the
Indies, a priest who contrasted sharply with those Jesuits who now
served as political mentors to James. By June the translation must
have been in press (it was advertised in the *London Gazette* for
July 13-16). On June 10, Queen Mary gave birth to a son, the
famous "warming-pan" baby who was to grow up as the "Old Pre-

tender." Dryden seized upon this opportunity to dedicate, in his most flattering vein, the *St. Xavier* to Queen Mary. At the same time he worked rapidly on a poem celebrating the birth of the prince. Entitled *Britannia Rediviva,* it was completed and in print within twelve days of the event.

Written in couplets and extending to three hundred and sixty-one lines, the poem contains a certain dignity but adds nothing to Dryden's stature as a poet. Its range is necessarily limited and its obvious political purpose strikes a curious note in the fateful week when it appeared. His extravagant praise of James is outdone only by his extravagant view that the "son of prayers" may "make us Englishmen again" and will join with his father

> To keep possession, and secure the line,
> But long defer the honors of thy fate:
> Great may they be like his, like his be late;
> That James this running century may view,
> And give his son an auspice to the new.

He further sees the "royal babe" as a "blessing sent you in your own despite" and proof that

> God is abroad and, wondrous in his ways,
> The rise of empires, and their fall surveys.
> More (might I say) than with an usual eye,
> He sees his bleeding Church in ruin lie,
> And hears the souls of saints beneath his altar cry.

Though he can poetically view the child as a pledge that might heal the widening breach between churches and parties, Dryden was well aware that it was too late for any such accommodation. And though he prays that after five months of "discord and debate" the remaining seven of the "infant's year" will be "prelude to the realm's perpetual rest" and that by living well and being humble, charitable, and forgiving, the country may repay God for his great gift, one feels that he speaks with a despairing voice.

The absence of any perceptive comment from Dryden on the large and crucial events of these months and of his relation to them leaves a curious vacuum. His almost determined insistence upon support of his religion and his King in works pitched in a minor key—and this in the face of the most momentous constitutional drama of the age—seems uncharacteristic of him. To explain his actions is probably impossible at this late date, but a suggestion may be advanced. For two years since his conversion, Dryden had doggedly devoted his talents to his new religion, which, there seems little doubt, he accepted with his whole mind and heart. Though his warnings to the King and his advisers had gone unheeded, if not indeed unnoticed, he seems to have been convinced that disaster was inevitable. In the prospect of total loss, no stirring of his could avert his ruin, in any case. And to give the lie to his enemies that he could easily be persuaded to change again he may have set his course in a direction of total commitment to a lost cause. With the certainty of James's destruction evident in all that was happening about him, Dryden could maintain a consistent and unwavering loyalty to King and Church and thus keep his self-respect; for no other course seems to have been possible at this juncture.

His services to the Stuarts and to the Roman Catholic cause, for whatever they had been worth, were at an end. Never again would he lend himself or his talents to either. And not again would he participate in any public cause. At fifty-seven he could look back upon more than a quarter of a century of consistent support of hereditary Monarchy. Despite the allegations of his enemies to the contrary, he had probably expected no reward except his own consciousness of loyalty to a principle. And he could also look back to literary achievements that he was sure posterity would not let perish. To the future he could look only with trepidation.

"Ruin" and Rehabilitation
1688-1691

T HE ACQUITTAL of the seven Bishops on June 30, 1688, gave final proof that the country was solidly against James and his policies. On the same day an invitation, signed jointly by leaders of both the Whigs and the Tories, was dispatched to William of Orange, to come to England with an armed force to take over the government, but with no offers of the crown. Financed by generous contributions from individuals of varying political and religious beliefs, William at once began his preparations. By September it was generally known that the feverish activities in Dutch shipyards were directed toward the invasion of England. The King finally took fright, and, in a last-minute attempt to salvage the situation, began to make a few concessions to public feeling which heretofore he had steadfastly refused. Within the next two months, for example, he abolished the Court of High Commission, restored some of the old city charters, which Charles had so carefully called in for remodeling, and he even courted University opinion by restoring the ejected fellows of Magdalen, in which process John Dryden, Jr., was dismissed from the fellowship he had been given only a year before. But James would not relinquish his dispensing power, and Catholics, including the poet laureate, retained their posts. In October, however, such concessions came too late. The sands were fast running out. Aided by a favorable, "Protestant" wind, William arrived at Torbay with his unmolested fleet in early November, and stepped ashore with twelve thousand troops on Guy Fawkes Day. The crucial weeks of November saw his triumphal, unimpeded march to London. Joined continually by Whig and Tory lords and leaders, William was assured of wide support. After a futile gesture of leading his troops to the field, James retired without a conflict to London in early December. The revolution without blood-letting was complete. By the eleventh of the month the King had stolen away, leaving his throne without a Regency, and his people and country to potential chaos. Rioting and looting of Catholic chapels and houses began on that day and continued (as Luttrell records) for at least two days. By that time a temporary citizens' committee took charge and restored a semblance of order. Dryden so far as is known was not molested, but he no doubt could have been prepared for reprisals: he had never treated the London mob with other than contempt.

The weeks following James's flight, capture, and second un-interrupted flight to France saw the rapid and immensely complicated remolding of English government and life in the Revolution Settlement. The election of the Convention Parliament, staunchly Protestant, settled first the question of the throne, which was declared "vacant." This conclusion ignored the principle of hereditary right as it ignored the existence of the "son of prayers," born on June 10. But though it enabled both Whigs and Tories to agree to accept William and Mary as joint monarchs, it failed to please many who could not and would not agree to the semantic juggling of the word "vacant." Some churchmen who maintained in this crisis their passive (not active) obedience to James, became in the new reign Non-Jurors; others like Dryden could and did, on grounds of principle, refuse to take the oaths to the joint sovereigns.

At the turn of the new year, 1689, Dryden's personal situation, though serious enough, was perhaps not so dire as that of many Catholics. He had of course burnt all of his bridges. The course of events made certain that he along with all others of his religion would be deprived of official positions. The last warrant for his pension payment had been issued in the previous July.[1] Before March he was removed from his two posts, and that of laureate was turned over to his old antagonist, the true-blue Thomas Shadwell.[2] Just what further punitive measures would come from the Convention Parliament now in session remained for the future to disclose. Yet Dryden might expect action against him as a member of the hated religion. In February, no doubt in preparation for some kind of action, petty constables began to take a census of the Papists who had not been three years' resident in their respective wards. In St. Ann's, Soho, they found in Gerrard Street twenty-four, including "Wm Dayton [sic] Housekeeper, a poet in Gerrard Street, having two sons, both of his own religion, and his wife."[3] On May 13, Luttrell recorded the issuance of a proclamation requiring all Papists to depart the cities of London and Westminster, and ten miles adjacent, "pursuant to the late act of Parliament."[4] In the same month Parliament passed the Act of Toleration, which gave Protestant Dissenters relief from persecution without removing their civil disabilities. To the Catholics and Unitarians no relief whatever was provided. Though this act left in force the Test and the penal laws, against which Dryden had fulminated, the disinclination of King William to persecute the Catholics, at this point a small and feeble group, meant that they went generally unmolested unless they were guilty of overt acts against the government. Even the private exercise of their religion was tolerated. So Dryden's "ruin" (the word is his) proved to be chiefly the loss of income and position and perhaps a loss of face. There can be little doubt that he began to suffer serious financial distress, for the largest part of his fairly adequate income was stopped. He had little to resort to now except his genius. Having eschewed both religious and political controversy, he now returned to the writing of drama.

Despite his adherence to the lost cause which placed him on the opposite side from that of most of his acquaintances and relations, Dryden continued to maintain friendly relations with them. And through their friendship his immediate adjustment to changed conditions must have been smoothed. Sir Robert Howard, appointed to the Privy Council in the new régime on February 13, 1688/89, very likely was able to help him, and so too was the Earl of Dorset, who on the next day was sworn in as Lord Chamberlain and a member of the Council. Both could have used their influence to blunt any reprisals that some members of the new government might have wished to level at the poet. Although one of Dorset's first acts was to remove Dryden from his official post and to install Shadwell, his good will and friendship were shown in what Dryden acknowledged three years later as "a most bountiful present, which, at that time, when I was most in want of it, came most seasonably and unexpectedly to my relief." Indeed there are numerous indications that Dorset continued to be a powerful friend at court in the immediate years ahead. Through Dorset as Lord Chamberlain, Dryden's return to the theater was without much question made far easier and more pleasant than it otherwise would have been.[5]

The theater, of course, presented the obvious means for Dryden to supplement the small income from his Northamptonshire rents. But the theater he returned to in 1689 was not the theater he had left a half-dozen years earlier. Control of the United Company had passed, in 1687, from Charles Davenant to his unscrupulous brother Alexander. Before the year was over, he had dismissed Betterton as the artistic head of the enterprise, and from that time until his forced flight from the country in late 1693, internal strife tended to disrupt the acting company. Yet Betterton remained Dryden's oldest friend among the players, and it was from him that he sought advice.

Between February, when he lost his positions upon the accession of William and Mary, and early winter, when his play *Don Sebastian* was acted, there remain no records of Dryden's activities or his whereabouts. It may well be that he lived quietly and unmolested in his house in Gerrard Street, taking stock of his changed position and laying plans for his resumption of playwriting. He may, of course, have thought absence from the scene more prudent, in view of the Proclamation of May 13, 1689, requiring all Catholics to move at least ten miles out of London, and have taken his family for an extended visit into Northamptonshire, where he could at leisure work on his new play. Wherever he lived during the summer, it is certain that he worked with extreme care to recapture his long-unused talent for drama. Before committing *Don Sebastian* to the players, Dryden sought the friendly criticism of both Betterton and the Lord Chamberlain. The play was acted on December 4, and within a fortnight it was entered in the *Stationers' Register*; and by January 6, 1689/90, it was on sale and advertised in the *London Gazette*. The extreme speed with which Dryden saw it through the cycle of acting, printing, and publication suggests that he felt either a great emotional or a great financial need to put the first play of his return before the public at once. It may indeed have been his financial distress which dictated the rapidity of the process. This is somewhat borne out by the fact that not Tonson but Hindmarsh published it for him. Why Dryden should have left Tonson, who had published for him for the past ten years, has never been satisfactorily explained. One suggestion (made by MacDonald, p. 120) that Tonson suddenly became cautious and timorous because of the political situation hardly fits the case; for there is no reason to believe that publishing a non-political play by Dryden at this time was fraught with danger. A more likely explanation is that Dryden discovered that Hindmarsh was willing to pay him more for the copy than Tonson was prepared to offer. This temporary shift perhaps proved salutary, for here-after Tonson published regularly for Dryden and, despite some bickering over financial matters, the poet usually received what he considered fair treatment.

The play, as Dryden might well have feared, did not please the first day's audience though it was endured with polite good humor. He admits, in the preface, that *Don Sebastian* as first acted, was too crowded with characters and incidents and was "unsupportably too long." Betterton, who acted the part of Dorax, lopped off twelve hundred lines for stage purposes, and presumably thereafter the play succeeded somewhat better. Some of these lines were replaced in the printing, so that the reader might more readily see the due connection of scenes and enjoy images and descriptions that had been pared away for the acting version. The prologue, preface, and dedication all provide an excellent, if somewhat mixed, impression of Dryden's feelings as he picks up the threads of his literary career. The prologue contains much of his old jaunty humor for the pleasure of the theater audience, but the serious and slightly acerb comments in preface and dedication contradict this seeming levity which might otherwise have given the impression that the experiences of the immediate past had left no mark upon him. Spoken "by a woman," the prologue carries the proper self-deprecatory tone, yet avoids any recourse to self-pity, and it wittily fixes the changed conditions under which the poet now appeals to his audience, conditions painfully well known to both. He begins:

> The judge remov'd, tho' he's no more my lord,
> May plead at bar, or at the council board:
> So may cast poets write; there's no pretension
> To argue loss of wit, from loss of pension.
> Your looks are cheerful; and in all this place
> I see not one that wears a damning face.
> The British nation is too brave, to show
> Ignoble vengeance on a vanquish'd foe.
>
> .   .   .   .
>
> Suppose our poet was your foe before,
> Yet now, the bus'ness of the field is o'er;
> 'Tis time to let your civil wars alone,
> When troops are into winter quarters gone.
> Jove was alike to Latian and to Phrygian;
> And you will know, a play's of no religion.[6]

As a petitioner for grace, he is prepared to make concessions. The prologue continues:

> I heard him make advances of good nature;
> That he, for once, would sheathe his cutting satire.
> Sign but his peace, he vows he'll ne'er again
> The sacred names of fops and beaus profane.
> Strike up the bargain quickly, for I swear,
> As times go now, he offers very fair.
> Be not too hard on him with statutes neither;
> Be kind; and do not set your teeth together,
> To stretch the laws, as cobblers do their leather.
> Horses by Papists are not to be ridden,
> But sure the Muse's horse was ne'er forbidden;
> For in no rate-book it was ever found
> That Pegasus was valued at five pound.

The last four lines wittily refer to the recent statute forbidding Catholics to own a horse valued at more than five pounds; so he turns the jest upon himself as poet. And he ends with a final couplet, the significance of which would not have been lost on his audience:

> Fine him to daily drudging and inditing,
> And let him pay his taxes out in writing.

As a Catholic, Dryden was subject to a doubling of his tax rate.

The dedication was addressed in most flattering vein to Phillip Sidney, third Earl of Leicester, who had always been on the opposite side to Dryden in politics and in religion. The reason for the dedication Dryden explains thus: "Neither has he so far forgotten a poor inhabitant of his suburbs, whose best prospect [from Gerrard Street] is on the garden of Leicester-House, but that more than once he has been offering him his patronage to reconcile him to a world, of which his misfortunes have made him weary. There is another Sidney still remaining, though there can never be another Spencer to deserve the favour. But one Sidney gave his patronage to the applications of a poet; the other offered it unasked." The extravagance in comparing the rather inconspicuous and innocuous Earl of Leicester to the noble Atticus cries reproach upon Dryden; and inadvertently ironic is a passage, with a touch of bitterness, on praise in dedications: "There are few in any age who can bear the load of a Dedication, for where praise is undeserved, it is satire; though satire on folly is now no longer a scandal to any one person, where a whole age is dipped together."

The preface, however, provides the most complete key to an understanding of Dryden's state of mind during this trying adjustment period. After admitting that the play was too long, he expresses his gratitude to the first day's audience who did not "explode an entertainment which was designed to please them, or discourage an author whose misfortunes have once more brought him, against his will, upon the stage. While I continue in these bad circumstances, (and truly I see very little probability of coming out,) I must be obliged to write. . . . I write not this out of any expectation to be pitied, for I have enemies enow to wish me yet in a worse condition." His long experience of the stage and his observations upon the difficulty of pleasing varying audiences, the low state of the theater, the worn-out themes of tragedy, and the growing number of "young men without learning set up for judges," all had been discouragements that "had not only weaned me from the stage, but had also given me a loathing of it. But enough of this: the difficulties continue; they increase, and I am still condemned to dig in these exhausted mines."

According to his custom, Dryden speaks at large of his purposes in the play, and of incident, and character portrayal. He acknowledges the criticism he has heard and finds it trivial, though admitting that the piece might well be criticized for faults not yet discovered by the cavillers. And his answer to them is that the "Earl of Dorset was pleased to read the tragedy twice over before it was acted, and did me the favour to send me word that he was displeased anything should be cut away." This is hardly a complete answer to his critics; yet the judgment of posterity has somewhat confirmed Dorset's view: the play has generally been regarded as one of Dryden's best. And indeed it contains scenes of power, particularly that between Dorax and Sebastian, leading to the reconciliation of king and subject. Though a modified heroic play, *Don Sebastian* contains little or no bombast, and its theme is far different from the love and honor of the earlier plays. Here Dryden is concerned primarily with sin—the sin of incest, on the one hand, and the "sin" of disloyalty, on the other. The latter is resolved by a recognition in the subject of the goodness of the Monarch, and in him by the realization of the essential honesty and loyalty of the subject. The involuntary sin of incest committed by Sebastian and Almeyda is expiated, not by death ("the most easy" solution as he calls it) but by divorce, exile, and the assumption of a life of piety and religious

contemplation.   In place of the conventional ending, Dryden introduces an intense ending, which he judged to be more artistic.

The generally favorable reception of his return to the stage by
persons whose judgment he respected emboldened him to proceed at
once on another play.   He now turned to comedy, and out of Plautus
and Molière took the groundwork for *Amphitryon*.   With a large
contribution of his own, containing liberal amounts of bawdy and
rollicking good wit, Dryden produced a rapidly-moving farce.
Jupiter's assumption of Amphitryon's shape to do the marital offices
of the returning general with the beauteous Alcmena, and the conse-
quent cross-purposes when the real Amphitryon returns home produces continual laughter.   But to this Dryden adds a second character
doubling, when Mercury takes the form of the servant Sosia, and
pursues his own amorous adventure with the gold-seeking Phaedra.
To add interest, Dryden utilized machines to let down the Gods from
the heavens, and dancing, song, and music.   The last was supplied
by Henry Purcell, who set the three songs and wrote the music for
the pastoral dialogue (Act IV), which gave particular pleasure to
the ladies in the audience on the third day.   Ready for presentation
before Royalty by April 30, its performance was for some reason
cancelled; it finds no place in the record of plays acted before the
court until October.   Yet all the evidence points to an early acting,
in the spring, on the public stage.[7]   As significant for Dryden as the
reception of the play was the relationship now established with
Purcell, for out of this association grew the far more important
collaboration of the poet and composer in the following year in
King Arthur.   What led to his immediate interest in Purcell seems
to have been the young composer's work with Betterton, whose opera
The Prophetesse Purcell was setting at the same time.[8]

During the summer of 1690, Dryden prepared *Amphitryon* for
publication, and began preliminary studies for several works which
were to keep him busy for more than a year.   In the meantime, we
catch glimpses of some aspects of his personal rehabilitation into
the literary life of the time.   He frequented the coffeehouses, particularly Will Urwin's, and here he was soon to become a fixture, an
arbiter on literary discussions, holding forth on poetry and drama
for the edification of some of the young men who clustered about
him.   His friends and acquaintances of these latter years, many of
whom he publicly names, include a large group of persons not directly
connected with his working life, and most of the younger men with
literary aspirations.[9]   Fortunately we have a partial record of his

friendship with one of them, William Walsh, whom he seems to have met at Will's sometime during 1690. The extant correspondence between them testifies in some measure to the homage paid him by the young and to the genuine interest and kindness he showered upon those, no matter what their religious or political complexion, whose devotion to letters matched his. During the next few years his benign dictatorship in wit and criticism at the meetings of Parnassian groups, though denigrated by some of the less accomplished among the inhabitants of the developing Grub Street, contributed significantly to the poet's virtual sovereignty in letters, to which his long practice and solid accomplishments so richly entitled him.

Following the success of Betterton and Purcell's collaboration on *The Prophetesse* in midsummer, Dryden apparently determined to revive his old plans to produce the large operatic work, of which *Albion and Albanius,* in 1684 and 1685, was only in the nature of an introduction. But much had happened since that time, and a complete remodeling as it turned out was politically necessary. Probably before the summer was over, composer and poet began to work closely with each other to refurbish the material which was to appear in the late spring of 1691 as *King Arthur.* At the same time Dryden addressed himself to translation, in the knowledge that he would not continue long in the theater which he had publicly expressed his dislike for and which in its present parlous state could not have been a particularly happy place for a man who had known it in better times.

By the last of October, *Amphitryon* was in print, accompanied by a short dedication, dated October 24, to Sir William Leveson-Gower. Years before Dryden had paid a visit to this gentleman in Staffordshire, which he now recalls. But it is not primarily the old friendship that is of importance to him now, but the continued proofs of Sir William's kindness to him since the Revolution. Sir William, he pointedly writes, has "not suffered the difference of opinions, which produce such hatred and enmity in the brutal part of human kind, to remove you from the settled basis of your good nature and good sense." Dryden has sought Leveson-Gower's permission to dedicate this play to him for a particular purpose; and in the following passage we find Dryden's deliberate plan to exploit, in the lowness of his fortunes, the friendship and the good will of men of contrary beliefs which awaits him for the asking:

It is upon this knowledge of you, Sir, that I have chosen you, with your permission, to be the patron of this poem; and as since the wonderful

Revolution, I have begun with the best pattern of humanity, the Earl of Leicester, I shall continue to follow the same method in all to whom I shall address, and endeavour to pitch on such only as have been pleased to own me in this ruin of my small fortune; who, though they are of a contrary opinion themselves, yet blame not me for adhering to a lost cause, and judging for myself, what I cannot choose but judge, so long as I am a patient sufferer, and no disturber of the government; which if it be a severe penance, as a great wit has told the world, it is at least enjoined me by myself, and Sancho Panza, as much a fool as I, was observed to discipline his body no farther than he found he could endure the smart. . . . I suffer no more than I can easily undergo, and so long as I enjoy my liberty, which is the birthright of an Englishman, the rest shall never go near my heart. The merry philosopher is more to my humour than the melancholick, and I find no disposition in myself to cry, while the mad world is daily supplying me with such occasions of laughter.[10]

The difficulty of Dryden's personal adjustment was without doubt shared by his family. The census returns for Papists in St. Ann's parish had shown that his household consisted of his wife and two sons. These were Charles and John. The former after Westminster had not taken up his election to Trinity College. In early 1686/87, through his father's friendships, Charles was in the office of the Earl of Middleton, one of the Secretaries of State.[11] After his removal from Magdalen two years before, John apparently remained at home, where both he and Charles—under their father's tutelage— were beginning to write poetry. The youngest son, Erasmus-Henry, left Charterhouse to embrace a religious life, and in October, 1690, took up his studies at the English college in Rome under the sponsorship of his kinsman, Cardinal Howard.[12] Within a few years Charles and John, having found no settled way of life in London, went to Rome, where both contracted illnesses of various kinds. Charles returned home in 1697 or 1698, but John remained in Rome, where he died in 1701.

The winter of 1690-91 saw Dryden engaged with Juvenal and with *King Arthur*. By February, he had completed his translations of Juvenal's first, sixth, and tenth satires, and on February 9, 1690/ 91, they were entered in the *Stationers' Register*. These were preliminary studies for a large volume to be published eighteen months later. Before its appearance Dryden added two more of Juvenal's satires, the third and the sixteenth. At the same time he was in correspondence with Walsh, who had now followed up their meetings at the coffeehouse with requests that Dryden read some of his verses and a discourse on women, which he assures Dryden was written in haste, "in obedience to the command of a fair Lady."[13] In answer, Dryden wrote a long letter in which he judiciously comments upon Walsh's verses and makes a suggestion for smoothing out the last two lines of one of his epigrams. He also read the "Discourse on Women," which he generally commends for its thought and style; but he cautions the young man about concluding sentences with prepositions and suggests that he make nicer distinctions in the use of the relative pronouns *who* and *that*. Pleased with the care and attention given his work by the master, Walsh becomes emboldened to ask a further favor. Confessing that his "Dialogue of Women" (as he now calls it) written to impress the fair lady may not succeed as he might wish, he is reluctant to put his name to it; yet without a name, it may not be read at all. Now, he asks, "if you would give yorselfe ye trouble to write some little preface to it, it might [*sic*] a very great means to recommend it to ye World."[14] To this request Dryden good-naturedly complied, and Walsh's *Dialogue Concerning Women* appeared in April 1691, with Dryden's foreword. Nor was Walsh reticent in using Dryden's corrections of his verses. In 1692, Walsh's *Letters and Poems, Amorous and Gallant* included without change the rewritten lines that Dryden had mentioned in his letter. How many more lines in these verses belong to Dryden we can only surmise. Had Dryden spent as much time with the work of other aspiring poets, he could hardly have found time to do much else.

In the meantime, Dryden wrote through the winter revising the dramatic opera that had been all but complete, though not acted, in 1684. With Purcell he worked closely on the songs, and although the two artistic tempers sometimes clashed, in general it proved a happy collaboration. Dryden's respect for Purcell's talents seemed to increase as the opera progressed, and to the public accolade he had given the young man in the dedication to *Amphitryon,* he added another in the dedication to the opera, addressed to the Marquis of Halifax and timed to appear in print immediately after the first run in the theater. The play was in print during the first week of June, when it was advertised in the *London Gazette*. "There is nothing better than what I intended," he wrote, "but the musick, which has since arrived to a greater perfection in England than ever formerly; especially passing through the artful hands of Mr. Purcell, who has composed it with so great a genius, that he has nothing to fear but an ignorant, ill-judging audience." He has not abandoned his characteristic generosity in praise of excellence. Indeed, his service to Purcell went far deeper. When John Carr's proposals of the preceding summer to print by subscription Purcell's vocal and instrumental music of *The Prophetesse* finally succeeded in drawing the necessary patronage, Carr issued the volume the last week of February. To serve the composer's interests, Dryden wrote a learned preface to it, which appeared with Henry Purcell's name subscribed.[15]

The allegorical story of Arthur in its original form had been designed to trace the descent of Charles II from Arthur and the Saxon forebears and to serve as a poem of triumph, for, he reminds Halifax, "it was indeed a time which was proper for triumph, when he had overcome all those difficulties which for some years had perplexed his peaceful reign." Part of that large design we have seen in the expanded prologue which was *Albion and Albanius*. But Dryden knew as well as any man that 1684 was a different world from that of 1691. Consequently much that had originally been included had of practical necessity to be sacrificed. He writes: "But not to offend the present times, nor a government which has hitherto protected me, I have been obliged so much to alter the first design, and take away so many beauties from the writing, that it is now no more what it was formerly than the present ship of the Royal Sovereign, after so often taking down and altering, is the vessel it was at the first building."

This passage, which thus publicly acknowledges the favorable treatment measured out to Dryden by the new government, was in its original form even more significant in the light it throws upon Dryden's character. Recently, Professor Fredson Bowers discovered a unique copy of the first edition of *King Arthur* (Bodleian, Malone, I, 38), which contains "the original, or cancellandum leaf A3, in addition to the conjugate fold of A2 and A3 used as cancellanus." The leaf apparently was cancelled to delete a short passage which, if retained, could have been a source of embarrassment to the government. After the words, "a government which has hitherto protected me" occurs the following, "(and by a particular Favour wou'd have continued me what I was, if I could have comply'd with the Termes which were offered me)," followed by the present text "I have been obliged," etc. What terms were proposed to him can only be imagined, but conceivably they would have compelled Dryden to abjure some articles of his faith, either by taking a modified oath of allegiance to the new joint sovereigns or by renouncing the principle of transubstantiation, that prime battleground between the Anglican and Catholic churches, about which Dryden had had much to say in

The Hind and the Panther. His refusal to compromise testifies to the strength of his present convictions. The suppression of the parenthetical comment may have been arranged by Tonson in consultation with the Earl of Dorset; and it may be that Dorset, an old friend and patron, was the source of the "particular Favour." However this may be, whoever arranged the suppression of the passage undoubtedly performed a service both to Dryden, who could have ill afforded at this juncture a new wave of attacks, and to the government, which would have been embarrassed to have it known that the unrepentant Catholic laureate had even been approached on such a matter.[16]

King Arthur appeared under the best of auspices, with a show of royal approbation. Dedicated to Halifax, an old acquaintance of Dryden's, and a staunch Tory and Anglican, and until February, 1689/90, Lord Privy Seal, the play was assured of a respectful reading audience. But even before it was acted, Dryden seems to have employed his friends in high places to elicit early approval of his revision. He had sent the manuscript to his "first and best patroness the Duchess of Monmouth" (soon to remarry "Jack" Churchill and thereby to become Lady Cornwallis). His patroness recommended it to Queen Mary, who read it and gave it "her royal approbation." And Dryden presumed "to guess, that her Majesty was not displeased to find in this poem the praises of her native country, and the heroick actions of so famous a predecessor in the government of Great Britain, as King Arthur." The combination of royal approval of the manuscript, the dedication to Halifax, and the artistic efforts of Dryden, Purcell, and Betterton made certain what Dryden hoped —that it would "be the chiefest entertainment of our ladies and gentlemen this summer."[17]

The Struggle for Solvency
1691-1694

BEFORE *King Arthur* was completed, Dryden had begun his next play. It is likely, though not certain, that he was well along with it by late spring. Evidently in one of his letters to Walsh he had mentioned it, for in a letter to Dryden, dated August 15, Walsh inquires whether *Cleomenes* is yet completed.[1] That the play was nearing completion is suggested by a comment of Thomas Southerne, in the preface to *The Wives' Excuse* (1692). He says that Dryden fell sick in the summer of 1691 and called him in to help write part of the last act. Certainly Dryden did suffer a continued illness during that time, as he himself testified in the address to Lord Abingdon prefixed to *Eleanora* in the following year. And the schedule was further disrupted by a rather new kind of literary exercise for him. On May 31, 1691, Eleanora, the first wife of James Bertie, Earl of Abingdon, died. In the succeeding months the Earl, searching for a more durable monument to her than stone, approached Dryden with the request that he memorialize Eleanora in verse. Such a "command" (as Dryden chose to call it) appealed to the poet—probably for two reasons, both quite valid at the moment. He needed money, and the Earl was apparently prepared to pay somewhat handsomely for eulogistic verses by the old poet.[2] The other reason was also compelling. The Earl of Abingdon, a prominent Anglican, and a royalist of some importance, had been among the first to invite William into England to *mediate* between James and his people. He had contributed £30,000 to the cost of William's expedition. When, however, William ceased to be the mediator and pressed his demands for joint sovereignty with Mary, Abingdon opposed him and exercised his influence against proclaiming the throne vacant. To have such a man as a patron—even though he was personally unknown to him—seemed to have been Dryden's hope in his planned rehabilitation.

So he undertook to write of Eleanora, whom he had never seen. He learned, by talking with her friends, that Eleanora had been in life a model sweetheart, a model wife and mother, a devout and humble Christian, and an inspiration to her generation. If precedent were needed for eulogizing a person whom he did not know, he found it in "Doctor Donne, the greatest wit, though not the best poet of our nation, [who] acknowledges, that he had never seen Mrs. Drury, whom he has made immortal in his admirable *Anniversaries*." He professes to follow Donne "in the design of his panegyric; which was to raise an emulation in the living, to copy out the example of the dead." As an apotheosis of Eleanora it is like Donne's eulogy to Elizabeth Drury; and like Donne's poems it contains a succession of tributes to Eleanora's charity, her prudent management, humility, conjugal virtues, and friendship. In the epiphonema Dryden injects himself, and begs Eleanora not to refuse

> This humble tribute of no vulgar Muse;
> Who, not by cares, or wants, or age depress'd,
> Stems a wild deluge with a dauntless breast;
> And dares to sing thy praises in a clime
> Where vice triumphs, and virtue is a crime;
> Where ev'n to draw the picture of thy mind
> Is satire on the most of humankind:
> Take it, while yet 'tis praise; before my rage,
> Unsafely just, break loose on this bad age;
> So bad, that thou thyself hadst no defense
> From vice, but barely by departing hence.

> (ll. 360-70)

The poem, in print in March, 1691/92, required some months to compose; for as he wrote to Abingdon in the foreword, "We, who are priests of Apollo, have not the inspiration when we please; but must wait till the god comes rushing on us, and invades us with a fury which we are not able to resist." Ovid, he points out, had said that good verses "never flow but from a serene and compos'd spirit." In the late months of 1691 and the following winter, his spirit was so vexed by a number of things that it was anything but serene.[3]

Dryden's difficulty in completing *Cleomenes* was followed by other trials that could not have been foreseen. Apparently it was ready by early October, for on the sixth of that month he wrote out a receipt for thirty guineas to Tonson, who had advanced him money for the copy.[4] After the play went to the company for rehearsal, gossip began to circulate that Dryden had written into the play a reflection on the government. His enemies at court apprised the Queen that it contained a topical parallel, not specified so far as can be learned but doubtless consisting of a suspected likeness between Cleomenes rusting away in exile at the foreign court of Egypt and James II in exile at the French court of Louis. The suspicious might indeed equate Egypt with France, for had not Dryden in *Absalom and Achitophel* called the French "Egyptians"? Some parallel might indeed be found by those who would see.[5]

The result was that as preparations for acting neared completion, word came from the court banning the play. At this point Dryden called upon his powerful friends. Laurence Hyde, the Earl of Rochester, arranged a meeting at his house, where the poet read *Cleomenes* to an assembly including Rochester's wife and daughters. Finding nothing subversive, Rochester, who was Queen Mary's uncle, made representations to his niece. As a consequence, the ban was lifted, and by February, 1691/92, Motteux (in the *Gentleman's Journal*) reported that *Cleomenes* would appear shortly.[6] The affair, however, dragged on. Finally announced for April 9, the play was again stopped by the Lord Chamberlain with word that the Queen absolutely forbade its acting.[7] Dryden then prevailed upon Lord Falkland to testify that as long ago as 1684 or 1685 he had presented him a French book in which "were the names of many subjects that I had thought on for the stage; amongst which this tragedy was one." Falkland's good office, in addition to the Lord Chamberlain's decision that the play contained nothing dangerous, brought about a reversal. Finally, on April 16, it was acted with applause.[8]

The negotiations had been exhausting, and Dryden avers in his preface that "had it not been on consideration of the actors, who were to suffer on my account, I should not have been at all solicitous whether it were played or no. Nobody can imagine that in my declining age I write willingly, or that I am desirous of exposing, at this time of day, the small reputation which I have gotten on the theatre. The subsistence which I had from the former government is lost; and the reward I have from the stage is so little, that it is not worth my labour." Though he is somewhat annoyed by the "superiours of the playhouse," who had "garbled" the play and were able "to geld it so clearly in some places, that they took away the very manhood of it," he nevertheless recognizes that he cannot "reasonably blame them for their caution, because they are answerable for any thing that is publickly represented." To them he ironically applies the words of Cassandra to Ptolomony (Act III):

> To be so nice in my concerns for you;
> To doubt where doubts are not; to be too fearful;
> To raise a bugbear shadow of a danger,
> And then be frighted, though it cannot reach you.

But the end was happy: the brilliant acting of the players Dryden commends, particularly that of "Mrs. Barry, [who], always excellent, has in this tragedy excelled herself, and gained a reputation beyond any woman whom I have ever seen on the theatre." The final success of his play, however, did nothing to relieve Dryden's disenchantment with the stage, and he made plans to leave playwriting at the earliest moment.[9]

During all these drawn-out exasperations, Dryden found time to proceed with his translations from Juvenal in preparation for the volume of satires which Tonson, under Dryden's general supervision, was planning to publish. The work was well advanced even before the acting of *Cleomenes,* for Motteux in his journal for February announced that "*Juvenal* and Persius englished by several hands will be printed in a short time, Mr. *Dryden* having done 4 Satyrs of the First, and 2 of the last. . . . Poetry is it seems hereditary in his Family, for each of his Sons have done one Satyr of *Juvenal,* which, with so extraordinary a Tutor as their Father, cannot but be very acceptable to the world." It is not possible to determine upon what basis the "several hands" were chosen or upon what principle the assignments were made.[10] Included with Dryden in the undertaking were his two sons, Tate, Bowles, Stepney, Creech, Harvey, Duke, Power (a fellow of Trinity College, Cambridge), and Congreve, whose translation of the eleventh satire was his first published work. Dryden may have been given enough editorial responsibility to enable him to suggest revisions, or even to make corrections in order to polish rugged lines. All of his coadjutors were young men, some of whom he had not known before. Congreve, only recently come to London and not yet embarked upon his playwriting career, seems to have made an immediate impression on Dryden: their friendship dates from this time. Prefixed to Dryden's translations of Persius, which had a separate title page in the volume, Congreve's verses "To Mr. Dryden" pay tribute to the older poet:

> Those sullen Clouds, which have for Ages past,
> O're Persius's too-long-suffering Muse been cast,
> Disperse, and flie before thy Sacred Pen,
> And, in their room, bright tracks of light are seen.
>
> .   .   .   .
>
> Old Stoick Virtue, clad in rugged lines
> Polish'd by you, in Modern Brilliant shines,
> And, as before, for Persius our Esteem,
> To his antiquity was paid, not him:
> So now, whatever Praise, from us is due,
> Belongs not to Old Persius, but the New,
> For still Obscure, to us no light he gives;
> Dead in himself, in you alone he lives.

Hardly more than a year later Dryden returned this tribute in "Verses to My dear Friend, Mr. Congreve on his Comedy called the Double-Dealer."

Though the Juvenal was a co-operative venture, Persius remained entirely Dryden's province. Either because of the difficulties which Persius presented to the English translator, or because Tonson believed that Persius by Dryden alone would increase the sales of his collection, Dryden undertook all six satires.[11] These, along with his translations of Juvenal, were probably ready by June; but publication was still some time away because of his decision to include a dedicatory discourse, to be addressed to the Earl of Dorset, concerning the "original and progress of satire." The need for rest and change must by then have been imperative; the last of the summer found him in Essex (at some unidentified friend's or relative's house) and perhaps even somewhat later in his native Northamptonshire.[12] During this pleasant exile from the city, he either wrote entirely or completed the long prefatory address to Dorset, which he dated August 15. This copy for the volume he must have turned over to Tonson (when he visited Dryden in Northamptonshire?). In the meantime, he probably was bringing to an end another task which had been laid aside until Juvenal and Persius were out of the way. As early as April he had shown Motteux the copy of a translation of Polybius' *History,* which had been given to him for correction and criticism by the translator, Sir Henry Sheeres, along with a request for a "Character" of the Greek historian.[13]

During Dryden's vacation Tonson met him and proposed terms for a new miscellany. In the preliminary negotiations Tonson had offered £50, which Dryden persuaded him to increase to fifty guineas. Dryden chose to translate Ovid, and began to turn portions of the first book of the *Metamorphoses* into English. From his retreat he wrote Tonson (then in London) on October 3, demanding twenty guineas for somewhat less than six hundred lines of Ovid. A week later, on October 10, Dryden returned to London, and apparently not having had explicit word from his publisher, took the Ovid to Peter Motteux in the hope of getting twenty guineas from that bookseller, who, however, refused to pay the asking price. Thrown back upon Tonson, Dryden completed more verses and sent them along. But Tonson felt himself bilked, for he had received a total of only 1,446 lines, for which he had agreed to pay fifty guineas. In a desperately serious remonstrance to Dryden, he points out that *proportionately* he was getting a far worse bargain than the "strange bookseller"; and he adjures the poet to use him at least as favorably as he had done in the Juvenal, which was a far more difficult job for the poet than Ovid.[14] Dryden's sense of fairness seems to have rescued the situation and brought about a compromise. He relented his apparent intransigent attitude and provided Tonson some 1,734 lines from Ovid, including the fable of "Iphis and Ianthe," from the ninth Book, and that of "Acis, Polyphemus and Galatea," from the thirteenth. For good measure he sent Tonson two songs, a paraphrase of "Veni Creator Spiritus" and 195 lines of translation from the sixth book of the *Iliad*—the last parting of Hector and Andromache.

When the *Satires of Juvenal and Persius* appeared in late October in a handsome folio, it was prefaced by a long and ambitious essay entitled "Discourse concerning the Original and Progress of Satire." Drawing heavily upon continental and English editors and commentators, the essay in effect becomes a piece of historical and critical scholarship, with fresh and acute observations of his own throughout. His purpose, as he explains to Dorset is four-fold: "to give you from the best authors, the origin, the antiquity, the growth, the change, and the complement of satire among the Romans: to describe, if not define, the nature of that poem, with its several qualifications and virtues, together with the several sorts of it; to compare the excellencies of Horace, Persius, and Juvenal, and shew the particular manners of their satires; and lastly, to give an account of this new way of version, which is attempted in our performance." He does not, however, address himself at once to this comprehensive plan, but uses up somewhat more than one-fourth of the entire essay in praise of his old friend and patron, and with a discussion of epic poetry and of earlier plans for his own long-abandoned epic. Among the numerous ideas on epic poetry, three notably important ones that impinge closely upon his career may be mentioned: his belief that a modern epic is possible, contrary to the expressed conviction of many critics that "Christianity is not capable of those embellishments which are afforded in the belief of those ancient heathens"; the proposal of his original "invention" to supply the machinery of tutelary angels to the modern writer of epic; and the detailed plans that he had once made for his own epic, nearly twenty years earlier.

Though he concedes that "in the severe notions of our faith" the Christian virtues of suffering, patience, humility, and resignation are patently not those that make for epic in the generally accepted sense, yet he believes that these are virtues of the "private Christian." Those of a king or of a general—the possible protagonists in an epic —are "prudence, counsel, active fortitude, coercive power, awful command, and the exercise of magnanimity, as well as justice." This being so, nothing is to prevent the creation of a modern epic: "the heroick action of some great commander, enterprised for the common good, and honour of the Christian cause, and executed happily." It may indeed be written now, "as it was of old by the heathens; provided the poet be endued with the same talents; and the language, though not of equal dignity, yet as near approaching to it, as our modern barbarism will allow."

Having demonstrated the reasonable possibility of the writing of a modern epic, he moves to his proposal of Christian "machinery." Poets in the Christian era have not fully known their own resources: "If they had searched the Old Testament as they ought, they might there have found the machines which are proper for their work. . . . The perusing of one chapter in the prophecy of Daniel, and accommodating what there they find with the principles of Platonick philosophy, as it is now Christianized, would have made the ministry of angels as strong an engine for the working up heroick poetry, in our religion, as that of the ancients has been to raise theirs by all the fables of their gods. . . ." That there is Christian belief in the existence of these tutelary angels admits of no doubt, "it is a doctrine almost universally received by Christians, as well protestants and catholicks." The epic poet need only utilize them according to his best judgment, as he will doubtless use the evil spirits in opposition, who can on occasion appear as angels of light. Milton, indeed "has given . . . an example of the like nature, when Satan [appears] like a cherub to Uriel."

With respect to his own plans for an epic, Dryden is more specific than he was from 1674 through 1676, when he was actually making detailed studies for his poem. It was to have been patriotic, "intended chiefly for the honour of my native country"; and of two subjects—King Arthur conquering the Saxons (which he subsequently embodied in short form in the opera) and Edward the Black Prince in subduing Spain and restoring Don Pedro—he rather favored the second because of the "greatness of the action, and its answerable event, for the magnanimity of the English hero . . . and for the many beautiful episodes, which I had interwoven with the principal design, together with the characters of the chiefest English persons." Among the last would have been included his living friends and patrons, after the example of Virgil and Spenser. The time for this great project, however, was long past, for not properly encouraged by Charles II he had, he points out, been forced to give it up. Now it is impossible, for "age has overtaken me, and want, a more insufferable evil, . . . has wholly disenabled me." His more faithful than remunerative service to two kings he sharply contrasts with the unsolicited and generous treatment accorded him by Dorset since the Revolution.

The main portion of this discourse, however, he devotes to his announced four-fold examination of satire and the satirists here translated. His plan of treatment is exemplary and considerably more formalized than in any other of his critical essays. Yet as we might expect, the neatness of his plan is often broken by the happy intrusion of numerous digressions, not only recognized by the author as such, but gloried in. Relying upon his "authorities"— Dacier, Casaubon, Rigault, Heinsius, Segrais, Barten Holyday, and Sir Robert Stapylton—Dryden traces the history of satire and describes its nature. Throughout, his individual judgments, as precise and shrewd and colloquially racy as ever, provide interesting sidelights in an otherwise sober performance. When he proceeds to the critical assessment, and comparison of Juvenal and Persius (Horace inevitably coming into his considerations), his maturity of judgment and his inherent good taste overrun the categorical pronouncements of the "authorities," whose vulnerable spot he unerringly exposes: "the critics," he observes, "who, having first taken a liking to one of these poets, proceed to comment on him, and to illustrate him;

after which, they fall in love with their own labours to that degree
of blind fondness, that at length they defend and exalt their author,
not so much for his sake, as for their own." So he does not permit
himself to be controlled by the partial judgment of a Casaubon or
a Heinsius: his ear and his taste were truer—and his interests less
involved—than theirs. Persius cost him much labor; he returns
again and again to the complaint that Persius is everywhere obscure
and the translation of him difficult. Yet in some respects he finds
Persius superior to Juvenal and to Horace, particularly in his recom-
mendations for a virtuous life and in his consistency of philosophical
outlook. But for all this, it is Juvenal and Horace who claim his allegiance in satire.

Such a detailed and extensive study of Roman satire might be
expected to lead him to a consideration of English satire, and of
his own. In digressive passages of varying length he includes many
comments which are of biographical importance. In treating the
relative merits of Juvenal and Horace, he, for example, excepts the
odes and epodes of the latter because they were not (to him) proper
representations of true Roman satire, but somewhat like the Greek
Silli, or "invectives against particular sects and persons." This leads
him to the examples of similar satiric pieces in England, there called
lampoons, "a dangerous sort of weapon, and for the most part unlawful." His reasons for arriving at such a conclusion are illumi-
nating: "We have no moral right on the reputation of other men.
It is taking from them what we cannot restore to them." In his
own writing (though he is often called a satirist) the only pure
example of the *Silli* or lampoon is *Macflecknoe*; though such poems
as *Absalom and Achitophel* and *The Medal* are of course partly
compounded of personal invective. Lampoon, he continues, can be
permitted for only two reasons, not always possible of justification:
first, "revenge, when we have been affronted in the same nature, or
have been any wise notoriously abused, and can make our selves no
other reparation"; second, to expose and to make examples of vicious
men when they "ought to be upbraided with their crimes and follies"
for the good of society.

The second he regards as the justifiable, if not the prescriptive,
function of the moral poet. But revenge as a motive he rejects as
incompatible with Christian belief: "all offenses are to be forgiven,
as we expect the like pardon for those which we daily commit against
Almighty God. And this consideration has often made me tremble,
when I was saying our Saviour's prayer." Many times, he goes on,

he has avoided answering attacks even when he has been notoriously provoked. "More libels," he points out quite accurately—and now statistically provable—"have been written against me, than almost any man now living; and I had reason on my side, to have defended my own innocence." Not, he hastens to add, would he defend his poetry, which would receive its proper judgment under other judges among posterity, for "interest and passion will lie buried in another age, and partiality and prejudice be forgotten." But his morals, "which have been sufficiently aspersed," and his reputation, which was dear to him, might well be defended, were he not deterred by his Christian sense of forgiveness. "I have seldom answered any scurrilous lampoon, when it was in my power to have exposed my enemies: and being naturally vindicative [sic], have suffered in silence, and possessed my soul in quiet." Of his own poetry he has little to say. The most significant comment is a short passage on the character of Zimri in his *Absalom and Achitophel*. Carried away at the moment in his need to illustrate delicate touches of fine raillery in satire—Horatian rather than Juvenalian in inspiration—Dryden cites the character of Zimri as "worth the whole poem"—an opinion he might not have voiced at another time. "I avoided the mention of great crimes," he points out, "and applied myself to the representing of blindsides and little extravagancies. . . . It succeeded as I wished; the jest went round, and he was laughed at in his turn, who began the frolick."

The concluding section—and the shortest of his long essay— consists almost entirely of an explanation of the principles of translation upon which the several translators proceeded. These are not, he emphasizes, literal translations, but combinations of paraphrase and imitation. A line by line rendering of the sense of Juvenal and Persius—as impossible as unsatisfactory—had already been attempted in the scholarly, unpoetic versions of Barten Holyday. While admitting that the present version is not so literally faithful to the original as those of Holyday and Stapylton—who indeed followed so closely their originals that "they trod on the heels of Juvenal and Persius, and hurt them by their too near approach"—Dryden is convinced that the new translations will be "far more pleasing to our readers." "A noble author," he points out, "would not be pursued too close by a translator." The final justification of the evident liberties taken with the originals is the pleasure and entertainment to be derived by the contemporary English reader, for the translators "endeavored to make [Juvenal] speak that kind of English, which [he] would have sopken, had [he] lived in England and had written to this age."

Six weeks after the satires were published, Samuel Briscoe published Sheeres' *Polybius,* with Dryden's "Character." Much of the material of the "Character" is derivative, as Dryden freely admits. He levies again upon the scholarship of the learned Casaubon. He had come to his task, however, not as a neophyte but as a longtime admirer of the Greek historian, whom he had read with pleasure before he was ten years old, in an English translation—probably Grimestone's folio of 1634. Even at that early age he had been able, he says, to assess the superiority of Polybius to other historians with whom he had early been acquainted. At his advanced age now, this early fondness for the author was confirmed, and he profited more from reading Polybius than from "Thucydides, Appian, Dion Cassius, and all the rest of the Greek historians together."

Dryden's busy autumn was punctuated by several events that looked to the past and to the future. On November 19 Thomas Shadwell died after holding his position of laureate for slightly more than a year and a half. Within the month the post was given not to the uncompromising Dryden but to Nahum Tate; and the place of Historiographer Royal, now dissociated from the laureateship, went to Thomas Rymer. Dryden could not have mourned overlong about Shadwell and he was to have little reason to be happy about Rymer, whose *Short View of Tragedy,* issued in December, fell severely upon Dryden's plays. As the winter passed, Tonson's progress on the new miscellany volume came almost to a stop, though Dryden proceeded to bring to completion his own work for *Examen Poeticum,* as it was to be called. Supplementary verse from other authors seems to have been very slow in coming in; and as late as the following June, Peter Motteux, announcing the volume for the autumn, inserts the publisher's invitation "to the ingenious to contribute to that choice and valuable Collection by sending him [Tonson] such pieces as may be properly inserted in it." Whether or not Tonson received all of the contributions he wished, he went ahead in July, the publication date having been postponed, much to Dryden's annoyance, since he was eager to go on his summer holiday in Northamptonshire.[15]

While the preparations for *Examen Poeticum* took their slow course, Dryden was faced with personal problems and decisions that we know of only through his correspondence with Walsh and Tonson. Sometime during the winter his two sons, John and

Charles, evidently faced with slight prospects at home, journeyed to Rome, where they were installed under the care of Cardinal Howard.[16] At home, the poet's generosity to a supposed friend resulted only in his being cheated of £50; and having had the man arrested, he is undecided whether to go through the long process of common law and Chancery to recover the amount.[17] He apparently decided to forgo prosecution. In the spring he began to plot and to write his new, and last, play. By May, when he wrote to Walsh, he had completed two acts and had conferred with Doggett, the actor, about the role of the lecherous old fool which he was to act. He had also arranged with Tonson to send Walsh some books which would be useful to him in writing a preface for the play. Apparently it was to be a critical essay upholding the claims of the moderns versus the ancients; but under Walsh's hand it became too long for inclusion and was not used. Interestingly, Dryden says that he "would be proud of your entring the lists, though not against Rymer"; he himself was writing an answer to that critic in the dedicatory epistle soon to appear with *Examen Poeticum*.[18] Toward the end of July, accompanied by Tonson, Dryden journeyed to Northamptonshire, their temporary differences over the payments for the translation of Ovid seemingly forgotten. In a friendly letter of August 30, he acknowledges his pleasure at Tonson's "good nature, in bearing [me] company to this place," especially since the publisher had gone to some expense and for the time had to neglect his business. "I will endeavour," writes Dryden, "to make you some amends; & therefore I desire you to command me something for your service."[19] The time was fast approaching when he could make those amends and repay in large measure the good nature of his publisher. Though Dryden makes no mention in this letter of his proposed translation of Virgil, there is little doubt that they were engaged in preliminary plans for it.

Dryden's most pressing piece of business, however, was to finish the new play, which he was to call *Love Triumphant*. After Tonson's return to London, Dryden remained alone in the country, his wife not having accompanied him. Although his movements cannot be traced, he appears to have spent most, if not all, of his vacation at the house of Sir Matthew Dudley, at the Manor of Clapton, only a short distance east of Titchmarsh, where his relatives lived. Indeed his inability to visit Titchmarsh more often brought considerable disappointment to him. His host, Sir Matthew, was busily wooing the daughter of the Earl of Thomond, who lived about twenty miles distant, and consequently was away from home much of the time, and with him the calèche, on which Dryden seems to have depended for transportation.   Otherwise, in a household which consisted of Sir Matthew and his brother, the poet seems to have been well cared for, and diverted by what pleasures the country provided, especially fishing.   He kept up correspondence with Tonson, the latter apparently doing most of the writing.   To the publisher he reports that he has translated "six hunderd [sic] lines of Ovid" [Virgil?], but he believes "his 772 lines" cannot be put in less than "nine hunderd [sic] or more of mine."[20]

When *Examen Poeticum* appeared in July it carried a dedication to Francis, Lord Radcliffe, who a few years later was to become Lord Derwentwater.   Dryden's connection with him remains most obscure, and the only link between them may have been their Catholicism.   From a sentence in Dryden's letter to Tonson from Northamptonshire one gathers that the publisher thought Radcliffe a likely patron, though Dryden believed otherwise: "I am sure you thought my Lord Radclyffe wou'd have done something: I ghessd more truly, that he cou'd not; but I was too far ingagd to desist; though I was tempted to it, by the melancholique prospect I had of it."   In spite of the fact that Dryden read to Radcliffe and his lady some portions of his translations from Ovid, the noble lord did not act the generous patron.   However, the importance of the dedication resides not in the fact that it was addressed to Radcliffe but that it becomes a sounding board to reflect Dryden's weariness and his contempt for government (coupled with another defense of himself), and an opportunity to answer his critics, notably Rymer, whose *Short View of Tragedy* had been published in the preceding December.

Why, he asks, "have I spent my life in so unprofitable a study? Why am I grown old in seeking so barren a reward as fame?"   The same abilities and energy, he thinks, could have raised him to "any honours of the gown; which are often given to men of as little learning and less honesty than myself."   Warming to his subject, which soon becomes an introduction to an attack on his critics, Dryden obliquely comments on the recent elevation (in December, 1692) of both Tate and Rymer to the offices of laureate and historiographer, vacated by the death of Shadwell.   "No government," he continues, "has ever been, or ever can be, wherein timeservers and blockheads will not be uppermost.   The persons are only changed, but the same jugglings in state, the same hypocrisy in religion, the same self-interest and mismanagement will remain for ever. Blood and money will be lavished in all ages, only for the preferment of new faces with old consciences. . . . I am not ashamed to be little, when I see them so infamously great." Yet he knows not "why the name of Poet should be dishonourable to me, if I am truly one, as I hope I am. . . . For the reputation of my honesty, no man can question it, who has any of his own; for that of my poetry, it shall either stand by its own merit, or fall for want of it."

He has now arrived in his essay at the object toward which he has been steadily moving: the censurers and detractors of poets, particularly of himself. The contemporary critics, he finds, are a far cry from their predecessors in antiquity. Then they were defenders of poets and commentators—really coadjutors who could and did shield the real poets from the ill-natured cavils of "those fellows, who were then called Zoili and Momi, and now take upon themselves the venerable name of censors." These were never called "critics" in ancient times. At best these cavillers are wits of the second order, entirely subservient to the fame of poets. How then have they, "from our seconds, become principals against us? Does the ivy undermine the oak, which supports its weakness?" Julius Scaliger he cites as a case in point, the very Scaliger who "wou'd needs turn down" Homer and would dethrone him, "after the possession of three thousand years." Though Scaliger has indeed pointed out imperfections in the great epic poet, "which are incident to human kind," yet, "who had not rather be that Homer, than this Scaliger?" Of Lucan, the same critic had written that "he rather seems to bark than sing." "Would any but a dog," asks Dryden, "have made so snarling a comparison?"

By easy transition he comes to a consideration of two kinds of such detractors in England. One group is made up of those who with seeming moderation and respect toward the dramatists of the Elizabethan age "only scorn and vilify the present poets, to set up their predecessors." They commend Shakespeare, Jonson, and Beaumont and Fletcher not to do them homage but to "throw dirt on the writers of this age." A "more venomous" kind of insect, however, he finds in those who manifestly seek the overthrow "of our poetical church and state"—those who allow nothing to their countrymen, and who "attack the living, by raking up the ashes of the dead. . . ." By exalting the ancient drama, and by this process subverting the Elizabethan title, these critics know that "we, who claim under them [the Elizabethans], must fall of course." As Dryden suspected, such attacks as these were aimed only too clearly at him, for no other man of the era had written so much drama or so much criticism of the drama. "If I am the man, as I have reason to believe, who am seemingly courted and secretly undermined, I think I shall be able to defend myself, when I am openly attacked." Rymer had provoked this spirited outburst by his remarks in *A Short View of Tragedy*.

Although Dryden had written bitter words about government, he had not made an overt attack upon the present government. Yet some were willing to believe he had done so; and in a letter from the country he relates to Tonson the gossip he has heard from London:

About a fortnight ago I had an intimation from a friend by letter, that one of the Secretaryes, I suppose Trenchard had informd the Queen, that I had abusd her Government, (those were the words) in my Epistle to my Lord Radclyffe; & that thereupon, she had commanded her Historiographer Rymer, to fall upon my playes; wch he assures me is now doeing. I doubt not his malice, from a former hint you gave me: & if he be employd, I am confident tis of his own seeking; who you know has spoken slightly of me in his last Critique: & that gave me occasion to snarl againe. In your next, let me know what you can learn of this matter.[21]

But Rymer did not return to the attack.

Dryden's last play, far advanced in May when he mentioned his progress on it to Walsh, must have been finished during his month and a half in the country. By the beginning of September his visit was drawing to a close, and on September 13, he wrote to Tonson that he had taken a place in the coach for the following Tuesday. Having learned from Tonson that Congreve and Southerne intend to meet his coach four miles from London and keep him company into the city, he is deeply touched by this evidence of their great affection for him. He happily looks forward to the diversion and hopes the weather will not prevent it. Indeed, he is full of good nature and writes his sincere gratitude to Tonson for his many recent kindnesses. Dryden reports that he has also done some kindnesses of his own. He confesses to being sleepy. On the night before, some benighted travelers had stumbled upon the Dudley household, to find only Mr. Dudley, one manservant, and the old poet—and no maid in the house. They made shift, however, to be hospitable. The "lusty pike," which Dryden had caught that day, provided supper for the four ladies and two gentlemen. But beds being scarce because of this casual intrusion of six people, Dryden relinquished his own to them, and so sat up most of the night.[22]   On the following Wednesday night, September 20, he was back in Gerrard Street.

Almost at once began the negotiations with the theater to produce the all-but-complete *Love Triumphant*.   The egregious Alexander Davenant had finally been caught up with, and his swindling operations as manager of the theater fully exposed.   On October 23 he fled England.[23]   Into this gap moved the shrewd Rich, who now began his exploitation of the theater and actors alike.   By December he was virtually in control, and it was under his management that the new play was produced.   At the same time both of Dryden's young friends, Congreve and Southerne, had plays of their own ready, so that we are treated to the experience of following the successive productions of Congreve's *The Double-Dealer,* Dryden's *Love Triumphant,* and Southerne's *The Fatal Marriage.*   Congreve's, put into rehearsal first, was acted about the beginning of December, not without a good deal of censure, induced (as Dryden said) because "the women thinke he has exposed their Bitchery too much; & the Gentlemen, are offended with him; for the discovery of their follyes."   But in spite of the cavilling, the play "took," and enjoyed a successful run.   In the cast were the greatest actors of the Company and of the age: Betterton, Underhill, Doggett, Powell, Williams, Kynaston, Ann Bracegirdle, Elizabeth Barry, and Mrs. Mountford.

When *The Double Dealer* appeared in print some months later, Dryden contributed, as prefixed verses, a gracious poem entitled "To My Dear Friend Mr. Congreve, on his Comedy Call'd the Double-Dealer."   It was a labor of love; and in it he demonstrates again not only his great generosity toward his friends but his shrewd critical sense in assessing literary excellence.   Congreve's great powers he recognized in this first play.   He writes:

> O that your brows my laurel had sustain'd;
> Well had I been depos'd, if you had reign'd!
> The father had descended for the son;
> For only you are lineal to the throne.

And he moves into prophecy:

> Yet this I prophesy: thou shalt be seen
> (Tho with some short parenthesis between)
> High on the throne of wit; and, seated there,
> Not mine—that's little—but thy laurel wear.

At the end he lays upon his young friend a charge which was fulfilled some years after Dryden's death:

> Already I am worn with cares and age,
> And just abandoning th' ungrateful stage;
> Unprofitably kept at Heav'n's expense,
> I live a rent-charge on his providence:
> But you, whom ev'ry Muse and Grace adorn,
> Whom I foresee to better fortune born,
> Be kind to my remains; and O defend,
> Against your judgment, your departed friend!
> Let not the insulting foe my fame pursue,
> But shade those laurels which descend to you;
> And take for tribute what these lines express:
> You merit more; nor could my love do less.

As soon as their run had ended, the same acting group, with the addition of Alexander, Mrs. Betterton, and Mrs. Kent, began rehearsals for *Love Triumphant*. By the middle of January the new play was ready for the stage.[24] Dryden had now made his final decision: this was the end of his career in the drama. He announces his retirement in the prologue—partly in the popular form of a last will and testament:

> He leaves you, first, all plays of his inditing,
> The whole estate which he has got by writing.
> The beaux may think this nothing but vain praise;
> They'll find it something, the testator says;
> For half their love is made from scraps of plays.
> To his worst foes he leaves his honesty,
> That they may thrive upon 't as much as he.
> He leaves his manners to the roaring boys,
> Who come in drunk, and fill the house with noise.
> He leaves to the dire critics of his wit,
> His silence and contempt of all they writ.

He cannot forbear to take one more cut at Rymer:

> To Shakespeare's critic, he bequeaths the curse,
> To find his faults, and yet himself make worse;
> A precious reader in poetic schools,
> Who by his own examples damns his rules.

Unlike Congreve's comedy, Dryden's play did not "take." Its ill-success puts an ironic capstone upon his career in the theater:

thirty years before, his first play, *The Wild Gallant,* had also been a failure. But between the two he had enjoyed many successes, enough for one man and one lifetime. Presumably *Love Triumphant* did not have a long run. Within two or three weeks many of the same actors were busy mounting Southerne's *The Fatal Marriage,* in which Elizabeth Barry, whose superb acting in tragic roles had already placed her among the pre-eminent actresses, won the applause of the town and carried Southerne's play to a great success. The failure of Dryden's last play, "coin'd from [an] old poet's addle-pate," did not, we feel sure, detract from his satisfaction at his young friend's good fortune.

Like most of his plays since the Revolution, *Love Triumphant* was published very soon after acting. It appeared (according to the advertisement in the *London Gazette*) about March 15, 1693/94. Included was a dedication to the Earl of Salisbury, a convert to Catholicism and a relative of Elizabeth Dryden through the Suffolk branch of the Howards. One of the least interesting of Dryden's dedicatory epistles, it acknowledges unspecified favors he had received from Salisbury before and after the Revolution. Viewing his last play as the youngest child of an old man, he points out that those that were born earlier have carried "away the right of patrimony by right of eldership." The play therefore must make its own way in the world; yet natural affection "calls upon me to put it out . . . into the best service which I can procure for it." And according to the "usual practice of our decayed gentry, to look about them for some illustrious family, and there endeavour to fix their young darling, where he may be both well educated and supported, I have herein also followed the custom of the world, and am satisfied in my judgment that I could not have made a more worthy choice." The ill-success of the play on the stage seems to demand a defense, which he supplies in token form, but without much feeling of conviction. His main concern is to justify modern practice which diverges from the theory of the ancients. Aristotle, he admits, has said that

the catastrophe which is made from a change of will is not one of the first order for beauty; but it may reasonably be alledged in defence of this play, as well as of the *Cinna* (which I take to be the very best of Corneille's) that the philosopher who made the rule, copied all the laws which he gave for the theatre from the authorities and examples of the Greek poets which he had read. . . . Had it been possible for Aristotle to have seen the *Cinna,* I am confident he would have altered his opinion; and concluded, that a simple change of will might be managed with so much judgment, as to render it the most agreeable as well as the most surprizing part of the whole fable; let Dacier, and all the rest of the modern criticks, who are too much bigotted to the ancients, contend never so much to the contrary.

With respect to the observance of the unities, he justifies his practice in *Love Triumphant* by pointing out that the action takes place within the limits of "an astrological day, which begins at twelve and ends at the same hour the day following." This concept he has never before cited, and one may find him writing with tongue in cheek; for he goes on to suggest, as he had years earlier, that the unity of place (never one of Aristotle's "unities") leads to multiple absurdities both in the attitude of playwrights and audiences: "it is an original absurdity for the audience to suppose themselves to be in any other place than in the very theatre in which they sit." Even so, there may be more absurdities in the practice of the playwright, who, to follow a ridiculous principle, curtails his "liberty of invention." But for Dryden these concerns were rapidly receding in importance; for the play had ended; and he turned to Virgil as to an old friend and to the translation as a labor of love.

The Great Translation: *Virgil*
1694-1697

T HE DECISION to undertake a translation of the whole Virgil was no doubt made during the late summer of 1693, when poet and publisher were together in Northamptonshire.[1] The autumn months were devoted to further planning, and, on Dryden's part, to a preliminary translation of the third *Georgic* as a sample which was to appear in Tonson's next (or fourth) miscellany volume, finally published the following July. The third *Georgic* was completed by December, when Dryden wrote Walsh about the early plans for Virgil. He tells him that present plans include a limited edition for first subscribers, each copy to cost five guineas and to include "an hunderd & two Brass Cutts, with the Coats of Armes of the subscriber to each Cutt." Another edition—the "inferiour subscription"— would have no coats of arms or cuts and would merely list the names of subscribers. Each copy of this edition was priced at two guineas.[2]

For the next six months his thoughts and energies were taken up with details of the *Virgil*. Both publisher and poet were soon aware of the magnitude of the task: the labor of collecting the first subscription and arranging for the coats of arms and the cuts was in itself formidable. Subscribers with part of their money paid in as earnest would not be willing to wait indefinitely for the finished work; a foreseeable completion date was necessary. Dryden, having already suffered periods of illness, knew that his physical condition might postpone a rapid completion of the translation. Since they had already had differences over finances, both Dryden and Tonson saw the need of a contract for their mutual protection. It was drawn up and signed on June 15, 1694. Congreve signed as Dryden's witness.

The legal document is carefully written and no doubt included those items of possible disagreement which both men could foresee. Dryden agrees to translate "with all convenient Speed" all the *Eclogues, Georgics,* and the *Æneid* and to prepare them for the press, with such notes, prefaces, and dedications as he shall think proper. He further articles that—in order to complete the task as rapidly as possible—he "will not write translate or publish or assist in the writing translating or publishing of any other book" except "a little French Booke of Painting which he hath engag'd to perform for some Gentlemen Vertuosoes and Painters." This was Du Fresnoy's *Art of Painting.* Dryden also agrees not to write any prose or poetry which when printed would exceed the cost of one shilling. This article would enable him to earn a few pounds by writing prologues or epilogues. Finally, he reserves the right to provide his son John's play, *The Husband his own Cuckold,* with prologue, epilogue, or songs. In good faith he thus voluntarily agrees to reserve nearly all of his energies, for an unspecified time, to the task of translating Virgil.

Tonson's responsibilities under the terms of the contract were, of course, largely financial. For the whole translation he agrees to pay £200—in installments: £50 for the *Eclogues* and *Georgics,* and £50 for each block of four books of the *Æneid.* This indeed looks like a great bargain for Tonson, until we examine more closely other terms of the contract. Dryden in addition to his "translation" money, was also to receive all collections in excess of the official subscription price. Such moneys would include gifts, payments for dedicatory epistles, and so on. Furthermore, Dryden's total remuneration was eventually to be increased by a clause enabling him to purchase from Tonson, at a low rate, as many copies of the less expensive edition as he wished and to advertise and sell them on his own account.[3] Accordingly, at the midway point of his work, he advertised for subscribers at the rate of two guineas. To supply the demand for these large paper copies, identical to the de luxe first subscribers' books, except for the omission of the cuts and the several coats of arms, Dryden ordered 250 copies. For these Tonson charged him, after a careful reckoning of accounts, £1 6s. 4d. each.[4] The poet's profit on these came, then, to 15s. 8d. each. If we add the total income from these—£195 16s. 8d.— to the translation money and to his share of the first subscribers' edition (£207 2s.), his returns from his contract with Tonson would amount to slightly more than £600. Presumably he received much more than this through gifts made to him by Chesterfield, Clifford, and Mulgrave, to whom he dedicated the three sections of the complete work. All in all, he probably received close to £1,400.[5]

This accounting, however, looks ahead to the completion of a long, hard task which, Dryden pointed out, he had undertaken "in my great Climacteric." How fatiguing it would prove he could hardly have known when he signed the agreement, nor could he have imagined the recurring periods of ill-health or the constant difficulties with subscribers and their payments, and the inevitable frictions with his publisher. The record of the following years of work is scanty, but enough is known to warrant a tentative reconstruction.

At the very beginning he was faced, of course, with the choice of texts and commentaries. Having already translated Juvenal and Persius and selections from Ovid, he knew the importance of selecting a satisfactory text with complete commentary and interpretation. For Persius he had used Isaac Casaubon's text of 1605, and had relied heavily upon the learned commentary of that great scholar. For Juvenal, he had found in the so-called "Dolphin" series, created in France for the use of the Dauphin, a text (1674) and commentary by Prateus (Louis Desprès) the best for his purpose. The text of Ovid and commentary by Borchard Cnipping (Leyden, 1670) he had used, along with others. For Virgil he was able to find a distinguished and authoritative text in the same "Dolphin" series, that of Carolus Ruaeus (Charles de la Rue), which had been published in 1675.[6] Dryden's good friend Gilbert Dolben turned over to him "all the several editions of Virgil, and all the commentaries of those editions in Latin."[7] What this group included we can only guess, though Dryden mentions that Fabrini (whom he rejected) was included, as well as Pontanus, and Ruaeus. In addition to these, he had available a considerable number of English translations of Virgil or parts of Virgil, upon which he was progressively to depend as time went on: those of May, Ogilby, Stapylton, Godolphin, Howard, Denham, Cowley, Waller, Lauderdale, Mulgrave, and others. With these about him, he was armed with the most authoritative texts of his century as well as with the best of the scholarly and poetic translations into English. Although not ignorant of his text, Dryden did not follow it scrupulously, and the commentaries and interpretations he used with care. To many readers, the translation has appeared expansive, incorrect, irresponsible, and chaotic.

Indeed, unfavorable criticism of the translation began upon its publication and has not yet ended. Dryden's heavy reliance upon his English predecessors has long been known, and though Dryden was candid in making general acknowledgments of indebtedness, his failure to spell out his frequent and detailed borrowings has led to charges ranging from ignorance of Latin and of Virgil to dishonesty and chicanery. Yet despite its many shortcomings—and Dryden was the first to point out many of them—its sharpest critics have found it a brilliant example of poetic translation. And as such, after two and a half centuries, it maintains an honored place among all translations into English.

As month succeeded month, and Dryden added more and more couplets to the growing copy that was being turned over to Tonson, he found himself more abstracted, though not more insulated, from the contemporary scene than he had ever been. The concentration upon his studies, and upon Virgil, was more intense and lasted for a longer period than he had ever known. Punctuated by periods of sickness and not greatly interrupted by other literary activity, the long stretch of thirty-six months might be expected to produce tension, discouragement, and irascibility. The petty details of the financial arrangements connected with the subscriptions, the anxiety induced by Tonson's negligence in arranging for coats of arms for the plates, the concern over saving a place for the Earl of Chesterfield or the Duke of Devonshire, the suspicion that some of the solicitors for subscriptions were not overly scrupulous, or that Tonson had driven too sharp a bargain, the worry over debased money that he was forced to accept—all these took a toll of the strength of the old poet.

From first to last his chief worries were lack of money and ill-health. By divorcing himself from the stage, Dryden had cut himself off from a steady, if not munificent, income. To take its place only Tonson's payments, called for in the contract, and the receipts from the second subscribers (not to be a reality until late in 1695) were available. The payment of £50 for the *Eclogues* and the *Georgics* came in the autumn of 1694—about four months after the signing of the contract. The second payment, due after the fourth *Æneid* was finished, could hardly have been made before April, 1695; for two months of that period had been used for the translation of Du Fresnoy. The early part of Virgil went rapidly; but after mid-1695, there is a noticeable slowing down in the delivery of the copy to Tonson. By June 8 after an (enforced?) idleness of a fortnight, he wrote Tonson that it was time to think of the second subscriptions, which according to the agreement, were to be advertised after the sixth *Æneid* should be complete.[8] It is therefore possible to surmise that this point was reached either in June or July, or that it was well within sight. He was looking far enough ahead to allow plenty of time, for as he wrote, "the more time I have for collecting them, the larger they are like to be." Those subscriptions were of great value to him, for, under the agreement, the second subscriptions were to be his opportunity to add measurably to his total income from the task. In the same letter he asks that Tonson inform him of the price of the paper and of the books: Dryden's profit was the difference between this cost and the two guineas he would receive for each book.

The advertisement for the second subscribers, however, (in spite of Dryden's foresight) seems to have been delayed for some months. Perhaps an extended illness prevented him from pushing his work as rapidly as he had thought possible, or perhaps the preliminary solicitation for subscribers proved so disappointingly slow or inept that it was thought prudent to withhold the public advertisement until a later time. At any rate, the announcement seems not to have been made for some time, probably not until the late spring of 1696.[9] In the meantime, in the summer of 1695, he pressed on with the sixth *Æneid,* and finished it, at least in preliminary draft, before one of his friends invited him to the country to pursue his studies in the comfort and leisure of a great country estate. John Cecil, fifth Earl of Exeter, whose great Burghley House stood less than twenty miles from the village of Dryden's birth, and from the villages where he was accustomed to visit during the summer—Aldwinckle, Titchmarsh, Oundle—offered him the hospitality of his house in the late summer and early autumn. It may be that Dryden had spent part of his summer in his accustomed haunts, and merely moved on to Burghley House. During his stay with Exeter, who was a fellow Tory and who, though an early supporter of William, had refused to take the oaths in 1689, Dryden must have thoroughly enjoyed himself. Certainly the political atmosphere he would have found congenial, and perhaps also the intellectual. Dryden's visit at Burghley House enabled him to complete the seventh *Æneid.* By the last of October he was back in London, ready to begin the eighth.

On the twenty-ninth of that month he wrote to Tonson, somewhat irascibly, unmollified by an apparently conciliatory letter which Tonson had dispatched to him while he was yet in the country.

Matters of money were at issue; and Dryden begins his letter: "Some kind of intercourse must be carryed on betwixt us, while I am translateing Virgil."[10] Not a happy beginning, this, nor does the letter become more friendly as Dryden proceeds to rehearse some details of their disagreements at this mid-point of their joint undertaking. He intends, within a few days, to begin the eighth *Æneid,* and gives Tonson due warning—not without a snarl—that he expects at the completion of that book £50, "in good silver; not such as I have had formerly. I am not obligd to take gold, neither will I; nor stay for it beyond four & twenty houres after it is due." His anger, indeed, feeds and grows upon itself, and he overflows with complaints which must certainly have been a lively subject of argument with them through the correspondence of the past few months. "I thank you," he writes, "for the civility of your last letter in the Country: but the thirty shillings upon every book remains with me." Apparently Tonson had, during the solicitation for the second subscribers, appropriated some of the initial one guinea payments (the guinea then being worth 30*s.*) to himself. These Dryden rightfully could claim; for his only obligation to Tonson—on this account—was the purchase price, *at cost,* of the 250 books eventually to be printed. This cost, of course, could not be determined until after the edition was complete and in print.[11] The second subscriptions, it appears, were not going well; and Tonson's suggestion made to Congreve—to have Sir Godfrey Kneller and John Clostermann (who were indebted to Dryden for the *De Arte Graphica*) solicit for them—did not impress the poet. "You always intended," he charges, "I shoud get nothing by the Second Subscriptions, as I found from first to last." Having aired these matters, Dryden ends his letter on a somewhat more placatory note: "But this is past, & you shall have your bargain if I live, and have my health." He is worried, at the same time, about the First Subscribers, and for places for some, like the Duke of Devonshire (the father of his hostess at Burghley House), who had not yet been included. The sharpness of his tone to his publisher is gathered up in the passage: "And I must have a place for the Duke of Devonshyre. Some of *your friends* will be glad to take back their three guinneys [italics mine]." And again: "I desire neither excuses nor reasons from you; for I am but too well satisfyd already. The Notes & Prefaces shall be short: because you shall get the more by saving paper." The curt "John Dryden" contrasts with his more usual polite close, and suggests the depth of his displeasure and a growing ill-temper.

As the months went on, relations between poet and publisher worsened. Tonson and Congreve, entrusted with the task of phrasing the proposals for the second subscriptions, were unconscionably slow; in November Dryden anxiously inquired when he might be able to see them. In the meantime, the copy of the completed portions of *Virgil* was being circulated, at Dryden's request, to certain selected persons, in order to generate among the knowledgeable an interest in the work and to encourage him by what he must have expected to be a semipublic approbation of his efforts.[12] As nearly as can be determined, he proceeded to the eighth book in November, 1695, about the time his son's play was being readied for the stage. The negotiations for its acting within the next month must have diverted somewhat his thoughts and energies from Virgil; so that the eighth book probably required three or possibly four months during the winter. Upon its completion he received a warrant from Tonson for the payment of £50; whether he had to wait more than "four & twenty houres" for it is not clear. Unfortunately he was forced to accept the whole amount in shilling and sixpenny silver pieces from the goldsmith, Mr. Knight, only to find that they would not "go." In desperation he sent them back and exchanged them for guineas at 27*s*. each. "Tis troublesome," he writes, "to be a looser."

Beyond money matters, he had several other complaints. Tonson having refused the poet's request for an additional payment for the notes he hoped to add to his translation, Dryden asserts that he is not sorry for the refusal; for "to make them good, wou'd have cost me half a yeares time at least." He will therefore include marginal notes to help the unlearned, "who understand not the poeticall Fables." The prefaces, however, he will make more learned. Indeed, now that he can look back upon a work more than two-thirds completed, he is convinced that it would require seven years to translate Virgil "exactly." He was weary; and perhaps not too extravagantly pleased with his performance. Yet he might have been mollified to reflect that in less than two years' time, beset by financial troubles and illness, and now in his sixty-fifth year, he had already performed a great labor. Anger at Tonson was tempered by his realization that "all of your trade are Sharpers & you not more than others; therefore I have not wholly left you." With the wisdom of hindsight, he upbraids Tonson for failure to publish proposals for the de luxe first subscription; for many persons, for whom now there is no room, are eager to subscribe. At this point in the translation he is prepared for a change of routine and desires Tonson to send transcribed copies of the *Eclogues, Georgics,* and *Æneids* I-IV, so that he can put the simple notes to them and send them along to the printer in order that the "press may stay as little as possibly it can." At the same time *Æneids* V-VIII are ready for Tonson. The seriousness of his financial distress of the moment is sharply pointed up by his request that Tonson send him his share of Lord Derby's subscription money—two guineas. "And let it be good," he concludes, "if you desire to oblige me who am not your Enemy, & may be your friend. . . ."[13]

At this stage of the translation Dryden began perceptibly to slow down. Though one gets little impression of feverish haste in his accomplishment thus far, his steady, if occasionally interrupted, attention to *Virgil* is impressive. If as seems probable he had by January (or February), 1695/96, arrived at the ninth *Æneid,* the same rate of speed might be expected to end the work by early autumn. Yet it was to require many months longer, and considerably more than a year was to pass before the book was published. The reasons for the delay may be inferred. Recurrent illness was one: he suggests as much, in the "Postscript" to the *Virgil* when he writes: "That I have [since completing the work] recovered in some measure the health which I had lost by too much application to this work, is owing, next to God's mercy, to the skill and care of Dr. Guibbons and Dr. Hobbs, the two ornaments of their profession." Another reason was mental fatigue from continued concentration upon one book and one unvaried technique. Even Virgil must have palled after months of such enforced intimacy. After so many thousands of lines already translated, the problem of varying line tone, of finding English rhyme-words, of making the couplet march on proper feet became acute. From the first he had relied upon his English predecessors for rhyme-words, but now he found himself turning to them more and more. Another reason was the practical necessity of keeping track of Tonson, as well as of the solicitors for the subscriptions. Though perhaps not dishonest, they were often careless or forgetful, as was indeed Ned Plowden, who, having been paid a subscription by the Countess of Macclesfield, forgot to turn in the money; and Dryden, who probably had been informed of her payment by the Countess (a near neighbor on Gerrard Street), was obliged to bring pressure to bear upon Plowden.[14] Holidays away from London, away from such petty, nerve-racking details, were necessary. Though definite evidence of his movements is lacking, it may be assumed that he found a welcome at country houses of relatives or friends.

As the early spring of 1696 wore on, Dryden continued his translation of the ninth *Æneid* and the tenth, probably completing the latter by June or July. Only two letters during these months survive to give us fleeting glimpses of his chief worries and concerns. Both are addressed to Tonson. The first, on May 26, is a mere note to ask how much Tonson is willing to pay for a copy of his son's play. It also informs Tonson that Sir Robert Howard has offered to help in the desperate coinage situation by changing clipped money for him at the Exchequer—if Dryden can gain anything by that procedure. The other letter (in June?) throws some light upon Dryden's family life. As an expression of his affection for his two older sons in Rome, Dryden had determined to send each a watch from the shop of the celebrated watchmaker, Thomas Tompion. The watches cost £22, a sum which he did not have but which he was sure he could get from Tonson as an advance on the next—and the last—payment of £50, due after the twelfth *Æneid* should be delivered. Consequently, he asks the publisher to send him a goldsmith's bill for £22 (Tompion had refused to accept gold) so that he can pay Tompion's man upon delivery of the watches in the afternoon of the day he was writing the note. Presumably Tonson complied. The cost of his gift was nearly half what he was to receive for translating four books of *Virgil,* more than a half year's work.

By early September he had completed the eleventh *Æneid,* and was ready to begin on the last.[15] Sir William Bowyer had again asked him to come to Denham Court, and thither he went to work on the twelfth book, most of which was done at this retreat. The anxiety and impatience of some of his subscribers must have been allayed as word circulated that the poet was nearing the end of the long task. In a letter to Tonson, dated September 30, Basil Kennett (who had just published his *Romae Antiquae Notitia*) wrote: "It's ye best News in ye world that your great Friend is so near the height of his glory: when 'twill be as impossible to think of Virgil without M^r. Dryden as of either without Mr Tonson."[16] Dryden spent probably not more than two or three months at Denham Court: he was back in London in late November.

At last the final *Æneid* was in English; and Dryden sent off the copy to Tonson with the request that it be transcribed in a legible hand and returned for final review. The notes, jotted on some of the margins, were incomplete and these he planned to enlarge before they should be transferred from the foul copy, which he feared could hardly be deciphered because it was so badly written. All the copy, then, was dispatched, including the fourth and ninth *Eclogues*, not newly translated but only slightly corrected in his wife's copy of the 1684 *Miscellany Poems,* where they had first appeared.[17] Though Virgil was translated, much yet needed to be done before eventual publication. Final choice of patrons to whom the various portions were to be dedicated still had to be made.

Dryden's selection of Lord Clifford for the *Eclogues* recognized the son of his early patron and a Catholic peer to whom tradition links him during his composition of *The Hind and the Panther.* Choice of Mulgrave, now Marquis of Normanby, for the *Æneid,* continued a long association of patron and poet; and Mulgrave had a proprietary right in the epic by virtue of his attempts to pave the way for Charles II's patronage of Dryden's proposed original epic, nearly twenty-five years before. The final choice of Chesterfield for the *Georgics* is rather more difficult to explain. That nobleman had hitherto not been conspicuous as a patron of literature, nor had he ever, to our knowledge, shown the slightest interest in Dryden, or Dryden in him. Chesterfield, however, by his first marriage with Elizabeth, daughter of the Duke of Ormond, and by his third (and last) with a daughter of the Earl of Carnarvon by whom he had a son, Philip (who in 1692 married Elizabeth, daughter of the Marquis of Halifax), had allied himself with the Ormond and Halifax families, both of whom were Dryden's patrons. He was, furthermore, a member of that group of nobles who, having early supported William, refused to take the oaths in 1689. Dryden had already paid special deference to other members of this group, so that the choice of Chesterfield may be partly explained on this score. Indeed when he came to inscribe the *Eclogues* to Clifford, Dryden particularly and pointedly began by saying: "I have found it not more difficult to translate Virgil, than to find such patrons as I desire for my translation; for though England is not wanting in a learned nobility, yet such are my unhappy circumstances, that they have confined me to a narrow choice." He was merely carrying out, perhaps, the policy he had set for himself in the first dedicatory epistles after the Revolution: to honor only those who had owned him in the decline of his fortunes, or those who by their actions had shown that politically they were on his side.

Fortunately, the slight correspondence between Dryden and

Chesterfield is available; and it is interesting to see what skill Dryden uses in phrasing his request for permission to dedicate the *Georgics*. Writing on February 17, 1696/97, Dryden first says his lack of confidence has delayed this letter "which I design'd almost a year together." Now time is pressing, for "my Translation of Virgil is already in the Press and I can not possibly deferr the publication of it any Longer than Midsummer Term at farthes." The sense of his own diffidence and of urgency are thus communicated to Chester-field. Even though the last books of Virgil were so recently com-pleted as hardly to give time for transcribing, not to mention his final review and the writing of notes, the impression he gives Chesterfield is that the *whole* work is in press. He then brings in the political side, to establish the fact of their mutual interests: "I have hinder'd it thus long in hopes of his return, for whom, and for my Conscience I have sufferd, that I might have layd my Authour at his feet." But the return of James II in 1697 was scarcely a probability, and though it may have been the vague hope of optimistic Jacobites, one may question that either Dryden or Chesterfield could have seriously entertained any such expectation. Dryden then says that both Clifford and Normanby had "desired" the *Eclogues* and the *Æneid*. "If I durst presume so farr, I would humbly offer the Georgiques to your Lordships patronage." And he hastens to add that they are Virgil's "Masterpiece in which he has not onely out done all other Poets, but him self." This assurance he reinforces by asserting that he has himself "labour'd and I may say I have cultivated the Georgiques with more care than any other part of him, and as I think my self with more success." With one more touch of subtlety, he clinches the matter: "Tis suitable to the retir'd life which you have chosen, and to your studies of Philosophy." Yet lest Chesterfield think this is broached merely as a mercenary trans-action, he adds: "And you may please to believe me as an honest man, that I have not the least consideration of any profit in this Address, but onely of honouring my self by dedicating to you." Of course, this is a direct bid for help—as Chesterfield no doubt would recognize. He ends his letter on a note of graceful humility, and yet of urgency.[18]

After Chesterfield's acceptance of the honor in a letter dated the very next day, February 18, Dryden could proceed toward the final details of getting his work through the press; he still, almost to the very week when the folio was issued, had to bestir himself about the subscribers and their payments.[19] The public expectation seems to have been keen, and every postponement merely increasd the interest,[20] but, finally, about the first week in August, *Virgil* in English, in a handsome folio, was distributed to the subscribers and put on sale for the general public.

The long task was done; and the poet, richer in prestige and somewhat better off financially, found himself poorer in health. It had been a grueling effort, and his extreme weariness breathes through not only his dedications but also the letters of the next few months. His illness he often alludes to: the gout bothered him, and he fell prey to colds and coughs and fevers of various kinds. He was beset with the physical complications induced by constant overwork and advancing age. "What I now offer to your Lordship," he writes to Clifford in the dedication to the *Eclogues,* "is the wretched remainder of a sickly age, worn out with study, and oppressed by fortune; without other support than the constancy and patience of a Christian." He is like a Tantalus condemned, not to hell, but to Elysium: "The fruit and the water may reach my lips, but cannot enter; and if they could, yet I want a palate, as well as a digestion." Wretchedness and old age he felt indeed: in wishing that the *Eclogues* will give pleasure in the reading, he adds, "though made English by one who scarcely remembers that passion which inspired my author when he wrote them."

Both the dedications to Clifford and Chesterfield are short, personal, and intimate; that to Normanby, prefixed to the *Æneid,* becomes an extended critical essay on epic poetry and its history. This is perhaps the learned "preface" he had alluded to months before when he wrote to Tonson. In writing to Clifford, he recalls the services of Sir Thomas, who "was that Pollio, or that Varus, who introduced me to Augustus." And he bespeaks favor by reminding Clifford that in Rome "patronage and clientship always descended from the fathers to the sons; and that the same plebeian houses had recourse to the same patrician line, which had formerly protected them. . . . so that I am your Lordship's by descent, and part of your inheritance." The dedication to the *Georgics* is full of flattery of Chesterfield's learning, judgment, good sense, and modesty; and it approaches, if it does not indeed attain, the fulsome. Part of it is taken up with a disquisition on the rise—and fall—of poetic vigor and genius in Virgil. In his view, Virgil had written the *Georgics* in the "full strength and vigour of his age, when his judgment was at the height, and before his fancy was declining." One cannot avoid the feeling that when he speaks of the gains and losses suffered by the Roman poet in his advancing years, he is really striking a kind of parallel balance sheet of his own career.

On the personal side, however, the most pertinent section of his dedication to Chesterfield is that in which he philosophizes on courts, courtiers, and men of affairs. Had he not, at various times before this, inveighed similarly upon such matters, his remarks might betray a post-Revolution bitterness at his own condition. Some of them, indeed, may be based on a sense of personal injury, but they seem rather to reflect his mature judgment reviewing nearly a half-century of informed participation in matters of great moment to his age: "I have laughed," he writes,

. . . when I have reflected on those men, who, from time to time, have shot themselves into the world. I have seen many successions of them; some bolting out upon the stage with vast applause, and others hissed off, and quitting it with disgrace. But while they were in action, I have constantly observed, that they seemed desirous to retreat from business: greatness, they said, was nauseous, and a crowd was troublesome; a quiet privacy was their ambition. Some few of them I believe said this in earnest. . . . They saw the happiness of a private life, and promised to themselves a blessing which every day it was in their power to possess; but they deferred it, and lingered still at court, because they thought they had not yet enough to make them happy.

Chesterfield, he points out, has not made the mistake of continuing in affairs, but has indeed made good his retirement. Yet, Dryden goes on, though the court is "a place of forgetfulness at the best, for well-deservers," it is not all bad; it has its positive values:

It is necessary for the polishing of manners, to have breathed that air; but it is infectious even to the best morals to live always in it. It is a dangerous commerce, where an honest man is sure at the first of being cheated. . . . The undermining smile becomes at length habitual; and the drift of his plausible conversation is only to flatter one, that he may betray another. Yet it is good to have been a looker on, without venturing to play; that a man may know false dice another time, though he never means to use them. I commend not him who never knew a court, but him who forsakes it, because he knows it. A young man deserves no praise, who out of melancholy zeal leaves the world before he has well tried it, and runs headlong into religion. He who carries a maidenhead into a cloister, is sometimes apt to lose it there, and to repent of his repentance.

The dedication of the *Æneid* to Normanby is a long, rambling essay dealing with epic poetry and other subjects. After an opening statement about epic, and a short comparison between epic and tragedy, Dryden states the method he proposes to follow in this discourse: "I design not a treatise of heroick poetry, but write in a loose epistolary way, somewhat tending to that subject, after the example of Horace in his First Epistle of the Second Book to Augustus Caesar, and of that to the Pisos, which we call his Art of Poetry; in both of which he observes no method that I can trace. . . . I have taken up, laid down, and resumed, as often as I pleased, the same subject; and this loose proceeding I shall use through all this Prefatory Dedication." And he keeps his promise. Coming within his purview are a multitude of ideas: a comparison of epic and tragedy, with the primacy given to epic; a long defense of Virgil, against the critics and criticasters who he thought had misread, misinterpreted, or unfavorably commented upon any aspect of the *Æneid*; a justification of particular lines, words, and episodes in the poem; a discussion of the armory of poetic talents needed by the epic poet; his own problems of versification and his projected *Prosodia* (not yet public because of Normanby's heeded advice not to print it); the genius of Spenser in heroic poetry; his own estimate of his achievement in the translation ("I will boldly own, that this English translation has more of Virgil's spirit in it than either the French or the Italian"); a justification of his use of neologisms and of a Latinized vocabulary; the increasing difficulties of translation as he came toward the end of his task, and the recognition of men, like Congreve, Addison, Chetwood, Moyle, and others, who had materially aided him with prefaces, summaries, suggestions; and finally the tributes, *passim,* to Normanby's learning, poetic accomplishments, and particularly his long continued patronage, and his kindly generosity to the poet, especially since the Revolution.

The very looseness of the essay endows it with a readability that it might well have lost had he digested such diverse materials by a more formal and conventional method. His happy and apt comments and illustrations, indicative of his still vigorously perceptive mind, contribute as always to the charm of his prose. On the marriage of Æneas and Dido, he remarks dryly, "that the ceremonies were short we may believe, for Dido was not only amorous, but a widow." On the chronology of events in the *Æneid,* he writes: "[Virgil's] great judgment made the laws of poetry, but he never made himself a slave to them: chronology at best is but a cobweb law, and he broke through it with his weight." On his desire to please—in this translation—the *judices natos:* "Without [it] I could never have been able to have done any thing at this age, when the fire of poetry is commonly extinguished in other men. Yet Virgil has given me the example of

Entellus for my encouragement; when he was well heated, the younger champion could not stand before him. And we find the elder contended not for the gift, but for the honour: *nec dona moror:* for Dampier has informed us in his Voyages, that the air of the country which produces gold, is never wholesome." And on the difficulty of translating: "Virgil called upon me in every line for some new word; and I paid so long, that I was almost bankrupt . . . the twelfth Æneid cost me double the time of the first and second. What had become of me, if Virgil had taxed me with another book? I had certainly been reduced to pay the publick in hammered money, for want of milled. . . ."

Amidst the many digressive passages made almost inevitable by his announced method, there appear some references which are personal and which allow us a glimpse of the man rather than the poet. He points out that Virgil wrote his great poem "in a time when the old form of government was subverted, and a new one just established by Octavius Caesar." Marius and Cinna "under the specious pretence of the publick good "had revenged themselves without form of law, on their private enemies." And Sylla, in proscribing "the heads of the adverse party . . . had nothing but liberty and reformation in his mouth; for the cause of religion is but a modern motive to rebellion, invented by the Christian priesthood, refining on the heathen." The destruction of senate and commons produced tyranny, the result of "altering fundamental laws and constitutions." The tyrannies and usurpations incident to elective monarchies he dismisses as not for him. As he had said years before, he is of Montaigne's opinion "that an honest man ought to be contented with that form of government, and with those fundamental constitutions of it, which he received from his ancestors, and under which himself was born."

In his analysis of Virgil's characterization of Æneas, Dryden examines with care (and with some relish) Book IV and the treatment of Dido's desertion. For the Carthaginian queen was Rome's enemy, and Virgil's comment on her who had forsaken her vows to Sichaeus when she succumbed to Æneas—*Varium et mutabile semper femina*—Dryden regards as "the sharpest satire in the fewest words that ever was made on womankind; for both the adjectives are neuter, and *animal* must be understood, to make them grammar." Indeed Virgil was well advised to put the words in the mouth of Mercury, for "if a god had not spoken them, neither durst he have written them, nor I translated them."

Although he is certain that his translation contains "more of Virgil's spirit in it than either the French or the Italian [Segrais' and Annibale Caro's]," he is by no means satisfied.   Recalling that Virgil had spent eleven years in composing the *Æneid,* he writes, "that, instead of three years, which I have spent in the translation of his works, I had four years more allowed me to correct my errours, that I might make my version somewhat more tolerable than it is. . . . Yet I will neither plead my age, nor sickness, in excuse of the faults which I have made.   That I wanted time, is all I have to say: for some of my subscribers grew so clamorous, that I could no longer defer the publication."   Even so, he has a lively awareness that his translation has superseded all others in English and that it can stand on its own merits as one of the distinguished translations of the age. Yet, it is also true that he preserved a becoming modesty when he compared his work with the original, whose greatness he continually proclaimed with characteristic enthusiasm: "Lay by Virgil [he tells Normanby] I beseech your Lordship and all my better sort of judges, when you take up my version, and it will appear a passable beauty when the original muse is absent; but like Spencer's false Florimel, made of snow, it melts and vanishes, when the true one comes in sight."

In order to complete the undertaking, there remained to be written only a postscript, in which he acknowledges his many and various obligations.   The first is to the Almighty Power for "the assistance he has given me in the beginning, the prosecution, and conclusion of my present studies, which are more happily performed than I could have promised to myself. . . ."   For, "what Virgil wrote in the vigour of his age, in plenty and at ease, I have undertaken to translate in my declining years; struggling with wants, oppressed by sickness, curbed in my genius, liable to be misconstrued in all I write; and my judges, if they are not very equitable, already prejudiced against me by the lying character which has been given them of my morals."   His other obligations, not already taken care of in the several dedications, he acknowledges in order, and with becoming scrupulousness.   They range from his sincere and appreciative words on the role of his physicians, Dr. Hobbs and Dr. Gibbons, in aiding him to recover his health, to his public thanks to such men as Sir William Trumbull, Secretary of State, who had "recommended" the twelfth book of the *Æneid* as his favorite, and to the Earls of Derby and Peterborough for their favors offered "to one of a different persuasion."

As soon as the folio appeared in the early days of August, Dryden apparently procured enough copies of the large paper first subscribers' issue to send, with appropriate covering letters, to the three men to whom he had dedicated the work, and possibly to other selected persons. Certainly Chesterfield was thus honored, and he wrote, on August 10, 1697, in grateful acknowledgement of the receipt of his copy, and included a gift which was designed to express, as he says, "some part of my resentments [i.e., appreciation] for the unvaluable Present that you have made me." That the gift was substantial is indicated by Dryden's reply in the following week: "I can not pretend to acknowledg, as I ought, the noble present which I have receiv'd from your Lordship, any more, than I can pretend to have deserv'd it." And he alludes to the "largeness" of the present. Some of the poet's other friends, too, we may believe, showed their appreciation in like fashion.[21]

Dryden's *Virgil* was now public property, and it was for the public to make its judgment. He might indeed expect a favorable response if the "better sort of judges" (to whom he was committing it) remained "equitable." The reception proved generally enthusiastic, and to many Dryden's *Virgil* took its place at the head of English poetic translations of the classics. But the chorus of praise was not destined to be universal; not all the judges (as he had foreseen) were to be equitable. He had, however, discounted in advance the dissident voices that he knew would arise. On the whole he was content—and very weary.[22]

Twilight of Honors
1697-1699

DRYDEN's fatigue must have been deep, perhaps deeper than he himself knew. For at sixty-six, he could not call upon the powers of renewal, especially after the pressures of the past decade, which he once had. Fortunately he had raised to himself enduring friends, and in his present need to refresh himself, one of them came forward with an invitation to spend some time with him. Sir William Bowyer asked him to partake again of the comforts and the beauties of Denham Court. Dryden no doubt was grateful for this opportunity to revisit "that delicious spot of ground," where he had earlier worked on the first *Georgic* and the last *Æneid*. By August 18 he was ready to take the coach; but before leaving he wrote a note to Sir William Trumbull (a neighbor in Gerrard Street), asking the Secretary to intercede in behalf of a Catholic bookseller, named Metcalf, who had been commanded to appear before the Council on the next day. Metcalf had been taken into custody for the printing of a short pamphlet in Latin, detailing a project of some of the Catholic clergy "to live in Common, that thereby they might be helpfull to Such of our Communion who are in want."[1] Dryden asks only that the Secretary, considering Metcalf's youth, will forgive the young man upon his asking pardon and promising to offend no more.

The ensuing weeks at Denham Court no doubt brought him needed release from his affairs in London, but they were not without their troubles. He came down with a cold in early September, which aggravated a deafness already troublesome before he had left town, an affliction that was to continue to get worse to the end of his life. From Denham Court he wrote a letter to his sons in Rome—the only surviving piece of the correspondence between them—containing a number of statements, which, had we access to his sons' letters to him, could more easily be interpreted. Some almost defy even a reasonable guess. One such, for example, is the charge "that by Tonsons meanes, almost all our Letters have miscarryed for this last yeare." It is hard to believe that Tonson was so villainous—or so careless—as to prevent Dryden from communicating with his sons. Dryden and Tonson, however, had disagreed on one item of importance. Tonson, Dryden writes, "has missd of his design in the Dedication [of *Virgil*]: though He had prepard the Book for it: for in every figure of Eneas, he has causd him to be drawn like K. William, with a hookd Nose."[2] Dryden's refusal to dedicate to the King, at Tonson's suggestion, emphasizes again his settled determination not to try to curry favor with a government to which he could not take the oaths. In a letter to him in the early summer, his sons had apparently suggested that he might make some such gesture of compromise. His answer is definite and unyielding: "I remember the Counsell you give me in your letter: but dissembling, though lawfull in some Cases, is not my talent: yet for your sake I will struggle, with the plain openness of my nature, & keep in my just resentments against that degenerate Order. In the mean time, I flatter not my self with any manner of hopes. But do my duty & suffer for God's sake, being assurd before hand, never to be rewarded, though the times shoud alter."

Though he was enjoying a needed holiday at Denham Court, he was not idle. He tells his sons that upon his return to London, he intends to alter an old play, *The Conquest of China by the Tartars,* written many years before by Sir Robert Howard, who has lately turned it over to him. By it he hopes to earn £100. This project he never completed. In the meantime, however, he is engaged in writing a "Song for St Cecilia's feast." This is "troublesome, & no way beneficiall: but," he adds, "I coud not deny the Stewards of the feast, who came in a body to me, to desire that kindness; one of them being Mr. Bridgman, whose parents are your Mothers friends." This was *Alexander's Feast,* and though not "beneficial" in the sense in which Dryden uses the word, the superb lyric won him more fame in his own day and later than several Conquests of China could have done. His chatty letter proceeds leisurely, and we are treated to an intimate glimpse of the affectionate relationship between him and his sons. He is concerned for Charles's health but is assured that he will begin to mend during the present month of September; for having cast the boy's Nativity himself, he is sure it is true: "all things hetherto have happend accordingly to the very time that I pred[icted them]," he avers, with some pride in his astrological knowledge and his skill in casting horoscopes. Of his *Virgil* he is able to give them gratifying news: it succeeds "beyond its desert or my Expectation." The profits, to be sure, might have been greater, but "neither my conscience nor honour wou'd suffer me to take them: but I never can repent of my Constancy; since I am thoroughly perswaded of the justice of the laws, for which I suffer." He knows that his sons need money; and he promises to remit them thirty guineas between Michaelmas and Christmas even though he is uncertain, at the moment, where he will get them.

Dryden sent this letter to Lady Elizabeth, in London, who appended a long note of her own, though she had written her sons the preceding week. She hopes they may return to England the following summer, for she points out, "you doe but just make shift to Live wheare you are: and soe I hope you may doe heare: for I will Leaf noe ston unturnd to help my beloved sonns." She is eager for the prayers of her youngest, now a priest; she sends a gift box, and hopes she may have something better for them when they return home. "My deare Jackes play," she thinks, is the best parcel in the box.

When Dryden returned to London from Denham Court in the autumn, his immediate task was to fulfill his promise to the Stewards of the St. Cecilia Festival, to have his ode ready for the celebration on November 22. Among the Stewards who had come to him in a body to petition him for the poem were two professional musicians, Francis Le Rich, who as late as 1689 had been a member of the King's Music,[3] and Jeremiah Clarke, a composer of some note and an associate of the more famous Dr. John Blow. With Purcell now two years dead, Dryden needed a new composer, and for the ode Clarke was chosen, either by the Stewards or by the poet. Through his collaboration with Draghi in the setting of the St. Cecilia Ode of 1687, and through his more extensive work with Purcell, Dryden, of course, was well aware of the composer's problems in setting the words of his poetry. With this experience Dryden created a libretto which gave ample scope for many varied effects. Clarke's score for *Alexander's Feast* has not survived; neither has that by Thomas Clayton, composed in 1711 at the instance of Steele, who had directed Hughes to make verbal changes in Dryden's poem.[4] Handel's popular and famous score of 1736, set to Newburgh Hamilton's almost "verbatim repetition of Dryden's ode," went through ten editions in twenty years. When the ode with Clarke's music was originally performed on November 22, 1697, the reception proved so enthusiastic that within the next month it was presented at least twice—on the sixth of December and again on the sixteenth, the latter for the benefit of the composer and Francis Le Rich.[5] Writing to Tonson, in this month, Dryden is "glad to heare from all Hands, that my Ode is esteemd the best of all my poetry, by all the Town; I thought so my self when I writ it but being old, I mistrusted my own Judgment."[6] The copy was turned over to Tonson for printing, with Dryden's admonition to remember to change the name *Lais* (twice written in the copy) to *Thais*: "those two Ladyes were Contemporaryes, wch caused that small mistake."[7] The ode appeared in folio apparently before the end of the year.

By this time relations between the poet and his publisher seem to have returned to their earlier cordiality. In December, Tonson sent Dryden some highly potable sherry, which Dryden acknowledges as "the best of the kind I ever dranke." In the same letter he bestirred himself about the thirty guineas which he had, in September, promised to send his sons. He would be glad, he writes Tonson, "if you could put me in a way of remitting thirty guineas to Rome; wch I would pay heer, for my Sonns to have the vallue there, according as the Exchange goes; any time this fortnight, will be soon enough to send the money." The sentence is ambiguous, but it is possible he is asking Tonson for an advance to be charged against his share of *Alexander's Feast*. Later in the month he reports to Tonson that he has broken off his studies for *The Conquest of China* (which he never mentions anywhere again and which he probably at this time abandoned) to review *Virgil* and to make corrections for the second edition. He spent nine days on revisions,[8] incorporating his changes on the printed copy which Tonson had sent him for that purpose. The poet's negotiations with the printer, Robert Everingham, had not been satisfactory, and apparently not very cordial, for he reports the printer "a beast, and understands nothing I can say to him of correcting the press." Consequently he asks Tonson to come for the revised copy himself. Within a day or two Tonson complied, and hard upon the meeting Dryden dispatched another note with a poem to be included in the second edition with the other commendatory verses Dryden had forgotten to give his publisher. This poem was by Lady Mary Chudleigh, a near neighbor of Lord Clifford at Ugbroke Park in Devon, and was perhaps transmitted to the poet by his patron. That afternoon he took it to the coffeehouse, where both Walsh and Wycherley read it and gave a favorable opinion of it.

For some reason, however, it was not included in the second edition and finally saw print five years later in the lady's *Poems on Several Occasions*. Other matters of moment find a place, particularly his advice about the order of the printing, so that Dr. Chetwood, whom he has written, may return the corrected preface to the *Eclogues,* which was full of errors in the first edition. "You can not take too great care of the printing of this Edition, exactly after my Amendments: for a fault of that nature will disoblige me Eternally." Tonson must look sharp to the printer; for Dryden writes: "I vow to God, if Everingham takes not care of this Impression, He shall never print any thing of mine hereafter. . . ."[9]

The poet's concern now over his son Charles's health seems more anxious than it had been in September: his assurance in the infallibility of his astrological readings must have been shaken, for Charles had not mended. Turning from astrology to conventional medicine, he had described his son's symptoms to his own physician, who now had sent Dryden his diagnosis. He fears a rupture; and Dryden begs Tonson to make speedy arrangements to send both the doctor's note and his own to Charles at once. "For a week lost," he says, "may be my Sonns ruine: whom I intend to send for, next Summer, without his Brother . . . if it please God that I must dye of over study, I cannot spend my life better, than in saving his."

The demand for a second edition of *Virgil* within six months testifies to its immediate popularity. But the popularity of the poet, though enhanced by both the *Virgil* and *Alexander's Feast,* was by no means universal. At the beginning of 1698 two books were either in press, or nearly ready, that were to take away some of the satisfaction that had come with the success of the *Virgil.* Attacks were nothing new to Dryden, and they had never ceased, even after he had exiled himself for three years in his work on the translation. In December, 1694, when Queen Mary died, most of the poets hastened to write their conventional elegies. Conspicuously absent from this universal lament was any poem by Dryden. His refusal to commemorate Mary, though understandable, occasioned some comment at the time.[10] Several months later, in February, 1694/95, appeared, in ten books, an epic poem by Richard Blackmore, a Fellow of the College of Physicians. In a preface to his long poem, entitled *Prince Arthur,* Blackmore launched a virulent attack on the poets of the age, especially the playwrights, who, he says, plead the necessity of writing lewdness, because of the degeneracy of the age. He sees indeed a deliberate attempt, on the part of the comic play-

wrights particularly, "to ruin all Opinion and Esteem of Virtue."[11]
The business of the poet, he says, is not to please but to instruct.
The clergyman and the poet, he argues, should touch hands, for
their function is identical. Dryden is not mentioned by name in this
attack that precedes (by three years) Collier's similar but more
detailed castigation of the stage. Nor does Blackmore take the
trouble to acknowledge his indebtedness to Dryden for the suggestion
of the Arthur theme for an epic or the discussion of "machinery"—
at hand for the use of a Christian poet—both treated at length in
Dryden's "Original and Progress of Satire" in 1692. Not content
to be thus unappreciative, Blackmore gratuitously attacked Dryden
(in Book VI of his epic, under the character of Laurus):

> The poets Nation, did obsequious wait
> For the kind Dole, divided at his [Dorset's] gate.
> *Laurus* amidst the meagre Crowd appear'd,
> An old, revolted, unbelieving Bard,
> Who thronged, and shov'd, and prest, and would be
> > heard.
> Distinguish'd by his louder craving Tone,
> So well to all the Muses Patrons known,
> He did the Voice of modest Poets drown.
> *Sakil's* [Dorset's] high Roof, the Muses Palace rung
> With endless Cries, and endless Songs he sung.
> To bless good *Sakil Laurus* would be first,
> But *Sakil's* Prince, and *Sakil's* God he curst.
> *Sakil* without distinction threw him Bread,
> Despis'd the Flatt'rer, but the Poet fed.

Such an attack upon his character Dryden had no public opportunity,
or perhaps desire, to answer at that time. That he was stung by it
there can be little doubt.

The two books in 1698 containing more serious attacks on him
were Jeremy Collier's *Short View of the Immorality and Profaneness
of the English Stage* and *Notes on Dryden's Virgil,* by Luke Milbourne, an obscure clergyman in Norfolk. The first—now the *locus
classicus* of attacks on the playwrights—achieved a great popular
success and elevated its Non-Juror author to a pre-eminence to which
his modest talents could, at another time, hardly have entitled him.
For many years Collier's book became a center of the controversy on
the function of the playwright and the questions of immorality and
morality as they impinged upon the drama and stage. Milbourne's

book, on the contrary, suffered almost a stillbirth: it had no popular
success, nor could it have been expected to appeal widely, since it
was a niggling examination, running to over two hundred pages, of
Dryden's statements in preface and dedications and of specific lines
in the *Eclogues* and the *Georgics*. He does not examine the *Æneid*.
Milbourne's continuous faultfinding tends to follow the pattern of
the age in controversial (but not in critical) literature. He extracts
sentences from the dedications, upon which he exercises his malicious
wit. For example, on Dryden's comment, "I'm afraid I have mistaken Virgil's sense more often and more grossly," Milbourne writes:
"Ne'er did Elvira make a truer Confession to her Spanish Friar.
But how could one Poet mistake another so much?" He praises
Tonson's honesty for entitling the volume "Dryden's Virgil," and
writes that the publisher's "ingenuity" is greater than the translator's,
"to let the Reader know, that this is not that Virgil so much admired
in the Augustan Age, an author whom Mr. Dryden once thought
untranslatable, but a Virgil of another Stamp, of a courser Alloy;
a silly, impertinent, non-sensical Writer, of a various and uncertain
style." Determined to blast the old poet's reputation as a man,
Milbourne drags in comments on matters that have no connection
with Virgil or with Dryden's role as translator. To Dryden's sentence,
"I am too much an Englishman to lose what my Ancestors have
gained for me," Milbourne appends, "i.e., Since acquaintance with
such, whom he can never praise enough. Things are mightily altered
with him since the Days of the Hind and Panther, and the Defence
of the Strong Box Papers. Thus tempora mutantur."[12] At the end
of his book Milbourne includes his own version of the first *Georgic*
to illustrate how Virgil should be translated. Dryden's answer to
this parson was postponed until the publication of the preface to the
Fables, two years later.

Collier's attack, though not directed solely toward Dryden, struck
more telling and juster blows than Milbourne's, as the poet later was
to acknowledge. Yet he made no attempt to answer Collier formally,
despite the fact that the clergyman had cited eight of his plays as
containing immorality and profaneness. Perhaps he was too tired
and too ill to engage in another battle, especially since his enemy
had already in a sense disarmed him. Furthermore, some of his
younger friends were at once beginning to write their rebuttals, and
he may have decided to leave to them the task of making an adequate
answer. Congreve, Filmer, and Vanbrugh all published answers
within the year.[13] But Dryden did not altogether ignore Collier or

his charges; and during the ensuing two years, he adverts to Collier and his position in four several pieces: "To my Friend Mr. Motteux"; Epilogue to the *Secular Masque*; Preface to the *Fables*; and the first forty lines of *Cymon and Iphigenia,* included in the volume of the *Fables.* The first of these (as verses prefixed to Peter Motteux' play, *Beauty in Distress*), in print by June, 1698, represents Dryden's immediate reaction to Collier's book upon its appearance. He begins:

> 'Tis hard, my friend, to write in such an age,
> As damns not only poets, but the stage,

and goes on to castigate the "Muses' foes" who

> Would sink their Maker's praises into prose.
> Were they content to prune the lavish vine
> Of straggling branches, and improve the wine,
> Who but a madman would his faults defend?
> All would submit; for all but fools will mend.
> But when to common sense they give the lie,
> And turn distorted words to blasphemy,
> *They* give the scandal; and the wise discern,
> Their glosses teach an age too apt to learn.
> What I have loosely or profanely writ,
> Let them to fires, (their due desert,) commit;
> Nor, when accus'd by me, let *them* complain:
> Their faults and not their function I arraign.
>
> (ll. 6-18)

Dryden's assessment of the purpose behind Collier's attack—to destroy, not to reform, the stage—agrees with that of Congreve in his *Amendments to Mr. Collier's False and Imperfect Citations.* Dryden's willingness to admit his former deviations from morality and good manners is tempered by his belief that, in spite of the distortions and untruths in the *Short View,* Collier had made his point. Yet even with such confession and such concession, he could not bring himself to accept Collier's premises concerning either the function of the stage or what constituted blasphemous portrayal of the clergy, whose "faults and not their function" he insisted were arraigned. On several occasions he was to repeat the same confession of his own faults and the same irreconcilable antagonism to Collier's essential position that "the business of plays is to recommend virtue, and discountenance vice."

While Collier's attack provided the wits at the coffeehouses material for heated discussion, Dryden had completed a prose translation of part of Tacitus, which seems to have been merely a potboiler for additional income. Information about his connection with the three-volume *Annals and History of Cornelius Tacitus,* published by Matthew Gillyflower in the early summer, is completely lacking. That he turned into English the first book of the *Annals* is attested by the title page of the edition. And that the volume was out by June 30 is shown by a letter of that date printed in the *Hatton Correspondence* (II, 234): "Here is a new translation of Tacitus his works done by several persons, as Mr. Dryden, Mr. Bromley, Sr Hen. Savil, Sr Roger L'Estrange, and others . . . How far ye translators have perform'd their parts I know not, for I but just cast my eye on ye bookes. . . ." Dryden's chief personal satisfaction in the late spring or early summer, however, was the fulfillment of his decision to bring back from Rome his son Charles, whose ill-health at Rome persisted in England; and before the summer was out they journeyed to Northamptonshire for rest and country air.

Before leaving London, however, Dryden and Tonson, encouraged by the enthusiastic reception of *Virgil,* agreed upon another volume of translations. An informal understanding must have been reached at this time, although it was not formalized into a written contract until the following March. According to their agreement Dryden was to furnish a total of ten thousand verses (more or less), the choice of authors to be entirely the poet's. On his part Tonson was to pay 250 guineas, this to be increased to a total payment of £300, should a second edition be called for. This was to be published as *The Fables.* Dryden's retreat to the country, as was usually true, became a time for work as well as for relaxation. He began at once to translate and continued at a consistent pace during the late summer and autumn and through the winter; by March, 1698/99, he had completed and turned over to Tonson about seventy-five hundred lines of the projected volume. In return he received the contract price of 250 guineas (a total of £268 15*s.,* the guinea being worth 21*s.* 6*d.* at this time).[14]

But his sojourn in Northamptonshire with his son became partly a round of visits to relatives. The repeated invitations of Elizabeth Steward, daughter of his cousin Mrs. John Creed (Sir Gilbert Pickering's daughter) to visit her at Cotterstock, Dryden finally accepted in a letter dated October 1, at Titchmarsh. "How can you be so good," he writes, "to an old decrepid Man who can entertain you with no discourse which is worthy of your good sense & who can

onely be a trouble to you in all the time he stays at Cotterstock?"
He begs that she will send her coach to Titchmarsh for him on the
following Tuesday, October 4. Except for a planned visit of one
day to his cousin John Driden at Chesterton, he hopes to spend the
entire week, until the tenth, with her. The visit was entirely happy,
and a repeated invitation for the following summer he accepts, "if I
have life & health, to come into Northamptonshyre."[15] His health,
not noticeably improved in the country, became worse by the time
he had arrived home. He must have left Titchmarsh for London
sometime during the last two weeks of October. A chatty and
amusing letter dated from London on November 23 to Mrs. Steward
relates his difficulties in the intervening weeks. The only woman
at Titchmarsh he could talk with was the Parson's wife, who "was
intended by Nature, as a help meet for a deaf Husband [and] was
somewhat of the loudest, for my Conversation." The long coach
journey home, both enlivened and made exasperating by the presence
of a very fat woman, proved tiring and uncomfortable. "When I was
ridd of her," he says, "I came sick home: & kept my House, for three
weeks together; but by advice of my Doctour, takeing twice the bitter
draught, with Sena in it, & looseing at least twelve Ounces of blood,
by Cupping on my Neck, I am just well enough, to go abroad in the
Afternoon."[16]

He gradually mended, and in his next letter to Mrs. Steward, to
thank her for a gift of food from the country, he does not mention
ill-health, except to note that Charles is still indisposed.[17] Not since
his return from Rome in the summer had his eldest son recovered
from that insistent malady which his father had once confidently
predicted, by astrological computation, would disappear. Between
intermittent attacks of colds and agues, Dryden pushed on with his
translations, which, because of their fragmentary nature and their
relative shortness, he was able to accomplish at the odd times when
he felt able. He could pick them up and set them aside when he
wished, for he no longer felt the urgency which had driven him to
complete the *Virgil*. As the winter of 1698-99 passed, he was "still
drudging on: always a Poet, and never a good one," as he wrote to
Mrs. Steward on Candlemass Day. Other ailments attacked him:
he began to have kidney trouble, for which he subjected himself to
periodic courses of physic and other remedies which he does not
name. During the intervals between treatments, he writes, "I pass
my time sometimes with Ovid, and sometimes with our old English
poet, Chaucer; translating such stories as best please my fancy; and

intend besides them to add somewhat of my own: so that it is not
impossible, but ere the summer be pass'd, I may come down to you
with a volume in my hand, like a dog out of the water, with a duck
in his mouth."[18]

By this time he had written almost two-thirds of the material he
had set for himself. Yet the burden of the letter to his young kinswoman was his ill-health. He hopes to visit her at Cotterstock in the
coming summer, but "my want of health may perhaps hinder me."
She will indeed be sure of a guest—"if," he adds, "I am well enough
to travell as farr north as Northamptonshyre." From his doctors he
was apparently receiving little help. They now suggest that both he
and Charles might be benefited by a sojourn at Bath, but he is not
yet convinced that they should go, "for that city is so closs and so ill
situated, that perhaps the ayr may do us more harm than the waters
can do us good." He is prepared to compromise on the treatment
advocated by his physicians: he may try the waters nearby (at
Islington Spa?) first, to note whether any good effects result. His
continuing ill health emphasized the fact of his own mortality. The
friends of his more vigorous years were passing away. The most
recent death among his long-time intimates was Sir Robert Howard's,
in September, 1698. Though the two had not always agreed on
literary matters, their friendship had remained intact. And though
only four years before his death Sir Robert had written his *History
of Religion,* in which he castigates Roman Catholicism and upholds
the Anglican Church, no breach seems to have occurred in their
personal relationship on account of religious differences.

As February moved into March, Dryden continued to drudge
(it is his repeated word) upon his translations and the few original
poems he intended to include. His relatives in the country continued their kindnesses and sent their gifts of produce to their eminent
but poor kinsman. Added to the bacon and marrow puddings of
Elizabeth Steward, came equally valuable gifts from Dryden's cousin
John, of Chesterton, who sent a turkey hen and eggs, and "a good
young Goose." This evidence of friendship, in addition to other
benefactions from his cousin, pleased the old poet, since they were
made to "so undeserveing a Kinsman, & one of another persuasion,
in matters of Religion." And he begs that Elmes Steward, living only
six miles distant from Chesterton, will often visit his Cousin John,
particularly before the hunting goes out, as a solace to him for the
recent loss of his younger brother (Beville?) who was a "Most
Extraordinary well Natur'd Man, & much my friend." This evidence

of an easy relationship with his Protestant relatives suggests again the great capacity for friendship possessed by Dryden throughout his life. His country relations could not but be impressed by the eminence of their distinguished representative in literature; and his ill-success in accumulating worldly goods (at which they were generally quite successful) gave them opportunity to exercise their generosity to one of their own.[19]

In addition to acknowledging the friendly interest of his kinsfolk, Dryden relates (in this letter of March 4) some of the city gossip and includes a short account of the events in town that might appeal to Elizabeth Steward. He records a revival of Congreve's *The Double Dealer* and the introduction of a new device—the printing of the author's name in the play bill. The impact of the recent attack on the stage, he implies, without mentioning Collier: several "expressions" were left out of Congreve's play, in recognition of the King's recent order on the reformation of the stage.[20] Dryden, however, was not so much concerned about this order as about the King's forthcoming proclamation—which appeared two days later, on March 6—against the Catholics. He is generous enough to believe that William "is very Unwilling to persecute us; considering us to be but an handfull, & those disarmd." And he informs her that he is "still drudgeing at a Book of Miscellanyes, which I hope will be well enough. If otherwise, three-score & seaven may be pardon'd."[21]

On March 20, Dryden signed the formal contract with Tonson for the miscellany volume, which was to be entitled *Fables, Ancient and Modern; Translated into Verse from Homer, Ovid, Boccace, & Chaucer: with Original Poems.* He then had about seventy-five hundred lines to deliver to his publisher, and the remaining twenty-five hundred would be forthcoming as rapidly as his obviously deteriorating physical condition would allow.

On July 11, writing to Elizabeth Steward, he complains of "many fitts of Sickness & so much other unpleasant business" that he has neglected to thank her for various gifts she has sent. He makes no mention of his book, but informs her of his intended visit to Cotterstock before the summer is out. He has sent a petition to her, by her sisters (who are bound for the country) that she "order some small Beer to be brewd for me, without hops . . . because I lost my health last year, by drinking bitter beer at Titchmarsh."[22] In the same week, on July 14, he is writing his friend Samuel Pepys, to let him know that the Character of Chaucer's Good Parson, recommended to him by the diarist at a dinner last year, is now completed:

"whenever you please, he shall wait on you, and for the safer Conveyance, I will carry him in my pocket." The state of the miscellany at this point in midsummer we learn from his note: it is nearly finished and he hopes that the "indifferent large volume in folio" will be in press during Michaelmas term. In answer to the poet's note Pepys dashed off a reply by return messenger, inviting Dryden "to a cold chicken and a sallade, any *noone* after Sunday, as being just stepping into the ayre for 2 days." Presumably the two old gentlemen ate their chicken and salad and perhaps discussed not only the good Parson, but also the "many lewd originalls" which gave "hourly offence" to Pepys.[23]

On August 10, accompanied as usual by Charles (a great favorite with the Cotterstock relations), but not by Lady Elizabeth (perhaps not a favorite), Dryden took a coach to Northamptonshire. In the kindly atmosphere of Elizabeth Steward's household, the "old cripple," as he called himself, relaxed and took his comfort, and drank his small beer. For more than a month—with side journeys to Chesterton and probably to Titchmarsh and perhaps even farther afield to Blakesley, where his land was situated—he idled in the country. By September 28, again in London, he was writing Elizabeth Steward an account of his trip back to the city, including his gratitude for their kindness to Charles and him. His holiday had been fruitful as well as pleasant. He had taken with him the completed manuscript of the verses written to his cousin John, by which he intended to honor his relative in the miscellany. In general his cousin had approved, but he made one objection: he disliked the satirical lines against the Dutch courage in the late war. These the poet agreed to omit, "out of the respect [his cousin] had to his Soveraign."[24] He left only the praises "due to the gallantry of my own Countrymen."

Not long after his return to London, probably in October, he wrote to Charles Montague, enclosing the epistle to John Driden for Montague's judgment, as he had some time before sent him the verses "To the Duchess of Ormond," which were likewise to be included in the new volume. Why Dryden felt impelled to send them to Montague may not be far to seek. Though he flatters the younger man by calling him "so great a Judge & Poet," Montague was neither. Twelve years earlier he had, with Prior, attacked Dryden in *The Hind and the Panther Transvers'd* and had said some uncomplimentary things about the then poet laureate. But time had softened both. In the interval, Montague's brilliant work in founding the Bank of England had secured him the Chancellorship of the Exchequer; and he had become one of King William's most influential ministers. It is perhaps to the politician Montague, not to an old friend, that Dryden addresses himself. He may need to make certain—in the face of new and more rigorous laws against Catholics —that nothing in his verses is likely to give offense to a government which he has no reason to love and no wish to offend. "I have consulted," he writes, "the Judgment of my Unbyassd friends . . . & they think there is nothing which can justly give offense. . . . I say not this, to cast a blind on your Judgment (which I cou'd not do, if I endeavourd it) but to assure you, that nothing relateing to the publique shall stand, without your permission." He is especially concerned to point out that in the description of a Parliament man he has not only justly described his cousin, a member from Huntingdonshire, but also his ideal of what an "Englishman in Parliament oughto [sic] be; & deliver it as a Memorial of my own Principles to all Posterity." Montague's decision seems to have accorded with that of the "unbyassd friends," among whom was the Earl of Dorset; for the verses found their way, doubtless without further significant change, into the volume now almost ready to go to press.[25]

Dryden's deference to Montague on the matter of acceptability— to the government—of the principles enunciated in the verses to his cousin, may help to explain a reference in the letter to Elizabeth Steward, written on November 7. His tardiness in writing her was not ill health, or "a worse thing ingratitude," but "a flood of little businesses, which yet are necessary to my Subsistence." Proposals perhaps by Montague and Dorset (no longer Lord Chamberlain) and possibly by Dryden's old patron and friend Normanby, seem to have been made to convince the King and his advisers that something should be done for the poet who had grown old in the service of two monarchs and had endured his share of suffering for maintaining unpopular opinions. Some progress had been made, but Dryden ruefully says: "the Court rather speaks kindly of me, than does any thing for me, though they promise largely: & perhaps they think I will advance, as they go backward: in which they will be much deceivd: for I can never go an Inch beyond my Conscience & my Honour." He still refused to compromise his principles:

If they will consider me as a Man, who have done my best to improve the Language, & Especially the Poetry, & will be content with my acquiescence under the present Government, & forbearing satire on it, that I can promise, because I can perform it: but I can neither take the

Oaths, nor forsake my Religion, because I know not what Church to go to, if I leave the Catholique; they are all so divided amongst them selves in matters of faith, necessary to Salvation: & yet all assumeing the name of Protestants. May God be pleasd to open your Eyes, as he has opend mine: Truth is but one; & they who have once heard of it, can plead no Excuse, if they do not embrace it. But these things are too serious, for a trifling Letter.[26]

He ends his letter with an account of literary and political gossip: a new play by Charles Hopkins ("who writes good verses without knowing how, or why") is to be acted; Congreve is at Barnet Wells for his gout; the Earl of Dorset has paid him a visit, and he in return has dined with the Earl; the King hopes to maintain a standing army, using the ferment in Scotland as an excuse.

Nearly three weeks later, on November 26, Dryden writes again to Elizabeth, having had a letter from her in the meantime. More gossip—the country woman seemed eager for it—of the poet's world. He speaks of the acting next week of a new tragedy called *Iphigenia,* by John Dennis, who "cryes [it] up at an Excessive rate." He has been lately to visit the Duchess of Norfolk (Mary, daughter of the Earl of Peterborough) who speaks of Elizabeth "with much Affection, & Respect." Gossip has it, he tells her, that Montague (her cousin) will be created Earl of Bristol. He reverts to his now forlorn hope of getting something from the court: "[Montague] I hope, is much my friend: But I doubt I am in no Condition of haveing a kindness done me; Haveing the Chancellour [Somers] my Enemy. And not being capable of renounceing the Cause, for which I have so long Sufferd."[27]

By this time he had turned over to Tonson the remaining copy to make up the verses agreed upon for the *Fables.* Actually, he gave his publisher good measure, for instead of delivering ten thousand lines, he sent more than eleven thousand. It is pleasant to observe that, after their numerous disagreements in previous years over the number of verses to be delivered and the payments for them, Dryden in his last considerable work was able to overpay his publisher. The book was finally in press by about the beginning of December, though Tonson made no great speed with it. By December 14 Dryden was again wracked by unexpected and apparently undiagnosed illness. His mind, he confessed to Elizabeth, was full of cares and his "body ill at ease." His was a house of illness: "I had last night at bed time, an unwelcome fit of vomiting; & my Sonn Charles lyes sick upon his bed with the Colique: which has been violent upon him for almost a week." Yet he tells her more news from the city. Dennis' play, *Iphigenia,* had been a dismal failure, and so too had been another play of the same title by Bowyer at the rival theater in the same week: they "clashd together, like two rotten ships, which cou'd not endure the shock; & sunk to rights." The Collier attack on the stage is still news, for he reports the appearance in print of the King's proclamation against vice and profaneness: "But a deep disease is not to be cur'd with a slight Medicine. The parsons who must read it, will find as little effect from it, as from their dull Sermons: tis a Scare-Crow, wch will not fright many birds from preying on the fields & orchards."[28] At the moment of writing this letter his verse attack on Collier was being printed (lines 1-41 of *Cymon and Iphigenia*), and the notice of Collier in his "other harmony of prose"—the preface to the *Fables*—was probably about to be written.

Within a fortnight, as a serious and fatal addition to the list of his physical ailments, which included gout, the gravel, and deafness, he contracted "a St. Anthony's Fire in one of [his] legs." This attack of erysipelas proved to be the beginning of the end.

The Last Harmony
1699-1700

A s the new year began, Dryden's condition seems to have shown but slight improvement: he makes mention of his illnesses in a letter to Mrs. Steward in February; and in March he can say, "I am neither in health, nor do I want Afflictions of any kind." About March 4 the *Fables* was published, though it was a week later before he had received copies for his own use. He immediately dispatched them to friends and to his relatives in Northamptonshire.

The reception of this "indifferent large volume in folio," he can write to Elizabeth Steward, has been generally favorable: "The Town encourages [it] with more Applause than anything of mine deserves."[1] Yet in spite of the initial reception, the *Fables,* partly perhaps because of its miscellaneousness, proved less popular than most of his other volumes: not until thirteen years later was a second edition called for. Of the pieces included in the volume, both the Town and Dryden himself thought most highly of the verses to John Driden. Whether his contemporaries enjoyed his preface we cannot know; but posterity has taken it for its own, finding in it one of the most felicitous examples of a supple and polished English prose style, admired, imitated, but rarely equalled, and hardly ever surpassed. Dryden's own term for it—"the other harmony of prose"—succinctly and accurately describes it.

Both the preface and the verses to his cousin, of course, are, biographically, the most significant portions of the volume. The verses are particularly so because they were written *con amore* and because they restate the principles that he had held for most of his adult life. The fact that his cousin served in the Commons as a member from Huntingdon provided him an opportunity to dilate upon the functions of the Parliament man:

Good Senators (and such are you) so give,
That kings may be supplied, the people strive.
And he, when want requires, is truly wise,
Who slights not foreign aids, nor over-buys,
But on our native strength, in time of need, relies.

(ll. 135-39)

He proceeds to laud the English valor in the continental wars, recently concluded by the treaty of Ryswick:

What has been done was done with British force:
Namur subdued is England's palm alone;

.   .   .   .

France, tho' pretending arms, pursued the peace;
Oblig'd, by one sole treaty, to restore
What twenty years of war had won before.
Enough for Europe has our Albion fought:
Let us enjoy the peace our blood has bought.

(ll. 151-59)

The Parliament man whom he celebrates becomes an ideal, who seems to represent his own convictions on government:

A patriot both the king and country serves;
Prerogative and privilege preserves:
Of each our laws the certain limit show;
One must not ebb, nor t'other overflow.
Betwixt the prince and parliament we stand;
The barriers of the state on either hand:
May neither overflow, for then they drown the land!
When both are full, they feed our blest abode;
Like those that water'd once the paradise of God.

(ll. 171-79)

But this nice balance, as he well knew, could not always maintain itself in practice; he recognizes the absolute necessity of flexibility of powers:

Some overpoise of sway by turns they share;
In peace the people, and the prince in war:
Consuls of mod'rate pow'r in calms were made;
When the Gauls came, one sole dictator sway'd.
Patriots, in peace, assert the people's right;
With noble stubbornness resisting might:

No lawless mandates from the court receive,
Nor lend by force, but in a body give.

(ll. 180-87)

This resistance of the individual to a tyrannic force leads him
into a eulogy of his (and his cousin's) grandfather, old Sir Erasmus,
whose "noble stubbornness" in resisting the government of James I
and Charles I, had put him twice into prison:

Such was your gen'rous grandsire; free to grant
In parliaments that weigh'd their prince's want:
But so tenacious of the common cause,
As not to lend the king against his laws;
And, in a loathsome dungeon doom'd to lie,
In bonds retain'd his birthright liberty,
And sham'd oppression, till it set him free.

(ll. 188-94)

The remainder of the 209 lines in the poem touch a number of
topics, including congratulations to his cousin on his successful
resistance to marriage—"better shun the bait than struggle in the
snare"—a comment on his cousin's wealth, inheritance, generosity,
and easiness of access, and his delight in hunting ("hunting," as he
had written his Cotterstock relatives, "is my cousin's life"). The
poet's own age and constant illness and his cousin's age (he was now
sixty-five) moves him to an extended comment on the infirmities
and ailments that beset man, and the role of the physician in curing
them:

So liv'd our sires ere doctors learn'd to kill,
And multiplied with theirs the weekly bill.
The first physicians by debauch were made;
Excess began, and sloth sustains the trade.
Pity the gen'rous kind their cares bestow
To search forbidden truths; (a sin to know:)
To which if human science could attain,
The doom of death, pronounc'd by God, were vain.
In vain the leech would interpose delay;
Fate fastens first, and vindicates the prey.

(ll. 71-80)

The physician in general reminds him of his own doctor, in whom
he has had some confidence, and another, his *bête noir,* Dr. Blackmore:

Gibbons but guesses, nor is sure to save;
But Maurus [Blackmore] sweeps whole parishes, and
    peoples ev'ry grave;
And no more mercy to mankind will use,
Than when he robb'd and murder'd Maro's Muse.
Wouldst thou be soon dispatch'd, and perish whole?
Trust Maurus with thy life, and M-lb-rne with thy
    soul.

                                        (ll. 82-87)

So Blackmore and Milbourne are partially repaid for their unpro-
voked attacks on him.   But Garth and his *Dispensary* come in for
special praise, which was soon to be returned by that doctor-poet.

Throughout the verse translations in the *Fables,* Dryden, following his usual procedure, inserted lines of his own, without textual
justification.   Two of the most striking of these interpolations are to
be found in *The Wife of Bath, Her Tale,* and *Cymon and Iphigenia.*
Both are consonant with his convictions in this twilight period.   The
first, consisting of four couplets, offers a justification and an apology
for the lubricity of the age:

Then courts of kings were held in high renown,
Ere made the common brothels of the town:
There, virgins honorable vows receiv'd,
But chaste as maids in monasteries liv'd;
The king himself, to nuptial ties a slave,
No bad example to his poets gave;
And they, not bad, but in a vicious age,
Had not, to please the prince, debauch'd the stage.

                                        (ll. 61-68)

The second interpolation is much longer, comprising the initial
passage of forty-one lines (marginally labelled "Poeta loquitur") of
Cymon and Iphigenia.   Though a direct and telling attack upon some
aspects of Collier's book of the preceding year, it nonetheless acknowledges the justice of the remonstrance against the looseness of
some of the comedy of the age.   "Old as I am," he begins, "for
ladies' love unfit,

The pow'r of beauty I remember yet,
Which once inflam'd my soul, and still inspires
    my wit.
If love be folly, the severe divine
Has felt that folly, tho' he censures mine;

> Pollutes the pleasures of a chaste embrace,
> Acts what I write, and propagates in grace,
> With riotous excess, a priestly race.
> Suppose him free, and that I forge th' offense,
> He shew'd the way, perverting first my sense:
> In malice witty, and with venom fraught,
> He makes me speak the things I never thought.
>
> (ll. 2-12)

The divine's "ungovern'd zeal," indeed, might suggest something other than the desire for good works:

> The world will think that what we loosely write,
> Tho' now arraign'd, he read with some delight;
> Because he seems to chew the cud again,
> When his broad comment makes the text too plain;
> And teaches more in one explaining page,
> Than all the double meanings of the stage.
> What needs he paraphrase on what we mean?
> We were at worst but wanton; he's obscene.
> I nor my fellows nor myself excuse;
> But love's the subject of the comic Muse:
> Nor can we write without it, nor would you
> A tale of only dry instruction view.
>
> (ll. 15-26)

If this be but special pleading, Dryden makes no great effort to exculpate himself; but the fundamental chasm between the two points of view remains crucial and unbridgeable.[2]

The tone, the quality, the savor of his preface to the volume can be no more than suggested by quotations. It must be read and reread in order to appreciate the special place it has held, and still holds, among all of Dryden's writing in the critical affections of posterity. The mellowness, the grace, the humor, and the penetration of it each reader discovers for himself; the spell of his felicitous prose is pervasive. In another connection he had written in a letter to Elizabeth Steward that he hoped "they will consider me as a Man, who have done my best to improve the Language. . . ." The preface to the *Fables* has helped succeeding generations so to consider him.

His delightful discursiveness he easily excuses by reminding his reader that the "nature of a Preface is rambling, never wholly out of the way, nor in it. This I have learned from the practice of honest

Montagne." He proceeds to ramble. Of his own original verses in the volume, he writes:

Whether they are equal or inferior to my other poems, an author is the most improper judge: and therefore I leave them wholly to the mercy of the reader. I will hope the best, that they will not be condemned; but if they should, I have the excuse of an old gentleman, who mounting on horseback before some ladies, when I was present, got up somewhat heavily, but desired of the fair spectators, that they would count fourscore and eight, before they judged him. By the mercy of God, I am already come within twenty years of his number; a cripple in my limbs, —but what decays are in my mind the reader must determine.

His memory, he goes on, is not impaired, and his judgment has not diminished: "Thoughts, such as they are, come crowding in so fast upon me, that my only difficulty is to choose or to reject; to run them into verse, or to give them the other harmony of prose: I have so long studied and practised both, that they are grown into a habit, and become familiar to me." In explaining his choice of poems for translation he assures the reader that he has taken such stories, "both ancient and modern, as contain in each of them some instructive moral." Of his verse he can say,

I have written nothing which savours of immorality or profaneness; at least, I am not conscious to myself of any such intention. If there happen to be found an irreverent expression, or a thought too wanton, they are crept into my verses through my inadvertency. . . . Thus far, I hope, I am right in court, without renouncing to my other right of self-defence, where I have been wrongfully accused, and my sense wiredrawn into blasphemy or bawdry, as it has often been by a religious lawyer, in a late pleading against the stage; in which he mixes truth with falsehood, and has not forgotten the old rule of calumniating strongly, that something may remain.

Dryden's critical analyses and estimates of Homer, Chaucer, Ovid, Boccaccio, which take up a considerable portion of his essay, have often been cited as examples of Dryden's enduring critical judgment.[3] Yet other important comments are less well known. In considering Ovid and Chaucer, for instance, he remarks: "The vulgar judges, which are nine parts in ten of all nations, who call conceits and jingles, wit, who see Ovid full of them, and Chaucer altogether without them, will think me little less than mad for preferring the Englishman to the Roman." His preference for Chaucer leads him to a shrewd and penetrating analysis of Chaucer's achievement.[4] Chaucer's skill in characterization he admires almost to excess, citing with evident relish a list of characters from the ribald Reeve to the "mincing Lady Prioress, and the broad-speaking gap-toothed Wife of Bath": "But enough of this: there is such a variety of game springing up before me, that I am distracted in my choice, and know not which to follow. It is sufficient to say according to the proverb, that here is God's plenty."

He justifies his rendering of Chaucer into "modern English"— against the counsel of some of his friends, among them the late Earl of Leicester—on the ground that the good things in Chaucer should not be denied his contemporaries merely because they are unable or unwilling to cope with the antiquated words of the original. "Words," he insists, "are not like landmarks, so sacred as never to be removed." Something, he admits, is lost in the translation of Chaucer, as it is in every translation. Yet the

sense will remain, which would otherwise be lost, or at least be maimed, when it is scarce intelligible, and that but to a few. How few are there, who can read Chaucer, so as to understand him perfectly? And if imperfectly, then with less profit, and no pleasure. It is not for the use of some old Saxon friends, that I have taken these pains with him: let them neglect my version, because they have no need of it. I made it for their sakes, who understand sense and poetry as well as they, when that poetry and sense is put into words which they understand.

A brief comment on Chaucer's religion ("he seems to have some little bias towards the opinions of Wycliffe") brings him effortlessly to priests. So much has been made of Dryden's attacks on the clergy, both in his day and ours, that his final testimony is of some significance; for it serves to remind us that he differentiated clearly between the office and the man. He writes,

I cannot blame him [Chaucer] for inveighing so sharply against the vices of the clergy in his age: their pride, their ambition, their pomp, their avarice, their worldly interest, deserved the lashes which he gave them . . . the scandal which is given by particular priests, reflects not on the sacred function. Chaucer's Monk, his Canon, and his Friar, took not from the character of his Good Parson. A satirical poet is the check of the laymen on bad priests. We are only to take care, that we involve not the innocent with the guilty in the same condemnation. The good cannot be too much honoured, nor the bad too coarsely used; for the corruption of the best becomes the worst. . . . If the faults of men in orders are only to be judged among themselves, they are all in some sort parties; for, since they say the honour of their order is concerned in every member of it, how can we be sure that they will be impartial judges? How far I may be allowed to speak my opinion in this case, I know not. . . . I would rather extend than diminish any part of [the reverence and esteem which priests have had]: yet I must needs say,

that when a priest provokes me without any occasion given him, I have
no reason, unless it be the charity of a Christian, to forgive him. . . . If
I answer him in his own language, self-defence, I am sure, must be allowed me; and if I carry it farther, even to a sharp recrimination, somewhat may be indulged to human frailty.

He has "with some pleasure" followed the character of a holy man
in the Good Parson, but he reserves the right "if I shall think fit
hereafter, to describe another sort of priests, such as are more easily
to be found than the Good Parson; such as have given the last blow
to Christianity in this age, by a practice so contrary to their doctrine.
But this will keep cold till another time."

As a "corollary" to the preface, he adverts to the three figures
(two priests and a doctor-poet), Milbourne, Collier, and Blackmore,
who most recently have been his attackers. Having "done justice to
others, I owe somewhat to myself," Dryden says, and he pens his
answer to each in turn. Milbourne, "who is in orders,"

pretends amongst the rest this quarrel to me, that I have fallen foul on
priesthood: if I have, I am only to ask pardon of good priests, and am
afraid his part of the reparation will come to little. Let him be satisfied
that he shall not be able to force himself upon me for an adversary. . . .
His own translations of Virgil have answered his criticisms on mine.
If . . . he prefers the version of Ogilby to mine, the world has made him
the same compliment; for it is agreed on all hands, that he writes even
below Ogilby. That, you will say, is not easily to be done; but what
cannot Milbourne bring about? . . . If I had taken to the church, (as
he affirms, but which was never in my thoughts,) I should have had more
sense, if not more grace, than to have turned myself out of my benefice
by writing libels on my parishioners. But his account of my manners
and my principles, are of a piece with his cavils and his poetry: and so
I have done with him for ever.

For "Quack Maurus" he reserves another bolt, to which he will add
yet another, in the last month of his life, when he writes the prologue
to *The Pilgrim*. "As for the City Bard, or Knight Physician," he
writes,

I hear his quarrel to me is, that I was the author of *Absalom and
Achitophel*, which he thinks is a little hard on his fanatick patrons in
London.

But I will deal the more civilly with his two Poems [*Prince Arthur*
and *King Arthur*], because nothing ill is to be spoken of the dead; and
therefore peace be to the *manes* of his Arthurs. I will only say that it
was not for this noble Knight that I drew the plan of an epick poem on
King Arthur, in my preface to the translation of Juvenal. . . . from that
Preface he plainly took his hint; for he began immediately upon the

story, though he had the baseness not to acknowledge his benefactor, but, instead of it, to traduce me in a libel.

Finally, he comes to Collier, repeating in prose elaboration what he had already expressed in the more condensed verses quoted above. Collier, he admits, in many things "has taxed me justly": "and I have pleaded guilty to all thoughts and expressions of mine, which can be truly argued of obscenity, profaneness, or immorality, and retract them. If he be my enemy, let him triumph; if he be my friend, as I have given him no personal occasion to be otherwise, he will be glad of my repentance. It becomes me not to draw my pen in the defence of a bad cause, when I have so often drawn it for a good one." Yet, he continues, it would not be very difficult to prove that Collier has perverted his meaning in many places. Collier's evident relish in his search for bawdry and immorality provokes Dryden to write: "I will not say, 'the zeal of God's house has eaten him up;' but I am sure it has devoured some part of his good manners and civility." After pointing out that "it became not one of [Collier's] function to rake into the rubbish of ancient and modern plays: a divine might have employed his pains to better purpose, than in the nastiness of Plautus and Aristophanes, whose examples, as they excuse not me, so it might be possibly supposed, that he read them not without some pleasure," he remarks that the drama of "the former age" contained bawdry too. "Are the times so much more reformed now," he asks, "than they were five and twenty years ago? If they are, I congratulate the amendment of our morals. But I am not to prejudice the cause of my fellow-poets, though I abandon my own defence: they have some of them answered for themselves; and neither they nor I can think Mr. Collier so formidable an enemy that we should shun him." And so he was done with Collier forever.

The interval of about six weeks between the appearance of the *Fables* and Dryden's death is almost a void. One letter only, to Elizabeth Steward, gives us merely a glimpse of his last days. On April 11, three weeks before the end, he writes her one of his gossipy and charming letters, relating the news of literary and political affairs, along with personal and family matters. His cousin John, he tells her, delighted with the verses honoring him, has sent a "noble present" which surprised him, for he "did not in the least expect it." He is "lame at home; & [has] not stirrd abroad this Moneth at least." The attack of erysipelas apparently had not been controlled, even by the best guesses of Dr. Gibbon. He tells Elizabeth of the imminent acting—"Within this moneth"—for his benefit, of *The Pilgrim*, cor--

rected by his "good friend Mr. Vanbrook." For this performance, he reveals, he has written a "New Masque, & [is] to write a New Prologue & Epilogue." With these yet to be written, it is clear that he was busy composing verse during the last fortnight of his life. And he was occupied with other concerns as well. Southerne's *The Revolt of Capua,* scheduled for production at Betterton's theater within this fortnight, he was asked to read—apparently as a consultant—but he writes, "I am out with that Company, & therefore if I can help it, will not read it before tis acted." He ends with an apology "for this slovenly letter; but I have not health to transcribe it."

The masque, then, was complete at this date, and very likely also the "Dialogue," or the "Song of the Scholar and his Mistress," relating their crossed love, who fall mad for each other and who meet in Bedlam.[5] The "Secular Masque," written while his body was full of pain and with the shadow of death upon him, remains a remarkable testimony not only to Dryden's vitality but to his continued command of his great poetic faculties. The mythological representation of the closing age he manages by the use of Janus, the God of Beginnings, Momus, the God of Derision, and, of course, Chronos. Janus appears first to command Chronos to mend his pace, for the goal is now in sight, and adjures him to "spread thy fans," that is, as a reaper spreads his winnowing fan to separate wheat from chaff, and to "wing thy flight," that is, to prepare for the journey through the next "secular" age. Chronos enters with his scythe and with a globe upon his back which on his entrance he sets down, with the words:

> Let me, let me drop my freight,
> > And leave the world behind.
> I could not bear
> Another year
> > The load of humankind.

Thereupon Momus enters, laughing:

> Ha! ha! ha! ha! ha! ha! well has thou done
> > To lay down thy pack,
> > And lighten thy back;
> The world was a fool, e'er since it begun,
> And since neither Janus, nor Chronos, nor I
> > Can hinder the crimes,
> > Or mend the bad times,
> 'Tis better to laugh than to cry.

Janus demands that Chronos begin the show to represent what changes the century has witnessed. Chronos calls in first Diana, who seems to represent the more peaceful life of the early part of the century:

> With horns and with hounds I waken the day,
> And hie to my woodland walks away;
> I tuck up my robe, and am buskin'd soon,
> And tie to my forehead a wexing moon.
> I course the fleet stag, unkennel the fox,
> And chase the wild goats o'er summits of rocks;
> With shouting and hooting we pierce thro' the sky,
> And Echo turns hunter, and doubles the cry.

Then, in recitative, the four figures comment:

> JANUS: Then our age was in its prime:
>
> CHRONOS: Free from rage:
>
> DIANA: And free from crime:
>
> MOMUS: A very merry, dancing, drinking,
>   Laughing, quaffing, and unthinking time.

These are repeated in chorus, followed at once by the entrance of Mars, who calls on the vocal brass, for the world is "past its infant age":

> Mars has look'd the sky to red;
> And Peace, the lazy good, is fled.
> Plenty, Peace, and Pleasure fly;
>   The sprightly green
>   In woodland walks no more is seen.

Civil war had arrived, and the scars were still fresh after half a century. To the warlike adjurations of Mars, Momus steps in to say:

> Thy sword within the scabbard keep,
>   And let mankind agree;
> Better the world were fast asleep,
>   Than kept awake by thee.
> The fools are only thinner,
>   With all our cost and care;
> But neither side a winner,
>   For things are as they were.

Venus then enters to represent Love as a counterbalance to War:

VENUS: Calms appear when storms are past,
        Love will have his hour at last:
        Nature is my kindly care;
        Mars destroys, and I repair;
        Take me, take me, while you may;
        Venus comes not ev'ry day.

The sardonic comments of Momus, repeated in chorus, bring the "Masque" to a close:

MOMUS: All, all of a piece throughout:
                Pointing to Diana
        Thy chase had a beast in view;
                To Mars
        Thy wars brought nothing about;
                To Venus
        Thy lovers were all untrue.

JANUS: 'Tis well an old age is out:

CHRONOS: And time to begin a new.

If the masque betrays a *fin de siècle* weariness and cynicism, the old poet was entitled to his feelings.

The old age was out, and Dryden's own life was fast ebbing. In the fortnight left to him after his letter of April 11, he wrote the prologue and epilogue to *The Pilgrim*—the last verse from his pen. The prologue he devotes almost entirely to a further attack upon Blackmore—Quack Maurus, whom he had already paid off in the preface to the *Fables*. But during this interval Blackmore had brought out *A Paraphrase on the Book of Job,* and it is to this that Dryden now directs his attention:[6]

    His man of Uz, stripp'd of his Hebrew robe,
    Is just the proverb, and *as poor as Job.*
    One would have thought he could no longer jog;
    But *Arthur* was a level, *Job's* a bog.
    There, tho' he crept, yet still he kept in sight;
    But here he founders in, and sinks downright.

Blackmore's dabbling with the epic in his *Arthurs,* his invasion of Scripture in this latest poetic effort, and his practice of medicine—all tend to defy classification and provide Dryden an irresistible target for satiric comment:

> We know not by what name we should arraign him,
> For no one category can contain him;
> A pedant, canting preacher, and a quack,
> Are load enough to break one ass's back:
> At last grown wanton, he presum'd to write,
> Traduc'd two kings, their kindness to requite;
> One made the doctor, and one dubb'd the knight.[7]

The epilogue to *The Pilgrim* should be read in conjunction with that section of the preface to the *Fables* in which he admits the justice of some of Collier's charges on the immorality of the stage. These verses serve as footnote to his former recantation; they attempt to deflect from theater and playwright some of the responsibility for the morality of the nation. For the first time he arraigns the court of Charles II as the first corrupter of morals, from which the stage took its cue. He begins:

> Perhaps the parson stretch'd a point too far,
> When with our theaters he wag'd a war,
> He tells you that this very moral age
> Receiv'd the first infection from the stage.
> But sure, a banish'd court, with lewdness fraught,
> The seeds of open vice, returning, brought.
>
> .　　.　　.　　.　　.　　.　　.　　.　　.
>
> The poets, who must live by courts, or starve,
> Were proud so good a government to serve;
> And, mixing with buffoons and pimps profane,
> Tainted the stage, for some small snip of gain.
> For they, like harlots, under bawds profess'd,
> Took all th' ungodly pains, and got the least.
> Thus did the thriving malady prevail,
> The court its head, the poets but the tail.
> The sin was of our native growth, 'tis true;
> The scandal of the sin was wholly new.
>
> .　　.　　.　　.　　.　　.　　.　　.　　.
>
> Nothing but open lewdness was a crime.
> A monarch's blood was venial to the nation,
> Compar'd with one foul act of fornication.

The origin, then, of the immorality that Collier inveighed against was, he thought, far otherwise than the clergyman pretended. Collier's attack on the stage will be wide of the mark:

Now, they would silence us, and shut the door
That let in all the barefac'd vice before.
As for reforming us, which some pretend,
That work in England is without an end:
Well we may change, but we shall never mend.
Yet, if you can but bear the present stage,
We hope much better of the coming age.

The dying poet read the age more shrewdly than the parson.

Dryden's physical condition became increasingly worse during the last ten days of April. The complications of the gout, the kidney condition, and the erysipelas in one of his legs, refused to respond to the treatment of Dr. Hobbs and Dr. Gibbon. Though they no doubt ransacked their pharmacopoeia and perhaps resorted to cupping (which could only aggravate a condition already grave), Dryden became steadily weaker. By April 29 his condition was critical; and word seems to have got about that the old poet was near death. In the issue of April 30, *The Post Boy* announced that "John Dryden, Esq.; the famous Poet, lies a dying." His condition became worse on Tuesday evening, April 30. Finally, at three in the morning of Wednesday, May 1, he breathed his last.[8] Long reconciled to his new religion, he died—as he had lived for nearly fifteen years—a firm adherent of the Roman Catholic faith. His death could hardly have been unexpected; and according to his relative, Mrs. Creed, "he received the notice of his approaching dissolution with sweet submission and entire resignation to the Divine Will." There is no record of attending priest or Catholic rites. He apparently remained conscious until the end, for Mrs. Creed testifies that "he took so tender and obliging a farewell of his friends, as none but he himself could have expressed."[9]

Although first plans for his interment at St. Anne's, Soho, were made at once, these were changed, and his body was sent to William Russell, an eminent embalmer, who prepared it for burial. From Russell's, Dryden was taken to the College of Physicians in Warwick Lane, where he lay in state for nearly a week. By May 6 it was generally known that a large funeral was being arranged and that his body would be buried in Westminster Abbey between Chaucer and Cowley. The day set for interment was Monday, May 13, and printed invitations were distributed widely, perhaps at the instance of his influential friends who had charge of arrangements:

Sir,—

    You are desired to accompany the Corps of Mr. John Dryden, from the College of Physicians in Warwick-Lane, to Westminster Abbey, on Monday the 13th of this instant May, 1700. at Four of the Clock in the Afternoon exactly, it being resolved to be moving by Five a clock. And be pleased to bring this Ticket with you.[10]

    The journals reported day-to-day developments from the time of his death until he was lowered into his grave. *The Post Boy,* which on May 7 had reported that his body was to "lye in State for some time in the Colledge of Physicians" and was to be conveyed to the Abbey on the following Monday, was able to inform its readers on May 9 that Dr. Garth, "that learned Physician and famous Orator," would speak a funeral Oration in Latin.[11]   After the event *The Post Boy, The Postman,* and *The Flying Post* carried descriptive accounts of the ceremonies.[12]   According to these witnesses, Garth spoke an eloquent tribute to the departed poet, which was followed by the singing, to mournful music, of the 30th Ode of Horace (Book III). According to *The Postman,* which was generally well-informed, "A world of people" attended, and the hearse, as it moved toward Westminster, was accompanied by "above one hundred coaches of the chief of the nobility and gentry." Mourners on horse (at least eight of them) preceded the hearse and nineteen walked beside it, to the harmonious strains of sad music, furnished by eight men in black scarves and hatbands, their instruments draped with black crêpe.[13] The black hearse, containing the double coffin, was drawn by six white Flanders horses, accoutered with velvet "plumes of feathers" and "velvet housings." It was an impressive *cortège,* even to London journalists. Ned Ward, whose report in *The London Spy* is more detailed than those in the journals, observed that "no Ambassador from the greatest Emperor in all the Universe, sent over with a Welcome Embassy to the Throne of *England,* ever made his Publick Entry to the Court, with half that Honour, as the Corps of the Great *Dryden* did its last *Exit* to the Grave."

Epilogue

Surviving Dryden were Lady Elizabeth and his three sons, to whom he had always been a loving and careful father. John, still resident in Rome, followed his father in death only three years later —on April 16, 1703.[1] Charles, the eldest, qualified as administrator of the estate, since Dryden had died intestate. Presumably he settled much of the small estate before his own death, by drowning, in 1704.[2] Erasmus-Henry, long on the continent, returned to England within a few years and followed his priestly vocation in Northampton-shire, where he died of a phthisis on December 3, 1710, having succeeded to the Dryden baronetcy upon the death of his uncle Erasmus only a few months before.[3] The poet's widow lived on for some years, dying enfeebled in body and in mind in the summer of 1714, in her seventy-eighth year.[4]

Public encomia began to appear the day after Dryden's death, and the attacks which he had borne in life continued without let. But as time rolled on and the new century grew older, rancor and bitterness fell away and perspective asserted itself. The greatness of his genius and his contributions to English letters became steadily more apparent. He was a man, and the limitations of his own humanity, with its strengths and weaknesses, he well knew and ac-knowledged. His more personal shortcomings and virtues lie partly hidden to our restricted and imperfect vision, as is proper. To Congreve, who would have known, shall be accorded the final word: "He was of very easy, I may say, of very pleasing access. . . . He was of a nature exceedingly humane and compassionate; easily for-giving injuries, and capable of a prompt and sincere reconciliation with them who had offended him. . . . To the best of my knowledge and observation, he was, of all the men that ever I knew, one of the most modest."

Appendices

APPENDIX A

THE COPE, DRYDEN, AND PICKERING FAMILIES

THE COPE FAMILY, into which the first John Dryden married, was prominent in Northamptonshire before the Drydens. Erasmus Cope, of whom little is known, may have acquired the old monastery of Canons Ashby and some of its lands, upon the distribution of Church properties by Henry VIII. At any rate the property was in the hands of his son and heir John Cope before May 3, 1547, when John was listed among those granted a general pardon for offenses before January 28 I Edward VI (*Calendar Patent Rolls, Edward VI*, II, 144). He is described as of Canons Ashby and later as sheriff of Northamptonshire. He had been created knight before 1550; and his considerable wealth is shown by frequent sale and transfer of land (*ibid.*, II, 192, 253; IV, 1; V, 261, 349, 356, 376, 414). Sir John died on January 22, 1558 (*Cal. Pat. Rolls, Elizabeth, 1558-1560*, p. 338), leaving Edward Cope his heir, whose wardship was granted to George Hennege.

In the meantime his daughter Elizabeth Cope had about 1550 married John Dryden, who, according to later family tradition, had migrated from Cumberland; he settled apparently in Adneston or Adston, a neighboring parish to Canons Ashby. He acquired at this time or soon thereafter considerable land in tenure (*Cal. Pat. Rolls, Phillip and Mary, 1553-1554*, I, 97). On September 15, 1554, he and his wife sold to Thomas Wilkes, merchant of the Staple of Calais, the rectory and church of Hoddenhull and the advowson of it (*A Descriptive Catalogue of Ancient Deeds*, VI, 515, no. C. 7738). Business and personal relationships between the Dryden and Wilkes families continued for many years. On November 12, 1578, "John Driden of Copes Ashebie" assigned to Sir William Catesby (in consideration of £1,500) the wardship and marriage of Margaret Wilkes, a sister and co-heir of Robert Wilkes. Dryden had held the wardship for more than a year, having been assigned it by Robert, Earl of Leicester, on May 4, 1577. A witness to the indenture to Catesby was John's son Erasmus (*ibid.*, V, 527, no. A. 13506). Within two or three years, Erasmus was to marry Frances Wilkes, who became the grandmother of the poet. For further references to this John Dryden, see *ibid.,* IV, 393, no. A. 9110; V, 335, no. A. 12537; V, 478.

After his marriage to Elizabeth Cope, John Dryden seems to have settled upon some of the Canons Ashby land, perhaps in a house known locally as "Wilkes Farm." Sir John Cope, of course, was still in residence at Canons Ashby (Public Record Office, *Inquisitions Post Mortem,* Chancery Series II, 207/54). Sometime after the death of Sir John Cope, in 1558, the Drydens moved into Canons Ashby, which henceforth was the Dryden seat. John Dryden died on September 3, 1584 (*ibid.*), leaving at least eight children and several grandchildren. Anthony, his eldest son, and perhaps other children appear to have predeceased him, for in his will (dated August 15 and proved September 10, Prerogative Court Canterbury, 24 Watson) he mentions Erasmus as his oldest son. To each of his children besides Erasmus—George, Elizabeth, John, Thomas, Bridget, Emma, Nicholas, and Stephen—he left £300.

The first son and child of Erasmus Dryden and Frances Wilkes was another John, born in 1580: he was sixteen years of age when he entered Broadgates Hall in 1596 (Joseph Foster, ed., *Alumni Oxoniensis: The Members of the University of Oxford 1500-1714* [London, 1891-92], 4 vols., I, 426-27). At least two other children, Frances and Elizabeth, were born before their grandfather's death in 1584, since they are mentioned in his will. William, the next son, was about ten years younger than John; he followed him to Broadgates and to the Middle Temple (Charles Henry Hopwood, ed., *Calendar of Middle Temple Records,* [London, 1903], 3 vols.; I, 420; II, 496). Erasmus, the third and youngest son, was born about 1602 or 1603, entered Emmanuel College, Cambridge, in 1618 (John and J. A. Venn, *the Book of Matriculations . . . in the University of Cambridge from 1544 to 1659* [Cambridge, 1913], p. 220). He left Cambridge in 1622 without a degree to enter Gray's Inn (Joseph Foster, ed., *Register of Admissions to Gray's Inn, 1521-1889* [London, 1889], p. 165).

Erasmus, as befitted a large landowner, was active in county affairs. He served as sheriff under Elizabeth and under James (Thomas Fuller, *The Worthies of England,* ed. John Nichols [London, 1811], 2 vols., II, 180, 181). References to him are frequent in contemporary documents. He was listed among contributions to the defense of the county in 1588 (he gave £50) (*Northamptonshire Notes and Queries,* I [1884], 46). Under date of August 4, 1599, in the "minute of Her Majesty's letters to the counties, for the sending up of voluntary horse," Erasmus was to supply one lance and one light horse (Historical Manuscripts Commission, 15th Report, Appendix, Part V, MSS of F. J. Savile Foljambe; see also H.M.C., Buccleuch and Queensberry MSS, III, 16, 53, 57, 134, 151, 170, 259, 358). The wholesale creation of titles by James I found Erasmus a customer. On November 8, 1619, he paid £1,100 for his baronetcy, which dignity was granted to him three days later (*Calendar State Papers, Domestic, James I, 1619-1623,* pp. 91, 92). In September, 1626, Charles I pressed for a general loan upon the subject, "according as every man was affected in the Rolls of the last subsidy." One provision of the resolution was that each person would be assessed £100 in money for every £100 in land. Those who refused to pay were arrested and committed in counties other than their own. Erasmus refused (he was then seventy-four years of age) and was committed to the care of Sir Cope Doyley, sheriff of Oxfordshire. Because there was no other "fit place" to keep him in the village of Nettlebed, the sheriff kept him at his own house (*Cal. S.P., Dom., Charles I, 1627-1628*, p. 310). Subsequently he was moved to the Gatehouse in Westminster, in company of his son-in-law, Sir John Pickering, John Hampden, Sir Edmond Hampden, and Sir William Wilmer. In February (1627) they joined in a petition to the Council for release (*Cal. S.P., Dom., 1625-1649, Addenda*, p. 198); but the King in Council had already (January 29) ordered that the resisters should be discharged—among them Erasmus Draiton (John Rushworth, *Historical Collections* [London, 1721-22], 8 vols., I, 418, 428, 472, 473).

Sir John, son of Erasmus, was likewise a sheriff of the county (Fuller, *Worthies*, II, 181) and during parliamentary rule had served on numerous commissions. He, along with his brothers William and Erasmus (the poet's father), helped collect county assessments in 1652/53 (*Antiquarian Memoranda and Biographies* [Northampton, 1901], and H.M.C., 14th Rep., App., Pt. II, Vol. III, p. 122). Having married Honor Beville, of a well-to-do family in Chesterton, Huntingdonshire, he had through marriage and purchase acquired two-thirds of the Manor of Chesterton (*The Victoria History of the County of Huntingdon* [London, 1926-36], 3 vols., III, 140). He lent money to the parliamentary government on the security of sequestered estates (*Calendar Committee for Compounding, 1643-1660*, pp. 28-31). In 1642, when drawings for Irish land were made, he paid in £600 (*Cal. S.P., Dom., Ireland Adventurers for Land, 1642-1659*, p. 31); in 1654, he was granted land in the barony of Eglish, King's County (*Cal. S.P., Dom., Ireland, 1647-1660*, pp. 490, 522).

The poet's father was not nearly so active as his uncle. In addition to Erasmus' county office of Justice of the Peace (*Northamptonshire Notes and Queries*, I [1884], 5) and membership on the committee mentioned above, he served on a committee in Northamptonshire to collect the Scottish loan in 1646 (*Calendar Committee for Compounding, 1643-1660*, p. 50). He seems not to have participated in governmental affairs as much as his father or his Pickering relatives.

The Pickerings were an older county family than the Drydens (*Victoria History of the County of Northamptonshire* [London, 1902-37], 4 vols., III, 144 ff.). They had settled in Aldwinckle and Titchmarsh in the early sixteenth century. On May 29, 1553, the Earl of Worcester transferred to Gilbert Pickering and his sons a grant of his manor of "Tychemarshe," along with 160 messuages, 100 cottages, watermills, and gardens, 3,000 acres of land, 800 acres of meadow, 1,200 acres of pasture, and Aldwinckle All Saints (*Cal. Pat. Rolls, Edward VI*, V, 114). Gilbert's son John had a son Gilbert, who died in 1613, to be succeeded by his son John (later Sir John), who married, in 1609, Susanna Dryden, daughter of Sir Erasmus (*ibid.*). Their son Gilbert became a knight in 1638 and took an active part in the governments of the Interregnum. This was "Noll's Lord Chamberlain." He married Elizabeth Montague, the sister of Edward Montague, later Earl of Sandwich. He acquired much land in Northamptonshire, including the Manor of Oundle.

The younger brother of Sir John Pickering, however, is of importance here. Henry was baptized at Titchmarsh, December 24, 1564. At eighteen years of age he matriculated at Christ's College, Cambridge, took his B.A. in 1586/87 and his M.A. in 1590. He was incorporated at Oxford in 1593 (*Biographical Register of Christ's College, 1505-1905*, compiled by John Peile [Cambridge, 1910-13], 2 vols., I, 174). In 1590 he was described as a "scholar of Cambridge . . . zealous, resourceful, pious." He participated in investigations regarding the alleged bewitching of his nieces, the daughters of Robert Throckmorton, and "helped to procure the execution of the 'Witches of Warboys'" (P. D. Mundy, "The Pickerings of Aldwincle All Saints, Northants," *Notes and Queries*, CXCVII [Nov. 8, 1952], 490-92). Since his father owned the advowson to Aldwinckle All Saints, Henry was installed as rector, a post he held for forty-four years, until his death in 1637. His will was dated August 1, 1636; he left, as a token, 10s. to his "loving son-in-law Erasmus Dryden" (*ibid.*). On December 1, 1600, he had been granted a license to marry Isabella Smith of Oundle (*Marriage Licences*, Peterborough. This reference is by communication from the late Mr. P. D. Mundy). Among his children was Mary (b. probably before 1610), who married Erasmus Dryden and became the poet's mother.

APPENDIX B

DRYDEN'S RELATION TO CROMWELL'S GOVERNMENT

THE TEMPTATION that besets literary scholars to identify the man best known to them with men of the same name referred to in contemporary documents is nowhere better illustrated than here. It may be pointed out that the name Dryden occurs in many documents and in many spelling variants: *Dryden, Drydon, Drydan, Dreydon, Drayden, Dreyden, Driden, Dridon, Dredon, Dreden, Dreiden, Dreidon, Draiden, Dradon,* and even *Dayton.* Whenever the name occurs, perhaps the safest procedure is to assume that it does not refer to the poet, unless it is accompanied by some distinguishing phrase. Even the inclusion of the Christian name *John* by no means makes identification safe or reasonable. The Drydens in their various branches were very prolific, and the presence of a John in each branch complicates enormously the problem of identification. For many years it was thought that the poet was collector of customs because a John Dryden was officially appointed to the post. This mistake was set right many years ago (Charles E. Ward, "Was John

Dryden Collector of Customs?" *Modern Language Notes*, XLVII (1932), 246-39). The belief that the poet was an employee of Cromwell's government likewise rests upon the discovery of the name John Driden on a receipt, and the appearance of the name, in different spellings, in two other documents. The first was printed by Masson in *The Life of John Milton*, V, 375, and is to be found in Public Record Office, *State Papers*, 18/180, f. 95. It reads:

> Received then of the right hono^{ble} Mr.
> Secretary Thurloe the sume of ffifty pounds
> by mee
> John Driden

It is dated October 19, 1657. Only the words *by mee* and the signature were written by the signer. But was this *John Driden* the poet? Only one undoubted holograph of the poet within this early period exists: that on the letter to his cousin Honor, where he signs *Jo: Dryden*. There are certain similarities—a large, clear loop on the *y*, a rather humped *m* and *n*, and the vertical line on the capital *D* rising above the, curved portion. Yet positive identification is complicated by the complete lack of signatures from other men who might have signed the document. One of these was John Driden, the poet's cousin and son of Sir John Dryden. He had entered Wadham College in 1651, and at this time was probably twenty-two or twenty-three years of age. Since his father had taken an active part in the government, it could be imagined that his son might also find a place. Another possible claimant was the John Dryden who took out a license to marry Elizabeth Lucke at St. John the Baptist, London, on June 15, 1663. He gave his age as twenty-seven (J. L. Chester, ed., *Marriage Allegations in the Registry of the Vicar-General of Archbishop of Canterbury* [London, 1886], Harleian Society, Vol. XXIII, June 15, 1663). Since a witness was Lewis Fossan, a Merchant Taylor, it is reasonable to suppose he became the woollen draper of St. Bride's Parish, who was many years later appointed collector of customs. He was a cousin of John Driden of Chesterton (P.R.O. C 9/445/77) and therefore was probably the grandson of William Dryden of Farndon, Northants, a younger brother of Sir John of Canons Ashby. Still another John Dryden—this one an attorney—bought the manor of St. Ives, Huntingdonshire, and the advowson in 1682 from Robert and Mullineux Audley (*Victoria History, Huntingdon*, II, 220). Since there is a suggestion that he had connections with Farndon, he may have been either a son or grandson of William.

The two documents which include the name Dryden in connection with Cromwell's funeral may be found in P.R.O. *S.P.*, 18/182, f. 90, and the British Museum, Lansdowne 95, No. 2, 11^{v}. The first (printed by Pierre Legouis in *André Marvell* [Paris, 1928], p. 214n.) reveals that a *Mr. Drayden* was on the list of persons scheduled to receive mourning cloth. This document is dated September 7, 1658. The other document lists *Mr. Dradon* walking in company with Milton and Marvell and other secretaries for the "French and Latin Tongs." (This was printed by W. Arthur Turner, "Milton, Marvell, and 'Dradon' at Cromwell's Funeral,"

Philological Quarterly, XXVIII [April, 1949], 320-23). See also *The Diary of Thomas Burton* (London, 1828), 4 vols., II, 524, where *Mr. Dradon* is also listed among the secretaries in the procession. The *Mr. Drayden* and *Mr. Dradon* of these documents I should suppose are the same person.

But I would not suppose that he is necessarily the poet. The *Mr. Drydens* who could qualify for these dubious honors were almost without number—and not only among members of the poet's Northamptonshire family. There were Drydens in Cornwall (see British Museum, Additional MS 813, f. 3, 10ʳ and 10ᵛ) and Drydens in Cumberland (see *Transactions of the Cumberland and Westmoreland Antiquarian and Archaeological Society* [Kendal, 1889], X, 176 ff., and I [N.S. 1901], 30)—one who spent an evening with Bishop Nicolson on Church business. Until further, irrefutable, evidence appears that the poet held a minor post in Cromwell's government, we might do well to reject such identifications; for mischievous interpretations easily follow the acceptance of such unprovable identifications.

APPENDIX C

THE HOWARD FAMILY

T HIS BRANCH of the Howard family came from Thomas Howard, First Earl of Suffolk. His second son, Thomas, was born about 1580. He proceeded to Cambridge (Magdalene) in 1598, and took his M.A. in 1605. From 1614 to 1619 he was Master of the Horse to Prince Charles. In 1614 he married into the Cecil family, taking as his wife, Elizabeth, daughter of William Cecil, second Earl of Exeter. Honors came to him continuously for the next forty years. On January 22, 1621/22, he was created Baron Howard of Charlton (his mother had been of the Knyvett family of Charlton, Wiltshire) and Viscount Andover, the latter a courtesy title, which was later held by his eldest son, Charles, until 1669, when he became second Earl. On February 7, 1625/26, he was created first Earl of Berkshire. On June 8, 1632, he was elected Steward of the city of Oxford, a post he held until beyond the Restoration. In 1638 he came into the Wiltshire estates at Charlton, which had been settled on him by his mother. From 1643 to 1646 he was Governor to Charles Stuart, Prince of Wales. He died, at nearly ninety years of age, on July 20, 1669, and was buried in Westminster Abbey.

The children of this marriage numbered at least fourteen: Charles (1617); Thomas (1619); Henry (1620?), who married Elizabeth, daughter of William Lord Spencer and sister of the Earl of Sunderland; William (1622), whose daughter Dorothy married James Grahme, and her sister Ann, Sir Gabriel Sylvius; Frances (1623), who married Conyers Darcy, Earl of Holderness; Edward (1624), the playwright; Robert (1625/26), the playwright and Dryden's friend; Maria (1627/28); Philip

(1628/29); Diana (1631); Algernon (1632/33); James (1634/35?), another minor literary figure; and Elizabeth (1636, 1638?), who married Dryden. Elizabeth was the second daughter of the family so named, an earlier Elizabeth having died on May 29, 1622 (J. V. Kelto, ed., *Register of St. Martin in the Fields, 1619-1636* [London, 1936]). See also Henry Howard of Corby, *Indications of Memorials, Monuments,* [etc.] *of the Howard Family* (1834 [41]), pp. 59-69; and Gerald Brenan and E. P. Stratham, *The House of Howard* (London, 1907), 2 vols., I, 72-73. Volume II, page 410, contains genealogical tables of the Howard family.

The Earl of Berkshire, like many another adherent of the Stuarts, suffered grievously during the Interregnum. He was forced to compound for his estates and he found it very difficult—at times impossible—to do so; he finally became a delinquent. In April, 1644, he asked the Aldermen of the city of Oxford for a loan of £200, which received their approval because of the "many favours by him done to this Cittie." In order to oblige the Earl they sold the city plate, fearing it would "be otherwyse disposed of." The generous aldermen were caught up three years later by the Council (*Oxford Council Acts, 1626-1665* [Oxford, 1933], pp. 152, 384-85). By 1655 he was petitioning the Treasury Commissioners for an order to allow him to continue on his old patent (granted by Charles I on January 13, 1640/41) as farmer of the post fines. After two years of deliberation the Commissioners approved the grant to him and his son, Sir Robert. These two agreed to pay £3,000 for this privilege, which was to net them between £1,000 and £2,000 per year (*Cal. S.P., Dom., 1655-1656*, pp. 35, 221, 252-53; *Cal. S.P., Dom., 1656-1657*, p. 46, *et passim; Cal. S.P., Dom., 1657-1658*, pp. 93-94, 102). In 1661 the patent was reissued to them for a term of forty-eight years (*Cal. S.P., Dom., 1660-1661*, p. 577).

After Charles came back, the Howard family expected recompense for their years of sacrifice. In addition to the farm of the post fines, the Earl and Sir Robert petitioned for other posts and patents. Viscount Andover was given an annuity of £1,000; Philip Howard petitioned for a grant for thirteen years of the office of making white and green glass; the Earl petitioned for a grant of "all the sea-wrack or sea-weed, driven on shore between high and low water in England and Scotland," for the office of Custos Brevium in the Court of Common Pleas, for a patent for a new invention "of which he is informed," for the boiling potashes for making soap (*Cal. S.P., Dom., 1660-1661*, pp. 386, 430, 188, 385, 523).

Sir Robert was granted a patent to the Office of Serjeant Painter to the King, and of the Office of Clerk of the Patents in Chancery (*ibid.,* pp. 55, 76). Within a year or two he had given up both places (*ibid., 1663-1664*, p. 58). By 1666-67, as a member of Parliament, he was becoming prominent among the younger members, and took a leading part in debates. He was particularly active in the group that forced the dismissal of Clarendon. In 1668, Howard was very close to Buckingham (one of the Cabal), who apparently tried to make him Secretary of State (E. S. DeBeer, "The Dictionary of National Biography," *Bulletin of the Institute of Historical Research,* III [1925-26], pp. 64-65). In October, 1671, he became Secretary of the Treasury under Clifford; and in March, 1672/73, Auditor of the Exchequer, a lucrative post which he retained until his death in 1698. In 1678/79 he appears to have supported the Exclusion Bill—a political position opposite that of Dryden. He continued as M.P. until James the Second's Parliament, in which he did not sit. After the Revolution, he sat for Castle Rising until his death. He was a staunch anti-Catholic, in the face of the Catholicism of his older brother and perhaps other members of his family. His uncle Philip, of course, became Cardinal Howard.

Petitions and warrants and farms and annuities, however, seem not to have been sufficient to rebuild the old Earl's fortunes. By December, 1662, he was addressing King Charles about the King's proposed purchase of Berkshire House, the great town residence of the Earl. He is "willing to part with his house to His Majesty, that he may give him no trouble in piecing up a broken fortune, occasioned by the persecution of his enemies" (*Cal. S.P., Dom., 1661-1662,* p. 606). The house was finally bought out of the moiety of the Excise formerly assigned to the Dunkirk Army. Berkshire House had a varied career thereafter. Clarendon resided in it after the great Fire (Pepys, *Diary,* November 19, 1666), and in 1668 it became the residence of Lady Castlemaine, later the Duchess of Cleveland (*ibid.,* May 8, 1668).

APPENDIX D

NOTES AND OBSERVATIONS ON THE EMPRESS OF MOROCCO

DESPITE Settle's rather uncertain identification of Dryden as one of the authors of *Notes and Observations,* it seems to me doubtful that Dryden was involved. In addition to Settle's statements about his supposed attackers, we have only the word of John Dennis, given more than forty years later from hearsay and gossip. Dennis, in 1673, was sixteen years old and had no connections with the persons or the events. In the *Remarks on Mr. Pope's Translation of Homer* (1717) Dennis "remembers" that Dryden, Shadwell, and Crowne "began to grow Jealous" of Settle's success and in confederacy wrote the "Remarks," as he calls them. Dryden became involved because, according to Dennis, "Mr. Settle was then a formidable Rival to Mr. Dryden." Settle, he says, answered their attack and had "by much the better of them." Yet he also adds that he has "utterly forgot the Controversy." But he has "remembered" enough perhaps to confuse the situation: he seems to be merely embroidering Settle's angry guess. For at no time—and certainly not in 1673 when Settle was only beginning his undistinguished career—was Settle ever a rival, formidable or otherwise, of Dryden; nor is there any evidence available to explain what would have been uncharacteristic of Dryden—a gratuitous attack upon the virtually unknown Settle. Nor has anyone ever offered any believable testimony about Shadwell's participation. A. S. Borgman (*Thomas Shadwell, His Life and Comedies* [New York, 1928], pp. 43 ff.) has accepted merely the early guess of Settle.

There is more substance to Settle's charge that John Crowne was implicated. Twenty-five years later, in the "Epistle to the Reader," attached to his play *Caligula* (1698), Crowne admits that "In my notes to a play called the Empress of Morocco (I call 'em mine because above three parts of four were written by me) I gave vent to more ill-nature in me than I will do again." If Crowne speaks the truth and indeed wrote more than three-quarters of the *Notes and Observations,* who was responsible for the remainder? If we suppose Dryden, what part and how much of it did he write? Nobody has seriously attempted to prove any of it his. Malone, who examined the tract to find Dryden, was most tentative in his conclusions: "[Dryden] appears to me to have had very little share in the composition of these Remarks; and as it is acknowledged that a great part of them was written by Shadwell and Crown, I have not thought it proper to give them a place in this collection of his prose works. But the Preface, I think, *from internal evidence,* [italics mine] is ascertained to be his composition; and one passage in the body of the piece, and the Postscript, may also with some probability be ascribed to him; and therefore these I have admitted, though I have some doubts concerning the latter" (Malone, ed., *Prose Works of Dryden,* II, 274).

The ascription of these parts to Dryden merely on the basis of internal evidence may be open to question. It seems to me that there is little or nothing one can point to, in the parts mentioned by Malone, as more characteristically Dryden's than Shadwell's or Crowne's. Until there is more clinching evidence available, I believe we may exculpate Dryden in this matter. In any case, it is hardly proper to call the *Empress of Morocco* the "cause of one of Dryden's most famous quarrels," as does Hugh Macdonald in *John Dryden: A Bibliography of Early Editions and Drydeniana.* Indeed, if Dryden were in such belligerent mood, we might more reasonably expect him to strike at Joseph Arrowsmith, whose *Reformation* (1673) burlesqued and satirized him in the figure of the Tutor, and at the numerous persons who were actively engaged in baiting him, rather than at the innocuous Settle.

APPENDIX E

ALBION AND ALBANIUS

Details of the collaboration between the poet and the composer, with Betterton forming the practical link with the theater, are lacking, and no amount of conjecture will supply the story of this first full-scale effort to create a new kind of opera in England. However, from the available data we can follow, to some extent, the plan they were working on. The piece apparently was to be modelled upon the successful French "ma-

chine" plays, which had achieved much success in Paris in the 1670's
and earlier. The chief plays in the genre were Corneille's *La Toison
D'or* (as early as 1660/61), Boyer's *Jupiter et Sémélé* (1660) and *Festa
de Vénus* (1669), Molière's *Amphitryon* (1668) and *Psyché* (1671), de
Visé's *Amours de Venus et d'Adonis* (1670) and *Le Mariage de Bacchus
et d'Ariane.* The usual, but not invariable, form of these consisted of a
somewhat extensive prologue (as in *Psyché*), which employed mythological characters and relied almost entirely upon allegory. Following the
prologue were the usual five acts, each of which contained an elaborate
scenic piece, or pieces, and intricate machines for the flying goddesses,
the chariots, the clouds, and lightning and thunder. A considerable number of such scenic devices had long been used by Betterton at the Duke's
Theatre. So too had dancing and music, the latter not greatly employed
in the French plays, because of an order restricting the acting companies
in France from engaging professional singers and musicians (H. C.
Lancaster, *A History of French Dramatic Literature in the Seventeenth
Century* [Baltimore, 1929-42], 5 vols., Vol. II, Part III, pp. 503-31).

The novelty of this forthcoming opera did not reside in the effects.
It lay in the conscious attempt to create *de novo* an English operatic
form. Heretofore the English opera consisted of applying to an already
existing play, like *The Tempest* or *Macbeth*, scenic displays, music, and
dancing. Songs had been set by one or more of the King's musicians,
engaged, as it were, on a piece-work basis. The purpose now was to give
one composer complete responsibility for the score, which was to be
finally achieved through a process of consultation and compromise with
the poet. Along with them was the stage manager and technician, who
would provide the scenes and machines proper to the book of the opera.
In form, it was to follow the French model, but with rather more music
and singing than was possible in Paris. It was to have an elaborate
allegorical prologue, followed by five acts, to be punctuated by scenic
devices, by singing and dancing, and by the introduction of allegorical
figures.

Such appears to have been the plan. Who decided finally upon the
theme remains unknown, but perhaps Dryden was responsible for it.
In his own words: "Every loyal Englishman cannot but be satisfied with
the moral of this, which so plainly represents the double restoration of
his sacred Majesty." Such a theme was particularly apt and timely, for
Charles's counterattack upon his enemies had now reached a triumphantly
successful conclusion through the drive upon the city Charters. He was
assured of complete control over the recalcitrant, and from the Tory
point of view, disloyal inhabitants of the capital. It was a second
restoration of Charles: he in a sense had regained kingly power and had
been reinstated in the affections of his people, after the struggles of the
past half-dozen years. The time for rejoicing and for commemoration
was clearly at hand.

The awareness that he was attempting something new appears in the
preface which Dryden wrote—even before the opera was acted. "It has
attempted," he says, "a discovery beyond any former undertaker of our

nation. Only remember, that if there be no north-east passage to be
found, the fault is in nature, and not in me . . . if I have not succeeded
as I desire, yet there is something still remaining to satisfy the curiosity
or itch of sight and hearing." But the opera *Albion and Albanius,* which
took the boards in 1685, was not the one for which these elaborate preparations were made. In the larger plan the first act of *Albion* (as we know
it) provided merely the prologue—after the French fashion. This was
to introduce a five-act play, which perhaps was intended to celebrate the
House of Stuart by tracing its noble forebears and by bringing the account
of the dynasty up to the moment of Charles's "second Restoration."
This play, as Dryden says in the dedication seven years later, was *King
Arthur,* which was "the last piece of service which I had the honour to
do for my gracious Master, King Charles the Second; and though he
lived not to see the performance of it on the stage, yet the prologue to it,
which was the opera of Albion and Albanius, was often practiced before
him at Whitehall." He admits that extensive revisions in the original
were necessary so as not to offend the government of William and Mary
in 1691/92, and we are left to conjecture what the original contained.
Perhaps it was a more complete laudation of the Stuarts than is now apparent in *King Arthur,* yet a careful reading will reveal a number of
traces of an original allegory which Dryden did not trouble himself to
remove; for Mary, after all, was Albion's niece and Albanius' daughter,
and she could hardly take offense at a celebration of her family.

What happened to force a change in the original plan is matter only
for conjecture. Dryden merely says that "some intervening accidents . . .
deferred the performance of the main design." These may have been (as
suggested above) connected with failure to find adequate financial support for the expensive production. To salvage what had already been
done, Dryden "proposed to the actors to turn the intended prologue into
an entertainment by itself, as you now see it, by adding two acts more
to what I had already written." The result was *Albion and Albanius.*
The description of the scenes, for which Dryden relied on Betterton
("who has spared neither for industry nor cost to make this entertainment perfect"), tends to corroborate Dryden's statement that "the new-
ness of the undertaking is all the hazard." Nothing like it had yet
appeared. The entirely new frontispiece for the stage, for example, was
elaborate beyond anything attempted hitherto by Betterton and must
have cost the company hundreds of pounds more than any other similar
work the companies had ever commissioned. On either side of the
stage was to be a great pilaster resting upon a base highly ornamented
with a shield in gold, one representing two hearts, a scroll, and an imperial
crown; the other, two quivers full of arrows saltire. And on each base
stands a figure larger than life, one representing Peace, with palm and
olive branch, the other Plenty, with the cornucopia. Beyond and above
these, are Corinthian columns decorated with flowers; and on the arch
above the stage are seen Poetry and Painting, the City of London,
Thames, the imperial figures of King and Queen, attended by Pallas and
the three Graces, Cupid, and so on. The opening scene discovers statues

of Charles I and Charles II on either side of the stage, and a street of palaces, the view, in perspective, continued as far as the limits of the deep stage would permit. Mercury descends in a chariot drawn by ravens, to discover Augusta and Thames, amid paintings of a city in chaos and destruction. New scene follows new scene in profusion. In Act I, the clouds divide and Juno appears in a machine drawn by peacocks; to symphonic music it moves forward and descends, opens, and discloses the tail of the peacock "which is so large, that it almost fills the opening of the stage between scene and scene." Act II opens with a scene of a "Poetical Hell," in which are seen Prometheus and the vulture, Sisyphus, and the Belides, surrounded by pyramids of fire and figures in torment.

To match this magnificence Dryden and Grabu apparently worked in close co-operation to adapt music to verse. Dryden's knowledge of French and Italian—and (as he says) of the best operas in both countries —enabled the poet to write in such a "variety of measures as have given the composer Monsieur Grabut what occasions he could wish, to shew his extraordinary talent in diversifying the recitative, the lyrical part, and the chorus." He adds that in the rehearsals, the King found "the composition and choruses . . . more just and more beautiful, than any he had heard in England." Indeed the "best judges and those too of the best quality . . . commended the happiness of his genius . . . and his skill." Dryden records this tribute to Grabu "because amongst some English musicians and their scholars, (who are sure to judge after them) the imputation of being a Frenchman is enough to make a party, who maliciously endeavour to decry him." Yet he points out that Grabu's knowledge of French and Italian operas, his skill in music, and his good sense "have raised him to a degree above any man who shall pretend to be his rival on our stage."

Dryden's defense of Grabu underlines the contemporary attacks upon him, part of which no doubt were made because the English musicians were affronted that a foreigner should have been chosen before one of them. Nicholas Staggins, successor to Grabu as Charles's master of the King's Violins, and Pelham Humphrey, to name only two, had had some experience in the theater and might have expected to be commissioned for what must have seemed reasonably enough to be the most exciting assignment of the time. In 1683/84, when the decision was made, Grabu obviously could bring a wider and more varied experience to this particular plan than anyone in England. Modern historians and music critics, like E. J. Dent, who calls *Albion* "a monument of stupidity," generally comment unfavorably on Grabu's score (which was printed in 1687). Some have thought that Henry Purcell should have done the music; but that young man, by 1684, had had practically no theater experience and had not yet reached his musical majority. However, when Dryden and Betterton, seven years later, revived the main part of the design, Purcell was entrusted with the score; the result is the King Arthur music, which constitutes one of Purcell's claims to musical fame.

Notes

CHAPTER I

1. The date of his birth has been a matter of considerable speculation. Edmond Malone, ed., *Critical and Miscellaneous Prose Works of John Dryden* (London, 1800), 4 vols., I, i, 5-8, reviewed the whole case for settling upon August 9, 1631, but rejected the evidence (cited by Pope) on the monument to Dryden, which was erected by the Duke of Buckingham. Recent discoveries, however, have corroborated the evidence for August 9. See the letter in the *Times Literary Supplement* by Roswell G. Ham, August 20, 1931, p. 633; and also further correspondence September 3, 10, 17, 24; November 12, 1931. More recently both the late P. D. Mundy and James M. Osborn have cited a part of the transcript of the Register of All Saints, Aldwinckle, to prove August 14, 1631, the date of the poet's baptism. See Mundy, "The Baptism of John Dryden," *Notes and Queries,* CLXXXIV (1943), 286, 352, and Osborn, *John Dryden: Some Biographical Facts and Problems* (New York, 1940), p. 270. There seems little reason to doubt that August 9 (19 N.S.) should be accepted.

2. See P. D. Mundy, p. 286. The paper recording the baptism of Dryden on August 14, 1631 (Bodleian, MS Top. Northants, c. 17, f. 167), Mundy points out, is in reality a portion of the All Saints Register transmitted to the Reverend Nathaniel Bridges, rector of the Wadenhoe Church from 1714 to 1747, by the Reverend Mr. Fleetwood, rector of Aldwinckle All Saints from 1721 to 1763. This seems to be a piece of clinching evidence that Dryden's birth did take place in Aldwinckle Parish.

3. Evidence for the marriage at Pilton on this date is to be found in a communication by one "H. W.," "John Dryden's Parents," to *N&Q,* 2nd Series, XII (1861), 207-8. He quotes from the register of Pilton Church: "Erasmus Dreydon, gent., and Mary Pyckeringe were married the one and twentieth day of October." No ready explanation is available for their marriage at Pilton, performed by the rector, William Allen, rather than at Aldwinckle by Mary's father.

4. See Appendix A, p. 321.

5. The first son, Anthony, was born about 1551; Erasmus, the second son, in 1553; Edward in 1555; George in 1562; John in 1564. Anthony, Erasmus, and Edward all matriculated at Magdalen in 1571, followed by George in 1574/75, and John in 1578 (see *Alumni Oxonienses,* ed. Joseph Foster [London, 1887-88], 4 vols., I, 426-27); Anthony matriculated at the Middle Temple in 1575, Erasmus in 1578, George in 1579 (Charles Henry Hopwood, ed., *Calendar of Middle Temple Records* [London, 1904], I, 205, *et passim*).

6. See James Bass Mullinger, *The University of Cambridge* (Cambridge, 1884), II, 310 ff., and F. J. Powicke, *The Cambridge Platonists* (London, 1926), Chap. I.

7. *Calendar State Papers, Domestic, 1603-1610*, p. 200.   James I had issued a proclamation for uniformity on March 5, 1604.

8. *Dictionary of National Biography*, "John Dod."

9. P. D. Mundy, "Cope, Dryden, Throckmorton, Oxenbridge and Allied Puritan Families," *N&Q*, CLXXX (1941), 182-83.

10. George Baker, *The History and Antiquities of the County of Northampton* (London, 1822-41), II, 24.   This land remained in the family until 1804.

11. The late P. D. Mundy possessed a copy of a letter to Alexander Stephens written in 1798 by the then Lady Dryden detailing information about this land.   It has in part been printed by James M. Osborn (*Dryden*, pp. 235 ff.), who also prints a letter written by the same Lady, on the same subject, to Edmond Malone.

Erasmus Dryden seems to have held more lands in freehold and reversion than this particular plot.   See the complaint of Edward Watts to Archbishop Laud, March 31, 1640 (*Cal. S.P., Dom., Charles I, 1639-1640*, No. 46, pp. 607-8), regarding Erasmus' refusal to grant to a new vicar of Blakesley "the herbage of the third part of the old churchyard"; he refuses to allow burials and pays only 6*d*. per year to the churchwardens for its use.   It is well worth 6*s*. 8*d*.   Furthermore, Watts alleges that Erasmus resists carrying on the long tradition of paying a man to ring the bow bell at 8 P.M. and 4 A.M.   As Watts says, his family has long held the reversion and rent of the rectory.   It had been granted to Thomas Watts in 1560 (*Calendar Patent Rolls, 2 Elizabeth, Part II, 1560*, p. 281).

12. From *Marriage Licences*, Peterborough.   I am indebted to the late P. D. Mundy for this reference.

13. The baptisms of Dryden's brothers and sisters, up to 1644, are recorded in the Register of Titchmarsh Church: Agnes, November 8, 1632; Rose, October 18, 1633; Mary, November 13, 1634; Lucy, January 17, 1635/36; Martha, April 10(?), 1637; Erasmus, May 16, 1638; Abigail, August 1, 1639; Hannah, December 26, 1644.   The Register does not include the other five children.   The reason for the omissions is difficult to determine.   On the basis of their later marriage allegations, Henry would have been born about 1643, James in 1648, Elizabeth in 1654—the year of her father's death.   Frances in her marriage allegation admits to being twenty-four years of age in 1680 (Joseph Chester and George Armytage, eds., *Allegations for Marriage Licences, issued by the Bishop of London, 1611-1828* [London, 1887], Harleian Society). She was obviously shading her age by several years.   Perhaps Elizabeth and Frances were twins.   There appears no record of Hester.   The brothers in later years were all domiciled in London.

14. Printed by Malone, ed., *Prose Works of Dryden*, I, i, 564 ff.

15. A. J. Shirren, "The Whitings of Etton and Aldwincle," *N&Q*, CXCVIII, No. 5 (May, 1953), 197.

16. Family tradition held that Spenser had been a friend to Sir Erasmus. Perhaps the connection was somewhat different.   Spenser's second wife, Elizabeth Boyle, was a cousin of Sir Erasmus (Douglas Hamer, "Some Spenser Problems," *N&Q*, CLXXX (1941), 206-9.

17. Malone, ed., *Prose Works of Dryden*, II, 358-59.

18. G. F. Russell Barker and A. H. Stenning, eds., *The Record of Old Westminsters* (London, 1928), 2 vols., I, 6-8, and II, 1076-78.   Sir John Dryden had already, in 1644, served on a committee to inventory, at the Collegiate Church at Westminster, "a list of plate [and] gilt plate" (Historical

Manuscripts Commission, 14th Report Appendix, Part II, Vol. III (1894), p. 122).

19. For detailed accounts of the regimen at Westminster school at this time, see Foster Watson, *The English Grammar Schools to 1660* (Cambridge, 1908); G. F. Russell Barker, *Memoir of Richard Busby* (London, 1895); John Sergeaunt, *Annals of Westminster School* (London, 1898); Barker and Stenning, eds., *Record of Old Westminsters*. Watson is particularly valuable for information on the texts and authors in use during the period. Standard for curriculum and methods is Charles Hoole's *A New Discovery of the Old Art of Teaching Schoole* (1660), ed. E. T. Campagnac (Liverpool, 1913).

20. Headnote to the "Third Satire of Persius." He also inscribed the "Fifth Satire" to Busby, acknowledging his debt for the "best part of my own education and that of my two sons." From Busby, he admits here, he received "the first and truest taste of Persius." Juvenal, Persius, and Martial seem to have been favorites of his master, for he wrote texts of them for use in his school: *Juvnalis et Persii Satirae in usum Scholae Westmonasteriensis* (1656), and *Martialis Epigrammata in usum,* [etc.], (1661).

21. The accomplishments of the boys who survived this rigorous discipline are writ large in the history of seventeenth-century culture and thought. The particular facility of these scholars at a slightly later period is noted in an interesting and amusing item by Evelyn (*Diary,* May 13, 1661), who had attended the election of scholars to Trinity and Christ Church in 1661, eleven years after Dryden had gone through such an election to Trinity. "I heard and saw," he writes, "such exercises at the election of scholars at Westminister School to be sent to the university in Latin, Greek, Hebrew, and Arabic, [the last added after Dryden's time] in themes and extemporary verses, as wonderfully astonished me in such youths, with such readiness and wit, some of them not above twelve, or thirteen years of age. Pity it is, that what they attain here so ripely, they either do not retain, or do not improve more considerably when they come to be men, though many of them do; and no less is to be blamed their odd pronouncing of Latin, so that out of England none were able to understand, or endure it."

22. See Hugh Macdonald, *John Dryden: A Bibliography of Early Editions and Drydeniana* (Oxford, 1939), pp. 1-2, for bibliographical data. There seems to have been no personal connection between John Dryden and Lord Hastings, though they came from the same county. To account for the contributions of the Westminster boys, it has been suggested, though there is no evidence, that Hastings was a student in the school. This would hardly explain the presence of all the other contributors. The volume, I think, was merely a "project."

23. To Mark Van Doren, who has written the best critical study of Dryden's poetry in *The Poetry of John Dryden* (New York, 1920), the Hastings poem seemed an "unhappy effusion" (p. 4). Yet he is prepared to praise certain lines for "readiness and a bound" (pp. 104-5). Edward N. Hooker and H. T. Swedenberg, Jr., eds., *The Works of John Dryden* (Berkeley and Los Angeles, 1956), comment that "it contains, for Dryden, an unusually large number of internal stops" (I, 174). For Dryden, the seventeen-year old beginner, or for Dryden, the fifty-year old master of verse?

24. See Ruth Wallerstein's study "On the Death of Mrs. Killigrew: The Perfecting of a Genre," *Studies in Philology,* XLIV (1947), 519-28.

25. See W. W. Rouse Ball and J. A. Venn, eds., *Admissions to Trinity College Cambridge* (London, 1911-16), 5 vols., II, 412.

26. Macdonald, *Bibliography,* p. 3.

27. P. 221. Now kept in the Muniment Room, where I was allowed to inspect it and copy out the citations concerning Dryden.

28. Dryden did not achieve the Honours List in 1653/54, or at any other time. See the *Early Honours Lists, 1498-1747,* ed. C. M. Neale (London, 1909). Neale points out (p. 16) that only one-seventh of the Senior Wranglers in this period later became eminent enough to find a place in the *DNB.*

29. See G. P. H. Pawson, *The Cambridge Platonists and their Place in Religious Thought* (London, 1930), pp. 21 ff.

30. Register at Titchmarsh Church. Mary Dryden was left in good enough financial circumstances to enable her to lend money. On May 10, 1667, she lent her brother, Sir Henry Pickering £1,300. Some repayment was made by Sir Henry, and, after his death, by his heir, another Sir Henry. But by 1699 the whole amount had not been repaid. Consequently, Elizabeth and Frances, executors of Mary Dryden's will, turned the whole problem of collection over to their brother Erasmus. Through their husbands, Charles Bennet and Joseph Sandwell, who signed an indenture, they sold the remaining debt to Erasmus for £200. The original bond of Sir Henry Pickering and the indenture are among the family papers at Canons Ashby and were copied out by the late P. D. Mundy, to whom I am indebted for a transcript of them.

31. *Northamptonshire Notes and Queries,* I (1884), 5.

32. *Cal. S.P., Dom., 1653-1654,* January 25, 1653/54, p. 368. He was appointed in the place of Sam Moyer.

33. The will was proved January 23, 1654/55, and is now in Somerset House. The precise wording of the bequest respecting the Blakesley land reads as follows: "I give my Sonne John two partes of my land in Blakesley: I give my wife one third parte of Blakesley during her life natturall to receive the rent thereof quarterley." It would appear by this that John was granted the land outright and his mother only the rent from one-third of the whole for her life. Whether this third reverted, upon her death, to John is not clear; but one may assume that to be the testator's meaning. The fact that Mary in her will (Somerset House, Hale 60), proved in June 1677, makes no mention of the Blakesley land suggests strongly that it was not in her power to devise it, that it was to pass to her son John.

34. Trinity College *"Conclusion Book,"* p. 237.

35. Dryden's income from his Blakesley land has never been satisfactorily estimated and perhaps it is impossible to arrive at a satisfactory figure. Malone (*Prose Works of Dryden,* I, i, 440 ff.), arguing from the size of the Blakesley estate in 1798 (186 acres) and from Account Books at Canons Ashby, concluded that the rent amounted to 6s. 6d. per acre and that the total income was £60—the base figure he uses throughout the Life. Malone, however, was using eighteenth-century calculations. Blakesley, as we have seen, consisted in Dryden's time of 330 acres. Although rents and taxes varied between 1654 and 1700 (the time when Dryden owned the land), it may be possible to arrive at an approximation. Farm land in Northamptonshire was among the best in the Midlands, and during these years, which saw a slow inflation, such land probably yielded about 5s. rent per acre. It was also taxed at amounts varying between 1s. and 4s. on the pound. Dryden, writing to Tonson in 1696 (Charles E. Ward, ed., *The Letters of John Dryden* [Durham, N.C., 1942], p. 83), mentions receiving the "remainder" of his rent—£16 10s. With this definite amount, we can work out the probable value of his land. He was receiving about 5s. rent per acre. This totals £82 10s. Taxes for such land would be at least 2s. on the pound; but Dryden as a Catholic would have been charged double—4s. His tax, £16 10s., would be paid by his tenant, who would then remit the net rent—or the "remainder" as Dryden referred to it—of £16 10s. per quarter. If these figures prove reasonably accurate, Dryden's land, at twenty years' purchase, had a capital value at that time of £1,650. (See Arthur H. Johnson, *The Disappearance*

of the Small Landowner [Oxford, 1909], and David Ogg, *England in the Reigns of James II and William III,* [Oxford, 1955].)

36. I think we can reject as apocryphal one explanation for his failure to return to Cambridge to proceed to his M.A. W. D. Christie ("Dryden's Departure from Cambridge University," *N&Q,* 4th Series, X [1872], 370) reprinted a letter by one Mr. Pain written about 1727, in which he quotes the recollection of the Reverend Dr. Crichton, then eighty-eight years of age, of his college days. The old gentleman remembered at that distance that Dryden did not stay for his M.A. because his head was "too roving and active" to confine himself to an academic life; consequently he "went to London into gayer company; and set up for a poet." Another guess, by Christie himself, is equally unsatisfactory. He conjectures that since Dryden, after his father's death, had an income of his own, he would have been deterred from taking a further degree because he would have been liable to a fee of £8 6s. 4d. in addition to regular fees (see W. D. Christie, ed., *The Poetical Works of John Dryden* [London, 1870], p. xx). I do not believe that this sum of money would have forced Dryden to abandon any plans to take an M.A.

37. See Appendix B, p. 324.

38. Hooker and Swedenberg, eds., *Works,* I, 187; and for the bibliographical problems involved in the *Three Poems* volume, Macdonald, *Bibliography,* pp. 3-7.

39. Godfrey Davies, *The Restoration of Charles II* (San Marino, Cal., 1955), p. 3.

40. David Ogg, *England in the Reign of Charles II* (Oxford, 1934), 2 vols., I, 1.

CHAPTER II

1. See Davies, *Restoration of Charles II,* for a detailed recital of the events leading up to the return of the King.

2. He was baptized at St. Martin's-in-the-Field on January 19, 1625/26. The "Panegyrick to the King," he says, was written when "the King deserved the Praise as much as now, but separated farther from the Power; which was about three years since, when I was a Prisoner in *Windsor-Castle*" ("To the Reader"). No documentary evidence has come to light to show that Howard was ever a prisoner.

3. In addition to panegyrics on the King and General Monck, Howard includes a section of "Songs and Sonnets," and translations of *Virgil,* Book IV, and of the *Achilles* of Statius. He adds learned notes to the translations, in which he quotes many ancient writers, and not a few moderns, including Meric Casaubon, Scaliger, and John Selden. Dryden's verses to Howard run from A6^r to A8^r.

4. Dryden's relation to Herringman (who became his publisher) has been a subject of much speculation. It has been thought that Dryden met Howard through Herringman (Macdonald, *Bibliography,* p. 8, n. 1), and that Dryden may indeed have been employed by Herringman. More than twenty years after these early poems of Dryden were printed, the author of the *Medal of John Bayes* alleged that

> He turn'd a Journey-man t'a Bookseller;
> Writ prefaces to Books for meat and Drink;

the bookseller was identified as Herringman. Osborn (*Dryden,* pp. 168-83) investigated the output of Herringman during these years to try to identify any prefaces that may have been written by Dryden. He was unable to certify any as being unmistakably Dryden's, even though some were signed

"J. D."   Seventeenth-century gossip did not suggest that Dryden and Howard met through Herringman.

5. In his address "To the Reader" Howard makes it appear that his verses to the King antedate by many months those of other poets which were coming out in great profusion between April and June (see *Thomason Tracts* [London, 1908], for lists of commendatory poems on the King which appeared during these weeks). "Yet I should a little be dissatisfied with my self to appear publick in his praise, *just when he was visibly restoring to power* [italics mine], did not the reading of the Panegyrick vindicate the writing of it, . . . It was written when the King deserved the Praise as much as now, but separated farther from the Power; which was about three years since, when I was Prisoner in Windsor-Castle, being the best diversion I could then find for my own condition; to think how great his Virtues were for whom I suffered, though in small a measure compar'd to his own, that I rather blush at it, than believe it meritorious."

Although Howard's loyalty, and that of his family, to the King was un-doubted, it may be pointed out that in 1657 (when this panegyric to the King was supposedly written) Howard and his father, the Earl of Berkshire, were treating with Cromwell for the continuation of one of their lucrative sinecures —farming of the post fines. From July, 1656, until September, 1657, they negotiated with the Treasury commissioners. On September 10, 1657, the Council—with His Highness, Oliver, present—approved a new lease of the post fines to Berkshire, if they thought it advantageous to the state; they had conferred with Sir Robert Howard and found him willing to advance the yearly rent from £2,275 to £3,000 if the "Earl may have a grant of all the post fines for the rest of the term hitherto granted." A week later, the commissioners were authorized to farm them to the Earl, "or to his son Sir Robert." (*Cal. S.P., Dom.*, 1655/56, pp. 35, 221, 252; 1656/57, pp. 46, 191, 313; 1657/58, pp. 93, 102).

6. At least thirty panegyrics were published between May and July. This poem had appeared by June 19, when it is dated in *Thomason Tracts,* II, 319. See also Hooker and Swedenberg, eds., *Works,* I, 215, and H. T. Swedenberg, Jr., "England's Joy: *Astraea Redux* in its Setting," in *SP,* L (1953), 30-44. Dryden, ll. 79-80, refers to Charles II as "banish'd David." In 1660 a curious tract was published, entitled *The Last Counsel of a Martyred King to his Son, by J. D. Esq.; a loyal Subject and Servant to His Majesty.* London, printed for J. Jones and are to be sold at the Royal Exchange in Cornhill, 1660. At the end of his advice, the unidentified author ends with a verse "Elegie on the Sufferings and Death of King Charles I" in which occur the lines:

> Thou England's David, how
> Did Shimeis Tongue not move thee?
> Where's the Man?
> Where is the King?

The Biblical parallel between David and his troubles and the Stuarts was a commonplace. See R. F. Jones, "The Originality of *Absalom and Achitophel,*" *Modern Language Notes,* XLVI (1931), 211-18.

7. Allardyce Nicoll, *A History of Restoration Drama, 1660-1700* (Cambridge, 1923), p. 270.

8. See A. H. Nethercot, *Sir William D'Avenant, Poet Laureate and Play-wright-Manager* (Chicago, 1938), and Leslie Hotson, *The Commonwealth and Restoration Stage* (Cambridge, Mass., 1928).

9. Brice Harris, *Charles Sackville, Sixth Earl of Dorset* (Urbana, Ill., 1940), pp. 24-27.

10. William S. Clark, "Dryden's Relations with Howard and Orrery," *MLN,* XLII (1927), 16-20.

11. *To His Sacred Majesty* appeared either at the time of the coronation on April 23 or shortly thereafter. Thomason records at least twelve poems which appeared on that event during the month, by such persons as Samuel Pordage, John Tatham, Dryden, and others.

12. Hooker and Swedenberg, eds., *Works,* I, 234 ff.

13. Clarendon's son became Dryden's patron and friend in the 1680's. See Letter 10, Ward, ed., *Letters,* pp. 20-22.

14. Thomas Birch's *History of the Royal Society* (London, 1756-57), covers the early years of the society, 1660-87. Thomas Sprat's *History* of 1667 is more a recital of the earliest beginnings and the aims of the group than a history. Extremely useful is *The Record of the Royal Society of London* (3rd ed.; London, 1912), which contains transcripts from the society's records. See also E. S. DeBeer, "The Earliest Fellows of the Royal Society," *Bulletin of the Institute of Historical Research,* XV (1937-38), 79-93, and Sir Henry Lyons, *The Royal Society, 1660-1940* (Cambridge, 1944).

Dryden, like the majority of the fellows, was not a scientist, but he seems to have found considerable interest in the inquiries of the group. Yet he took no great part in the deliberations. He was dropped from the rolls, in 1666, upon nonpayment of his fees, as were others. He was appointed to one special committee (December 2, 1664), which was to investigate the improving of the English language. Among the other twenty-one members were John Evelyn, Thomas Sprat, and Sir Joseph Williamson, founder of the *London Gazette.* For a detailed study of this group and its purpose, see O. F. Emerson, *John Dryden and A British Academy* (London, [1921]).

15. See *DNB,* "Walter Charleton."

16. Anthony Powell, *John Aubrey and his Friends* (New York, 1948), p. 107*n.*

17. *DNB,* "Walter Charleton."

18. *The Record of the Royal Society* (3rd ed.; London, 1912), p. 30. Earl Wasserman, "Dryden's Epistle to Charleton," in the *Journal of English and Germanic Philology,* LV (1956), 201-12, suggests that science is not the central theme, but only a function of it. He sees the main theme as political.

19. The letters of Orrery are quite explicit in respect to these early conversations and the role of Charles II. See William S. Clark, ed., *The Dramatic Works of Roger Boyle, Earl of Orrery* (Cambridge, Mass., 1937), 2 vols., I, 23 ff.

20. See Hotson, *Commonwealth and Restoration Stage,* pp. 242 ff.

21. Miss Boswell believes that the first performance may have been given at court rather than at Gibbons' Tennis Court (Eleanore Boswell, *The Restoration Court Stage* [Cambridge, Mass., 1930], p. 281).

22. Dryden's possible dependence on another's work for this play has been commented on by others as well as by Dryden himself. Alfred Harbage in "Elizabethan-Restoration Palimpsest," *Modern Language Review,* XXXV (1940), 287-319, points out the "interesting possibility" that *The Wild Gallant* is an adaptation of a lost play by Brome. Dryden, he says, "has as much as told us that he has adapted an English play whose author was unknown to him. Had the original play been in print, it would have been identified; *ergo,* it reached Dryden in manuscript." As Harbage makes clear in this article, Sir Robert Howard was finding manuscript plays a source for adaptation. There is at the same time a possibility that Dryden was using Howard's work directly. Carryl N. Thurber, in *Sir Robert Howard's Comedy "The Committee"* (Urbana, Ill., 1921), p. 37, quotes from the *Session of the Poets* to suggest such indebtedness:

> Sir Robert Howard, called for over and over,
> At length sent in Teague with a packet of news,

Wherein the sad knight, to his grief did discover
How Dryden had lately robbed him of his Muse.

Each man in the court was pleased with the theft,
Which made the whole family swear and rant;
Desiring, their Robin in the lurch being left,
The thief might be punished for his 'Wild Gallant.'

23. See George Thorn-Drury, *Review of English Studies,* "Dryden's Verses 'To the Lady Castlemain upon Her Incouraging His First Play,' " VI (1930), 193-94, and Hooker and Swedenberg, eds., *Works,* I, 254, 383-84.

24. Ethel Seaton, "Two Restoration Plays," *TLS,* October 18, 1934, p. 715, cites evidence that places Howard's play in July, 1663, nearly three years earlier than the commonly accepted date.

25. Charges of moral turpitude against her are based on the ambiguous and inconclusive evidence of the following letter to the Earl of Chesterfield. It may well be that she merely protests that she has said nothing reprehensible and wishes a meeting to explain that her words have been misinterpreted.

My Lord   1658
I received yours, though not without great trouble, but am not guilty of any thing you lay to my charge, nor will I ever alter from the expressions I have formerly made, therefore I hope you will not be so unjust as to believe all that the world sayes of mee, but rather credit my protestation of never having named you to my friends, being allwayes carefull of that for my own sake as well as yours; and therefore let it be not in the power of any, nor of your own inclinations, to make mee less. If you will meet me in the old Exchange, about six o'clock I will justifie myselfe.
Your very humble servant.

This is in the manuscript *Letterbook of the Earl of Chesterfield* (British Museum, Additional MS 19253, f. 179b) and there indicated as coming from "E. Howard." Chesterfield, in 1659, married Lady Elizabeth Butler (his second wife), daughter of the Duke of Ormond. In 1669, he married, for the third time, Lady Elizabeth Dormer, daughter of the Earl of Carnarvon. The charges made by Shadwell and others that Dryden was hectored into marriage by Elizabeth's brothers and that she was "a teeming matron ere she was a wife" are, I think, suspect. The lack of corroborative evidence of Elizabeth's lack of propriety may permit us to question the charges made through the malice of those who envied or feared her husband, twenty years later. (See, for example, *Azaria and Hushai,* an attack of 1682, which carried a number of malicious items against the Drydens.)

26. In a letter to Sir Robert Long, dated August 14, 1666, Dryden gives him credit for convincing the Earl that he should assign the patent. (See Ward, ed., *Letters,* pp. 6-7.)

27. Joseph Foster, ed., *London Marriage Licences, 1521-1869* (London, 1887), p. 423.

28. Robert Bell, ed., *Poetical Works of John Dryden* (London, 1854), 3 vols., I, 24.

29. "Relations with Howard and Orrery," *MLN,* pp. 16-20; Charles E. Ward, "Some Notes on Dryden," *RES,* XIII (1937), 298-300; and William S. Clark, Letter to Editor, *RES,* XIV (1938), 330-32.

30. See Osborn, *Dryden,* pp. 192-97, for a discussion of Dryden's London residences. Although it is not possible to identify the place of residence, Osborn on the basis of the letter from "J. Driden" to Major Richard Salwey, which he reproduces, facing p. 256, suggests that the couple were living in

rented quarters. Salwey recorded that he notified the writer that he "would attend him at his lodging early on the morrow." A close examination of this letter suggests that it is in a hand quite dissimilar to the poet's.

31. Pepys, *Diary*, January 27, 1663/64; he saw it on February 1.

32. See John H. Smith's "The Dryden-Howard Collaboration," in *SP*, LI (1954), 54-74. *The Indian Queen* was entered in the *Stationers' Register* on February 4, 1663/64.

33. *The History of Henry V* was acted in August, 1664, and *The General* in September. His *Mustapha* came out in the following April. See Clark, ed., *Orrery*, I, 102-3, 226.

34. It was advertised in *The Newes*, No. 86, for November 3.

35. Dryden was already an habitué of this new institution. On February 3, 1663/64, Pepys records seeing him "and all the wits of the town," at the "great Coffee-House" in Covent Garden. The coffeehouse was to be his critical sounding board for nearly forty years, as he was to be its chief literary arbiter.

36. The date of the acting of *The Indian Emperour* is uncertain. Nicoll, *History*, p. 359, supposes April, 1665. In general this approximate time is accepted. The play was entered in the *Stationers' Register* by Herringman on May 26. Very often—but not always—registration followed shortly after a play had been acted.

CHAPTER III

1. *Cal. S.P., Dom., 1665-1666*, p. 459.

2. Ward, ed., *Letters*, pp. 6, 145.

3. The complicated, and perhaps not complete, record of the warrants and petitions connected with Lady Elizabeth's grant leaves a payment of £450 unaccounted for. It may be that the Drydens finally settled for £2,550. But this may be doubted, since the warrant of August 11, 1669, specifically states that the original grant of £3,000 is paid in full (*Calendar Treasury Books, III, Part I, 1669-1672*, p. 265. See also *ibid., II, 1667-1668*, pp. 68, 160, 385, and *Cal. S.P., Dom., 1666-1667*, p. 76).

The affairs of the Earl of Berkshire are too tangled to attempt to follow. His original grant of £8,000, dated April 12, 1662, was to have been paid in annual installments of £1,000. Within three months of this date (on July 24) he had assigned the grant to one Dame Mary Graves, conditioned on her payment to him of £5,000. On October 21, he signed a bond to her for £7,400 to secure a loan of £3,700 (*Cal. S.P., Dom., 1661-1662*, p. 523). Whether Dame Mary had actually paid him £5,000 for his grant is not clear. At any rate he had received no part of his grant from the Treasury by August 31, 1666 (*Cal. Treas. Books, 1667-1668*, II, 160). On the following August 21, Sir Robert Howard attempted to have the unpaid remainder of Lady Elizabeth Dryden's grant incorporated with the Earl of Berkshire's, which at that time must have had a fair chance of being paid (*ibid.*, p. 68).

4. Charles was born August 27 (O.S.), 1666, according to a "Figure on Nativity of Mr. Dryden the Poet and his son." This gives Dryden's birth as August 19, 1631, and his son's as September 6, 1666. Both are New Style (Ashmolean MS Bodleian, No. 243, f. 209).

5. Hooker and Swedenberg, eds., *Works*, I, 258-59. Hooker first suggested this interpretation in "The Purpose of Dryden's *Annus Mirabilis*," *Huntington Library Quarterly*, X (1946), 49-67. Whether Dryden's purpose was primarily or even largely to nip sedition and support the government may fairly be questioned. Several points should be noted:

(1) Why does Dryden omit treatment of the plague—"one of the greatest 'wonders' of 1666?" (*Works*, I, 289). Perhaps it is a quibble, but the plague was over before 1666 began. Dryden, having already admitted to his heroic poem the event of the fire—thus destroying the original poetic unity adumbrated by the choice of one argument—would have utterly destroyed his poem by admitting a third action. The plague would have been, artistically, completely antipathetic to the heroic actions to be seen in the war and the fire. It was hardly "heroic" to be laid low by an unseen killer like the bubonic plague; nor was it "heroic" for the King, the Parliament, or Dryden to flee the stricken city for safer places.

(2) The pamphlets and tracts advanced in evidence for this interpretation are few in number and obviously written by persons on the lunatic fringe. Are there any others to suggest a widespread dissatisfaction with Charles and the royal Parliament? Where is the fear of the populace to be found? Only in John Spencer, an Oxford scholar, or the off-hand remark in Sprat's *History of the Royal Society*, not yet in print? Do we not need more evidence to demonstrate that the government was so weak as to need to fear opposition pamphlets? After all, were such tracts not a constant factor in seventeenth-century England? It might, further, be supposed that Pepys or Evelyn, never loathe to express their doubts and fears—or the gossip—might have made reference to the matter. Pepys records a comment on Dryden's poem (on Feb. 2, 1666/67, soon after its appearance): "I am very well pleased this night with reading a poem I brought home with me last night from Westminster Hall, of Dryden's upon the present war; a very good poem." For Pepys, then, the poem was not to help out a government faced with a limited number of tracts put out by very few of the discredited and powerless minority in the English society of the time.

(3) "It is difficult to avoid the suspicion that *Annus Mirabilis* was a major factor in Dryden's appointment, little more than a year after the publication of the poem, as poet laureate" (*Works*, I, 259). I doubt that it was a major factor. By April, 1668, when he was appointed laureate, Dryden's poetic and dramatic and critical writing far surpassed that of any other man of his age, both in quantity and quality. *Annus Mirabilis* was only one of a number of works from his pen, and perhaps not the most important. In 1668 he was almost alone in his claim to the post of laureate.
6. W. P. Ker, ed., *Essays of John Dryden* (Oxford, 1900), 2 vols., I, 14-15.
7. *Ibid.*, I, 20.
8. Hotson, *Commonwealth and Restoration Stage*, p. 249.
9. *Ibid.*, p. 250; Nicoll, *History*, p. 287. Evelyn saw *Mustapha* at the Royal Cockpit on October 18. Apparently both theaters were planning to reopen on November 29.
10. Pepys, January 14. See also Boswell, *Court Stage*, p. 283, and Nicoll, *History*, p. 305, for a record of a performance of January 22.
11. It was a favorite of the court; and it was acted there at least once by the court ladies and the Duke of Monmouth. Pepys records the gossip, under date of January 14, 1667/68. "To Mrs. Pierce's, where my wife and Deb is; and there they fell to discourse of the last night's work at Court, where the ladies and Duke of Monmouth and others acted 'The Indian Emperour;' wherein they told me these things most remarkable: that not any woman but the Duchesse of Monmouth and Mrs. Cornwallis did any thing but like fools and stocks, but that these two did do most extraordinary well." Pepys, possibly because of Nell Gwyn's appearance in the cast, saw it four times: August 22,

November 11, 1667; March 28, April 21, 1668. He also bought a copy of the printed play, then just out, on October 28, 1667.

12. Pepys saw it on March 2, when the King attended.

13. "Royal Society," *Bull. of Inst. of Hist. Research*, pp. 79-93. Dryden was dropped from the rolls on October 29.

14. Nethercot, *Sir William D'Avenant*, p. 202 ff.

15. H. T. E. Perry, *The First Duchess of New Castle and Her Husband* (Boston, 1918), pp. 150-52.

16. John Downes, *Roscius Anglicanus* (London, 1708), p. 28.

17. Pepys, *Diary*, August 16, 1667.

18. Macdonald, *Bibliography*, p. 100.

19. *Cal. Treas. Books, II, 1667-1668*, p. 68.

20. *Ibid.*, pp. 83, 186.

21. Public Record Office, *Exchequer*, 403/2772, p. 109.

22. Malone, ed., *Prose Works of Dryden*, I, ii, 317-21.

23. Nicoll, *History*, p. 306.

24. I have been unable to find any document that will fix more certainly the date of John's birth. In lieu of one, I accept this time, as given in the *DNB*. It is fairly close, as can be determined by the known dates of the births of his older and younger brothers.

25. Ker, ed., *Essays of John Dryden*, I, 299-302; Ned B. Allen, *The Sources of John Dryden's Comedies* (Ann Arbor, 1935), pp. 154-70.

26. "Elizabethan-Restoration Palimpsest," *MLR*, pp. 287-319. Harbage persuasively demonstrates that Howard's play was a remodeling of a play by Ford.

27. Pepys, *Diary*, February 22.

28. John H. Smith advances another view. He sees Dryden's prologue as an attack on the Duke of Buckingham in reply to the Duke's epilogue to his revision of Fletcher's *The Chances* in 1667. But the Duke did not try to pass off the play as his own, as Howard was doing ("Dryden and Buckingham: The Beginnings of the Feud," *MLN*, LXIX [1954], 242-45).

29. *Cal. S.P., Dom., 1667-1668*, p. 341 (date of April 13); and Eleanore Boswell, "Chaucer, Dryden and the Laureateship," *RES*, VII (1931), 337-39.

30. Hotson, *Commonwealth and Restoration Stage*, p. 244, *et passim*.

31. The text of the agreement has often been printed. See Osborn, *Dryden*, pp. 184-91, for the text and a discussion of the later complaint against Dryden.

32. Printed in full by Malone, ed., *Prose Works of Dryden*, I, i, pp. 554 ff. There seems no evidence to suggest that an honorary degree was a perquisite of the laureateship. See E. K. Broadus, *The Laureateship* (Oxford, 1921).

33. Dedication, to the Earl of Dorset, of *The Original and Progress of Satire*.

34. Indeed not since early 1665 (in *The Indian Emperour*) has he employed rhyme: *Secret Love* contains only a few scenes in rhyme; and none is found in *Sir Martin Mar-All, The Tempest*, or *An Evening's Love*. Not until *Tyrannic Love* (1669) does he return to rhyme in sustained fashion.

35. Ker, ed., *Essays of John Dryden*, I, 23-27.

36. See George Williamson, "The Occasion of an *Essay of Dramatic Poesy*, *MP*, XLIV (1946), 1-9. Williamson believes that Sorbière "raised issues which remained central to the controversy represented by the *Essay of Dramatic Poesy*." Of course he did; but the wits were already discussing the same things. Sorbière and Sprat may reinforce, but they do not provide the issues, which were already present.

37. The first—and most confusing—attempt to identify the speakers was Malone's. He made two guesses. He first (*Prose Works of Dryden*, I, ii,

34) identified Eugenius as Lord Buckhurst; Crites as the Earl of Roscommon; Lisideius as John Sheffield, Earl of Mulgrave; and Neander as Dryden. Later (I, ii, 116-17) he changed his mind, and found Crites now to be Sir Robert Howard; Eugenius remained Lord Buckhurst; and by an inspiration, Malone now saw Lisideius as an anagram of Sedley (I, i, 64-67). He substituted Sir Charles Sedley for Mulgrave; and Neander remained Dryden. His last identification has remained "scholarly truth," with only a dissenting voice or two, for 150 years. It must be emphasized that these identifications remain guesses. Professor George R. Noyes in "Crites in Dryden's *Essay of Dramatic Poesie*," *MLN,* XXXVIII (1923), 333-37, argued cogently that Crites could not conceivably be meant to represent Sir Robert Howard. But without clinching evidence, he suggested Roscommon as the figure to take the part of Crites. More recently Professor Frank L. Huntley in "On the Persons in Dryden's *Essay of Dramatic Poesy*," *MLN,* LXIII (1948), 88-95, working on a fresh approach, has suggested that quite possibly no actual persons are to be seen under the Greek names. Crites, in this view, becomes "not so much an individual as he is a typical ultra-conservative. The name is appropriate for a person who is a strong defender of Greek and Latin literature, but a carping criticaster of anything new" (p. 90). Eugenius signifies "well-born" (p. 91). Lisideius, however, is a stumbling block. Huntley suggests that it comes from "Le Cid," plus a Latinized-Greek masculine ending (p. 93). Neander, no longer Dryden, allegorically becomes the "new man" from *neo* and *andros* (p. 95). I believe it is unreasonable to try to identify actual persons in the *Essay.* Many who certainly could qualify for consideration have never been mentioned: Edward and James Howard, Etherege, Orrery, Davenant, Lord Vaughan, Sprat, Waller.

38. Frank L. Huntley, "On Dryden's Essay of Dramatic Poesy," in the University of Michigan *Contributions in Modern Philology,* No. 16 (March, 1951), p. 68.

39. Reprinted in D. D. Arundell, *Dryden and Howard, 1664-1668* (Cambridge, 1929), pp. 93-98.

40. A. S. Borgman, *Thomas Shadwell, His Life and Comedies* (New York, 1928), pp. 121-36. See also R. Jack Smith, "Shadwell's Impact upon John Dryden," *RES,* XX (1944), 29-44.

41. "R. F." has never been identified. Because of the initials, Richard Flecknoe has been the leading contender. Nor has a satisfactory explanation been advanced for his addressing the attack to Edward Howard, Sir Robert's older brother and himself a playwright. Until some evidence becomes available, speculation seems useless.

42. Ker, ed., *Essays of John Dryden,* pp. 110-14. Dryden refers to a debate in Parliament on a bill for importing Irish cattle, in January, 1667. Howard and others spoke repeatedly on the word *nuisance,* which became a crucial semantic problem for the members. On January 9, Pepys attended a conference of the two houses, and summarized their discussion (*Diary,* January 9, 1666/67). Though the Lords wished to expunge the word, Commons won and it was retained. See *Journal of House of Commons,* VIII, 675, and *Journal of House of Lords,* XII, 74.

CHAPTER IV

1. *Cal. Treas. Books, 1668,* pp. 340, 385, 410, 607, and *ibid., 1669-1672,* p. 265.

2. Malone, ed., *Prose Works of Dryden,* I, i, 149, on the evidence of the notation of his admission to the Charterhouse on February 5, 1682/83:

"Erasmus-Henry Dryden, admitted for his Majesty (in the room of Orlando Bagnall); aged 14 years, 2^d of May next."

3. The rate books for St. Martin's parish (properly "The Poor Rate Overseers Accounts") are available at the City of Westminster Library, Buckingham Palace Road. The book for 1668/69 is missing, but Dryden appears in that of 1669/70, as "Jon Drayton." His assessment is set at £1 per half year. His semiannual assessments fluctuate somewhat from year to year; the yearly payments range between 18s. and £2 8s.—one of the largest assessments on the street. For some years his next door neighbors were Lady Lumley and Francis Browne. In the book for 1680 (F 408) a curious notation appears: not *John* but *Edward* Dryden is assessed 18s. for that year (Osborn, *Dryden,* p. 196, notes this discrepancy but assigns 1682 as the year; it was 1680). It might be a clerical error, but the names are not easily confused. I once thought Edward was the poet's nephew, son of his brother Erasmus. This boy, however, was only twelve years old, since he was baptized on May 28, 1668 (L. E. Tanner, ed., *Register of St. Margaret's: Westminster, 1660-1675* [London, 1935]). Could it have been a cousin who occupied his house? If so, where did Dryden and his family spend the year?

4. It has been said that alterations were made in it before publication; but no evidence is adduced to show more than minor change (See Macdonald, *Bibliography,* p. 100; *The Works of John Dryden,* ed., Sir Walter Scott, revised and corrected by George Saintsbury [Edinburgh, 1882], 18 vols., II, 86; Montague Summers, ed., *Dryden: Dramatic Works* [London, 1931-32], 6 vols., I, xxxiv).

5. An extended discussion and analysis may be found in Allen, *Sources of Comedies,* pp. 1-49. A suggestion has been made that the contemporary Dr. John Pell might have been the prototype of the "humourous" Lord Nonsuch. See Frank H. Moore, "Dr. Pelling, Dr. Pell and Dryden's Lord Nonsuch" in *MLR,* XLIX (1954), 348-51.

6. Hotson, *Commonwealth and Restoration Stage,* pp. 250-53; the Bills and Answers are printed on pp. 348-55.

7. Again, the problem of identification is difficult. But the increased income, the permanent residence and settled family life, the later close connection with Blanchard—all point to the poet. The ledgers of Blanchard and Child contain the details of purchases and payments. In all, the purchases amounted to £86 17s. 1d. See F. G. Hilton, *The Marygold by Temple Bar, being a History of the Site now Occupied by No. 1 Fleet Street, the Banking House of Messrs. Child & Co.* (London, 1902), pp. 28 ff.

8. Ker, ed., *Essays of Dryden,* p. liii.

9. *Diary and Correspondence,* ed. William Bray, III, 213 ff. Evelyn worked for several years, but his history was not published. Only the preface was made public (1674), entitled *Navigation and Commerce, their Original and Progress.*

10. P.R.O., *Signet Office,* 3/16, p. 331; P.R.O., *E.,* 403/1777, p. 232; H.M.C., 10th Rep., App., Pt. IV, p. 151. For Dryden's function as historiographer, see Roswell G. Ham's "Dryden as Historiographer-Royal," in *RES,* XI (1935), 284-98. Ham offers proof, since generally accepted, that the anonymous "His Majesties Declaration Defended," 1681, came from Dryden. He also advances the claim that the *Narrative of the Reign of James II* was transcribed or corrected by Dryden. In attempting to discover the kind of works the historiographer might be expected to produce, Ham cites James Howell's experience while in that position. Howell, he says, "writes of himself as a 'free historian'; and, indeed, his published works, especially those issued immediately upon his appointment, were of such a character. Tractarian

and in general the political apologetics for royalty, they utilized history as a justification of theory" (p. 285). Among Dryden's works, which may have been a part of the historiographer's duties, he cites *The Duke of Guise, The Vindication of the Duke of Guise, The History of the League, Defense of the King's Papers, etc.,* and the *Life of St. Xavier.* Ham also conjectures, and I think with good reason, that Dryden either "supervised or composed a number of the tracts published 'by Royal Command'" during the reign of James II.

11. It was advertised in *Term Catalogues* for November 22.

12. Malone, ed., *Prose Works of Dryden,* I, ii, 344.

13. Louis I. Bredvold, *The Intellectual Milieu of John Dryden* (Ann Arbor, 1934), pp. 88-89. Bredvold points out that Tillotson (*Rule of Faith,* 1666), Stillingfleet (*Rational Account of the Grounds of the Protestant Religion,* 1665), and Joseph Glanvill (ΛΟΓΟΥ ΘΡΗΣΚΕΙΑ: or, *A Seasonable Recommendation, and Defence of Reason,* etc., 1670) and others were answering the Catholic attacks and maintaining the primacy of a rationalistic approach to matters of faith.

14. Scott-Saintsbury, *Works,* III, 438-39.

15. George H. Sabine, *A History of Political Theory* (New York, 1937), p. 357. Sabine points out that the doctrine of passive obedience "became the modernized version of monarchical divine right." In England it served the Anglican Church until 1688, when the Bishops' resistance to James crushed it beyond repair.

16. Sabine summarizes the course of this conflict: "Only slowly and under the compulsion of circumstances that permitted no other solution did a policy of religious toleration emerge, as it was discovered that a common political loyalty was possible to people of different religions" (*ibid.*).

17. *Stationers' Register,* January 8, 1669/70; *Term Catalogues,* February 17, 1669/70. This edition of *The Tempest* has often been confused with the 'operatic' version of 1674. For a discussion of the problem, see Charles E. Ward, "*The Tempest:* A Restoration Opera Problem," *Journal of English Literary History,* XIII (1946), 119-30.

18. See Cyril Hughes Hartmann, *Clifford of the Cabal* (London, 1937), and Clifford in his *Schema,* which contained advice to Charles about his expected Declaration of Catholicity, advocating putting Catholics in as heads of the colleges and universities. This proposal James II seems to have revived in 1687/88, when Dryden himself was mentioned as having been selected for such a post.

19. Nicoll, *History,* p. 42.

20. H.M.C., 12th Rep., App., Pt. V, Rutland, p. 22.

21. H.M.C., 10th Rep., Pt. 4, p. 151; *Cal. S.P., Dom., 1669-1672,* p. 772; P.R.O., *E.,* 403/1777, p. 232.

22. *Ibid.,* P.R.O., *E.,* 403/2772, p 109.

23. Malone, ed., *Prose Works of Dryden,* I, ii, 190-206.

24. For a discussion of the sources and of Dryden's own contributions, see Allen, *Sources of Comedies,* pp. 110 ff.

25. See Charles E. Ward, "The Dates of Two Dryden Plays," *PMLA,* LI (1936), 786-92.

26. So much has been written of *The Rehearsal* that it is unnecessary to go over the ground again. The reader is referred to Dane Smith, *Plays About the Theatre in England* (New York, 1936); Montague Summers, *The Playhouse of Pepys* (London, 1935), *The Restoration Theatre* (London, 1934), and his edition of *The Rehearsal* (Stratford-upon-Avon, 1914); Nicoll, *History;* George R. Noyes, ed., *Selected Dramas of John Dryden* (New York, 1910).

27. Hotson, *Commonwealth and Restoration Stage,* pp. 253-54.

28. *Ibid.,* p. 254. The company petitioned the King for a subsidy and for arrears due them for court performances. There seems to have been little direct financial help from the King, probably because of his extreme need for money to prosecute a war which was to break out almost any day.

29. George R. Noyes, ed., *The Poetical Works of Dryden* (Boston, 1909), pp. 64-65. In spite of the wretched condition of the company, the old actors Hart, Mohun, and Kynaston appear to have insisted upon certain prerogatives with regard to their liveries. On March 6, 1671/72—hardly a fortnight after the company had opened in Lincoln's Inn Fields—an order was sent to the Lord Chamberlain that "It is His Ma^{es} pleasure that Mr Mohun Mr Hart, and Mr Kynnaston be^e continually furnished at the charge of the Master and Company of His Ma^{es} Comoedians with [perruques, cravats, silk stockings, shoes, hats, shirts, and plumes of feathers]." See Nicoll, *History,* p. 327, quoting from P.R.O., *Lord Chamberlain Papers,* 7/1 and 5/140, p. 5. If the company complied with this order, the financial charge against it must have been heavy.

30. Noyes, ed., *Poetical Works,* p. 65. The identification of the French troupe mentioned here is complicated by the impossibility of fixing a date for the acting of *Arviragus.* A troupe had come to London in 1669 (Nicoll, *History,* p. 241) and another in late 1672. Still another seems to have come the following year, and one still later. (See the *Cal. S.P., Dom.,* and the *Cal. Treas. Books* for these years, *passim*). It may be that some of these visits overlapped, for there is not always evidence of the time of their departure or, for that matter, of their arrival.

31. John Pollock, *Cambridge Modern History* (London 1902-12), 13 vols., V, 207.

32. For the problem of the time of production, see "The Dates of Two Dryden Plays," *PMLA,* pp. 786-92. Other pieces of propaganda came out about the same time: W. de Britaine, *The Dutch Usurpation,* Henry Stubbes's *Justification of the Present War against the United Netherlands,* Andrew Marvell's *Character of Holland.*

33. Malone, ed., *Prose Works of Dryden,* I, ii, 355-60.

34. J. V. Rundle, "The Source of Dryden's 'Comic Plot' in *The Assignation,*" *MP,* XLV (1947), 104-11. Frank H. Moore, in "Heroic Comedy: A New Interpretation of Dryden's Assignation," *SP,* LI (1954), 585-98.

35. Quoted in Macdonald, *Bibliography,* p. 205.

CHAPTER V

1. The French players arrived in late 1672, perhaps in November. An order was issued to the customs commissioners on December 17, to admit their goods without duty (*Cal. Treas. Books, 1672-1675,* p. 14). Two other orders, on January 1 and 9 refer to the same problem of getting their scenes and costumes out of customs (*ibid.,* pp. 24, 29). By the end of April they had completed their acting and were ready to return home. On May 1, an order to customs directed that the luggage of Sir Leoline Jenkins and Sir Joseph Williamson (who were preparing to go as ambassadors to the treaty of Aix-la-Chapelle) be inspected and also that the goods of the French comedians be examined for export, "whom the said ambassadors are directed by the king to receive into their train" (*ibid.,* p. 127). On May 4, Lord Arlington wrote Sir Joseph Williamson: "The French Comedians complain they shall find little or no convenience for the transportation of their goods and persons on board the ships. You understand the King's mind enough

towards such occasions to afford them all possible facility and to assure them yourself of it" (*Cal. S.P., Dom., 1673,* p. 209).

The Italians arrived in April and somewhat overlapped the French. Customs again is directed to admit their goods duty free (*Cal. Treas. Books, 1672-1675,* p. 119). They stayed until early September (*ibid.,* p. 392).

2. Ogg, *Reign of Charles II,* I, 369.

3. *Cal. Treas. Books, 1672-1675,* p. 81.

4. H. R. Steeves, "The Athenian Virtuosi and the Athenian Society," *MLR,* VII (1912), 358-71; Macdonald, *Bibliography,* pp. 201 ff. In *A Description,* the author is visiting the coffeehouse where the Virtuosi meet; on p. 13 is a description of the room before the entrance of the Virtuosi:

> But a little further we beheld many engins of torture: here indeed was the scene of death, here was one book suspended, another torn upon a tenterhook, a third dead from a stab receiv'd from a cruel Penknife; drawing nearer, I found them all belonging to Mr. Dryden. Here lay *Almanzor* stretcht upon the rack, that pain might force out words far distant from his thoughts; here the *Maiden Queen* lay deflour'd, and there the *Indian Emperour* was defac'd with the scratches of a barbarous stile. . . ."

5. Ward, ed., *Letters,* pp. 9-10. Dryden's letter to Rochester I dated before May, 1673. I now believe this to be an error: it probably dates rather late in the summer. Two or three items in the letter suggest the latter date: the report of the success of the players at Oxford; the remark that Rochester's friends are ready to envy him his leisure in the country, "though they know you are onely their Steward, and that you treasure up but so much health, as you intend to spend on them in Winter." Although officially Buckingham became Lieutenant General on May 13, the likelihood is that Dryden heard about the appointment only weeks later. Furthermore, the references in his prologue and epilogue, given at Oxford by the Theatre Royal group, point to a later date than April or May for this letter.

6. Malone, ed., *Prose Works of Dryden,* I, ii, 375.

7. The play was registered on June 26 and must have been printed almost immediately. Clifford retired from his position as Lord Treasurer by June 19, when Evelyn congratulated Sir Thomas Osborne, the new Lord Treasurer. Clifford's retirement was "voluntary" in that he could not qualify for position under the Test Act. Evelyn visited him in Tunbridge Wells (July 25) and found him greatly troubled in mind. Within a little over three weeks he was dead by his own hand. See Evelyn, *Diary,* passim.

8. P.R.O., *E.,* 403/2772, p. 109. Nearly twenty-five years later, when Dryden dedicated the translation of Virgil's *Pastorals* to Clifford's son, he calls Clifford "the patron of my manhood, when I flourished in the opinion of the world." And he points out that he was "that Pollio, or that Varus, who introduced me to Augustus."

9. Boswell, *Court Stage,* p. 285, gives the date of the Whitehall performance as March; Nicoll, *History,* p. 371, inexplicably writes, "probably produced at Court in 1671."

10. See Appendix D, p. 328.

11. Joseph Arrowsmith, *The Reformation* (London, 1673), pp. 46-49.

12. W. D. Christie, ed., *Letters Addressed from London to Sir Joseph Williamson at the Congress of Cologne,* Camden Society Publications, N.S. VIII-IX (London, 1874), 2 vols., II, 23-24.

13. Details of these financial problems may be found in Hotson, *Commonwealth and Restoration Stage,* pp. 254 ff.

14. There can be little doubt that Dryden worked with the stage in mind. Descriptions of the operatic scenes and the various "machining" effects are

described with enough care to show that he was preparing the opera for performance. The detailed description of the setting of Act I, scene 1, for example, illustrates how the operatic elements were adapted to the material:

> Represents a Chaos, or a confused Mass of Matter; the stage is almost wholly dark: a Symphony of warlike Music is heard for some time; then from the Heavens (which are opened) fall the rebellious Angels, wheeling in Air, and seeming transfixed with Thunderbolts: The bottom of the Stage being opened, received the Angels, who fall out of sight. Tunes of Victory are played, and an Hymn sung; Angels discovered above, brandishing their Swords: The Music ceasing, and the Heavens being closed, the Scene shifts, and on a sudden represents Hell: Part of the Scene is a Lake of Brimstone, or rolling Fire; the Earth of a burnt Colour: The fallen Angels appear on the Lake, lying prostrate; a Tune of Horror and Lamentation is heard.

In the ensuing scene, the fallen angels rise from the burning lake and fly again to dry land. Lucifer gives order that a "golden palace" rise; as by magic, it appears. To fill the interval between Acts I and II, Dryden suggests an added tentative scene:

> Betwixt the first Act and the second, while the Chiefs sit in the palace, may be expressed the sports of the Devils; as flights, and dancing in grotesque figures: And a song, expressing the change of their condition; what they enjoyed before, and how they fell bravely in battle, having deserved victory by their valour, and what they would have done if they had conquered.

In Act II, after Raphael appears to Adam, they both "ascend to soft music, and a song is sung." At once the scene changes—

> . . . and represents, above, a Sun gloriously rising, and moving orbicularly: at a distance, below, is the Moon; the part next the Sun enlightened, the other dark. A black Cloud comes whirling from the adverse part of the Heavens, bearing Lucifer in it; at his nearer approach the body of the Sun is darkened.

This spectacle, after a twenty-line speech by Lucifer, is superseded by another, which in numerous variations had often been presented in masque and opera:

> From that part of the Heavens where the Sun appears, a Chariot is discovered drawn with white Horses, and in it Uriel, the Regent of the Sun. The Chariot moves swiftly towards Lucifer, and at Uriel's approach the Sun recovers his light.

Compared with these, and others to follow, the Paradise scene is quite simple, consisting in all likelihood of a painted drop with "Trees cut out on each side, with several fruits upon them; a Fountain in the midst: At the far end the prospect terminates in Walks."

In the temptation scene, Lucifer discovers Adam and Eve asleep in their Bower (which is merely described as a "night piece of a pleasant Bower"). He sits down by Eve and seems to whisper in her ear. At once is presented to view a Vision—

> . . . where a tree rises loaden with fruits; four Spirits rise with it, and draw a canopy out of the tree; other Spirits dance about the tree in deformed shapes; after the dance an Angel enters, with a Woman, habited like Eve.

The splendor and cost of these scenes, plus the charges for singers, dancers, and musicians, would have required much more money than the company was able to raise.

W. J. Lawrence ("Dryden's Abortive Opera," *TLS,* August 6, August 13, October 1, and November 24, 1931) advanced the idea that the opera represented Dryden's attempt to provide a marriage gift to Mary D'Este, whom the Duke of York actually married, as we have seen, on November 21. It was not a very convincing argument. Had it been so intended—in spite of its lack of performance—it no doubt would have been published at once. Nearly four years elapsed before it saw print. It was dedicated to the lady in 1677.

15. Noyes, ed., *Poetical Works,* pp. 73-74.

16. Nicoll, *History,* pp. 88, 123, 316-17.

17. See my article, "*The Tempest:* A Restoration Opera Problem," *ELH,* pp. 119-30, in which I advance Betterton's claims to the "operatic" *Tempest.*

18. For details concerning the appearance of these critical works and their impact on Dryden, see Frank L. Huntley, "Dryden's Discovery of Boileau," *MP,* XLV (1947), 112-17, and A. F. B. Clark, *Boileau and the Classical Critics in England, 1660-1830* (Paris, 1925); and, for a larger view of epic theory in England, H. T. Swedenberg, Jr., *The Theory of Epic in England, 1650-1800* (Berkeley, Calif., 1944).

19. *Calisto,* though not presented until after the middle of February, 1674/75, had long been prepared for. Costumes were being arranged for in the preceding September; in November the Whitehall Theatre was being readied for rehearsals on "Saturday, Tuesday and Thursday nights." Documents relating to the preparations and arrangements are printed in Nicoll, *History,* pp. 319-21. See also Boswell, *Court Stage,* for a fuller account. There is a suggestion by Crowne that Dryden might well have been chosen, in his place. In the preface to the printed masque in November, he says in part: "had it been written by him, to whom by the double right of place and merit the honour of the employment belonged, the pleasure had been in all kinds complete" (Macdonald, *Bibliography,* p. 210).

20. The copy for *Aureng-Zebe* was entered in the *Stationers' Register* on November 29, 1675, the play already having been acted on the seventeenth. Though no notice is to be found in *Term Catalogues* until May 5, 1676, it appears to have been in print several months earlier, for an advertisement for it appears in the *London Gazette* for February 17-21.

21. See John Harold Wilson, ed., *The Rochester-Savile Letters, 1671-1680* (Columbus, Ohio, 1941), and *The Court Wits of the Restoration* (Princeton, N.J., 1948). Wilson points out that from the autumn of 1675 to the summer of 1676, Rochester was at Woodstock, where he wrote numerous satirical pieces. The assumption is that the *Allusion* circulated in manuscript. If so, it could possibly have come to Dryden's attention before he addressed Mulgrave, who—as Wilson so well documents—was at this time a great enemy of Rochester. Though a specific date is not assigned to the writing of the *Allusion* or to its circulation, the letter of Rochester to Savile in April, 1676, seems to provide the *terminus ad quem.* It is the well-known "Black-Will-with-the-Cudgel" letter, indicating then that Savile had informed Rochester that he was out of favor "with a certain Poet." Dryden's strictures in this dedication could have been his first answer to Rochester's attack; but like much else in this period, it must remain for the moment in the limbo of the unproven.

22. Malone, ed., *Prose Works of Dryden,* I, ii, 415-27.

23. A reflection of the current political situation may possibly be seen in Dryden's juxtaposition of concepts of kingship in *Aureng-Zebe.* The old Emperour represents the absolute tyrant; Morat (the young son) can justify usurpation and deny rights of succession to the older son, Aureng-Zebe. The latter, Ruth Wallerstein ("Dryden and the Analysis of Shakespeare's Techniques," *RES,* XIX [1943], 165-85), sees as arguing "for the responsible

monarch bound by the ideal of public welfare and using his prerogative to that end; . . . he sums up more than a century of reflection on monarchy."

24. Nicoll, *History,* p. 307.

25. Hotson, *Commonwealth and Restoration Stage,* pp. 257-60.

26. Mary Dryden's will is in Somerset House, Hale 60. No mention is made of the Blakesley land, which she, with a one-third life interest, could probably not devise. Hereafter, I assume, he enjoyed the full income from it.

CHAPTER VI

1. *Term Catalogues,* February 12; the *London Gazette,* February 8-12.

2. In addition to his desire to dedicate the unacted opera to the Duchess, Dryden says he was induced to publish it for another reason: "Many hundred copies of it" were dispersed abroad and became "a libel against me; and I saw, with some disdain, more nonsense than I, or as bad a poet, could have crammed into it at a month's warning, in which time it was wholly written, and not since revised." Nat Lee's laudatory verses published with it urge that Dryden proceed with his plans for an epic to celebrate "majestic Charles."

3. He levied particularly upon Chapters 27 and 33 of Peri Hypsus, but he also ranged through other chapters in Boileau to find illustrations: note, for instance, his use of Chapter 31 (for Longinus' use of Herodotus for hyperboles); Chapters 22 and 38 (for boldness of figures); Chapters 16-18 (on "aggravations"); Chapter 13 (on imaging). In passing it may be said that Dryden only sparingly used Rapin: in one place he misread him by asserting that he taxed Tasso for introducing heathen deities; he taxed, not Tasso, but Sannazaro (in his poem *De Partu Virginis*).

4. Ker, ed., *Essays of John Dryden,* I, lx. About Dryden's refusal to accept the decisions of poetry arrived at by common sense and his attack upon the critics' ideas of fustian, Ker remarks: "Dryden, like Tasso before him, is compelled to stand up against the scholars who have learned their lesson too well; it is as if he foresaw the sterilizing influence of the prose understanding, and the harm that might be done by correctness if the principles of correctness were vulgarized" (p. lix).

5. On July 2, a minute of the grant was entered in the Treasury accounts. The official documents may be found in P.R.O., *E.,* 403/2576, p. 49, and P.R.O., *S.O.,* 3/17, p. 376.

6. Hotson, *Commonwealth and Restoration Stage,* p. 238. The receipts of £100 for May contrast sharply with those of the preceding months, which went no higher than £50 and as low as £8.

7. Nicoll, *History,* pp. 62, 292-94.

8. Ward, ed., *Letters,* pp. 11-12, 147-48.

9. Robert J. Allen, "Two Wycherley Letters," *TLS,* April 18, 1935, p. 257.

10. Ward, ed., *Letters,* pp. 13-14, 148-49.

11. The date is accepted on the authority of the accounts of the performance given in Percy Fitzgerald's *A New History of the English Stage* (London, 1882), 2 vols., I, 145.

12. British Museum, Add. MS 28955, f. 12; Roswell G. Ham, "The Authorship of *A Session of the Poets,*" *RES,* IX (1933), 319-22; John Harold Wilson, "Rochester's 'A Session of the Poets,'" *RES,* XXII (1946), 109-16.

13. Shaftesbury was committed on February 15 and remained until February 26, 1677/78. See W. D. Christie, *A Life of Anthony Ashley Cooper, First Earl of Shaftesbury, 1621-1683* (London, 1871), 2 vols., II, 229-32, 257.

14. Osborn, *Dryden,* p. 187. The petition is reproduced in facsimile by Osborn, who provides a complete analysis of the situation.

15. The opening day's performance was given before Royalty, as indicated by the list printed by Nicoll, *History,* p. 311. But never again is there a record of performance. It is curious that no contemporary gossip seems to be extant about the circumstances which led to its demise. There is, however, a good deal of comment after the play was published. Most of it reflects upon the lubricity of the play, as known in print; the acting text must have been bawdy in the extreme. One typical example of comment occurs in John Tutchin's *Poems on Several Occasions* (1685):

> Well might the audience, with their hisses, damn
> The Bawdy Sot that late wrote *Limberham*:
> But yet you see, the Stage he will command,
> And hold the Laurel in's polluted hand.
>   (Macdonald, *Bibliography,* p. 250)

16. See Mark Van Doren, *Poetry of Dryden,* pp. 339 ff.; the articles by George Thorn-Drury in "Dryden's 'MacFlecknoe,' A Vindication," *MLR,* XIII (1918), 276-81; and R. Jack Smith, "The Date of MacFlecknoe," *RES,* XVIII (1942), 322-23. The fact that it was printed four years later and then by a pirate, the fictitious "D. Green," and not under Dryden's auspices, strongly suggests that it was intended for manuscript circulation among the wits of the town. Had not the conflicts of 1681-82 made such copy valuable to a pirate, it is at least arguable that it might not have been printed for many years, if ever.

CHAPTER VII

1. Noyes thought it might have been acted in August, since the Woollen Act, mentioned in the prologue, went into effect on the first of that month. Nicoll conjectures January 1678/79 as the probable date of acting. Since the copy for publication received L'Estrange's imprimatur on January 3, 1678/79, it very likely had already been acted. I should suggest November or December. The final lines in the epilogue:

> Charm! song! and show! a murder and a ghost!
> We know not what you can desire or hope
> To please you more, but burning of a Pope

probably allude to the traditional Pope burning on Queen Elizabeth's birthday (November 17), which this year had a special significance.

2. Downes, *Roscius Anglicanus,* p. 37.

3. "C. April" is usually given as the probable acting date, by Nicoll and others, on the basis of its entry in the *Stationers' Register* on April 14, 1679. Though the practice was not invariable, the possession of copy by the publisher and its registration in the *Stationers' Register* followed performance of the play. No record is available to set more accurately the date of *Troilus and Cressida.*

4. Narcissus Luttrell, *A Brief Historical Relation of State Affairs, 1678-1714* (Oxford, 1857), 6 vols., I, 19.

5. Others in addition to Dryden were interested about this time in attempts to improve the language. The project of an English Academy found support of a number of persons soon after Dryden's proposal here. The Earl of Roscommon, now translating Horace's *Ars Poetica* and later to write an *Essay on Translated Verse,* envisaged an academy; and associated with him were Dryden, the Earl of Dorset, Lord Cavendish, Sir Charles Scarborough, and the Earl of Lauderdale. The idea, however, came to naught. See Carl Niemeyer, "The Earl of Roscommon's Academy," *MLN,* XLIX (1934), 432-37.

6. Both plays were advertised in *Term Catalogues* for November. The dedication to Vaughan, Earl of Carbery, must have been written and in print before the Earl's return to his governor's post in Jamaica on November 10.

7. The edition included twenty-three epistles; the names of sixteen contributions are listed; the authorship of three epistles is not announced.

8. *Domestick Intelligence* ran the offer of a reward again on January 2. It seems to me a tenable idea that Dryden received information from an assailant. The lack of public announcement in the matter may indeed argue as strongly for this point of view as for the negative. In any case, no publicity would be given. If Dryden knew the identity of the instigator of his beating, what course could he have taken? In law, probably no recourse was to be had, for he was bound to protect the informer, who, even if betrayed by the poet, could have lied his way out. Dryden then would have been a figure of ridicule. If he did not prosecute, but let it be known who had attacked him, he would have been subject not only to more ridicule but doubtless to another attack, which could have been murderous. Any revenge he might have taken would have been more cautiously done through his pen. The long-held belief that Rochester instigated the attack was based upon a misdated letter of Rochester. It is no longer tenable. See John Harold Wilson, "Rochester, Dryden, and the Rose Street Affair," *RES*, XV (1939), 294-301.

9. H.M.C., 7th Rep., App., Pt. I, 477b.

10. Wilson, ed., *Rochester-Savile Letters,* p. 73.

11. H. C. Foxcroft, *A Character of the Trimmer* (Cambridge, 1946), pp. 96-97.

12. More than half of the preface is taken up with a derivative account of Ovid's life and career, from Sandys, Heinsius, and perhaps Borchard Cnipping, whose text of 1670 he may have used. See Hooker and Swedenberg, eds., *Works*, I, pp. 323-30, for various comments and opinions.

13. Roscommon's *Art of Poetry* was published by Herringman and was advertised in *Term Catalogues* in May (Easter Term). Dryden quotes twice from his friend's translation, doubtless from his manuscript, which may have been turned over to him for advice and comment.

14. Bredvold has discussed the play and some of its political manifestations in "Political Aspects of *Amboyna and The Spanish Fryar*," *Essays and Studies in Language and Literature,* University of Michigan, VIII (1932), 119-32.

15. Edward N. Thompson, ed., *Correspondence of the Family of Hatton* (London 1878), Camden Society, I, 240. It may be recorded here that the anti-Catholic feeling in the play did not later please James II. Through the Lord Chamberlain it was effectively suppressed by order of December 8, 1686: "that ye play called Ye Spanish Friar should be noe more acted" (Nicoll, *History,* p. 10, n. 3).

CHAPTER VIII

1. Ll. 17-18. Noyes, ed., *Poetical Works,* pp. 98.

2. Patient and careful scholarship has already made a beginning in identifying Dryden's prose contributions to the paper scuffles of his time. "Dryden as Historiographer-Royal," *RES*, XI (1935), 284-98, has broken ground in this practically unknown part of Dryden's literary career.

3. R. W. Blencowe, ed., *Diary of the Times of Charles the Second by the Honourable Henry Sidney* (London, 1843), 2 vols., II, 188.

4. Barker and Stenning, eds., *Record of Old Westminsters,* I, 6-8, and II, 1076-78.

5. Sir John Pollock, *The Popish Plot* (2nd ed.; London, 1944), pp. 61-64.

6. *Ibid.,* p. 182.

7. The tract carries no imprint and no date. The final line of text, however, dates the writing of it as the last day of June.

8. H.M.C., 12th Rep., Pt. VII, Le Fleming MS, p. 175.

9. Osborn, *Dryden,* pp. 200-1. The information is contained in a newsletter, dated August 31, from Tonson, Dryden's publisher, to Luttrell.

10. Coleman S. Parsons, "Dryden's Letter of Attorney," *MLN,* L (1935), 364-65. Parsons, who discovered the paper in Watson Autograph Collection in the National Library of Scotland (583), prints it complete.

11. See Bredvold, *Intellectual Milieu,* pp. 139-43, and Dryden's numerous prefaces, addresses, and postscripts of these years.

12. The material for this section comes from Pollock, *Popish Plot,* pp. 251-53.

13. Macdonald, *Bibliography,* pp. 157-58, points out that Saunders was elected to Trinity College, Cambridge, from Westminster School in 1680. It is possible that he was a friend of Charles Dryden, through whom he was able to meet the poet. Saunders in the preface to his printed play said that it had received "some rules for correction from Mr Dryden himself."

14. Noyes, ed., *Poetical Works,* pp. 903-4. W. G. Hiscock, on the authority of an item in the *True Protestant Mercury* for March 19-23, 1680/81, identified the play given on March 19, as Saunder's *Tamerlane,* Dryden's epilogue, entitled "The Epilogue Spoken to the King at the opening of the Playhouse at Oxford on Saturday Last, Being March the Nineteenth 1681" occurs in two rare broadsides, described and printed by Ham, *TLS,* December 27, 1928, and the *London Mercury,* March, 1930; and by Hiscock, *TLS,* October 13, 1932, and *A Christ Church Miscellany* (Oxford, 1946), pp. 113-15. See also Autrey Nell Wiley, ed., *Rare Prologues and Epilogues, 1642-1700* (London, 1940), pp. 33 ff.

15. Roger North, *Examen: or, an Enquiry into the Credit and Veracity of a Pretended Complete History* (London, 1740), pp. 100-1.

16. Pollock, *Popish Plot,* p. 259.

17. Arthur Bryant, *King Charles II* (London, 1932), p. 317.

18. Luttrell, *State Affairs,* I, 87.

19. Macdonald, *Bibliography,* p. 167, and "Dryden as Historiographer-Royal," *RES,* pp. 284-98. *The Observator* was launched in April as a Tory mouthpiece and was Roger L'Estrange's paper. For the role of this effective sheet in the events of 1681, see George Kitchin, *Sir Roger L'Estrange* (London, 1913), pp. 260-88.

20. Pp. 4-5, 10-11.

21. Pp. 12-13.

22. P. 20. On page 7, Dryden quotes his adversary's sentence: "The Duke of York, the Queen, and the two French Dutchesses are the great support and protectors of the Popish interest in these Kingdoms," and finds capital humor in it. "How comes it to pass," he asks, "that our Author shuffles the two French Dutchesses together? Of which the one is Italian, the other a French Woman, and an English Dutchess?" These of course are the royal mistresses—the "beastly brace" of Mulgrave's *Essay upon Satire*—the Duchess of Portsmouth and the Duchess of Mazarin. Portsmouth, Dryden reminds his author, seems hardly the protector of Catholic interests in England, for she has connived with the factions against the Duke: "Is she so quickly become an old acquaintance, that none of the politick assignations at her Lodgings are remembered? After this, who will trust the gratitude of a Common-wealth?" As for the Italian Mazarin: "She is one who loves her ease to that degree, that no advantages of Fortune can bribe her into business. Let her but have

wherewithall to make merry adays, and to play at cards anights, and I dare answer for her, that she will take as little care to disturb their business as she takes in the management of her own. But if you will say that she only affects idleness, and is a grand Intriguer in her heart, I will only Answer, that I should shew you just such another as I have describ'd her Grace, amongst the heads of your own Party: indeed I do not say it is a Woman, but 'tis one who loves a Woman."

23. North, *Examen,* pp. 91-95, explicates in detail the legal organization within the city which enabled the sheriffs to empanel juries of their own choosing.

24. Foxcroft, *Trimmer,* p. 150.

CHAPTER IX

1. Luttrell, *State Affairs,* I, 111.

2. North, *Examen,* p. 111.

3. Ogg, *Reign of Charles II,* I, 629.

4. Nicoll supposes March 1681/82 (*History,* p. 373); Macdonald dates it February 7, 1681/82. The latter date is arrived at by the fact that Luttrell so dated his copy of a folio broadside of the prologue and epilogue which Tonson published—probably after the play had been performed. Luttrell's acquisition of the sheet on "February 7" may well mean that performance was considerably earlier. I believe it must have been in the autumn because of the materials included: the reference to petitions and remonstrances takes us back before the time of Shaftesbury's trial; and the comments on the "next Queen Bess's night" (with a description based upon a tract dating from the celebration of either 1679 or 1680) would have more relevance immediately before the Pope burning of November 17, 1681, than immediately afterwards, in February, 1681/82.

5. It was advertised on November 9 in *The Loyal Protestant and True Domestick Intelligence,* No. 79.

6. Macdonald, *Bibliography,* p. 20.

7. H.M.C., Ormond MSS, N.S. VI, p. 233. Another letter from the Earl of Arran alluding to the poem is to be found on p. 236: "Mr. Dryden's late poem will divert you [by] characters he gives of the worthies here." More than a month later, on December 21, a newsletter carries the information that: "In Dryden's poem, called Absalon and Architophel [*sic*], are represented the lively character of the Duke of Monmouth and Shaftesbury, also Howard, Sir William Jones, Bethel, Winnington and most of that party, under Jewish names, together with the Doctor of Salamance as Corah. After which are nobly described the Duke of Ormond, Halifax, Hide, Seymour, and most of the loyal party. Dryden has already been presented with 100 £" (H.M.C., 10th Rep., App., Pt. IV, p. 174).

8. See Richard F. Jones, "The Originality of *Absalom and Achitophel,*" *MLN,* XLIV (1931), 211-18.

9. A. W. Verrall, *Lectures on Dryden,* ed. Margaret De G. Verrall (Cambridge, 1914), p. 59. See also Morris Freedman, "Dryden's Miniature Epic" in *JEGP,* LVII (1958), 211-19.

10. Ogg, *Reign of Charles II,* II, 630-31.

11. See Hugh Macdonald, "The Attacks on John Dryden," *Essays and Studies, The English Association,* XXI (1935), 41-74, for a detailed listing of the tracts against Dryden in this controversy and others.

12. Macdonald, *Bibliography,* pp. 226-27.

13. Ralph B. Long, "Dryden's Importance as a Spokesman of the Tories," *Studies in English,* University of Texas Publications, No. 4126 (1941), pp. 79-99.

14. Barker and Stenning, eds., *Record of Old Westminsters,* I, 288.

15. *Cal. S.P., Dom., 1682,* p. 436. The King to the governors of Charterhouse mentions letters of July 12 being procured for one Henry Levett, but they are not to prejudice the former grant to Dryden, who is to be elected and admitted at the first vacancy "at our disposal" notwithstanding any other letters for anyone. Also, *ibid.,* January 1—June 30, *1683,* p. 33.

16. *Ibid.,* pp. 43, 445. Henry Keymer asserts that his grandson has had the King's appointment since June 22, 1678, and that Dryden has obtained a special letter which will prejudice his boy.

17. It was advertised in the *Loyal Protestant and True Domestick Intelligence* for January 14. For a discussion of Father Simon's work and Dickinson's translation, see Bredvold, *Intellectual Milieu,* pp. 98-107, and Charles E. Ward, "*Religio Laici* and Father Simon's *History,*" *MLN,* LXI (1946), 407-12.

18. Malone, ed., *Prose Works of Dryden,* I, i, 163, and *Cal. S.P., Dom., 1682,* p. 128, where under date of March 16 is a notation: "A medal has been lately engraved for the Earl of Shaftesbury. The author of *Absalom and Achitophel* made a severe satire on it."

19. For a complete survey of *The Medal of John Bayes,* see the valuable contributions of Osborn, *Dryden,* pp. 155-65, and George Thorn-Drury, ed., *Covent Garden Drollery* (London, 1928), pp. 135-37, and "Some Notes on Dryden," *RES,* I (1925), 190-92.

20. Malone, ed., *Prose Works of Dryden,* II, 73, and Macdonald, *Bibliography,* p. 125 and n. 6.

21. H.M.C., 15th Rep., Pt. VII, p. 108. This newsletter alleges that the acting of the play was forbidden by Charles.

22. During these months Dryden wrote several special prologues which were spoken at performances before the Duke and the King. See Noyes, ed., *Poetical Works,* pp. 133-34, and Wiley, ed., *Rare Prologues and Epilogues,* pp. 100 ff.

23. Ward, ed., *Letters,* pp. 18-20, 150-51. The letter here printed (p. 150) from Elizabeth Dryden to Busby regarding other aspects of the boys' school life is of interest, too, in showing the mother's concern for their health, their religious observances, and their "cleanliness."

CHAPTER X

1. Luttrell's copy, now at Yale, carries this date. At least one other tract of this year also included the imprint of D. Green—*Satyr to his Muse,* which has been fathered on Shadwell, without sufficient evidence. Malone (ed., *Prose Works of Dryden,* I, i, 169) printed the advertisement included at the end of the pirated *Macflecknoe* which suggests that someone with a collection of old satires was prepared to make a small business of printing them: "A gentleman having a curious collection of poetry by the most ingenious of the age, intends to oblige the world with a poem every Wednesday morning, and with all the new ones as they come to his hand." For bibliographical data, see Macdonald, *Bibliography,* pp. 28 ff.

2. Dryden's contribution was made known in 1716 by Tonson in a note "To The Reader," prefixed to the edition included in the *Second Part of Miscellany Poems.* Scott thought that Dryden also wrote other sections and that he contributed a good deal to the entire poem (Scott-Saintsbury, *Works,* IX, 321).

3. Luttrell so dated his copy, and "under the word Poem on the title wrote 'Atheisticall' " (Macdonald, *Bibliography*, p. 33, n. 2). A sidelight on Dryden's interests in religious questions during the weeks when he was writing *Religio Laici* is offered by the list of items he purchased at auction in May and June, when Richard Smith's library was sold in Great St. Bartholomew's Close. Dryden bought twenty-eight lots, a considerable proportion of them on religion. Among them were Forbes's *Irenicum in Ecclesia Scotia;* Duarenus' *de Sacris Ecclesial Ministeriis, History of the Bohemian Persecution;* William of Occam's *Tractatus de Sacramento Altaris.* See Bernard Quaritch, *Contributions towards a Dictionary of English Book-Collectors* (London, 1892-1921).

4. See Bredvold, *Intellectual Milieu,* pp. 98 ff., for a summary of Father Simon's book and Dickinson's translation, and also *"Religio Laici* and Father Simon's *History,"* MLN, in which supplementary details are printed.

5. Bredvold, *Intellectual Milieu,* p. 117.

6. *Ibid.,* pp. 117-29.

7. Hotson, *Commonwealth and Restoration Stage,* pp. 277, 280-82.

8. The date of first performance remains uncertain. Malone (ed., *Prose Works of Dryden,* II, 63) gives December 4, on the authority of a manuscript note on the (separate) printed prologue then in Bindley's collection. Macdonald (*Bibliography,* p. 126) gives November 30, on authority of P.R.O., *L.C.,* 5/145, p. 120.

9. Quoted passages are from Tonson's advertisement prefixed to Volume I. Malone (ed., *Prose Works of Dryden,* II, 424-25) believed, no doubt correctly, that Dryden wrote it for Tonson.

CHAPTER XI

1. Evelyn, *Diary,* June 17, 1683.

2. Ward, ed., *Letters,* pp. 20-22.

3. As Ogg points out (*Reign of Charles II,* II, 447), customs and excise were the soundest sources on which money grants could be founded: the goldsmiths favored the customs as the base for their loans. For evidence that the "John Dryden" appointed to a collectorship was not the poet, see Louis I. Bredvold, "Notes on John Dryden's Pension," MP, XXX (1933), 267-74, and Charles E. Ward, "Was John Dryden Collector of Customs?" MLN, XLVII (1932), 246-49.

4. H.M.C., 7th Rep., App., pp. 288A, 290A, *et passim.* Numerous letters passed from Lord Preston to Sunderland and the Duke of York with respect not only to the transporting of opera, but also the engaging of Italian players to come to England again.

5. See p. 107.

6. H. C. DeLafontaine, ed., *The King's Music* (London, [1909]), pp. 190, 284, 319, 384. Eventually—in 1687—all of Grabu's arrears were paid.

7. The delay may have been occasioned by printing problems, which will no doubt be cleared up by the editors of the California edition of Dryden. Macdonald gives an incorrect bibliographical description of the *History of the League,* which was pointed out by James M. Osborn, "Macdonald's Bibliography of Dryden: An Annotated Check List of Selected American Libraries," MP, XXXIX (Aug.-Nov., 1941), p. 97. Another explanation for its delay may be attributed to the unexpected (?) decision of Dryden to include the "Postscript," which may have come along to Tonson after most or all of the book has been printed. L. W. Cameron has investigated Dryden's translation of Maimbourg. The English text is a faithful translation, showing Dry-

den's skill in maintaining the tone of the original. See "The Cold Prose Fits of John Dryden," in *Revue de Littérature Comparée*, XXX (1956), 371-79.

8. Ward, ed., *Letters*, pp. 22-24.

9. Dryden's translations of the Odes of Horace did not raise envy in the young Creech, who on May 25 had written from All Souls, Oxford, a Dedication to Dryden of his *Odes, Satyrs, and Epistles of Horace*. It is addressed "To the Very Much Esteemed John Dryden, Esq." Among other things Creech "begs a Name [for patron] whose Luster might shed some Reputation on his Work," and he asks, "Where can this trifle find a corner that hath not been fill'd with Mr. *Dryden's* name?" He also testifies to a quality in Dryden's character that becomes increasingly apparent in later years: "that Candor and Goodness have the greatest share in your Composition, I dare appeal to every one whom You have any way honored with your Conversation; These so fill your Mind, that there is no room left for Pride, or any disobliging quality: This appears from the Encouragement You are ready to give any tolerable attempts, and reach out a helping hand to all those who endeavour to climb that height where You are already seated." Dryden's generosity and kindness, attested to by Creech, showed itself in November in his ode, "To the Memory of Mr. Oldham," prefixed to the *Remains of Mr. John Oldham in Verse and Prose*. It is a magnificent tribute to his fellow poet, whose satiric genius was akin to his own. See Van Doren, *Poetry of Dryden*, pp. 158-60, for an account of this poem.

10. Ward, ed., *Letters*, p. 23.

11. H.M.C., 12th Rep., App., Pt. V, p. 85.

12. See Appendix E, p. 329.

CHAPTER XII

1. The British Museum copy of the poem is dated, in Luttrell's hand, March 9. (Macdonald, *Bibliography*, p. 39). It was advertised in *The Observator* for March 14.

2. *Cal. Treas. Books, VIII, Part I, 1685-1689*, pp. 139-40, and P.R.O., *S.O., 3/18*.

3. Bredvold, *Intellectual Milieu*, p. 128. Like all students of Dryden, I am greatly indebted to Bredvold's superb study of Dryden's skepticism and the analysis of his religious problems.

4. "Dryden's Conversion: The Struggle for Faith," *TLS*, April 17, 1937, pp. 281-82.

5. The volume was advertised in *The Observator* for November 2, and the *London Gazette*, for November 9-12. See "On the Death of Mrs. Killigrew," *SP*, XLIV (1947), 519-28.

6. Evelyn, *Diary*, October 2, 1685.

7. *Copies / Of Two / Papers / Written by the Late / King Charles II. / Together / With a Copy of a Paper written by the / late Dutchess of York. / Published by his Majesties Command.* It was published by Henry Hills late in the year.

8. H.M.C., Downshire MS, I, i, 95. It seems to have been the general Anglican view that Charles never composed them, though they were written in his hand. Gilbert Burnet expresses the same opinion: "All that knew the King when they read them, did without any sort of doubting conclude, that he never composed them: for he never read the Scriptures, nor laid things together further than to turn them into a jest, or for some lively expression" (*History of His Own Times* [Oxford, 1823], II, 471-72).

9. Stillingfleet had entered St. Johns, Cambridge, the year before Dryden entered Trinity. He early began to write on Church history and problems.

Irenicum came out in 1659, *Origines Sacrae* in 1662. He was a Latitudinarian, and after 1689 was criticized by some Anglicans for his failure to adhere to the doctrine of passive obedience or nonresistance, and for his willingness to take the oath of abjuration in order, it was alleged, to obtain preferment. He was made Bishop of Worcester.

10. It is a quarto pamphlet of seventy-two pages, with the imprint of Richard Chiswell, dated 1686. It carries an imprimatur dated 1685.

11. Cambridge University Library, Add. MS 45(12). There is no suggestion of the authorship. The letter extends over thirteen closely written sheets.

12. The Harvard Library copy carries the date "July 15," written in a contemporary hand—perhaps Luttrell's. It was published by Henry Hills, the official printer to James, a fact which supports the supposition that it was an official reply by the historiographer royal.

13. Malone's attribution of only the third part to Dryden has, erroneously I think, generally been accepted. Who wrote the other two parts neither Malone nor anyone else has ever suggested. Part of the "evidence" used by Malone for this partial attribution rests upon Dryden's rather obscurely phrased statement in "To the Reader," attached to *The Hind and the Panther,* the pertinent section of which reads: "I refer myself to the judgment of those who have read the *Answer* to the Defence of the late King's Papers, and that of the Duchess, (in which last I was concerned) how charitably I have been represented there." This is obscure, and remains so until we recall that three tracts belong to the controversy, published in this order: (1) Stillingfleet's *Answer* to the King's Papers; (2) Dryden's Defense of them against Stillingfleet; and (3) Stillingfleet's rebuttal entitled *Vindication of an Answer.* Now we can understand Dryden's phrasing by reading: "I refer myself to the judgment of those who have read the *Answer* [i.e., Stillingfleet's *Vindication of an Answer*] to the [i.e., my] Defence of the late King's Papers, and that of the Duchess [i.e., to Dryden's tract], (in which last [i.e., *A Defence*] I was concerned) how charitably I have been represented there [i.e., in Stillingfleet's *Vindication of an Answer*]." Embedded in *A Defence* are numerous indications that Dryden is the author, and that he is writing all three parts. On page 1, for example, he says: "As I think the Answerer may, with as little need of Apology, become the Antagonist, as I the Champion of *a King and Princess* [italics mine] . . . I shall lose [no time] in scanning the Preliminary Discourses of my Adversary. . . ."

14. P.R.O., *E.,* 403/3035/ pp 146-47. On the same date a warrant was issued for £225 on his current pension, though a money warrant was not issued until September 30.

15. P.R.O., *S.P.,* 44/71, *Petitions,* p. 341.

16. Barker and Stenning, *Record of Old Westminsters,* I, 288-89.

17. Ward, ed., *Letters,* p. 27.

18. Malone, ed., *Prose Works of Dryden,* I, i, 149.

19. See Bredvold, *Intellectual Milieu,* pp. 164 ff., for a complete account of English Catholic opinion during these months.

CHAPTER XIII

1. Ward, ed., *Letters,* p. 123.
2. *Ibid.,* p. 27.
3. British Museum, Add. MS 28569, f. 63.
4. *Ibid.,* f. 65v.
5. Noyes, ed., *Poetical Works,* pp. 232-33.
6. Malone, ed., *Prose Works of Dryden,* II, 541.

7. In the Buzzard, Dryden seems to have embodied some of the worst features—as he saw them—of certain members of the clergy, notably the Latitudinarians. Burnet, originally a Scotch Presbyterian, went to England after the Restoration, became a Chaplain to Charles, and finally preacher at the Rolls Chapel, from which he was ejected in November, 1684, for his attack on Papists and Popery. He left for the continent, traveled through France, Italy, Switzerland and wrote a book of these travels which became a *succès de scandale,* because of the unfavorable view he expressed on the life in countries controlled by Papists and managed by arbitrary rulers. He finally went to Holland, was recommended by Halifax and others to King William, to whom he now attached himself. He was considered by many English to be bumptious, impudent, and pushing. From Holland he let loose a succession of blasts against the Catholics and James II's policies. He returned with William to England, and became Bishop of Salisbury. But even William despised him, never saying a good word for him and even calling him "a dangerous man without principles who would do more harm than twenty men could do good." He actually once called him "een rechte Tartuffe." See *A Life of Gilbert Burnet, Bishop of Salisbury,* by T. E. S. Clarke and H. C. Foxcroft (Cambridge, 1907), pp. 205-40.

8. See Bredvold, *Intellectual Milieu,* pp. 172-84.

9. Ogg, *Reigns of James II and William III,* p. 183.

10. George Macaulay Trevelyan, *The English Revolution, 1688-1689* (London, 1938), p. 71.

11. H.M.C., Downshire MS, I, i, 251. Other pertinent references may be found in John Gutch's *Collectanea Curiosa* (Oxford, 1781), 2 vols., II, 52; H.M.C., 14th Rep., App., Pt. II, Vol. III, Portland MS, p. 397; *ibid.,* 7th Rep., App., Pt. I, 504b; J. A. W. Bennett, "Dryden and All Souls," *MLN,* LII (1937), 115-16; Louis I. Bredvold, "Dryden and the University of Oxford," *MLN,* XLVI (1931), 218-24; Roswell G. Ham, "Dryden and the Colleges," *MLN,* XLIX (1934), 324-32; J. R. Bloxam, ed., *Magdalen College and King James II, 1686-1688* (Oxford, 1886), p. 225; and British Museum, Add. MS 38671, f. 31b.

12. He was appointed on December 31. Barely ten months later, on October 25, 1688, he was ejected along with other Catholics (Bloxam, *Magdalen College,* pp. 225, 265).

13. See Macdonald, *Bibliography,* pp. 253 ff., for a list of these attacks following *The Hind and the Panther.*

14. British Museum, Add. MS 36707, f. 11.

15. British Museum, Stowe 969.

16. In the library of Trinity College, Cambridge, is a copy of *The Works of that Famous English Poet Mr. Edmond Spenser* (London, 1679), which contains, in addition to the marginal note, several interlinear corrections and emendations.

17. For a full and excellent account of the ode and Dryden's poetic relationship to Draghi, see E. Brennecke, Jr., "Dryden's Odes and Draghi's Music," *PMLA,* XLIX (1934), 1-36. Dryden's connection with Grabu, it may be here pointed out, had not yet ended. On June 9, 1687, after a long delay, Grabu's music to *Albion and Albanius* was published, and the volume carried a dedication to King James, signed by Grabu, but written, I believe without doubt, by Dryden. The Frenchman could hardly have written such a finished and graceful address. Dryden was to do the same service for another musician, Purcell, when the music to his *Prophetess* was published. I print the dedication to *Albion* here in full:

Albion and Albanius: An Opera. Or Representation in Musick. Set by

Lewis Grabu, Esquire; Master of His late Majesty's Musick, Lic. March 15, 1686/7.

To The King.

Sir,

After the Shipwrack of all my fairest Hopes and Expectations, in the Death of the late King my Master, Your Royal Brother of ever Blessed Memory, the only Consolation I have left, is that the Labour I have bestowed in this Musical Representation, has partly been employ'd in paying my most humble Duty to the Person of Your most Sacred Majesty. The happy Invention of the Poet furnish'd me with that Occasion: The feigned Misfortune of two Persecuted Hero's, was too thin a Veil for the Moral not to shine through the Fable; the pretended Plot, and the true Conspiracy, were no more disguis'd on the private Stage, than they were on the publick Theater of the World. Never were two Princes united more straightly together in common Sufferings from ungrateful and Rebellious Subjects. The nearness of their Blood was not greater than the conformity of their Fortunes: But the Almighty has receiv'd the one to his Mercy in Heaven, and rewarded the Constancy and Obedience of the other here below: Vertue is at last Triumphant in both places. Immortality is actually possess'd by one Monarch; and the other has the Earnest of it, in the Type of Earthly Glory. My late Gracious Master was pleas'd to encourage this my humble Undertaking, and did me the Honour to make some Esteem of this my part in the Performance of it: Having more than once condescended to be present at the Repetition, before it came into the publick View, Your Majesty has been also pleased to do me the same Honour, when it appear'd at Your Theater in greater Splendour, and with more advantages of Ornament: And I may be justly proud to own, that You gave it the particular Grace of Your Royal Protection. As the Subject of it is naturally Magnificent, it could not but excite my Genius, and raise it to a greater height, in the Composition, even to surpass it self: At least, a vertuous Emulation of doing well, can never be so faulty, but it may be excus'd by the Zeal of the Undertaker, who laid his whole Strength to the pleasing of a Master and a Soveraign. The only Displeasure which remains with me, is, that I neither was nor could possibly be furnish'd with variety of excellent Voices to present it to Your Majesty in its full perfection. Notwithstanding which, You have been pleas'd to pardon this Defect, as not proceeding from any fault of mine, but only from the scarcity of Singers in this Island. So that I have nothing more at this time to beg, than the continuation of that Patronage, which Your Princely Goodness hath so graciously allow'd me: As having no other Ambition in the World, than that of pleasing You, and the desire of shewing my self on all possible occasions, and with the most profound Respect, to be

Your Majesty's
Most humble, most obliged, and
Most obedient Servant,

Lewis Grabu.

18. *Rate Books,* St. Anne's, Soho, Leicester Fields Division. The books for Gerrard Street begin in 1691.

19. See Bredvold, *Intellectual Milieu,* pp. 180-84, for evidence of Dryden's fear and prophetic accuracy about the course of events in religious matters.

20. See Trevelyan, *English Revolution,* for a detailed analysis of the revolutionary half year that followed.

CHAPTER XIV

1. *Cal. Treas. Books,* VII, p. 1985, dated July 6, 1688.

2. The warrant to swear Shadwell into the position was dated March 9, 1688/89 (D. M. Walmsley, "New Light on Thomas Shadwell," *TLS,* April 16, 1925). The actual patent was issued on August 29, 1689.

3. H.M.C., *House of Lords,* Rep. 12, App., Pt. VI, p. 8 and note.

4. Luttrell, *State Affairs,* I, 533.

5. In 1709 Prior, in dedicating his *Poems on Several Occasions* to Lionel, Earl of Dorset, said that when the sixth Earl was Lord Chamberlain and "was obliged to take the Kings Pension from Mr. Dryden . . . My Lord allowed him an Equivalent out of his own Estate: However displeased with the conduct of his old acquaintance, he relieved his necessities." Prior seems to have confused Dorset's immediate gift to Dryden with a continued and regular largess, for which there is no evidence.

6. Noyes, ed., *Poetical Works,* p. 259.

7. In the warrants for plays presented by the United company before Royalty (printed by Nicoll, *History,* pp. 305-14) occurs a notation for *Amphitryon* on April 30. But the word "cancelled" is placed beside it; and on that date royalty witnessed, at the Whitehall Theatre, Crowne's *Sir Courtly Nice.* The next date is October 21, and the next play on the list is *Amphitryon.* The latter date has often been accepted as the first acting of the play, erroneously I think. For the Dedication to Leveson-Gower is dated by Dryden "October 24," and the play with Purcell's music was printed by October 30, when it was advertised in the *London Gazette,* October 30—November 3, 1690. In the Dedication, there is every indication that the play was acted not three days before, but considerably earlier. If the notation in the play list, referred to above, is accurate, there seems no reason to doubt that the play was ready by the last of April.

8. The date of *The Prophetesse* is uncertain. June, 1690, the time usually assigned to it, may be somewhat late, for proposals for publishing the music, vocal and instrumental, by subscription were advertised in the *London Gazette* as early as July 3-7 by John Carr, who in the following winter finally published Purcell's music for this opera.

Dryden wrote a prologue to *The Prophetesse,* which did not appear in print until 1707 in the *Muses' Mercury* for January, and the next year in the *Annual Miscellany* (the *Fourth Miscellany*). A note appended to the printing of it in the *Muses' Mercury* says that Shadwell (then poet laureate) had prevented its being spoken on the second night. See Roger P. McCutcheon, "Dryden's Prologue to *The Prophetess*," *MLN,* XXXIX (1924), 123-24.

9. His friendly relations with Congreve, Southerne, Addison, Dennis, Vanbrugh, Aubrey, and others may be found in many references included in the text. But beyond these are many others, both among titled persons, whom he has long known, and others whom he meets through his wife's family. Other groups to which he has easy access would include musicians, artists (like Kneller and Closterman), stationers, scientists, and persons of prominence like Pepys, Evelyn, Dolben, and others.

10. An interesting comment on Dryden's play is to be found in Laurence Echard's preface to his translation of Plautus' *Comedies,* published in 1694: "I'm afraid Amphitryon will bear the worse in our Tongue, upon the account of Mr. Dryden's, whose improvements are very extraordinary. . . . I must do that great man justice in saying, that he has not only much improved the

humour, wit, and design in many places, but likewise the thoughts. I'll mention one . . . Alcmena in the second act complains thus [a section of Dryden's blank verse on how poor and short are life's pleasures]. I mention this the rather, because it may serve for one instance of what improvements our modern poets have made on the ancients, when they built upon their foundations" (Preface, sig. B3ᵛ. *Plautus's Comedies, Amphitryon, Epeidicus, and Rudens, made English; with Critical Remarks upon each Play* [London, 1694]).

11. Ward, ed., *Letters,* pp. 27, 155.

12. *Publications of the Catholic Records Society,* Vol. XL. *Liber Ruber Venerabilis Collegii Anglorum de Urbe. Nomina Alumnorum, A.D. 1631-1783* (London, 1943). Item No. 1120 concerns Erasmus: "Henricus Dryden [his mother apparently called him "Harry"] vero nomine, Londinensis Filius Ioannis et Elizabethae Annorum 22 Habeus Confirmationem Venit ad Collegium 25 Octo 1690 et enter Alumnos Ssᵐⁱ Dni N Alexandri 8ˡ Admissos est de mandato Emᵐⁱ Howardi Protectoris sub R P Antonio Luca Rectore Venit ad Theologiam studuerat Philosophiae Duaci discessit 1º Martii 1691 Florentiam ad Novitiatum PP Praedicatorum, non suscepto iuramento." John Kirk, in his *Biographies of English Catholics in the Eighteenth Century,* eds. John Hungerford Pollen, S.J., and Edwin Burton (London, 1909), seems to have had access to these records, for he includes in English the gist of this notice, pp. 66-67. He adds that Erasmus returned to England and "laboured on the mission in Northamptonshire, his native county"; and he further states that in the Dominican Obituary Erasmus is styled *"Haud degener filius poetae Dryden,* though I do not find that any specimen remains." The unhappy end of Erasmus' life is cleared up by another document in the *Publications of the Catholic Records Society,* Vol. XXV (1925). On p. 129 is given his obituary notice: "PFr Thomas [his religious name] Dryden, S. T. Lect. died Dec. 3, 1710, Canons Ashby, aet 42. Profession 19." On pp. 108 and 110, the same volume, a more detailed notice of his death occurs—a report of a visitation by Father Worthington: "Sept: Fr. Thomas Dryden now lay dying among his Protestant kinsfolk at Canons Ashby in Northamptonshire. There I betook myself, and his relations kindly received me. . . . He was buried on Dec. 3 among his ancestors in the church hard by, once that of a monastery." Finally, p. 146, is given the cause of death—"a slow phthisis." Here he is said to be in "the 44th year of his age, the 19th of his religious profession, and the 17th of his priesthood." Though the accounts differ very slightly, there remains little doubt that he did not die insane, as has often been stated. He had inherited the baronetcy upon the death of his uncle Erasmus only a few months before his own death. Both his older brothers had predeceased him.

13. Ward, ed., *Letters,* p. 32.

14. *Ibid.,* pp. 33-40.

15. Although publicly Purcell's name was attached to it, the Preface in Dryden's handwriting—even to Purcell's signature—is in the British Museum, Stowe 755, ff.34-35. Roswell G. Ham first made it public, and discussed the ideas in it as related to similar ideas of Dryden's on art and painting, music and poetry. See his article, "Dryden's Dedication for the *Music of the Prophetesse,* 1691," *PMLA,* L (1935), 1065-75.

16. Fredson Bowers, "Dryden as Laureate: The Cancel Leaf in 'King Arthur,' " *TLS,* April 10, 1953.

17. No doubt because of Purcell's music, *King Arthur* continued its successful life far into the eighteenth century and became Dryden's most often revived play.

CHAPTER XV

1. Ward, ed., *Letters*, p. 44.

2. Christie says, without documentation, that Dryden received five hundred guineas for the poem. Dryden's financial difficulty in 1691 may be seen in a document printed, without comment, by George Thorn-Drury in "Notes on Dryden," *RES*, I (1925), 83. It is a notation of a gift of £5 to Lady Elizabeth Driden "in Charitye" by Thomas Howard, son of Sir Robert and of course her nephew. It was dated January 16, 1691/92.

3. Even if his spirit were not serene, he must have been pleased with the notice given him in John Dunton's *Athenian Mercury* (Vol. 5, Nos. 1 and 2, December 1 and 5). Here were asked—and answered—the questions: "Who is the best English Satyrist now living?" and "Whom do you think the best Dramatick Professor in this Age?" To the first the answer was: "Strephon is now no more, and Oldham is dead . . . to give our Judgment impartially as to the present; as long as either *Absalom* and *Achitophel,* or *Albian* and *Albianus* [*sic*] are left, we must conclude Mr. D—— not only Satyrist, but the best every thing else except the best Christian, and even for that he's now of the best Religion for a Poet of any in the World."

In answer to the second question, comment is limited to *Don Sebastian, OEdipus,* and *King Arthur.* The conclusion is: "On the whole, we need say no more than as we did in the last *Mercury,* that in general Mr. *Dryden* is in our Judgment by far the most *compleat Dramatick Writer* not only of our Age, but of all the *English* Poets that went before him."

4. The manuscript receipt signed by Dryden and by his son John as a witness is now in the Folger Shakespeare Library.

5. John Robert Moore believes that Dryden's later plays contain reflections on the government. See "Political Allusions in Dryden's Later Plays," in *PMLA,* LXXIII (1958), 36-42.

6. The *Gentleman's Journal,* February, 1691/92, p. 27.

7. Luttrell, *State Affairs,* II, 413.

8. *Ibid.,* p. 422.

9. Soon after the acting of *Cleomenes,* Tonson began to prepare it for publication. In view of the difficulties of its approval, he apparently sought, and gained, Dryden's consent to include Creech's Life of Cleomenes (from Plutarch) so that any further criticism that the play departed too far from the source might be blunted. The play was in print and was advertised in the *London Gazette,* May 2-5, 1692.

10. That Dryden, who acted probably as adviser to Tonson and as supervisor of the edition, made the assignments is clear from a letter of George Stepney to Leibnitz (in J. M. Kemble, ed., *State Papers and Correspondence* [London, 1857], p. 121) dated in March, 1693, not long after it was in print. See also Thomas and Elizabeth Swedenberg, *George Stepney's Translation of the Eighth Satire of Juvenal* (Berkeley and Los Angeles), 1948, p. 7.

11. Motteux in the *Gentleman's Journal* for May 14, p. 25, says that Tonson has delayed publication to enable Dryden to do *Persius* because he thought "it would conduce most to his advantage, to have the *Persius* wholly done by Mr. *Dryden.*"

12. His trip to Essex is known only through Tonson's letter to him in the autumn (See Ward, ed., *Letters,* pp. 49-52). Although the letter is ambiguous at this point, I am inclined to think that after his Essex trip, Dryden proceeded to Northamptonshire, where he was joined by Tonson, who eventually returned to London in September. By October 2 Dryden had written in answer to a letter from Tonson.

13. The *Gentleman's Journal,* April, 1692, p. 22. *The History of Polybius,*

published by Sam Briscoe, presumably appeared in early December; it carries an imprimatur dated November 25. In the *London Gazette,* November 28-December 1, it was advertised to be published "next week."

14. Ward, ed., *Letters,* pp. 49-52.

15. *Ibid.,* pp. 56-57.

16. *Ibid.,* pp. 54, 164-65.

17. For other friends he was doing services which were appreciated. On April 4, John Aubrey wrote to Anthony Wood: "I have been here before March but never so much entangled or ingaged in business . . . and partly in publishing my Booke [his *Miscellanies*]. I am exceedingly obliged to my Old Acquaintance Mr. John Dreyden for his friendly advice and recommendation. He would have had his bookseller print it: but *he* will print only Plays and Romances. So I am obliged to do it by Subscription" (Anthony Powell, *John Aubrey and His Friends* [New York, 1948], pp. 225-26).

18. Dryden had apparently done numerous favors for Walsh. The young man had asked the poet to use his influence in getting him a position as Teller of the Exchequer. In July, Dryden reported that, through Lord Leicester, he discovered that the post had already been given to another man: "I suppose that you imagind the place of that benefit, being now worth 1500th y annum, wou'd not be long voyd: & therefore set not your heart upon it" (Ward, ed., *Letters,* pp. 56, 165). See H. H. Adams, "A Note on the Date of a Dryden Letter," *MLN,* LXIV (1949), 528-31, for a suggested new date for this letter to Walsh. He thinks, with good reason, that July 20 is a better date for the letter than August 17, 1693. This, I agree, fits better the sequence of events of this year as rehearsed by Dryden in his extant letters.

19. *Ibid.,* p. 58.

20. I believe that "Ovid" is a slip of the pen for "Virgil." The preceding sentence has adverted to Lord Radcliffe's failure to respond to the Dedication of *Examen Poeticum,* which contained all the Ovid translations. Why Dryden should now—after that volume was in print—be translating hundreds of additional lines of Ovid (which were never printed) remains most obscure. His thoughts, almost certainly, were upon the forthcoming translation, which was Virgil—not Ovid. Before December, he writes Walsh, he had already completed the third *Georgic;* if on August 30, when he wrote Tonson about his translation of "Ovid," he had finished 600 of 772 lines, he could have completed the remainder in the autumn upon his return to London, and polished the entire work before the end of November. The third *Georgic,* in modern texts, contains 566 lines—not 772. In Dryden's English text, it contains nearly the 900 lines he guesses it will require—actually 844. He may have suffered temporarily a lapse of memory when he wrote "772 lines"; or he may have included one or more of the Pastorals in his stint. Though it is obscure, I cannot believe he meant to write "Ovid."

21. Ward. ed., *Letters,* p. 59.

22. *Ibid.,* pp. 60-61.

23. Hotson, *Commonwealth and Restoration Stage,* p. 293.

24. Evelyn, on January 11, records that he supped at Edward Sheldon's, where Dryden read them the prologue and epilogue to this valedictory play, "now shortly to be acted."

CHAPTER XVI

1. More than a year before this time it had been suggested in print that Dryden should translate all of Virgil. In the preface to his *Poems on Several Occasions* (London, 1692), Thomas Fletcher wrote: "Tho' I am unable to perform so great a Task [to translate Virgil], yet I perswade my self that, if

a *Dryden* (a Master of our Language and Poetry) would undertake to Translate *Virgil* in blank Verse, we might hope to read him with as great pleasure in our Language, as his own."

2. Ward, ed., *Letters*, p. 64.

3. Both Tonson's copy and Dryden's are extant: British Museum, Add. MS 36933 and Add. Charter 8429.

4. These accounts may be found in Percy J. Dobell, *The Literature of the Restoration* (London, 1918).

5. As James Graham testified in later years. Since Graham was the husband of Dorothy Howard, Elizabeth Dryden's niece, it is possible that he had learned from acquaintance with Dryden the approximate amount. See John Taylor, "Drydeniana," *N&Q*, 5th Series, VII, (May 8, 1877), 386, for Graham's statement.

6. For the whole question of texts, his use of his sources and Dryden's Latin scholarship, see J. McG. Bottkol, "Dryden's Latin Scholarship," in *MP*, XL (1943), 241-54, and also his unpublished Harvard dissertation, *Dryden's Translations from Classical Verse* (1937). William Frost's *Dryden and the Art of Translation* (New Haven, 1955), is a perceptive study of Dryden as translator. Frost's analysis of Dryden's methods and accomplishment is important for a proper assessment of the *Virgil*. What needs to be remembered is well expressed by Frost: "Dryden's aim was to translate poetry, not simply the words of poems" (p. 49). See also a larger study of the *Æneid* and its background, by L. Proudfoot, *Dryden's Æneid and its Seventeenth Century Predecessors* (Manchester, 1960).

7. Postscript to *Virgil*.

8. Ward, ed., *Letters*, pp. 76-78.

9. See "Some Notes on Dryden," *RES*, XIII (1937), 297-306, where I printed the manuscript advertisement. I there dated it "between April and June, 1696." Though the date is conjectural, it still seems to be reasonable. The statement that the "Whole Work will be finished by Lady Day next" must be taken to refer to March 25, 1697; for no more than eight books, or possibly nine, were completed by Lady Day, 1696.

10. Ward, ed., *Letters*, pp. 77-78.

11. It was to be amicably settled in March 1698 by Dryden's payment of 6s. 4d. for each book—which left him a profit of at least 14s. 8d. on each book, or, if the value of the guinea was then still at 30s., a profit of 23s. 8d. See C. E. Ward, "The Publication and Profits of Dryden's *Virgil*," in *PMLA*, LIII (1938), 807-12.

12. After the fourth *Æneid* he wrote Tonson that he was "willing some few of my Friends may see it; & shall give leave to you, to shew your transcription to some others, whose names I will tell you." After the seventh *Æneid* he asked Tonson to make sure that the manuscript copy was delivered to Sir Robert Howard before he left for the country.

13. Ward, ed., *Letters*, pp. 80-81.

14. *Ibid.*, pp. 77-78.

15. See the letter from Daniel Bret to the Earl of Huntingdon, dated September 3, in H.M.C., Hastings MS, II, 280-81.

16. Manuscript letter in the Folger Shakespeare Library.

17. Ward, ed., *Letters*, pp. 84-85.

18. *Ibid.*, pp. 85-87.

19. As late as July 6, for example, he was writing to Tonson to inform Mr. Pate (a woollen draper and a solicitor for the *Virgil*) that "I can print no more names of his Subscribers than I have money for, before I print their names" (Ward, ed., *Letters*, p. 88).

20. On July 29, Thomas Burnet was writing to the Electress Sophia: "We are every hour impatiently expecting the coming out of Mr. Dreydens laborious versione of Virgil into English." Although Burnet highly praises Dryden for "his vast learning, perfectione in our langwodge, noble fancie, richnesse of thought, rypenesse of age, and experience of more as 50 years in the practice," and says that he "heth the fairest pretences to the immortal laurels of Virgil, as prince of all our english, poets," he fears that because "the author heth bein so many yeirs about this work, as his last and cheifest work, our witts will criticise the same the more." See Kemble, *State Papers,* p. 193.

21. Ward, ed., *Letters,* pp. 89-90.

22. While he was translating Virgil, Dryden took limited advantage of the clause in his contract with Tonson to publish some anticipated work, some not anticipated in the summer of 1694. For convenience, I include them at this point.

The first is the epistle "To Sir Godfrey Kneller," included in the *Fourth Miscellany.* Kneller, the popular portrait artist, had recently sent him as a gift a copy of the Droeshout portrait of Shakespeare in the First Folio, and in return Dryden memorializes the painter and the poet, whose genius is bound by the times, and who both suffer from the attacks of critics. In the following year Dryden fulfilled an early promise to Kneller and other artist friends to write a "Parallel betwixt Painting and Poetry," which he published with his own translation of de Piles' French version of du Fresnoy's Latin poem *de Arte Graphica.* It was entered in the *Stationers' Register* on April 10, 1695, and was in print by the end of June. The "parallels" important to him are those which he has often cited: perfection of characters; pleasure and instruction; the imitation of nature; the need of the artist for invention, judgment, and taste; design and form; coloring.

Dryden's next—and unanticipated—work was called for by the early death of Henry Purcell on November 21, 1695. Within the next few months he composed his elegy *Ode On the Death of Mr. Henry Purcell,* perhaps in collaboration with John Blow, who set it to music. In June, 1696, Henry Playford published poem and music. A piece of paternal love, provided for in his contract, was his contribution of preface, prologue, epilogue, and songs for his son's play, *The Husband His Own Cuckold,* which John had sent from Rome. In the epilogue, which he considered not the worst he had written, the old poet warns the fledgling playwright

> That if his play be dull, he's damn'd all o'er,
> Not only a damn'd blockhead, but damn'd poor.

The last and most ambitious undertaking beyond his agreement—and I think unauthorized by Tonson—was a "Life of Lucian," written in 1696 to accompany a projected edition promoted by the bookseller Samuel Briscoe, but not finally to be in print until 1711. It is a derivative account, relying heavily upon Zvinger's life, the *Elogium* of Gilbertus Cognatus, and a Latin translation of the life of Suidas (see Hardin Craig, "Dryden's Lucian" in *Classical Philology,* XVI [1921], 141-63). Like his other performances of this kind, the "Life of Lucian" contains numerous digressions which afford an intimate glimpse into Dryden's personal situation at the moment. Here one finds a confession that like Lucian (in "The Dialogue of the Harlots") he too has made "vice too amiable" and is "little able to defend" himself; a tribute to John Eachard for his skillful handling of the dialogue form; a swinging attack upon the booksellers, who sell "titles, not books." "While translations," he says, "are thus at the disposal of the booksellers, and have no better judges or rewarders of the performance, it is impossible that we should make any progress in an art so very useful to an enquiring people."

CHAPTER XVII

1. Ward, ed., *Letters,* pp. 91-92. See the notes to this letter for an account of the pamphlet and the official examination of Metcalf.

2. *Ibid.,* pp. 92-96.

3. DeLafontaine, *The King's Music,* passim.

4. Malone, ed., *Prose Works of Dryden,* I, i, 301-5. See a more detailed treatment of the musical settings and changes in Dryden's ode by Robert Manson Myers, *Handel, Dryden & Milton* (London, 1956); and Myers' article, "Neo-Classical Criticism of the Ode for Music," *PMLA,* LXII (1947), 399-421.

5. Malone, ed., *Prose Works of Dryden,* I, i, 296-97.

6. Ward, ed., *Letters,* pp. 98-100.

7. *Ibid.,* p. 96.

8. *Ibid.,* p. 97.

9. *Ibid.,* pp. 98-100.

10. See Macdonald, *Bibliography,* pp. 279 ff., for titles of poems taking Dryden to task for his silence on this occasion.

11. *Prince Arthur,* preface (London, 1695).

12. Luke Milbourne, *Notes on Dryden's Virgil. In a Letter to a Friend. With an Essay on the Same Poet* (London, 1698). Milbourne in 1687/88 had translated and published the first book of the *Æneid,* which Dryden nowhere mentions. At one time, Milbourne seemed to have thought highly of Dryden's poetry. See Malone, ed., *Prose Works of Dryden,* I, i, 314-16.

13. An analysis and history of the Collier controversy may be found in Sister Rose Anthony's *The Jeremy Collier Stage Controversy, 1698-1726* (Milwaukee, Wis., 1937), and Joseph Wood Krutch, *Comedy and Conscience after the Restoration* (New York, 1924). Among the pamphlets dealing with the controversy between 1698 and 1700 were the following: Congreve's *Amendments to Mr. Collier's False and Imperfect Citations* (1698); Edward Filmer's *A Defence of Dramatic Poetry, being a Review of Mr. Collier's View, etc.* (1698); Vanbrugh's *A Short Vindication of the Relapse and the Provok'd Wife* (1698); Collier's *Defence of the Short View* (1699) [a reply to Congreve and Vanbrugh]; James Drake's *The Ancient and Modern Stages Survey'd* (1699) [dedicated to Earl of Dorset]; Collier's *Second Defence of the Short View* (1699/1700), a reply to Drake.

14. The formal agreement, printed by Malone, ed., *Prose Works of Dryden,* I, i, 560, was dated March 20, 1698/99. The agreed payment was made four days later, which Dryden formally gave receipt for. Written in Dryden's hand and witnessed by Charles Dryden, the document is now in the Folger Shakespeare Library.

15. Ward, ed., *Letters,* pp. 101-3.

16. *Ibid.,* pp. 103-5.

17. *Ibid.,* pp. 105-6.

18. *Ibid.,* pp. 108-10.

19. Cousin John Driden, in particular, was exceedingly generous to his relations. At his death in 1708 he left a long list of bequests to innumerable nephews, nieces, and cousins. Charles, the poet's son, was bequeathed £500, which became a lapsed legacy, since he had died in 1704 (P.R.O., C 9/445/77).

20. The order was printed in the *London Gazette* only a few days before— on Monday, February 27. Nahum Tate, then poet laureate, had drawn up, on February 7, his own proposals for reforming the stage. (Lambeth Palace Library, MS, Vol. 933, item 57.) It has been printed by Krutch, *Comedy and Conscience,* pp. 177-78. In many quarters, of course, Collier's attack was being applauded. In September, the Archbishop of Canterbury, Dr. Tenison,

had sent Collier his thanks for writing against the profaneness of the stage (Luttrell, *State Affairs,* IV, 427).

21. Ward, ed., *Letters,* pp. 112-13.

22. *Ibid.,* p. 114.

23. *Ibid.,* pp. 115-16.

24. *Ibid.,* pp. 120-21.

25. The order in which he completed the translations and the original pieces which make up the *Fables* is difficult to determine. The evidence contained in the letters suggests that he did the selections from Ovid, Chaucer, and Boccaccio as his fancy at the moment dictated. This is borne out too by his statement in the preface to the volume. The original poems—again from the evidence of the letters—appear to have been the last composed.

26. Ward, ed., *Letters,* p. 123.

27. Elizabeth Steward's grandmother, the wife of Sir Gilbert Pickering, was Charles Montague's aunt. Dryden was misinformed: Montague was not created Earl of Bristol, but Baron Halifax.

28. Ward, ed., *Letters,* pp. 130-31.

CHAPTER XVIII

1. Ward, ed., *Letters,* p. 134. The volume contained eighteen separate pieces, ranging from Chaucer's *Palamon and Arcite,* in three parts and totalling 2,431 lines, to the "Pygmalion and the Statue" (from *Metamorphosis,* X) of 101 lines. Four selections come from Chaucer, plus the supposititious *The Flower and the Leaf;* eight are from Ovid; three from Boccaccio; and one—the first book of the *Iliad*—from Homer. The one original poem (except the dedicatory verses to the Duchess of Ormond) was "To my Honor'd Kinsman, John Driden."

2. Christie's comment that "unable to make a good defense, Dryden resorts to abuse, and, a Roman Catholic convert, he denounces the marriage of Protestant clergymen," seems to miss the point of the passage.

3. See John C. Sherwood, "Dryden and the Rules: The Preface to the *Fables,*" in *JEGP,* LII (1953), 13-26. His analysis demonstrates that the preface contains many of the conventional judgments that conform to the neo-classical rules, but with the usual displays of independence.

4. It is hardly to be expected that all of his judgments, or his acceptance of the then Chaucer canon, could survive the impact of later scholarship. That he failed to understand the principle of the Middle English syllabic *e* (as his critics still point out) is true. Yet—though Speght, upon whom the poet depended, had adumbrated the solution of the Chaucerian line—the whole principle was not to be fully understood until Tyrwhitt's analysis in 1775.

5. Noyes suggested (*Poetical Works,* p. 899) that this song was probably inserted in Act III of the play. The masque, Malone thought, may have been designed for performance on March 25, the first day of the new year and the new century; hence the word "secular" prefixed to it. There is, however, no indication, in Dryden's letter of April 11, that a postponement of the performance had taken place. The meaning of the masque would retain its pertinence even though it achieved performance after the official commencement of the new century.

6. It was advertised in *Term Catalogues* for Trinity Term.

7. Luttrell records on March 20, 1696/97, that "Dr. Blackmore having writt a poem called King Arthur and dedicated it to the King, his Majestie hath conferred the honour of knighthood upon him" (IV, 199).

8. I have assumed that the cause of his death was a complication of the diseases which we know from his last letters he was suffering from. This

assumption does not completely rule out Ned Ward's circumstantial account in the *London Spy*, the second volume, published within a few weeks of the event. Ward there gives as the cause of death gangrene in one leg, induced by the neglected inflammation of flesh growing over one of the toenails. This could have been the unchecked erysipelas in the one leg. Ward further states that Dryden refused to submit to an amputation, which had been demanded by his physician. Because the journalist may be relating second-hand and perhaps unauthenticated hearsay—and embroidering a report for journalistic purposes—I prefer to question this account and the suggested cause of death.

9. Part of the memorial notice written by Mrs. Creed and included on the tablet in the church at Titchmarsh. See Malone (*Prose Works of Dryden*, I, i, 564-66), for a transcript.

10. British Museum, 1878, d. 12. 18—a photostatic copy of the original invitation.

11. *The Post Boy*, Nos. 792 (May 4-7) and 793 (May 7-9).

12. Malone, ed., *Prose Works of Dryden*, I, i, 378-79.

13. *Ibid.*, pp. 378-79, 562-63, where is printed Russell's itemized bill for the funeral.

EPILOGUE

1. H.M.C., Buccleuch MSS, II, Pt. II, 768, and Osborn, *Dryden*, pp. 265-66.

2. Charles's power of administration may be found in Somerset House, Admõn Act Book, Middlesex, June 1700, f. 122b.

Thirteen years later, in May, 1713, Lady Ann Sylvius (Lady Elizabeth Dryden's niece), qualified to administer those effects not already administered by Charles before his death (Somerset House, Admõn Act Book). When the poet's cousin John Driden died in 1708, he left Charles (it would have become a lapsed legacy) £500 and his brother Erasmus-Henry 100 guineas (P.R.O., C 9/445/77). He also remembered Elmes and Elizabeth Steward by leaving them £100 each. This last bequest, one can believe, would have pleased Dryden.

3. *Publications of the Catholic Records Society*, XXV (1925), 129.

4. Malone, ed., *Prose Works of Dryden*, I, i, 396-97. Malone supposes that in her last years she was a lunatic. His proof, however, is not conclusive. The presence of the phrase *durante lunacia*, incorporated in the letters of administration of Lady Ann Sylvius, may mean only that the widow, then seventy-seven, had become enfeebled in mind, so that she could not attend to civil transactions and needed a nurse to look after her and a relative to manage her affairs.

Index